Rural
Santo Domingo

Rural
Santo Domingo
Settled, Unsettled,
and Resettled

MARLIN D. CLAUSNER

TEMPLE UNIVERSITY PRESS · *Philadelphia*

Temple University Press, Philadelphia 19122
©1973 by Temple University. All rights reserved
Published 1973
Printed in the United States of America

International Standard Book Number: 0–87722–012–3
Library of Congress Catalog Card Number: 72–95881

To Doña Mélida

CONTENTS

Appendixes

Maps

PREFACE

The world today suffers all too frequently and unnecessarily from a lack of human understanding. Yet the more I observe other peoples and other lands the more I realize that the similarities among men far outweigh the dissimilarities, once the insulating screens of the respective cultures are pierced. The problem appears to lie with the difficulty in stripping away the apparent differences in order to perceive what really lies beneath them.

Over the past several years I have had unusual opportunity to live—not merely travel—among people whose customs and traditions were either entirely Spanish or close adaptations of the Spanish. Deeply impressed by the attractiveness of these cultures, I am at the same time distressed at the persistency of mutual misconceptions which still exist between so many North Americans and their neighbors to the south. I honestly regret that many Latin Americans still conceive of the typical North American as a hard-driving, overorganized, unemotional technician who has absolutely no appreciation of the arts or human feelings, or else as a loud, overly friendly salesman whose life ambition is tied exclusively to the pursuit of the dollar. I regret even more that a surprising number of Latin Americans overlook the fact that they are just as busily and enthusiastically engaged in similar material pursuits in their own countries and, what is more, are depositing their profits in safer foreign banks. The "imperialistic" American dollar is publicly attacked but privately cherished. Equally if not more unfortunate is the tendency of many North Americans to deprecate the political, cultural, and economic idiosyncrasies of the Latin Americans. That is not to say, for example, that the periodic scandals in the political institutions of the individual Latin countries should be minimized, obscured, or ignored, but only that they be recognized for what they frequently are: the growing pains of an oppressed and uneducated majority whose historic political traditions were inconsistent with the political institutions adopted for them well along into the nineteenth century. After almost 200 years of national independence, North Americans, who are relatively well educated, should be careful to remember that they are still encountering serious difficulties making their own far from perfect system function equi-

ix

tably and responsively. Small wonder that similar systems have been all but unworkable in lands where habitually only a few men were privileged to think and act for the many who have been unprepared for any role other than that of follower. But even if the political system of any country were nearly perfect, no amount of legislation could completely inhibit the selfish acts of individuals who place themselves above the law. In a completely democratic setting, the law will be what an articulate majority wishes to make of it, not as it is interpreted by a few leaders, self-appointed or otherwise. However, the achievement of such democratic maturity in many Latin American republics, according to their own definitions and aspirations, is, in my opinion, at least a generation away. The missing ingredient is not a more modern constitution, a massive AID program, or even free elections. As was clearly recognized at Punta del Este, a critical factor is the lack of popular education.

Someday the majorities in the Latin American democracies, especially the poorer classes and those who live in the undeveloped rural areas, will, at a minimum, be able to enjoy the benefits of ten to twelve years of good education. Someday these majorities will have learned that political responsibility is built on the supremacy of institutions rather than individuals, on a willingness to compromise for the good of the majority, and on a respect for the rights of others. When this day comes, these countries will be on the road to liberation from the misfortunes of their historic pasts. By no means do I imply that United States' institutions be the models. On the contrary, a strong flavor of authoritarianism might well prove to be the successful formula. Each of the Latin American republics is distinct; each has its peculiar problems. The examples set long ago in Chile and Costa Rica and within the past fifty years in Mexico have shown that, through the adaptation of basic political principles to local conditions, national aspirations can best be achieved. But the citizens must have the maturity to adapt, adopt, and unwaveringly support the system most suited to their needs.

Two years ago the Dominican Republic, for the first time in its modern history, experienced an essentially peaceful and constitutional transfer of presidential power. Those who were deeply concerned about the continued economic and social progress of the nation realized the importance of the 1970 elections and the subsequent presidential inauguration. These same observers appreciated the frailty of the evolving post-Trujillo political institutions and the need to nurture them carefully.

I think, however, that too many North Americans are unfamiliar with events which are transpiring in the Dominican Republic and still regard it as being beset by revolution, financially untrustworthy, and incapable of progress. I also think that too many Dominican political candidates campaign irresponsibly among the uneducated and easily swayed *campesinos*, threatening blood reprisal on their opponents if they are not elected, promising benefits and advantages they are obviously incapable of delivering, invoking some sort of revolution as the rightful and righteous path to peace and social progress, and calling on their partisans to vote if necessary with weapons, not ballots.

Dominican history is as fascinating, complex, and exciting as the country itself. Since 1844 the relations of the Dominican Republic and the United States have reflected every major historical issue between the United States and the Caribbean area. Even a casual review of the impact on the United States of events in the Dominican Republic during 1861–65, 1904–5, 1911–16, and the late unpleasantness of 1965, reveals the sensitivity of our foreign policy to what takes place within the borders of this Latin American neighbor. The national interests of the United States and the Dominican Republic are inextricably tied by geography. Cultural differences make it difficult to achieve mutual appreciation of those interests. Average Americans and average Dominicans (if such people exist) ought to know more about each other, and this sort of knowledge cannot be easily acquired by an unrepresentative sampling of life in New York City or in the tourist spots of Santo Domingo city. I think that a historical approach would be useful. Lamentably, good standard histories of the Dominican Republic written by Dominicans and translated into English are conspicuously absent from the shelves of even the largest libraries in this country. The perspectives of such eminent scholars as José Gabriel García, Antonio del Monte y Tejada, Max Henríquez Ureña, Américo Lugo, and Pedro Henríquez Ureña, if made more widely available to students and interested general readers here, would provide invaluable material for the understanding of the Dominican background as interpreted by Dominicans themselves. The contemporary scholarly works of Joaquín Balaguer, Manuel Arturo Peña Batlle, Emilio Rodríguez Demorizi, Pedro Troncoso Sánchez, and others highlight many more Dominican perceptions which are essential to an appreciation of their social or cultural values. There is also a Marxist interpretation of Dominican history, such as that of J. I. Jiménez Grullón. It is a matter of regret that more is not known in the United States of Dominican authors and their contributions.

An educated rural population is essential to the future prosperity of the Dominican Republic. This book is intended for American readers who want to be more informed about some of the factors which have shaped Dominican rural society and its political traditions, especially regarding the handicaps under which the landless campesinos have lived. The book is also intended—without affront to Dominican readers—to emphasize the inevitable results of the combination of irresponsible government and an illiterate citizenry. North Americans ought to understand that the Dominicans have progressed, although slowly and painfully, despite the heritage of the Trujillo years from which the country is still suffering. On other the hand, Dominican leaders should demonstrate to the world that they are capable of providing the responsible leadership and honest government which the people need. In short, while the political and social institutions of the Dominican Republic are maturing and evolving, there is an acute need for mutual understanding between the two countries, not only among leaders but between peoples, an understanding which will be achieved most effectively by frequent and full cultural exchanges.

In this book I have examined some of the historical factors affecting land tenure in the Dominican Republic, factors which are not widely known in the United States and may not be fully understood in the Dominican Republic. If the book sheds some light on Dominican history for the readers of both countries, I will be happy to believe I have been able to speed up the cultural exchange process.

A complete list of all the good people who have helped me along the way during the past few years would overburden these pages. Yet I am sincerely impelled to name some of them, Dominicans and Americans, without whose cooperation and assistance this book could not have been written. *Licenciado* Emilio Rodríguez Demorizi, president of the Dominican Academy of History; Dr. Ramón Ramírez Baez and his staff, of the Secretariat of Education and Fine Arts; D. Victorino Alvarez Arévalo of the Institute of Agrarian Reform; Dr. Diógenes del Orbe Rodríguez; Licenciados Pedro Troncoso Sánchez and Wenceslao Troncoso Sánchez; Dr. Freddy Prestol Castillo; Señorita Rosa Elena Despradel Batista, director of the University of Santo Domingo library; and the distinguished director of the National Archives, Dr. Vetilio Alfau Durán and his assistants—all were most cooperative in making available a wide variety of research material.

To those *Veganos* who gave so freely of their time I can only express my warm appreciation: Monseñor Juan Antonio Flores, Bishop of La Vega, D. José Salcedo Rodríguez and his family, D. Francisco Gómez Estrella, D. Francisco de Moya Franco, D. Rogelio Jiménez García, D. Epifanio Espaillat de la Mota, and D. Ramón E. Conde Peralta and his family are but a few—there are indeed too many to name individually.

I would also like to thank Dr. Charles B. Green, Mr. Wayne Miles, and Mr. Melvin B. Morris of the AID Mission, U.S. Embassy, Santo Domingo, and Dr. William J. Morgan of the Office of the Naval Historian for their courtesies.

It is difficult to express adequately the deep respect and admiration I have for Dr. Clement G. Motten, who has been simultaneously a mentor, teacher, and friend, whose wise counsel and cheerful countenance helped me more than he realizes.

For his continuous personal interest and encouragement I will always be grateful to Dr. Edwin P. Adkins, who better than anyone else knows how this all started.

As we all realize sooner or later, few men can go far without support at home, and for her patience and understanding, which at times must have all but passed the point of no return, I wish to thank my wife, María del Socorro.

Extensive translation of Spanish language sources, as well as some French, has obviously been necessary. Any translation errors are my own, since I alone am responsible for this work.

Rural
Santo Domingo

1

INTRODUCTION

This is a study of rural land settlement and its evolution in the Dominican Republic. Such a scrutiny must spotlight the campesinos, the country folk, who, throughout Dominican history, have constituted the country's majority. Accordingly, the study will emphasize both old and new institutions and attitudes that have exerted influence mutually among landowners, landusers, and their governments.

This study is not highly specialized, nor is it intended to be. I am neither an economist, sociologist, agronomist, nor lawyer. As a student of history, however, I have examined a variety of written source materials in these fields and have conducted independent field research in the Dominican Republic in order better to exploit not only written sources but living sources as well. Because the effectiveness of the current Dominican agrarian reform program will elude definitive evaluation for many years, I have arbitrarily established a terminal date of 1966 for the purposes of research. The year 1966 marks the fifth after the death of Trujillo, the fourth after passage of the Agrarian Reform Law, and covers the initial efforts of the Dominican government to carry out that reform.

The Spanish Crown settled Española under mercantilist policies which brought the small colony periods of prosperity and long years of depression. Its characteristics were those of an established agricultural economy, and these remained through the unsettled years of early independence, subsequent decades of political instability, and into the twentieth century. Today the Dominican Republic is still an agrarian state. About 70 percent of the population are rural or dependent on agriculture. The present government is essentially democratic by Western standards, but it is built on an economic base characterized by a lack of diversity, distorted land tenure relationships, a high degree of rural illiteracy, and one of the fastest growing populations in the world.[1] These are clear indicators of a faulty agrarian structure which many Dominicans claim is going to be

---

1. 3.6 percent between 1950 and 1960. República Dominicana, *Cuarto censo nacional de población 1960*.

3

the vehicle for a social revolution, not necessarily peaceful. If their observations are correct, who will be leading the change?

Embracing the position that an understanding of the past will contribute to a better understanding of the present, I suggest that certain elements of the Dominican agrarian structure be examined historically in order better to appreciate the social and economic problems of the present and future. Two major, interrelated elements can be distinguished throughout all or most of the rural land history of the country: the basis of ownership or control of the land, and growth of population, or the lack of it. Certain institutions appear to be significant from time to time—for example, the Church, and rural education, which, over the long haul, will probably prove to have been the most important factor of all. This book will focus principally on these elements, some aspects of which are typical of the history of land problems elsewhere in Latin America and some of which are atypical. The main purpose is to trace the history, in the light of law and actual practice, of the relationship of the Dominican farmer to the land he works. This book is not intended to be a complete history of all the elements of agrarian reform, at least not in the current sense of this dynamic phrase. Agrarian reform is far too comprehensive a subject; the research needed to treat all its ramifications adequately would be monumental both in scope and time required.

The time frames are defined as follows: colonial, from discovery in 1492 to 1795, when Spain ceded Santo Domingo to France by the Treaty of Basel; the middle period, which includes the background and events of the Haitian invasions of 1801 and 1805, the return to Spanish colonial status in 1809, the third Haitian invasion of 1822, and independence, from 1844 to the eve of the American military occupation of 1916; and, finally, the modern period, from 1916 to 1966. The only references to military and political events will be those needed for an understanding of the land problems. For purposes of clarity the colonial designations of either Española or Santo Domingo will be used to identify the land until 1844, after which it became the Dominican Republic. When appropriate to make the distinction during the colonial period, the designation of Saint Domingue will apply to the French colony, Santo Domingo to the Spanish. The reader may notice occasional use of the colonial designation even during the modern period. This is an admitted technical inaccuracy which can be best and simply explained by the enduring fascination of readers of all ages with the colorful, romantic history of the Caribbees and the first of the Spanish conquests there.

An adequate history of landownership in the Dominican Republic can be developed only from the colonial background. The Catholic rulers of Spain, whatever might have been their doubts about the morality of the conquest of the Indians, showed little indecision concerning the land. Royal policy in this matter was clear and simple. All newly discovered lands, as defined by papal authority, belonged to the king, to be used or disposed of as he saw fit. The correspondence of the colonial period provides some arresting insights into the motives and purposes of the Spanish rulers as they continually sought to formulate land policies which would support their fiscal, economic, and political objectives.

The colonies existed for the purpose of exploitation. The initial chapters of this book, accordingly, explain with respect to Española how the model for land policies was evolved and how certain local land practices were established. The differences between *derecho*, the law, as theorized in Spain, and *hecho*, the law, as practiced in Santo Domingo, became apparent relatively early in colonial history. Neither the top-heavy administrative apparatus of the Hapsburgs nor the more enlightened bureaucracy of the Bourbons was ever able to force the colonies to comply fully with royal policy toward the Indians, labor, or land. This dichotomy was to be found in every region in Spanish America where land was rich or plentiful and the indigenous labor supply abundant.

Within this framework a careful study of the Hapsburg kings' directives throughout the sixteenth century shows frequent enlightened appreciation of the problems of settlement, distribution of land, agricultural productivity, and land tenure. For several reasons royal policies in these matters as they were applied in Española assumed a special significance, especially prior to 1530. First, Santo Domingo was the colonial center in the New World until well into the century, and served as an administrative proving ground on which to develop a mature colonial policy; second, after the importance of the gold and silver mines of the island began to diminish, effective usage and productivity of the land offered the main road to further economic development; third, as the exportation of West Indian sugar began to achieve an essential role in the economy of the mother country, the Crown was obliged to pay special attention to the needs of its sugar islands; and, fourth, in the age that began with Drake, Hawkins, and other freebooters of many nationalities, the strategic value of the Spanish Caribbean islands demanded that the Crown stabilize and promote their growth. Yet the Crown itself was largely responsible for the serious economic decline in Española throughout a long period of over 150 years.

Under the later Bourbons the little colony began to prosper, only to be ceded to France in 1795 to become part of Saint Domingue. Removed thus from the main arena when the Spanish empire began to dissolve, Dominicans passed under a succession of Haitian, French, Spanish, and again Haitian rulers before acquiring a tenuous independence in 1844. Since that year the more notorious aspects of Dominican history overshadow the brief periods of enlightened government.

There have been liberal, progressive Dominican leaders who could visualize the importance of a broader public education base, of improved agricultural techniques, and of public policy administered for the benefit of the majority of Dominicans without corruption. Nevertheless, these men have been few in number and they have left no permanent mark, not so much because their objectives were faulty but because the supporting social and political structures of the nation suffered from the same defects which at one time or another have plagued all of Spain's former colonies. In Dominican history there has never existed a popular, deep, and enduring respect for government by law. The best interests of the state have frequently been subordinated to the personal interests of the patriotic *caudillo*. Competent public administrators have been all too few. The vast bulk of the illiterate population and many literates either have not understood or have failed to recognize the importance of individual political responsibility inherent in democratic processes. The traditional minority ruling groups have been unwilling to accept the responsibility to educate the rural majority for the burdens of self-government. Dominican constitutions have unceasingly proclaimed the country's democratic ideals, standards and values; yet at times—and for prolonged periods—nowhere in Latin America has the practice differed so widely from the theory. Nowhere has government been so consistently dependent on armed force for survival. And yet, there have been good men who have tried to bring progress to their land.

The military occupation of the Dominican Republic by the United States in 1916 incurred the sharp censure of anti-imperialists, especially in Latin America, and of all Dominicans. Yet businessmen and farmers among the latter, whose security depended on internal peace and political stability, tended to be somewhat less critical of the occupation. The more informed citizens had accurately analyzed and admitted the defects of their institutions, had predicted the American intervention, understood its inevitability, and while criticizing American injustices and excesses, also recognized the benefits the intervention brought.[2] The United States wanted no land and took no land. The mission of the military government of Santo Domingo was to introduce badly needed reforms which would permit the Dominicans to stabilize their fundamental institutions of government. Among these the need to reform the systems of land tenure and public education, both of which directly affected the campesino, had been generated by the traditional, backward administration in the rural areas. As a tribute to the efforts of their creators, most of whom were Dominican, the elements of these reforms withstood the passage of the next fifty years without significant change. The Dominicans regained control of their own affairs in 1924 with the withdrawal of the last of the occupation forces. They lost that control when Rafael Leónidas Trujillo was elected president in 1930.

Although the first permanent European colony in the New World was founded in this land, the Dominican Republic is in a sense one of the newest of all the Latin American republics. The assassination of Trujillo in May 1961 unchained a whole nation which for thirty-one years had existed essentially as the dictator's feudal estate. The "Era of Trujillo" was an era of material progress and stability. It was also half a lifetime of *personalismo*, terror, and repression of individual rights. Trujillo monopolized the national economy for his own private purposes. He encouraged the destruction of the moral fiber of Dominican life, and he and those about him were guilty directly or indirectly of untold, unwarranted criminal acts against defenseless private citizens. He claimed eternal glory as the supreme patriot, yet his departure exposed an exploited people to the weaknesses of the corrupt system he had erected. This unfortunate legacy may well have been Trujillo's greatest crime. At a time when new states were beginning to form, or, as elsewhere in Latin America, when unstable governments were beginning to achieve, albeit slowly, a measure of political maturity, the Dominican Republic remained firmly under Trujillo's personal and greedy dictatorship. With his death the country was suddenly placed in a different environment in which the Dominicans themselves would have to determine the meaning of such words as "progress" and "freedom."

In 1961, as has been the case in other Latin American lands and in other years, the demise of dictatorship was followed by a period lacking not in ambitious leaders but in discerning followers. An essentially rural body politic, the majority illiterate, poorly fed, almost completely unfamiliar with the working of honest representative government, had become accustomed to universal corruption in high places. They could hardly be expected to exercise sophisticated political discrimination when the moment arrived to shape the lines of future national development. Yet these laborers and tenant or subsistence farmers could now participate in the affairs of state. Furthermore, technology

---

2. The criticism reached its peak about 1920–21 as it began to appear that the United States would be slow to withdraw its forces. The Dominican nationalists organized a society called the National Dominican Union and began a campaign in the republic, elsewhere in Latin America, and in Europe to force the United States to return control of their government to Dominicans. Ousted President Francisco Henríquez y Carvajal was especially active, even making informal visits to the State department to discuss the question of withdrawal of U.S. forces. State department files for these years contain many reports from Uruguay, Argentina, Cuba, Colombia, Venezuela, and France. United States, Department of State, *Records Relating to Internal Affairs of the Dominican Republic, 1910–1929* (hereafter referred to as *Internal Affairs of the D.R.*). Sumner Welles was the chief of the Latin American Affairs Division of the State department during 1921–22 and writes in detail of the nationalist activities in his *Naboth's Vineyard*, 2:821–35.

had brought them within easy reach of political policy-makers. The Dominican Republic is not large; a centrally located ten-kilowatt radio transmitter will easily reach the most remote village in the country. Almost without having to leave his fields, the campesino could not only hear what the *jefes* in the capital were saying but could also be reached by ideas transmitted from other countries. In short, he could be influenced by any political group that possessed a radio transmitter inside or outside Dominican borders.

The political events of the immediate post-Trujillo period will be outlined later in appropriate detail. What is relevant here is the fact that tens of thousands of rural inhabitants, either landless or owners of tiny, uneconomical parcels of land, now had a political voice. They, as well as the urban poor, could and would cast their votes for the man who would most effectively satisfy their desires for a better life. To the campesino a better life began with ownership of land. Since the state owned considerable property, some of it of prime agricultural quality, the significance of "land for the landless" was recognized by the Balaguer government even before the first free political campaigns of 1962. Balaguer took advantage of an opportunity to win campesino support within a few months after Trujillo's death by ordering the initial redistribution of government-held land. The Council of State, which replaced Balaguer in January 1962, further developed a full-fledged agrarian reform program based on recognition of overdue rural social evolution. The current 1966 Constitution recognizes these same social values in the land. The issue of agrarian reform, therefore, is now firmly embedded in national political and social institutions. The need for reform has been recognized, and enabling legislation has been passed. Will the government lead a peaceful change by its plan to resettle rural land, or will it drift, possibly into a revolutionary situation?

The question cannot be answered at this time, but there is enough evidence in the history of land relationships to provide an indication.

2

THE LAND

Raymond Aron has provided an appropriate introduction to the brief survey of Dominican geography in this chapter:

> Human geography depicts the societies in a given territory, in a given climate; it attempts to understand and explain the action which the characteristics of the setting have exerted over the life style and social organization at the same time as the modifications wrought in the former by the societies which have established themselves there. The environment which geography studies and defines is both natural and historic.[1]

This land contains within its modest physical limits a startling variety of geographical qualities: tropical lowlands, high rugged mountain peaks, cactus as well as rain forests, bubbling mountain streams, an inland salt lake, mangrove swamps, extensive natural underground caves of depths and limits still unknown, grassy slopes, and one of the richest agricultural plains in the West Indies. That portion of the island of Española with which this book is concerned lies south of the Tropic of Cancer between parallels of latitude 17.6 north and 20 north and meridians of longitude 68.2 west and 71.4 west. It covers an area of 19,325 square miles and has a coastline of approximately 940 miles. From east to west it measures 260 miles; at its western limit along the frontier of Haiti today, its greatest width is about 170 miles. To the Indians who occupied the island of which it was a major part, the land was known variously as Aiti (mountainous country), Bohío (home), or, better known today, as Quisqueya (mainland).

The dominant feature of Dominican terrain is the five mountain ranges, all of which run in a generally southeast-northwest direction and which cover approximately sixty percent of the country. The Monte Cristi, sometimes called the Septentrional Range, occupies a twenty-mile-wide strip five to ten miles inland on the north coast from Monte Cristi, near the Haitian border, to the flat swampy Gran Estero just to the west of the Samaná Peninsula. This is a distance of over 125 miles, nearly all of which

1. Aron, *Peace and War*, p. 182.

8

is rugged and irregular. The highest peaks of this range near Santiago reach almost 4,000 feet. The slopes are steep and the valleys are deeply cut by erosion.

The most extensive and largest range is the Cordillera Central, which dominates the central part of the country. Extending from within Haiti eastward to the Atlantic, a distance of about 160 miles, this range is a jumble of irregular ridges and peaks. The highest, Pico Duarte, is well over 10,000 feet. At the Atlantic the range dwindles to a series of low hills. The central mountain mass not only contains many different kinds of rock, but is also faulted along different axes. At its widest point, the Cordillera Central is about 130 miles.

Other ranges include the Sierra de Neiba, which is separated from the Sierra de Martín García by the Yaque del Sur River. Both ranges lie in the west and are parallel to the Cordillera Central, but to the south of it. The Sierra de Neiba is made up of fairly regular limestone ridges reaching 3,200 to 4,800 feet above sea level. There are few peaks. The Sierra de Martín García is a short range, geologically identical to the Neiba range. Its highest ridges ascend to about 4,000 feet above sea level.

The Sierra de Baoruco in the extreme southwest lies below the Neiba and Martín García ranges and dominates the Barahona, or Southern, Peninsula. Peaks in this region rise to about 6,400 feet above sea level. The mountains are covered with open pine forests; the southern slopes are grassy and well suited for cattle pasturage. The north front of the range is massive, steeply tilted, and characterized by overturned and faulted limestone. There are extensive beds of rock salt, gypsum, shale, and sandstone.

Interspersed between parallel mountain ranges are a number of fertile valleys. Thus, lying between the Monte Cristi range and the Cordillera Central is a large "royal plain," or valley, 135 miles long and 9 to 25 miles wide. This is the rich Vega Real, drained in its western expanses by the Yaque del Norte River and the Yuna River to the east. Although the Vega Real is nearly divided into two equal parts at Santiago where the two ranges come closest together, it is nevertheless a continuous district. With black, loamy topsoil up to twelve feet deep, this rolling, open expanse may well rank among the world's finest agricultural land. In the central and eastern portions of the plain and on the adjacent interior slopes of both mountain ranges are produced cacao, tobacco, coffee, rice, and tropical fruits of a quality unsurpassed anywhere in the Caribbean. The ascent to the Cordillera Septentrional is over low foothills; the frost line, which determines the limit of coffee cultivation, starts at 3,600 feet. Fed by a plentiful rainfall, the Yuna, its main tributary the Camú, and many smaller tributaries provide ample water except in times of general drought. To the east, the plain extends all the way to the Gran Estero. In the west, the Vega Real becomes progressively more arid as grassy meadows give way to the cactus and mesquite plains of the Monte Cristi. Here, where rainfall is extremely sparse, the Yaque del Norte is virtually the only reliable source of water. The soil of the region is about as rich and fertile as that of the eastern portion, but until major irrigation projects are completed the western part will continue to be devoted primarily to cattle-raising.

In the southwest, between the Cordillera Central and the Sierra de Neiba and Sierra Martín García ranges lies the valley of San Juan de la Maguana, fifty miles long and averaging fifteen miles in width. Here are low hills, rolling flatlands, and large tracts of nearly level savannas. Just to the east of the valley of San Juan de la Maguana lies the Azua Plain. It forms a rough rectangle thirty-five miles long in an east-west direction, by twenty miles wide. Its eastern border is the hinterland of the port of Azua on the Caribbean Sea. Although its soil is fertile, the Azua Plain must be classified as hot and semi-arid; there is more rain there than the vegetation indicates, but it is poorly distributed during the year. As a result, during the rainy season the run-off of torrential precipitation is excessive. Water conservation practices will increase the productivity of the soil significantly.

Extending along the entire eastern half of the south coast from Baní all the way to the Atlantic Ocean is the third major lowland area—the Coastal Plain. The width of the plain at Baní is only about 6 miles, but along its 145-mile stretch the width increases to about 10 miles at Santo Domingo and 50 miles at its eastern extremity. From the shoreline inland it gradually reaches a height above sea level of 325 feet. West of Santo Domingo the plain is almost arid; east of Santo Domingo the soil is more humid and supports extensive forest and savannas. Almost as fertile as the Vega Real, though with less topsoil, the eastern coastal plain includes the major sugar-producing area in the country. Agriculture is devoted almost exclusively to sugar cane along the coast and river banks, and to cattle and sugar further inland on the savannas of the extreme eastern provinces of La Altagracia and El Seibo.

The Samaná Peninsula, which was an island at one time according to geologists, is now joined to the main island by the Gran Estero and is composed of mangrove swamps and irregular natural canals threading indiscriminately throughout marshy flatland. In times of heavy rainfall the Gran Estero is nearly impassable. The Samaná Peninsula itself is essentially a low-lying mass of fairly rugged mountains reaching to elevations of 1,500 to 1,800 feet above sea level. The southern shoreline along the Bay of Samaná is a fringe of flat to rolling lowlands. The peninsula projects thirty miles to the east of the Gran Estero and is about eight to ten miles wide throughout.

In the extreme western part of the country, nestling between the southern slopes of the Sierra de Neiba and the northern slopes of the Sierra Baoruco, lies one of the most unusual features of Dominican geography—Enriquillo Basin. This depression is an extension of the east-west cul de sac region of Haiti; in its center is Lake Enriquillo. Bearing the name of the last of the Indian *caciques* (chiefs), the flatly elliptical lake covers an area of about 180 square miles and is saltier than the ocean. Although a geologist reported in 1892 that the lake was approximately at sea level,[2] through evaporation its surface has dropped to about 150 feet below sea level. In its center is narrow Cabritos Island, about six miles long, the site of the final treaty between the Spaniards and Enriquillo in 1533.

There are four main rivers in the Dominican Republic, some of which have already been mentioned. All have their sources in the Cordillera Central, the main watershed of the country. The Yaque del Norte and the Yuna both originate in the high slopes on the northern side. The former originates near the highest peak, Pico Duarte, flows for a total distance of 126 miles, first eastward and then rapidly north at Jarabacoa through Santiago, thence northwest through the Vega Real to the Atlantic at a point in Manzanillo Bay about three miles south of Monte Cristi. At this point there is a considerable delta; at its mouth the river is about 100 yards wide.

The Yuna, 135 miles long, runs north and slightly east from its source toward Cotuí, then east through the Vega Real to its mouth in Samaná Bay just below Sánchez.

The next two largest rivers are the Yaque del Sur, which originates on the high south slopes of the Cordillera Central's Pico Durate and runs generally south, and the Artibonito, which also has its source on the south slope of the Cordillera Central but in the far west. The swift Artibonito is over sixty feet wide, 142 miles long, and develops the

---

2. Thomas W. Vaughan et al., *A Geological Reconnaissance of the Dominican Republic*, p. 39.

greatest volume of water of any of the Dominican rivers; it drains the large area of the western Cordillera Central and flows westward into Haiti. The Yaque del Sur is 120 miles long and performs two special functions. First, it crosses the valley of San Juan de la Maguana and separates the Sierra de Neiba from the Sierra de Martín García; and, second, on its route to the Caribbean at the Bahía de Neiba it forms the western boundary of the Azua Plain. This river and its tributaries feed the provinces of Barahona and Azua. During the low water season from January to April, however, the tributaries usually dry up.

In addition to the four principal rivers, the country possesses a number of smaller ones which run year-round, such as the Ozama–Isabela confluence whose estuary forms the port for the city of Santo Domingo, and the Yuma, which drains the easternmost province of La Altagracia and empties into the Caribbean Sea. The Barahona Peninsula, south of the Sierra de Baoruco, is the only extensive region of the country with no major river system; throughout the region smaller streams are likely to be completely dry during the dry season.

Nearly the entire economy of the Dominican Republic has always been dependent on rainfall, which determines not only the capacities of the river systems to support agriculture, but also in modern times prescribes the amount of water that will be available for irrigation and hydroelectric power systems.

The average annual rainfall in the watershed of the Yaque del Norte varies from 20 to 40 inches on the floor of the Vega Real to 60 to 80 inches in the mountains. The average rainfall in the region drained by the Yaque del Sur varies from below 20 inches in the arid valley of San Juan de la Maguana to about 100 inches in the heights of the Cordillera Central. The Yuna system has an average of 50 to 95 inches on the floor of the eastern Vega Real, with 100 inches or more in the mountains. Elsewhere in the country, the average annual rainfall varies widely—22 inches at Pedernales on the southwestern Haitian border, 26–28 inches at Monte Cristi and Azua, 70 at Puerto Plata, 56 at Santo Domingo, and 93 inches at Samaná (the highest in the country except for mountain areas). The relationship of the above figures to agricultural productivity should be apparent. The importance of irrigation and water conservation projects to the economy of the fertile but arid regions is easily appreciated.

Generally, the climate in the lowlands is tropical, and subtropical to temperate at higher elevations. At sea level the average annual temperature is between 77.5 and 79.5 degrees Fahrenheit. July and August are the warmest months, with temperatures averaging between 78 and 84 degrees. The following table will give an indication of the normal variation in temperature found at several of the principal meteorological stations.[3] The winter, or cooler, season generally begins in December and lasts until March or possibly April. Heavy rains usually occur in May and often in September. The chief exception to this generalization is at Puerto Plata, where, according to records of the past sixty years, the months of heaviest rainfall are November through May; however, even the months of June, July, and August are not dry in Puerto Plata, which nestles at the foot of the abrupt northern face of the Cordillera Septentrional. During this three-month period, Puerto Plata will receive on the average about nine inches of rain, which is more than that measured at any one of the stations at Azua, Barahona, El

---

3. Rayford W. Logan, *Haiti and the Dominican Republic.* Travelers have occasionally experienced lower minimum temperatures, especially at Constanza, and higher maximum temperatures, especially in the capital, but those shown here are the normal ones.

Temperature Variation

	Min.	Max.	Comment
	(Degrees F.)		
Puerto Plata	49–69	79–104	20 feet above sea level; center of north coast
Santo Domingo	60–73	88–93	46 feet above sea level; center of south coast
La Vega	58–76	80–91	300 feet above sea level; inland, in the heart of La Vega Real
Constanza	32–55	76–89	3,900-foot elevation; in the Cordillera Central

Seibo, La Romana, Monte Cristi, Neiba, Pedernales, San Juan de la Maguana, or Santo Domingo during the corresponding three months of their dry seasons. The records also indicate that rainfall at Samaná, Puerto Plata, the San Juan de la Maguana, and in the eastern Vega Real is more evenly distributed throughout the year than in other regions.

These geographic and climatologic data are given in only sufficient detail for an understanding of the development of the history of land in the Dominican Republic. The geography of the country may be summarized as follows: The Dominican Republic is divided into three agricultural regions: a tropical zone with normally ample rainfall and fertile lowland fields; the grassy plains region found at sea level and slightly higher elevations; and the subtropical and temperate uplands and highlands. A fourth region might be included—the arid lowlands which are productive only with man-made assistance.

The principal commercial crops are sugar cane, grown in the eastern Cibao[4] and throughout the coastal lowlands; cacao, grown mostly in the deep topsoil of the central Vega Real; coffee, grown on the slopes and uplands of the Vega Real, Barahona, and in the southern uplands of the Cordillera Central; tobacco, which flourishes at the foot of the southern slopes of the Cordillera Septentrional in the Vega Real; rice, in the central part of the Vega Real; and tropical fruits, in the Vega Real and the coastal lowlands.

Cattle and other livestock are raised principally on the eastern savannas, in the Vega Real, and on the south-central plains west of the capital. Stock-raising is also a major activity in the valley of San Juan de la Maguana.

Two-thirds of the country is still forested; the most valuable woods are mahogany, pine, oak, and ebony.

The Dominican Republic's mineral resources have yet to be fully exploited, except for the gold and silver mines of the Cibao and San Cristóbal, which have been closed for over four centuries for lack of production. Other mineral resources either proven or under exploration have considerable potential. Nickel-, copper-, and iron-mining have been accelerating since the 1920's, although the quantities exported have not been significant. Most of the mining concessions are located in the Cordillera Central. Gypsum and alum have long been mined extensively in Barahona Province and exported, and there are extensive natural salt mines in Neiba. Of considerable potential impact on the

---

4. *Cibao*, in the language of the indigenous inhabitants, meant "the place of the rocks." Since colonial times "the Cibao" has generally meant the central portion of the Vega Real, today the provinces of Santiago, La Vega, Sánchez Ramírez, Duarte, Salcedo, and Espaillat.

economy of the country are reliable indications of oil in Neiba and Azua provinces. The Dominican Republic has been favorably treated by nature. The general description of his country by an observant Dominican writer in 1785 is worth repeating today:

> Its advantageous location, its availability for commerce, its pleasant climate, its rainfall and irrigation, its rivers and waters, its mountains and valleys, its abundance of animals and fish, its variety and fertility for agriculture, and, finally, the riches not yet fully investigated that lie deep in its interior and which reach to the surface—all herald a country where nature beckons and arouses envy of a delightful abode.[5]

A description of transportation facilities is not necessary here except to mention the fairly numerous natural ports and harbors which could service the country's external trade: Manzanillo Bay, Monte Cristi Roadstead, and the port of Puerto Plata on the north coast; Samaná Bay, with an excellent port at Sánchez on the east coast; Santo Domingo, La Romana, San Pedro de Macorís, and Barahona on the south coast.

One aspect of inland transportation should not be overlooked, at least from an historical viewpoint—the inadequacy of interior roads. As late as 1921 there was no road connecting the northern half of the country with the southern half.[6] If one wished to travel from the capital of Santo Domingo to Santiago, one had several choices—to travel by local steamship, taking a week to make all the stops between Santo Domingo and Puerto Plata, then by horseback over the Cordillera Septentrional to Santiago; or by horseback over the narrow winding Bonao Trail across the Cordillera Central; or take an alternate route via Cotuí, bypassing the village of Bonao—in either case a trip of several days. In the wet season the Trail was exceedingly difficult, even dangerous. On his trip from Santiago to assume the presidency in Santo Domingo in 1876, Ulises Espaillat took the mountain route via Cotuí, leaving Santiago on the morning of April 22 and arriving in the capital on April 27, having covered a distance of 125 miles.[7] Such almost primitive communications between the country's richest agricultural region and the seat of government constituted a serious enough political and economic barrier in the second decade of the twentieth century; in the colonial period and during the tumultuous years of the nineteenth century, the internal communications problem could spell life or death for the government.

This chapter was introduced by the reference of Raymond Aron to societies in a given

---

5. Antonio Sánchez Valverde, *Idea del valor de la isla Española*, p. 93 (hereafter referred to as *Idea*). Further reference will be made to this late-eighteenth-century author and his work. He was born in Española and was proud of the natural richness of his native land. Sánchez Valverde made a habit of traveling extensively to study the geography, climate, natural resources, agriculture, general economic activity, and the inhabitants of Española. His book, written in 1785 and probably the most valuable and useful of the period written by a Dominican, was intended to stimulate his contemporaries to increase agricultural productivity.

6. The first road connecting Santo Domingo with the Cibao was opened on May 6, 1922. This was a major public works project of the U.S. military government. United States, Department of the Navy, *Records of the Military Government of Santo Domingo, 1916–1924*, Quarterly Report, April 1–June 30, 1922. (Hereafter referred to as *Military Government*.)

7. Emilio Rodríguez Demorizi, ed., *Papeles de Espaillat*, p. 147. Almost fifty years later, geologists of the United States government commented that nearly all overland traffic used trails that were absolutely impassable for wheeled vehicles and that appeared to have received few repairs since the time of Columbus. The sharp hooves of innumerable mules and burros heavily laden with the varied products of the country had cut the soft stretches of road into remarkably even, transverse furrows, some nearly belly deep. With frequent rain at the higher altitudes, the furrows were converted into deep mudholes, slippery and precarious at best. Vaughan et al., *Geological Reconnaissance*, p. 44.

territory; it would not be complete without a few words concerning the inhabitants Columbus met. These were the Taino Indians of the Arawak culture. The Arawaks, about whom anthropologists still know comparatively little, probably originated in South America, drifted up through Venezuela and into the Lesser Antilles. Toward the end of the fourteenth century they were displaced by the ferocious Caribs.[8] The Arawaks in turn moved north and northwest into the Greater Antilles, where they encountered and drove out the pacific Ciboney. In 1492 there was a small isolated tribe of the Ciboney still inhabiting the remote southwest Peninsula of Española, today a part of Haiti.

The Tainos, typical representatives of the Arawak culture, were the principal inhabitants of Puerto Rico, Española, northern and eastern Cuba, and the Bahamas when the Spaniards first arrived in the New World. In the absence of an offshore continental ledge or extensive reefs to support fishing as a major activity, and lacking big game in the interior of the island, the Tainos for the most part turned to farming for their food rather than to fishing or hunting. On the land that was to become the first Spanish colony in the New World they tended to live away from the seacoasts in scattered villages of various sizes, some with as many as 3,000 inhabitants. Their political organization consisted of a hierarchy of independent chiefs, or caciques, each possessing the power of life or death over his sub-chiefs and subjects in all civil, military, and religious affairs.

The Tainos were a copper-skinned, well-proportioned people, of medium height, with broad heads and strong bones. Their distinguishing facial characteristics were high cheekbones, flat noses with broad nostrils, thin to moderately thick lips, and generally poor teeth. Their hair was straight, black, and soft. They were basically a peaceful people, hospitable, intelligent, and expressive. Intratribal warfare usually occurred only over some personal infringement or affront to an individual chief. The Tainos practiced a religion based on a belief in the existence of spirits or souls in both animate and inanimate objects. To gain control over the spirits of nature and thus acquire supernatural power, the Tainos constructed idols of wood and bone, called *zemi*, whose worship was the basis of their religious ceremonies. Unlike the warlike Caribs, the Tainos did not practice cannibalism or human sacrifice.

As farmers, the Tainos used a slash-and-burn technique, changing fields every few years. Ash from burned trees was used as fertilizer. They used irrigation, but otherwise their techniques were hardly more advanced than those of the Stone Age. Plows were unknown; their principal farming tool was the *coa*, a sort of wooden hoe.[9] Corn was an important food, together with potatoes, peanuts, yams, arrowroot, and other tubers, the most important of which was the *yuca*. Española abounded with tropical wild fruit: pineapple, *guayaba*, *mamey*, *papaya*, *chirimoya*, *guanábana*, and *zapote* (whose black seeds the Indians used for adornments) were only a few. Cacao, *aguacate* (avocado), and cotton were also indigenous.

The Tainos did no painting, but were able to carve well in wood, bone, and shell; they had sufficient knowledge of rudimentary metallurgy to be able to work gold by hammering it. There is some doubt as to whether they could weave. Most of the everyday work was performed by the women, who cultivated the crops, prepared food, and

---

8. For anthropological details, I have relied heavily on Julian H. Steward, ed., *Handbook of South American Indians*, vol. 4., *The Circum-Caribbean Tribes*.

9. The elementary stage of agricultural techniques used by the Tainos is one of the factors that has led Rosenblat to place the Indian population of Española at about 100,000 in 1492. Angel Rosenblat, *La población de América en 1492*, p. 16.

carried water. The men hunted for small game (iguana and *hutía*, a small rodent), fished, cleared the fields, and helped with the harvests.

Travel by land was not common. As the Spaniards discovered, there were a few narrow one-man paths for overland transportation, but the series of rugged cordilleras effectively isolated one tribal region from another, especially for north-south movement. Coastal and interisland transportation in dugout canoes was the usual means of communication. Four hundred years later, the water route was still superior and preferred.

Estimates of the size of the indigenous population on Española range from three million, by Bartolomé de Las Casas,[10] to one million or less, by Oviedo, down to 100,000, by Angel Rosenblat among the modern authors. Steward gives no island-by-island breakdown, but has calculated that the Arawak population of the Greater Antilles in 1500 was 225,000, with a population density of 2.5 per square mile.[11] Since Rosenblat puts the Cuban indigenous population at 80,000 and that of Puerto Rico at 50,000, his total for the Greater Antilles would be 230,000 in 1492, which is close to Steward's figure. The modern anthropologists' estimate of about 100,000 for Española at the time of discovery seems reasonable,[12] although it is doubtful that the evidence will ever permit definitive calculation. Rugged western Española (modern Haiti) was very sparsely inhabited compared to the eastern two-thirds of the island, where the bulk of the Indian population was.

Columbus found Española divided into five main tribal regions, or *cacicatos,* which were generally located as follows: Cacique, or Chief, Guacanagarí ruled in Marien, along the north and northwest coast of the island; Guarionex ruled in Magua, which was the most populous and included nearly all of the Vega Real, extending eastward to the Atlantic; Caonabo ruled in Maguana, the west-central and southwest-central region; Behechio and his famous sister Anacaona, who was also the wife of Caonabo, ruled in Jaragua, or Aniguayagua, the wealthiest region located in the southwest and along the southwestern coast; and Cayacoa governed in Higüey, or Yguayagua, the eastern and southeastern portion of the island. The Spaniards' first contact was with Guacanagarí, who, according to Las Casas, was hospitable, friendly, and always loyal to the admiral. Guarionex was initially friendly but soon became belligerent as his people of La Vega Real began to experience firsthand the greed and cruelty of the early conquerors. Eventually the remainder of the Indians followed the example of Guarionex as the Spanish governors set about to pacify the colony.

Nicolás de Ovando, appointed governor of Española in 1501,[13] completely crushed the Indians in two short but harsh campaigns, the first in Jaragua and the second in Higüey

---

10. Las Casas, *Historia de las Indias*, vol. 1 (hereafter referred to as *Historia*). Del Monte y Tejada has noted that three million is a probable estimate, but he offers no support for his conclusion. Antonio Del Monte y Tejada, *Historia de Santo Domingo*, 1: 360. Sauer agrees with those who place the 1492 population at 1,100,000, since this figure was derived from a tribute census conducted by the Spaniards in 1496. Carl Ortwin Sauer, *The Early Spanish Main*, pp. 64–67.

11. Steward also considered the limitations of Taino farming techniques to support the population.

12. Other factors which have entered into this calculation include the inherent difficulty in counting remote and dispersed groups and the tendency of the Spanish conquerors to exaggerate numbers. Rosenblat supports his calculations with considerable analysis in Annex V to his *La población indígena*, pp. 87–92.

13. Ursula S. Lamb has contributed to the history of this period with her book, *Frey Nicolás de Ovando, gobernador de las Indias, 1501–1509.*

in 1503. With the surrender of Cacique Cotubanamá the surviving Indians came permanently under the control and administration of the Spaniards. The peace was disturbed in 1520 by the revolt of the converted Christian, Cacique Enriquillo, who, fleeing from injustice,[14] sought refuge in the mountains of Baoruco. There he was joined by a number of other Indians, and together they refused to surrender despite periodic campaigns by the Spaniards to capture them. Finally, in 1533, after negotiating under a flag of truce, the Indians signed an honorable treaty of peace which stipulated the abolition of slavery. Honoring their agreement with Enriquillo, the Spaniards relocated him and approximately 4,000 others at Santa María de Boyá, twenty-five miles north of the city of Santo Domingo. From this point in time the Indians simply lost their identity and slowly slipped out of existence. By the mid-seventeenth century the last full-blooded Indian had disappeared.[15]

---

14. The Spaniard to whom Enrique had been assigned in *encomienda* outraged his wife. The cacique appealed for redress but was denied it. Thereupon he declared himself in revolt. José Gabriel García, *Compendio de la historia de Santo Domingo*, 1:98 (hereafter referred to as *Compendio*). The most famous Dominican novel of the colonial period takes this "Last of the Caciques" as its protagonist and is well worth reading. The work is Manuel de Jesús Galván, *Enriquillo*. Galván does not ignore Ovando.

15. Sánchez Valverde, *Idea*, p. 109. The Indians may well have disappeared earlier. Rosenblat calculates that as early as 1570 there were only 500 remaining. Rosenblat, *La población indígena*, p. 81.

The Colonial Period

3

DISCOVERY AND EARLY SETTLEMENT

Christopher Columbus' early correspondence about the discoveries of his first voyage revealed how deeply the beauty of Española had impressed him. On February 18, 1493, he reported having taken departure eastward from Cape Maisí at the tip of the island he had named Juana [Cuba], only to encounter within a few miles a new island, like all the others "most fertile to an excessive degree," which he named Española. The north coast of the new discovery abounded with good ports and large rivers. The land was high, and the trees tall, full-foliaged, and as beautiful as those in Spain in May. The Admiral continued:

> There are palm trees of six or eight varieties which one admires the sight of because of their beautiful form, even as the other trees and crops and grasses: here there are pine trees to marvel at, and there are extensive fields, and there is honey, and many kinds of birds, and many kinds of fruit. In the soil there are many mineral mines, and there is an incalculable number of inhabitants. Española is a marvel: the mountain ranges and peaks and fields and land are beautiful and ripe for planting and sowing, to raise flocks of all kinds, to build villages and towns. The seaports have to be seen to be believed, and the many great rivers of sweet water, the largest of which are gold-bearing. The trees, crops, and grasses differ greatly from those of Juana: on this island there are many varieties and large mines of gold and other metals.[1]

Back of what today is the port of Monte Cristi, Columbus later named the beautiful lowlands reaching to the southeast La Vega Real—the royal plain. This was the western extension of the Cibao, which was not only one of the principal nuclei of the Indian population in northern Española but also, to the great interest and delight of the Spaniards, was reported to be the location of rich gold mines. Columbus tried to verify

---

1. Genero H. de Volafán, *Primera epístola de almirante Don Cristóbal Colón, dando cuenta de su gran descubrimiento a Don Gabriel Sánchez, tesorero de Aragón*, pp. 5–6.

the reports of gold personally when he reconnoitered the Monte Cristi beaches in the vicinity of the wide mouth of the Yaque del Norte.

The initial contacts between Spaniards and Indians set the pattern of conquest which has been recorded elsewhere throughout Spanish America; the details need not be repeated here. When he departed for Spain in January, 1493, Columbus left thirty-nine men under the command of Diego de Arana at the fortified villa[2] of Navidad, between the present-day Haitian towns of Cape Haitien and Fort Liberté. This was his first attempt to establish a permanent settlement on the island. When he returned in November of the same year on his second voyage, he found the settlement in ruins, the men gone, and nearly all of the northwestern Indians up in arms. Guacanagarí, who perhaps was the only ally the Spaniards could rely on, reported to the apprehensive Columbus that his thirty-nine men had quarreled and fought among themselves, had carried off Indian women, and had gone about independently searching for gold. Without competent organization their settlement had disintegrated, and the Spaniards themselves had met death either from tropical diseases or at the hands of the aggressive Caonabo, cacique of Maguana and lord of the Cibao gold mines.[3]

Columbus had brought with him on this voyage some 1,500 men, mostly soldier-workers and artisans, a few priests, and about 20 gentlemen—nearly all from Seville. The expedition was equipped to some extent for farming and mining, and included livestock, fruit and vegetable seeds, and sugar cane cuttings taken on board at Gomera in the Canary Islands. But their primary objective was survival in the new and unknown world. Conquest and consolidation claimed priority. In these tasks they were successful, but if the colony were to be populated and made to flourish, the Crown would have to take additional measures. The Crown took the next decision toward colonial settlement on April 10, 1495,[4] even before Columbus had returned to Spain after his second voyage. Some citizens of Seville had petitioned the rulers to form another expedition to explore the Indies. Subject to certain commercial conditions, they received permission, but no further action took place until the following year.

Columbus arrived in Cádiz on June 11, 1496. He had left in Española a dispirited, rebellious force of Spaniards, unhappy and mutinous over the discipline enforced upon them. But they did enjoy the benefits of a well-established defense system consisting of seven strategically located military posts strung between Isabela and the southern Cibao. These small fortresses protected the Spaniards' internal lines of communication. Reports of Indian gold mines along the Haina River on the south coast had been confirmed late in 1495, and to defend this area Columbus had ordered a fortress to be built near the mouth of the Haina. He had also ordered his brother Bartholomew to begin construction of a port town about twenty-five miles to the east on the west bank of the Ozama River

2. As used by the Spaniards, the term "villa" referred to small population centers which enjoyed certain privileges that distinguished them from other hamlets. Lara Fernández notes that Columbus gave de Arana the same full authority that he had been given by the Spanish sovereigns. This delegation may have constituted the privilege. Carmen Lara Fernández, *Primera ciudad cristiana del Nuevo Mundo, la Isabela*, p. 11.

3. This is the explanation given by Columbus' early historian, Bartolomé de las Casas. Incháustegui says that the Indians' anger was caused by the outrages committed by the Spaniards on the Indian women, but does not mention other factors. J. Marino Incháustegui, *Historia dominicana*, 1:42. García cites the Spaniards' avarice, sensuality, poor discipline, and even mutiny. He then describes a midnight Indian attack which overpowered and wiped out the last Spanish defenders. García, *Compendio*, 1:32–33.

4. Las Casas, *Historia*, 1:423.

estuary.[5] With these additional strong points, the Spaniards could easily control the heart of the island from north or south. The potential value of the land titillated royal interest and produced concrete results. The Crown authorized an expedition of 40 gentlemen-at-arms, 100 foot soldier-workers, 30 sailors, 30 ship's boys, 20 goldworker artisans, 50 field hands, 10 gardeners, 30 women, and 20 professionals and tradesmen, including a physician, an apothecary, and an herbalist. Salaries and subsistence were specified, and even business loans were provided for some of the merchants among the 330 Spaniards who were to emigrate to the New World. Realizing that hunger would be as great a threat to colonial existence as would be the Indians and the strange tropical diseases, the Crown specifically ordered Columbus to develop farms and raise stock at Isabela, east of Monte Cristi. For this purpose, the Crown lent the farmers fifty bushels of wheat for planting and twenty pairs of cattle, horses, and mules.

Complementing the provision of material support to the settlers, the Crown then issued the first royal order[6] to Columbus to grant land to them. Columbus was told to apportion land, slopes, and rivers, to construct homes, and to establish farms, orchards, vineyards, cotton fields, olive groves, cane fields, sugar mills, and other farm structures. Increasing the population of the colony was given the highest priority; settlers would be required to remain on the island for four years. Land would be distributed under the old *ejido* system,[7] under which the Crown would retain unassigned lands, and local authority would take civil and criminal jurisdiction only over specified homesites walled off for private use and over unfenced pastures intended for common use. Gold, silver, and brazilwood were reserved as monopolies of the Crown, as were any other minerals found in the earth.

The expedition did not sail until August 1498, but the king and queen of Spain renewed their faith, confidence, and support of Columbus in writing prior to this, his third voyage. Included in their favors was an additional special royal *merced*[8] which, had

---

5. Bartholomew Columbus, in command of the colony after the admiral had departed for Spain, began work on the Ozama port on August 4, 1496. The new town was named Nueva Isabela. A few months later the name was changed to Santo Domingo de Guzmán. Because of its strategic location, it became the capital and seat of colonial government in the New World. This is the modern city of Santo Domingo.

6. June 22, 1497. Las Casas, *Historia*, 1:438. Haring suggests that had this order been given earlier, Columbus might have avoided much of the opposition he encountered from individual colonists already on Española. Clarence H. Haring, *The Spanish Empire in America*, p. 9.

7. The ejido, or common land, system had been instituted in Spain during the Wars of the Reconquest to repopulate as quickly as possible the land retaken from the Moors. Under this system, dispersed, frontier-type population centers were established behind the protection of walls which sheltered the settlers' homes. By day, they worked the land outside the walls. Here all property was held in common and could thus be made more productive sooner by the common effort. Although the system is collectively referred to as ejido, there were separate classes of common land according to the purposes: ejido, fields and land for growing and threshing grain, slaughtering yards, and playgrounds; *pastos comunes*, for pastures; *montes*, uncleared land and forests for lumber and fruit trees; and *propios*, land for management by municipal authorities to develop revenue. Bailey W. Diffie, *Latin American Civilization*, p. 72. Occasionally royal correspondence from Spain would contain the expression *dehesa boyal*, meaning cattle pastures; these were usually subdivisions which had been marked off from the whole. The phrase was rarely used on Española.

8. Merced, or gift, was basically a concession of free title made by the Crown as compensation for extraordinary military service. It was in the nature of a grant, a prize, a guerdon, a keepsake, or favor, differing from a sale in that a sale involved a legal obligation. Manuel R. Ruiz Tejada, *Estudio sobre la propiedad inmobiliaria en la República Dominicana*, p. 15 (hereafter referred to as

it been accepted, would have made the admiral the first great *latifundista*,[9] or large estate owner, of Española. The grant of land ran fifty leagues in an east-west direction and twenty-five leagues from north to south, thus giving Columbus no less than 11,250 square miles of land, or fifty-eight percent of what today is the Dominican Republic.[10] However, as Las Casas quotes the admiral:

> I begged their Royal Highnesses not to make me take it, in order to avoid criticism of evil tongues for settling my own land instead of the Crown's and also for having taken the best, for because of all this the anger aroused would be certain to hurt me; since their Royal Highnesses have given me the grants of one-tenth and later one-eighth of the tribute of all the Indies, I do not desire more.[11]

As the pacification of the island entered its final phase, the process of settlement accelerated concurrently. New villages were established; farming, mining, and commerce began to flourish. The most important population centers developed around the port of Santo Domingo and several of the original military posts in the north: Bonao, Concepción de la Vega, Santiago de los Caballeros, and Puerto Plata, all in or adjacent to the rich and fertile Cibao. In accordance with royal instructions, Columbus began to distribute land, including that cultivated by the Indians, and awarded it to the Spaniards.[12] Individual grants were usually made on a basis of ten to twenty thousand "plantings."[13] Yuca, yams, corn,[14] and other crops were cultivated in each planting. Each

---

Estudio). There was an important relation between the grant of *merced* and the *amparo real*, which will be discussed in Chap. 6.

9. *Latifundismo* refers to the existence of *latifundios*, or extensive land holdings, commonly found in most of the Spanish colonies in the New World and still persisting in some Latin American countries today. The term usually implies that the holdings are of uneconomical size, that is, not fully utilized for agricultural production and therefore socially unjustifiable in countries where many small farmers are unable to acquire enough land to support themselves. In this context, the latifundios have become primary targets for agrarian reformists, and properly so. Not all latifundios, however, are necessarily evil. Landowners who maintain all their holdings in effective production are not *latifundistas* in the uneconomical sense. Furthermore, certain essential agricultural enterprises, such as raising cattle and sugar cane, require large holdings if they are to be efficient. Criticism of latifundia should be based on the factors of land usage and productivity, not size alone.

The opposite of latifundismo is *minifundismo*, a term used to describe the existence of tiny landholdings (*minifundia*) too small to be of economic significance—for example, insufficient to support a family.

10. Based on Castilian measurement of one league equaling a little over three statute miles.

11. Las Casas, *Historia*, 1:474.

12. As the king's attitude toward his Indian subjects developed, his policy on seizure of their land changed. At first, according to his own criteria, the king was only distributing unoccupied land which had no other legitimate owner. Although the area actually worked by the Indians was limited, later instructions specified that land distribution would be impartial and without injustice to them. They were finally considered to be legitimate owners not only of their individual land but also of the communal areas they worked and of the waters which were used therewith. As Phillip II said later, Spaniards in the Indies exceeded their instructions and did much harm to the Indians' persons and property, taking them against their will. Rafael Gómez Hoyos, *La iglesia de América en las leyes de Indias*, p. 84.

13. Antonio de León Pinelo describes the Spanish measurement of land based on *montones*, or plantings, as follows: "For good yields, they formed round plantings of soil, about half a yard high and eight or ten feet in circumference, so close that they almost touched each other, as Gonzalo Fernández Oviedo indicates; although the bishop of Chiapas, Fray Bartolomé de las Casas, says that each montón was four hand breadths high and twelve feet square . . . and one *peonía* [about 46 acres; see Chap. 6, n. 16] of 100,000 montones laid out in a square

assignment of land was substantiated by a *cédula,* or written decree, given by Columbus, stating that the individual named had been given so many thousands of plantings in a designated *cacicato* and that the cacique named, along with a given number of Indians, would perform the labor. Here were the seeds of a long-term *repartimiento,* or forced labor system, for the phraseology of the cédula pertaining to Indian labor did not specify how much or the precise nature of the work the Indians were supposed to accomplish; nor was the overall period of labor assignment given. Hence the Spanish landowner was quick to retain the Indians indefinitely rather than merely to see the crops through the first harvest. He also used the authority of the cédula to divert the Indians to labor in the mines. A license to extract ore which could be extended was usually granted for a fixed period, but in the requests for extension of operations, the owner asked only for additional time, supplying no other details. Once conceded the extension, he would on his own initiative then force the Indians to provide mine labor, since he had never been specifically prohibited from doing so by the terms of his cédula.[15]

Anxious to stimulate prosperity and avoid quarrels and dissatisfaction among the settlers, Columbus responded favorably to their requests for Indian labor. According to Las Casas, Columbus intended to limit the period of such service to one or two years—just long enough to see the colony well established.[16] As it made clear within a short time, the Crown saw no inconsistency with its instructions to treat the Indians well, not to antagonize them, and to punish anyone ignoring the instructions.[17]

In effect, then, the caciques and their people were steadily converted into forced laborers, there being no local authority strong enough or willing to prevent the Spaniards from increasing their holdings at the expense of the Indians. It was enough for the admiral that the settlers were planting and harvesting and laying by; to Columbus, the immediate need to provide food for the colonists assumed greater importance than the morality of the colonists' exploitation of the Indians. Columbus and his successors, who followed his example, were doing no less than even the great viceroys of New Spain and Peru were to do later in the colonial period—place the interests of the Crown and colony ahead of those of the Indians.

In addition to land, the Crown also granted Columbus the right to create as many entailed estates, or *mayorazgos,* as he saw fit and in any manner he desired, in order to "preserve his memory" and that of his lineage.[18] In language the Crown was to employ generally for this purpose, the royal merced provided that the estates so created would be irrevocable and indivisible forever and that the person or persons who might receive the estates could not sell, give, bestow, decrease, divide, partition, or lose them because

---

had 316 montones on a side with 144 left over. . . . " José M. Ots Capdequi, *El régimen de la tierra en la América española durante el periodo colonial,* pp. 61–62 (hereafter referred to as *Régimen de tierra*).

14. These were all indigenous plants. Yuca, a tuber, is still a major item in the rural diet.

15. Las Casas, *Historia,* 2:104–5.

16. Ibid., 2:89.

17. Instructions of the king and queen for Christopher Columbus, May 29, 1493, *AGI, Indiferente* 418. *Lib.* 1, *fol.* 192v, quoted in Richard Konetzke, ed., *Colección de documentos para la historia de la formación social de Hispanoamérica, 1493–1810,* 1:1. (hereafter referred to as *Formación social*).

18. Las Casas, *Historia,* 1:477–78. Mejía Ricart has a complete quotation of the letter granting this authority. The royal letter was written in Seville. Gustavo Adolfo Mejía Ricart, *Historia de Santo Domingo,* 3:225–29.

of debt or any other reason, including the commission of any crime except heresy or treason.

Thus by 1498, only six years after the discovery of the New World, much of the basic settlement pattern had been established: the royal merced granting free land; the enforced distribution of Indian labor; the mayorazgo; and material support for the settlers recruited from Spain financed by the Crown. The Crown, however, was still uncertain as to the legal status of the Indian[19] and his right to the land which was now claimed by the king of Spain. Had Indian land been captured in a "just" war of conquest, to be disposed of as the king desired, or were the Indians to be considered as subjects of the king, with legal rights equal to those of the conquistadores themselves? Far removed from the scene, the Crown would have to make a decision based on circumstances for which there was no exact precedent.

In 1500 the Crown finally decided that the Indians were free vassals,[20] but in its hierarchical approach to social organization gave the Indians legal status below the Spaniards themselves. Thus the Indians, though not slaves, could be ordered to work for the Spaniards.[21] This consideration was a practical one. At the turn of the century the Spaniards in Española, as later elsewhere in the New World, could not afford to treat the Indians as equals in all respects. If not the Indians, who would perform the labor? Only in Costa Rica, considered a poor land for exploitation, where neither Indian nor Negro slavery ever gained a wide institutional foothold, would the sixteenth-century Spanish settlers be disposed to create a livelihood out of the soil by their own personal labor. Elsewhere—in Española, Cuba, Puerto Rico, Tierra Firme, or wherever Indians were found—they were usually treated as slaves despite Crown policy.

Unfortunately for the Indians, Columbus was returned to Spain in disgrace in 1500 by Francisco Bobadilla. With precedent for treatment of the Indians set, Bobadilla, and even more so his successor, regularized the policy of forced labor on the farms and in

---

19. As early as April 16, 1495, the Crown had cautioned the Council of State to hold the money derived from the sale of the Indians whom Columbus had shipped to Spain, pointing out that the Crown itself was not sure it had the right in all good conscience to sell the Indians as slaves. The decision would depend on Columbus' as yet unknown reasons for having sent the Indians and on the opinions of learned men, theologians, and canonists the Crown would consult. Royal letter, April 16, 1495, *AGI, Patronato* 9, *Ramo* 1, *fol.* 85v., quoted in Konetzke, *Formación social*, 1:2.

20. The decision is reflected in the royal cédula of June 20, 1500, ordering that the Indians Columbus had shipped to Spain be freed. Similar instructions were sent to Francisco de Bobadilla, governor of Española. Royal *cédula, AGI, Contratación* 3249, *fol.* 242, quoted in ibid., 1:4.

21. Instructions to Frey Nicolás de Ovando, September 16, 1501, *AGI, Indiferente* 418, *Lib.* 1, *fol.* 39, quoted in ibid., 1:4–6. In one paragraph of these instructions, the Crown describes the Indians as "our good subjects and vassals" (*nuestros buenos súbditos y vasallos*). Later in the document, the Crown tells Ovando that it will be necessary to compel the Indians to work, but to pay them a just wage. These points were repeated in the Provision of December 20, 1503. The Crown referred to earlier orders that the Indians be free and not subject to slavery (*servidumbre*), but now noted that the Indians enjoyed so much freedom that they were fleeing from the colonists and were refusing to work and become Christians. Therefore, in order to provide the necessary labor which must be performed, and to convert the Indians, the Crown ordered the governor to compel the latter to associate and converse with the settlers and work for them. For their labor on buildings, in the gold mines, and on the farms, they were to receive a fair wage. Again, however, the governor was directed to insure that the Indians were treated justly as free men and not slaves (*siervos*). *AGI. Indiferente*, 418, *Lib.* 1, *fol.* 121v., quoted in ibid., 1:16–17.

the mines. Nicolás de Ovando is generally credited with the establishment of the administrative device known as the *encomienda*. Developed in response to Ovando's instructions from the Crown, the colonial encomienda took the form of patronage over the lives of specific numbers of Indians assigned to the individual Spaniards, literally "committed to their protection." The Spaniards' duty was to protect and civilize the Indians and insure that they received religious instruction. In return for these benefits, the Indians were obliged to labor for the settlers, theoretically not as slaves but as paid workers. In practice, the Indians were not treated as workers, were rarely if at all paid and were given little religious instruction. Thus, despite the best intentions of the Crown, the rights of the Indians were increasingly abused as the colony began to develop. By 1509 the Crown found it necessary to instruct the governor to limit the *repartimiento*,[22] or assignment, of Indians to no more than two or three years; to treat the Indians as free workers, not slaves; and to inform him that the royal conscience could not accept repartimiento for life as a policy.[23]

With the foregoing as background, the remainder of the colonial period will be treated more or less topically, to permit the study of specific Crown policies and their application in Española.

---

22. The Crown's use of the phrase "repartimiento of Indians" in this case referred to the assignment of Indians for work and therefore was synonymous with the term "encomienda." In another context, the word "repartimiento" could also apply to a distribution of services, lands, taxes, or goods. See Frederick A. Kirkpatrick, "Repartimiento-Encomienda."

23. Royal cédula to Diego Columbus, August 14, 1509, *AGI, Indiferente* 418, *Lib.* 2, *fol.* 47v., quoted in Konetzke, *Formación social*, 1:22.

4

LAND AND EMIGRATION

By the end of Nicolás de Ovando's administration in 1509 life in the colony had begun to stabilize. Gold and silver mines were producing. The cattle industry was beginning to show a hint of economic potential, and a number of colonists were moving to develop a sugar industry. Columbus had brought in sugar cane from Gomera in the Canary Islands in 1493, but it was not until 1503 that Pedro de Atienza and Miguel Ballester built the first small mill, or *trapiche*, at Concepción de la Vega. Technically it was not a sugar mill, since the owners were interested only in producing *melaza*, or blackstrap molasses. Later, Gonzalo de Vellosa[1] brought in technicians from the Canaries to promote the production of sugar. But commencing about 1510, disconcerting reports began to reach the king. Las Casas had begun his long public battle on behalf of the exploited Indians; from the colonists came complaints of a shortage of labor; but, most disconcerting of all, the population growth seemed not only to have halted by actually contracted. Uncertain of the true situation, the regent, Cardinal Francisco Jiménez de Cisneros, dispatched three royal commissioners to Española in 1516 with orders to investigate crimes against the Indians and to report how the Crown might best administer the colony for the benefit of both Spaniards and Indians. The royal commissioners were also to advise on any other matters which might be useful, especially those having to do with population growth and the development of a strong economy.[2] The commis-

---

1. In 1515 Vellosa put the first small mill into operation at Yaguate, about thirty miles southwest of Santo Domingo. He then formed a partnership with Cristóbal and Francisco de Tapia to erect a larger mill on the lower Nigua River. Sugar production on a commercial basis began here in 1517. The Crown encouraged sugar production by recruiting mill technicians and by exempting from import taxes the machinery and materials needed for mill construction. By 1535 more than thirty mills had been built. See Mervyn Ratekin, "The Early Sugar Industy in Española."

2. Ratekin's description of a typical plantation is most interesting and illustrates the need for land and labor. Twenty-five to thirty acres of cane could produce 125 tons of sugar, but another equal quantity of forest land was needed to provide wood for fuel. To produce 125 tons of sugar, 200 workers were employed, of which 150 were slaves and the remainder Euro-

sioners had full authority to take corrective action, including the removal or suspension of colonial authorities from office. The commissioners, three Hieronimite fathers, arrived in Santo Domingo on December 20, 1516, and until recalled in 1519 were a source of valuable, detailed information to the officials in Spain. Their first report, dated January 20, 1517, included a description of the land and living conditions:

> The land, as it all appears, is very good and fruitful, and it produces in full abundance the things which are usally found in it, and it is believed that if the people of Castile were here on this island and if they were to till and work the soil here as they do elsewhere, their Royal Highnesses would have as much income from it as from Castile.
>
> There are at present very few Spanish settlers and few Indians, so that as a result the land is so scarcely populated that if God does not so dispose it and Your Most Reverend Lordship does not remedy it in some manner, it seems that it will never be populated . . . . As to what we feel about the capacity of the Indians, and if they ought to be put into villages, or what other thing should be done with them, we will not write for the present until we have better information about them and about the Spanish settlers here, and the state and quality of the land, because this matter is so serious and weighty there is need to observe much before one talks of it.[3]

Later in the year, after having been able to evaluate local conditions with more certainty, the fathers reemphasized the need for the Crown to develop the agricultural potential of the island.[4] Granting that the land was almost completely uncultivated and that knowledge of planting cycles and native crops was still sketchy, they were of the opinion that with human diligence and the help of God, the island of Española could become the best and richest of all the royal domains. They pointed out that perhaps the greatest obstacle to the development of Española was the scarcity of settlers. There were few settlers there and they were searching for or mining gold, which in itself was not improving the colony's financial condition. The colonists' food and clothing had to be imported at great expense, with the result that the workers were continually in debt to the Crown or to the Church.[5] The fathers specifically recommended that Portuguese residents of the Canary Islands be permitted to settle in Española because the Portuguese were better farmers.

Pointing to the need for an expanded labor force, the fathers then urged the Crown to grant general permission to the colonists to bring in Negro slaves whose work experience and numbers would augment the labor of Indians in encomienda.[6] The fathers

---

pean foremen and technicians. Mill owners charged other sugar landowners fifty percent of the finished sugar as their grinding price. Most of the mills around Santo Domingo were owned by government officials; thus, although they were influential, their source of power did not stem from their agricultural enterprises alone.

3. Report of Father Ludvigo, Father Alfonso, and Father Bernardino to Cardinal Cisneros, *AGI, Patronato Real, Leg.* 174, *Ramo* 4, quoted in J. Marino Incháustegui, comp., *Reales cédulas y correspondencia de gobernadores de Santo Domingo,* 1:13 (hereafter referred to as *Reales cédulas*).

4. Letter of June 22, 1517, ibid., 1:24–29.

5. In a few words these very observant priests had pinpointed a fundamental economic weakness of the Spanish colonial system as it existed in 1517, as it was to continue for three centuries, and as it is still reflected in the major economic ailments of most of Latin America today.

6. "There is a third necessity, as we have already written at great length, for Your Most Reverend Lordship to order that general permission be given these islands, especially San Juan, so that they may bring in recently captured slaves, because experience has demonstrated their great value in assisting these Indians, should these remain in encomienda to help the Spaniards, which they should not, because of the great profit that will come from them to Your Highnesses;

could only concur with the colonists, that the continued practice of the encomienda was necessary. In this connection, they also observed that landowners absent in Spain had no right to Indians in encomienda; only those who lived in the Indies and had the will to remain should be so privileged. In those cases where the owner was absent, the Indians had suffered, as well as the land. For similar reasons, the settler who lived in one of the islands should not have Indians in another. Here was the first official criticism of absentee ownership in Dominican land history.[7]

The Crown reacted favorably to the commissioners' recommendations. To spur emigration and increase agricultural production, the Crown offered to provide future emigrants a number of special mercedes, including:

> Free passage and maintenance from the time they left their homes until they reached the Indies;
> Free passage and free supplies of medicines for doctors and pharmacists who would go to the Indies;
> Free supplies of flour, other foodstuffs, cows, pigs, horses, chickens, and other subsistence according to their initial needs;
> Exemption for 20 years from all taxes, except for the *diezmo*,[8] for all agricultural workers who would go to the Indies;
> Assignment of Indians to the new settlers to help them build homes and villages, on the condition that the settlers maintain the Indians and that the labor of the Indians be moderate;
> Assignment of land and homesites needed by the settlers for their existence, to belong to them, their heirs, or successors forever; the quantity of land so assigned to be great, in accordance with the individual's desire to work the land;
> Provision of all plows, hoes, and spades needed, as well as plants, vegetables, seeds,

---

we beg that Your Most Reverend Lordships be gracious enough to concede this, and immediately, because these settlers are bothering us about this, and we can see that they are right." Ibid. 1:26.

7. "And because we believe that it was not the will of Your Most Reverend Lordship to undo what we had done here as you ordered, which was to have taken the Indians from the absentee owners who never lived here, among whom was one Oviedo, we agreed that this action be suspended insofar as it concerned the assigning of Indians to him the said orders were being applied, until Your Most Reverend Lordship could be informed of the fact. . . . It seemed to us that in this way we would be serving Your Most Reverend Lordship. And thus we beg you that, as it concerns these Indians, because we know that Your Most Reverend Lordship will be besieged by requests to grant mercedes of Indians to some, since they are to remain in encomienda, that you do not grant them because it will do great harm." Ibid.

8. The diezmo was the tithe, or ecclesiastical tax, of 10 percent which the Crown collected. Nearly all this income was used to support the Church. Pope Alexander VI had, in the *Eximae Devotionis* Bull of November 16, 1501, granted the Crown the right to use the tithes in the New World. In turn, the Crown was obliged to pay for the costs of maintaining and spreading the faith. J. Lloyd Mecham, *Church and State in Latin America*, pp. 14–17. The first cédula prescribing payment of the diezmo on Española was issued about 1503. These instructions, applicable to Española and other islands, were comprehensive, detailed, and very explicit. *AGI, Estante* 139, *Caja* 1, *Leg.* 4, quoted in Spain, Academia Real de la Historia, *Colección de documentos inéditos relativos al descubrimiento, conquista y organización de las antiguas posesiones españolas de ultramar*, 2d series, vol. 5, book 1, *Documentos legislativos*, p. 23. From the time of Charles V, in 1541, the tithes were divided into two equal parts. Of one part, half went to the bishop of the diocese, and half to the dean and chapter of the cathedral. The other half was divided into nine parts. Two were set aside for the royal exchequer, four for the parish clergy, and three for the administration, construction, and repair of churches and hospitals. Thus the Crown received only one-ninth of the diezmo. Haring, *Spanish Empire in America*, p. 266. The *quinto*, or royal fifth, was a twenty percent tax which the Crown collected on precious metals. The quinto might also be levied on other valuable properties such as slaves and war booty.

and other agricultural supplies, and to each worker a cow and a pig for breeding; and
Prize money for the first settler who could produce twelve pounds of silk, ten pounds
of cloves, ginger, cinnamon or other spices not then growing in the Indies, or fifteen
quintales[9] of woad,[10] a quintal of rice, or a quintal of olive oil.[11]

The Crown went to great lengths to announce throughout the empire the need to
send farmers to populate the Indies. Surprisingly modern relocation concepts were
adopted. For example, in those cases where individuals were eager to emigrate but who
first had to sell their present farms, local authorities were urged to serve the king by
persuading the neighbors of the prospective settler to buy his land. It was expected that
fair means of persuasion would be employed on the former and that fair prices would be
offered the latter.[12]

Careful and detailed instructions were given the royal comptroller at the *Casa de Contratación* (House of Trade) in Seville to provide the emigrants with the incentive to
remain in the Indies.[13] He was completely informed of the provisions of the royal
mercedes and told to fulfill as diligently and rapidly as possible those which committed
the Crown to provide supplies, equipment, services, or concessions. At the same time,
however, the Crown left no doubt that it wished to minimize costs of travel subsidies
such as preembarkation living expenses in Seville. Evidently there were some doubts as
to the sincerity of some of the travelers, because the comptroller was specifically
instructed not to advance money, but to pay expenses on a day-to-day basis.

The comptroller was to insure that each embarking settler had with him the appropriate supply of seeds for planting, including wheat, barley, chick-peas, beans, lentils,
and rice. He was also to make an effort to ship out individuals experienced in silk production. The necessary silkworms were available in the Granada area. Similarly, the
settlers were to be provided with plowshares, spades, and hoes, but these tools were to
be forwarded directly to the authorities in the Indies to be distributed to the settlers
upon their arrival.

The inventory seems to have been complete. The king appears to have planned the
program with commendable thoroughness: first, motivate the settler to start a new and
productive life in the Indies; second, pay all his travel expenses, if necessary helping him
to sell his farm in Spain; third, provide him with an ample quantity and variety of tools,
seeds, plants, and farm animals; fourth, give him a generous farm site on which to build
a home and grow his crops; fifth, supply him with native labor; and sixth, provide
financial assistance in the form of tax remission. As a final precaution, the king warned
the royal comptroller to look after the outward-bound passengers, subjecting them at no
time to harsh treatment.

On the same day that the royal cédula announcing the emigration policy was signed,
the king sent general instructions to all Crown officials throughout the empire, advising
them of the concessions offered and enjoining all to carry out the royal orders.

---

9. One quintal equaled approximately 100 pounds.
10. A European herb of the mustard family (*Isatis tinctoria*) grown for the blue dyestuff
yielded by its leaves. The Spanish name is *pastel*.
11. Royal cédula, September 10, 1518, *AGI, Indiferente General, Leg.* 419, *Lib.* 7, *fols.* 91–92v.,
quoted in Incháustegui, *Reales cédulas*, 1:94–97.
12. Royal cédula to all officials throughout the empire, September 10, 1518, *AGI, Indiferente
General, Leg.* 419, *Lib.* 7, *fols.* 94 and 95v., quoted in ibid., 1:99.
13. Royal instructions for Juan López de Recalde, comptroller for the Indies, September
10, 1518, *AGI, Indiferente General, Leg.* 419, *Lib.* 7, *fols.* 93 and 93v., quoted in ibid., 1:97.

By any standards, modern or otherwise, the royal concessions appear to have been well conceived, not only in the enticements offered to prospective settlers but in the basic assumption that the secret of the future prosperity of the colony lay in its agricultural potential rather than in precious metals. The weaknesses of the policy became apparent only after 1518, commencing with the discovery of new land and of colonial development elsewhere in the New World.

There is ample evidence, however, that even the immediate execution of the plan was less successful than the Crown might have hoped. Some of the difficulties could be attributed to the inevitable mistakes of inexperience at all administrative levels, to the long, slow, perilous voyage under miserable living conditions, and to living conditions in the Indies. One of the most debilitating environmental factors over which the Crown unfortunately had little control was that of disease. Epidemics of smallpox carried off thousands of Indians, and this, as well as other tropical diseases, was no less a threat to the settlers. The *peninsulares*[14] seemed to suffer far fewer fatalities from smallpox but were very vulnerable to tropical diseases, a not surprising consequence of the acculturation process. In one group of thirty-seven who arrived in Santo Domingo at the end of June 1520, with wives, children, and servants, all became ill shortly after arriving.[15] None died, and although within two weeks the men in the group had begun to regain their strength, convalescence of the others was slow. As if this unfortunate reception were not sobering enough, nearly all the seedlings, plants, and seeds the settlers had brought with them had either died enroute or were out of planting season. (The Crown was accordingly requested to order the Casa de Contratación to let no ship sail without a consignment of plants which could be sown in the current season.) As their health permitted, members of this particular group of new arrivals were moved to a point fifteen miles from Santo Domingo to settle, but they lacked the numbers and the vitality to make any real headway in building homes and beginning farm activity. By November, after six months of illness, rain, an occasional destructive hurricane, high humidity, and inactivity, could this group have been criticized for a lack of colonizing enthusiasm?

By 1518 sugar production had become important to the economy, and by 1520 sugar was being exported commercially.[16] There were about twelve mills in operation. Although the production of the mills increased as more land was placed under cultivation, there developed such a shortage of labor by about 1521 that twelve additional mills already near completion could not be put into operation for lack of manpower. The labor shortage continued. After thirty-five years of settlement, several important economic factors became so painfully apparent that *Oidores* Espinosa and Zuazo of the *Audiencia*[17] at Santo Domingo undertook to advise the Crown in a long and analytical

---

14. Penisulares is one of the colonial terms frequently used to refer to Spanish settlers born in the Iberian peninsula.

15. The first report of the condition of these emigrants reached Spain in a letter sent by Rodrigo de Figueroa on July 6, 1520. Later, Figueroa's letter of November 14 to the Crown concerning government matters also included a paragraph reporting on the convalescence of the group. Letter, Figueroa to His Majesty, July 6, 1520, *AGI, Patronato Real, Leg.* 74, *Ramo* 19, quoted in ibid., 1: 165–70; and letter, Figueroa to his Majesty, November 14, 1520, *AGI Patronato Real, Leg.* 172, *Ramo* 19, quoted in ibid., 1: 170–172.

16. Incháustegui, *Historia dominicana*, p. 127.

17. An oidor was a member of the royal tribunal or *Audiencia Real*. The Audiencia, which in Santo Domingo was composed of a president and three judges (oidores), functioned variously in a political, judicial, or administrative role. In any of its functions it was the supreme decision-making body in the colony. Some of its corporate political and administrative power

report of current conditions and the causes thereof, and to recommend a number of solutions.[18] First, the bulk of the Spanish settlers were not of the stock best suited for populating new lands. Too many were adventurers or worse, colonists who were likely to seek only mineral wealth, acquiring it by rapid and wasteful exploitation of the mines and afterward moving on to other adventures. Second, the settlers, regardless of their economic activity, were in large measure apparently unconcerned that their negligence and treatment of Indian labor, compounded by the epidemics of disease, were fast reducing the Indian population to extinction. Third, the Crown was caught between two conflicting economic exploitation policies: extraction of mineral wealth, on the one hand, and on the other, settlement, stability, and growth of Española based on agricultural resources. A fourth economic factor of concern to the more thoughtful officials in the colony was the wave of discoveries and settlement of new lands in the New World: Panama, New Spain, Honduras, and Nicaragua. The manpower needed for the expeditions, campaigns, and conquests of these regions was supplied largely from Española, as the oidores complained. Five villages on the island had been depopulated and eight others almost completely changed into ghost towns as ship after ship stripped these centers of their labor force without permission of the Audiencia. The letter written by the two officials was an observant one and worthy of study, for it is an excellent survey of the land and labor situation. In it were certain recommendations and comments concerning the lower classes which, if followed, would probably have changed the entire political and economic future of Santo Domingo. The oidores reported the following essential background facts:

The Indians and the laboring population of Española could no longer support the drain caused by new discoveries without soon disappearing altogether.

In many of the islands there were very few Spanish families or homes built. Most of the Spaniards were not interested in permanent establishment, being willing to remain only so long as they had Indian labor at their disposal.

The city of Santo Domingo, because of the presence of Negro slave labor in the nearby sugar mills, was the only stable population center on the island.

In order to increase the population Espinosa and Zuazo proposed:

> That the Crown adopt settlement policies based on permanency of settlement by emigrants rather than on temporary settlement dependent upon the continued availability of Indian labor;
> That as a matter of policy the Crown seek a totally different class of emigrant, one less likely to be itinerant, that is, married men accompanied by their wives, children, servants, and relatives, all resolved and willing to certify their intention to remain permanently in the New World, and further, that the land given them be so granted on condition that they keep this promise to be true settlers;

---

was shared with the governor, who was also president of the Audiencia. At other times the Audiencia served only as an advisory body to the governor. Judicially the Audiencia functioned as the highest court of appeal in the colony, although in the city of Santo Domingo it might also serve as a court of original jurisdiction. Unless the governor was a trained lawyer, he did not sit as president in legal cases. Oidores were, of course, trained lawyers.

A number of governors and presidents of the Audiencia in early colonial history were Church or Church-related officials, such as Frey Nicolás de Ovando (1501), Archbishop Ramírez de Fuenleal (1528), and Archbishop Alonso de Fuenmayor (1539). The Audiencia of Santo Domingo was created on October 5, 1511. After the signing of the Treaty of Basel in 1795 the Audiencia moved to Havana where after much delay it began to function on July 31, 1800. García, *Compendio*, 1: 280.

18. *Relación de los oidores licenciado Espinosa y licenciado Zuazo al Consejo de Indias*, March 30, 1528, *AGI, Patronato Real, Leg.* 172, *Ramo* 35, quoted in Incháustegui, *Reales cédulas*, 1: 200–212.

That in this manner there would be thefts neither of land nor of person by adventurous gold seekers, nor would there be disillusionment on the part of the settlers;

That, prepared with their families to settle in the New World, the emigrants would quickly forget their past and would become citizens of the new lands they would populate and which would flourish instead of decay;

That the first and main solution for permanent settlement would be for the Crown to decentralize its administrative control and establish in the New World a single agency to make all of the regional administrative decisions, including military defense details, subject only to the authority of one of the audiencias;

That a settler be entitled to only one encomienda of Indians and one assignment of farmland and homesite, except by express permission of the Crown, and that after a six-month residence in any island or province of the Indies, a move to another island would bring immediate expulsion and forced return to Spain.

As their final observation, the oidores added that under the existing policy, the rapid disappearance of the Indians would inevitably result in the complete ruin of the island as the Spaniards moved to other lands where labor was available. Under the conditions they proposed for setttlement, the colonists would treat the Indians as assets, not animals, knowing that a second encomienda would not be granted.

The two oidores submitted these proposals in light of their knowledge of affairs on Española, but their thoughts could well become policy considerations applicable throughout all new colonies. They also made a number of recommendations related to landownership and land usage which were specifically designed to populate and perpetuate the Crown's most important holding, their own island of Española. These special recommendations are also noted here in order to facilitate the analysis of an important cédula issued a year later.

To reverse the decaying process which was taking place, the oidores proposed that selected, qualified citizens of the island undertake at no direct cost to the Crown a settlement plan similar to the early Portuguese *donatário* system for the settlement of Brazil. The qualified citizens selected by the Crown would each assume the responsibility for carving out a new village, without prejudice to any existing one, to be populated by fifty married settlers from Spain or Portugal. Half would be free Spaniards[19] and half would be Negroes, the latter specifically not to be diverted to other already established villages. The principal would pay the costs of passage and initial maintenance, which for each settler would include ten cows, two bulls, fifty sheep, a mare, ten pigs, and equipment and supplies for planting and harvesting. Also, a village church would be constructed of stone, and a fortified building for defense. Everything was to be organized and self-sufficient within five years.

Of economic interest was the proposal to locate the new villages near mines or other work centers in order to provide the new arrivals with a source of outside employment while they developed their land. This was a solution aimed at mutual support of both mining and agriculture in the colony.

To recompense the principals for their expenditure of effort and money, the Crown was asked to grant to each of them permission to import 100 Negro slaves tax-free and a mayorazgo consisting of the ordinary jurisdiction of the new village and one-twentieth of the royal revenues from the village. The plan also called for the Crown to delegate to

---

19. The Spaniards were to be accepted as "Gentlemen, sons of illustrious families, of recognized lineage and with all of the qualities of those who are gentlemen, sons of illustrious families, and lords of Spain." Ibid., p. 208.

the Audiencia the right to determine the amount of land to be given to the new villages and to the settlers.

Thus the principals would assume all the responsibilities for settlement previously held by the Crown, except for the distribution of land, which would fall to the Audiencia. By selecting only families who would contribute favorably to the permanent growth of the colony, by emphasizing the long-term economic aspects of the venture, and by removing the distant Crown from interference or participation in the local decision-making process, or at least by minimizing such participation, the two planners hoped to convert a withering colony into a flourishing one.

The oidores also recommended the increased importation of Negro slaves needed for sugar production, the opening of several port cities to export and import trade, and closer regulation of mine labor.

The constructive recommendations of these two men touched on important weaknesses of the Crown's administrative machinery, immigration and settlement policies and procedures, land distribution, land usage, treatment of the Indians, and trade policy within the empire. But the Crown's reaction to the letter was highly favorable. Nine months later the royal administrative process had ground out a new policy for the founding of towns.[20] Details need not be given, but there were several important elements which faithfully followed the local recommendations:

> The quality of Española-bound settlers was upgraded to the category of *caballeros y hijosdalgo;*
> Permission was given to form colonizing groups headed by a founder under the terms which had been proposed;
> Within five years of the time settlement began, the settlers in each village would have to complete the construction of at least twenty-five houses of stone;
> Failure to fulfill the Crown's conditions would result in total loss to the settlers of the village and its facilities; in addition, there would be a forfeit of one thousand gold pesos;
> Villages founded within a distance of a little over thirty miles from the capital (ten leagues) or other population centers would be limited to an area of thirty-six square miles or less; at more than ten leagues from the capital, the area would be eighty-one square miles;
> Port areas were closed to settlement;
> The Crown reserved to itself the royal quinto on gold, silver, fishing, and pearl industries;
> Settlers and founders would have to commit themselves to remain permanently in the newly founded villages, and this commitment would be carefully examined by the Crown;
> The Audiencia was authorized to assign village land to the settlers, subject to the limitations prescribed in the cédula. Duplicate copies of the land grants would be forwarded to the Council of the Indies for inspection. The authority to distribute land was given personally to the president, and could not be delegated. This was an administrative step in the right direction so long as it did not lead to local abuses.

In decreeing this the Crown confined itself to the subject of founding new towns. There was no comment on the recommendation that 1,000 slaves be imported to bolster the labor supply for the mines. Neither was there any discernible royal reaction to the idea put forward by the two oidores of decentralizing the tight administrative control

---

20. Royal cédula conceding gifts and grants to the founders of new towns on the island of Española, January 15, 1529, *AGI, Patronato Real, Leg.* 18, *Ramo* 5, quoted in Konetzke, *Formación social,* 1:120.

exerted by the Crown and the Council of the Indies. The obvious advantages of administrative flexibility and responsiveness suggest now that perhaps the whole history of the Caribbean, or even all of Spanish America, would have been radically changed if an agency competent to make decisions in the name of the Crown had been established in the New World. Shorter time and space factors alone would have immeasurably simplified the mechanics of policy administration. Decisions would have more accurately reflected the actual conditions and true needs of the colonies. Despite the Crown's best intentions, a distant hierarchy in Spain could not always be expected to understand in detail, or even in principle, colonial problems previously unheard of. In hindsight, perhaps the most significant implication of the suggestion for decentralization lay in the events of the independence period in Spanish America. Had there been a viable, regional policy-making agency representing the Spanish Crown in the New World, this agency could have cushioned the impact of the events at Bayonne in 1808 and could have carried on with colonial affairs.

In the hands of competent administrators such as Antonio de Mendoza or José de Gálvez, Spanish America might well not have disintegrated at all. And with even a moderate display of initiative by the king's regional representative, the breakdown might have been so gradual that the restoration of Ferdinand to the throne in 1814 could have checked the erosion. What might have been the political evolution of the Spanish colonies, given the added years in which to mature? Would there have been reason for statesmen in Washington to fear European intrusion in the New World? Would the Monroe Doctrine have been enunciated?

Difficulties in the settlement of Española centered on the age-old relationships between man and the land. By 1528 a number of associated problems had been raised and recognized. Thinking men had proposed solutions to the Crown, which were in part accepted. Those accepted were economic and social; those of a political nature or which contained major political implications were not acted upon because of the Crown's jealous determination not to relinquish its tight control over the distant, rich subdivisions of the empire.

The Crown's stated desire to populate and stabilize Española was not an empty one. The Cédula of 1529, as well as later ones, encouraged men of character from outside the Indies to become emigrant-founders. One of the earliest complete records of such an enterprise is that of Francisco de Mesa of the Canary Islands. Shortly after 1540 de Mesa applied for royal permission to colonize in the vicinity of Monte Cristi. The Crown gave its permission on September 12, 1545, subject to a detailed *capitulación*,[21] or terms of reference, which set forth the regulations for civil organization and administration in the proposed settlement, special entry tax concessions for the settlers, and a number of clauses relating to land usage. De Mesa, with thirty Canary Islanders and their families, some 200 people in all, would found a settlement at Monte Cristi at no cost to the Crown. De Mesa would be named governor and high constable (*alguacil mayor*).

These were the terms under which the settlement would be founded:

The governor would distribute farmland and homesites to the settlers in the quantities

---

21. *AGI, Audiencia de Santo Domingo, Leg.* 868, *Lib.* G. 2., *fol.* 257v., quoted in Incháustegui, *Reales cédulas,* 1: 341–52. Also included on these pages are cédulas to the *Casa de Contratación,* two to the *presidente y oidores* of the Audiencia of Santo Domingo, one to Francisco de Mesa announcing the Crown's grant of title to the city of Monte Cristi, and a second to de Mesa granting him the title of lifetime governor of Monte Cristi.

and in accordance with the orders to be given by the Audiencia of Santo Domingo. Settlers receiving land would be obligated to occupy it for eight years or lose it.

The governor would not be permitted to distribute concessions to build sugar mills or water rights or land in addition to that specified, these being royal prerogatives which would be delegated to the Audiencia.

A square of land sixteen and a half miles on a side would be granted; all settlements which might be developed within the square would fall under de Mesa's jurisdiction.

Mineral rights would accrue to the settlers, provided they paid the Crown in perpetuity five percent of the value of the mined metal, except for gold and silver, of which the Crown would collect the usual fifth.

Once the governor had fully complied with all of the terms of the capitulación, the Crown would order the president and oidores of the Audiencia to reward de Mesa with a mayorazgo, consisting of the rights to build two sugar mills and to the land for them.

The above terms were reasonably consistent with the principles established in the Cédula of 1529: land was to be permanently occupied and developed; founders would be amply compensated for settlement expenses; the president of the Audiencia was given authority to designate the location of the land to be settled, subject to the maximum area limit set by the Crown; he would also indicate to de Mesa how the land should be redistributed; and the Crown retained its historic interest in precious metals.

The Cédula of 1529, followed by a similar order in 1560, set the pattern for emigration policy and practice. Unfortunately, the long economic depression of the seventeenth and eighteenth centuries[22] stunted the colony's growth and frustrated the Crown's plans. Some emigration took place even throughout the worst years of the depression[23] but never enough to stimulate the moribund economy of the island. Living conditions in remote, bypassed Española could hardly attract many new settlers. During these long years the Crown directly subsidized emigration from the Canary Islands, contributing as much as 16,000 silver pesos annually for aid to settlers. But despite this and other makeshift measures, only the later Bourbon liberalization of trade regulations in and with the Indies brought about a resumption of emigration and consequent increase in agricultural productivity. With this revitalizing policy of Charles III and under the competent and energetic leadership of Governor Isidoro de Peralta y Rojas, the population of Española climbed by 1785 to 152,640, including 30,000 slaves, the highest estimated total population of the colonial period.[24]

---

22. Spanish inability to protect colonial sea trade routes was an important factor responsible for the decline in Española. One of the earliest reactions to the threat of French, English, or Dutch attacks on Spanish commerce was the Spanish navy's adoption by the mid-sixteenth century of the fleet convoy system.

23. During the forty-four years from 1720 to 1764 fewer than 2,500 immigrants of both sexes and all ages arrived in Santo Domingo. *AGI, Audiencia de Santo Domingo, Leg.* 1020, cited in Sánchez Valverde, *Idea*, p. 132. Sánchez Valverde, a contemporary observer, was highly critical of the Crown's failure to promote emigration, especially since the economy of Santo Domingo was suffering by comparison with the affluency of Saint Domingue. He also informs us that during the lean years the Crown nevertheless spent more than twenty-five million pesos to pay for public expenses and salaries of the Audiencia and garrisons of the little colony. With no money coming into the royal treasury in Española, these annual subsidies were sent from New Spain beginning in 1608 and continuing almost to the end of the eighteenth century, hardly an indication of complete disinterest by the Crown.

24. García, *Compendio*, 1:220.

5

LAND AND LABOR

The Crown's first instructions to Nicolás de Ovando in 1501 were clear: Indians were to be treated well, would be free to travel throughout the land, and would receive the same protection from the Crown as any other subjects. The Crown, however, also recognized the importance of Indian mine labor to the royal treasury and made the following exception to the policy of "freedom for the Indians": "Because in order to mine gold and perform the other labors which we order, it will be necessary to utilize the services of the Indians, to force them to work in our service, paying to each a just salary which you feel they should have, according to the quality of the land . . . ."[1] Two years later, additional royal instructions to Ovando included orders to establish the Indians in villages rather than let them live alone "out in the woods" distant from the Church. The Crown also prescribed that Indian workers be permitted to live with their families, as did royal subjects elsewhere in the empire, and that near the Indian homes there be set aside a definite plot of land for each Indian to support himself and his family, raising flocks and farming without interference from his neighbor "so that each might exercise greater care in working and maintaining what was his own."[2] Viewed from the point of land tenure, this was a striking policy. The Instructions of 1503 contained many of the important elements of a modern agrarian reform program: distribution of land to individual owners; increased agricultural production; precise measurement and identification of land, a fair working wage, recognition of the social values of the united family, and recognition of the fact that the independent small farmer would probably maintain his land and achieve higher production than the man who labors in a commune. The Crown quite unknowingly anticipated some of the turn land tenure policies and agricultural production would take in twentieth-century Latin America, especially in Mexico under Cárdenas. It is unfortunate that these initial principles were gradually

---

1. Instructions to the *comendador* Fray Nicolás de Ovando, September 16, 1501, *AGI, Indiferente* 418, *Lib.* 1, *fol.* 39, quoted in Konetzke, *Formación Social*, 1:6.
2. Royal instructions for the governor and officials concerning the government of the Indies, March 29, 1503, *AGI, Indiferente* 418, *Lib.* 1, *fol.* 94v., quoted in ibid., 1:9.

weakened and lost as the Dominican national entity evolved over the succeeding centuries.

In 1509 instructions to the new governor, Diego Columbus, showed the same urgent royal desires, repeated the previous instructions given Ovando, and carried an implication that the earlier orders may not have been fully obeyed, or at least if they were, the Crown was not positively informed. Diego Columbus' instructions included this lengthy sentence:

> Similarly, because we ordered the aforesaid comendador mayor to attend with much diligence to the Indians of that island of Española living together in villages as do our subjects in these lands, and that each one have his home apart and wife and children and designated land, you will find out what has been done about this, and if there is anything needed to be done, work to have this accomplished as quickly as you can, ordering the establishment of the villages wherever you feel best for the settlers there.[3]

The Crown had good reason to issue these instructions. Ovando had been an excellent administrator and organizer, but he had also been an unrelenting exploiter of Indian labor. During his administration, which ended in 1509, the practice of encomienda had become a permanent institution, the equivalent of little more than uncompensated slavery. In the history of their own land, Dominicans remember Ovando as honest, straightforward, and exacting with Spaniards, but despotic and cruel to the Indians, whose numbers decreased rapidly under the mistreatment they suffered at his hands. The last testament of Isabel the Catholic, which urged fair treatment of the Indians, found no fulfillment in Ovando's Española.[4]

The Crown's anxiety over the colonists' disregard of instructions concerning Indian labor found a fuller expression in the comprehensive Ordinances for the Treatment of Indians, the so-called Laws of Burgos, issued on December 27, 1512.[5] There were thirty-five of these laws. One of the main reasons the Crown gave for their issuance was the fact that living so far apart from the Spanish colonists, the Indians were not adapting themselves satisfactorily to the way of life the Crown wanted to impose on them. Specifically, the Indians were receiving religious teaching while serving as laborers, but upon returning to their distant villages they would immediately revert to their customary unvirtuous ways of freedom. As the Crown viewed the problem of Indian indoctrination, the most suitable solution would be to move the Indian villages closer to the Spaniards. The Indians would be able to continue their religious training, receive medical treatment, waste less time going to and from work, and suffer less mistreatment at the hands of the most lawless of the Spaniards.

Accordingly, the Crown ordered the *encomenderos* to build four *bohíos*,[6] each thirty feet long by fifteen feet wide, for every fifty Indians in encomienda and to provide them with land sufficient for 5,000 plantings of sweet potatoes, 3,000 of yuca plus 250 feet of peppers

---

3. Instructions to Don Diego Columbus, admiral and governor of the Indies, May 3, 1509, *AGI, Indiferente, Leg.* 418, *Lib.* 2, *fol.* 19, quoted in ibid., 1:19.

4. Bernardo Pichardo's evaluation of this grim military friar reflects the consensus of Dominican historians: "The rapid flourishing of Española was due to his economic measures, but history will recall his memory for the bloody and unremitting anathema of the repartimientos and will curse his name. . . . " Bernardo Pichardo, *Resumen de historia patria,* pp. 28–29.

5. *Las ordenanzas para el tratamiento de los indios, AGI, Indiferente* 419, *Lib.* 4, *fol.* 83, quoted in Konetzke, *Formación social,* 1:38–57.

6. Arawak term for "dwelling" or "home." Over the years the word has come to mean "hut," and in the Caribbean is still frequently used to refer to a poor farmer's home.

and 50 of cotton. The Indians would be required to plant eighty acres of corn, and to each of the Indians assigned him, the encomendero would provide a dozen chickens and a rooster. The Crown intended that all the above property and its produce be used exclusively for the Indians. This land was not to be subdivided, but was to be made available to the Indians for common use to replace the land they had previously cultivated in their remote villages. It could not be sold, nor could the Indians be removed from it. Once the Indians were established on their land, their old villages would be burned to the ground.[7]

Crown policy on Indian land tenure had shifted away from the idea of individual occupation of land outlined in the 1503 Instruction toward a communal, or ejidal, idea.[8] In 1503 the Crown was concerned primarily with the physical welfare of the Indians and that they be treated the same as other subjects of the Crown. By 1513 the difficulties inherent in bringing the Faith to the Indians had become more obvious. Accordingly, the Crown resorted to the idea of communes in order to promote more effectively the important interests of the Church. The Crown appeared to be upset mostly at the failure of the encomenderos to provide churches and religious training for the Indians and, concurrently, at their continued abuse of mine laborers, their failure to provide the Indians in encomienda with the means to support their families or even with a place to sleep, failure to pay them for their labor or to provide the prescribed special perquisites for the caciques. The Crown also included in the new ordinances a series of instructions intended to increase the investigative obligations of *visitadores*[9] with respect to the living and labor conditions of the Indians, as well as a number of clauses forbidding such illegal actions by these officials as retaining "stray" Indians for their own personal service.

Despite the fact that during the next five years thirty Indian communes were established, treatment of the Indians did not improve materially. A careful reading of the Crown's instructions in 1518 to Rodrigo de Figueroa, president of the Audiencia of Santo Domingo, shows that, if anything, the Spaniards there had imposed increasingly onerous working conditions on the Indians, thus effectively reducing them to a slave status. The instructions to Figueroa not only repeated the earlier Laws of Burgos but, on the basis of reports which had reached the court, added several new ones such as the prohibition of Indian labor for children under fourteen and provision for freeing Indians who in the judgment of the president were capable of living an independent Christian life.

By the beginning of 1519, according to the Hieronimite Fathers, the Spanish population had reached 53,000,[10] but that of the Indians was rapidly dwindling because of

7. The requisites specified in this paragraph are all contained in the first of the Burgos Laws.
8. These laws support the conclusion that the granting to a settler of an encomienda did not carry with it title to land. In both laws it was intended that the Indians retain full land rights, either as individuals or as a community, as appropriate, and that they be protected from encroachment. The consequences of the colonists' disregard of these Indian rights is discussed in Chap. 13.
9. Law number 29 prescribed that in each town of the colony there be two official visitors, or inspectors (visitadores), whose responsibility it was to visit all surrounding villages, mines, ranches, shepherds, and swineherds. The visitadores were to observe the employment, treatment, and religious instruction of the Indians and to observe the degree of compliance with the Crown's orders in these matters. Laws 30 through 34 described in more detail the manner in which the visitadores were expected to function. The governor was told to investigate the performance of their duties once every two years.
10. Letter from the Hieronimite Fathers to the Crown, January 10, 1519, *AGI, Patronato Real, Leg.* 174, *Ramo* 11, quoted in Incháustegui, *Reales cédulas,* 1:134. The figure seems high, but the Hieronimites were not given to exaggeration or to submitting unsubstantiated reports.

disease and harsh working conditions. At the end of the year only fifty percent of the original Indian population was alive.[11]

The complaints by the colonists during the first three decades of the sixteenth century over the lack of Indians for mine, sugar mill, and other labor did not necessarily mean that there were no more Indians on the island. Years of continued mistreatment of the working Indians had, in exhausting the ready supply, left none available for new installations which were being built as the economy expanded. Thus, instead of permitting the Indians to spend part of their work year in encomienda and part, albeit a minor part, on their own lands as the law required, the Spanish *terratenientes*[12] forced the Indians to work practically full time. Dependent on the labor of women and children, Indian food supplies fell to inadequate, or at best marginal, levels, with the result over sustained periods of physical debilitation of both the Indian laborer and his family, leading to early death from illness or disease or simply from physical exhaustion. These conditions were most typical of the Indians assigned to work in the mines of the Cibao and on the sugar estates. Elsewhere, on the cattle ranches and farms, the Indian could adjust somewhat better to his working environment. Even here, however, he fell easy victim to smallpox, measles, and dysentery.

By the end of the sixteenth century the Crown had become unable to resolve the dilemma—a dilemma that characterized the entire history of the relationship between the Spaniards and the Indians and between both and the land. On the one hand, the Crown had for almost a century[13] been trying to put an end to the evils of encomienda and mistreatment and neglect of the Indians, who were free, legitimate subjects of the Crown. On the other hand, slave or forced labor be it Indian or Negro had become the economic keystone of the colony. Since mid-century this keystone had been crumbling because of vicious working conditions which placed progressively heavier work loads on a steadily diminishing work force.

The Crown conceded the superiority of economic considerations over moral ones and grudgingly recognized the colonial facts of life:

11. First report of the new president of the Audiencia on conditions in Santo Domingo, March 1520, *AGI, Patronato Real, Leg*. 172, *Ramo* 17, quoted in ibid., 1:147.

Based on Rosenblat's estimate of the total Indian population in 1514 of 30,000 and that of Father Bernardino, one of the Hieronimites, who estimated 10,000 heads of families *(vecinos)* in 1516, I would place the total Indian population in 1520 at about 6,000. Rosenblat cites the first repartimientos by Diego Columbus of 33,523, the 1514 repartimiento by Roderigo de Albuquerque of a total of 22,336 Indians not including children and the aged, and a report by Governor Zuazo in 1518 of an Indian population of 11,000. Rosenblat, *Población indígena*, pp. 87–92.

12. Terrateniente, which means "landowner," is the term which is still used in the Dominican Republic to refer to a medium or large landholder.

13. During the sixteenth century the Crown issued dozens of cédulas, instructions, and ordinances concerned with the just treatment of the Indians. The Ordinances for Good Treatment of the Indians, dated November 17, 1526, are an excellent example of the Crown's awareness that Indians were being cruelly exploited, contrary to the Laws of Burgos and many other royal decrees. *AGI, Indiferente, Leg*. 421, *Lib*. 11, *fol*. 332, quoted in Konetzke, *Formación social*, 1:89–96.

Other communications of the Crown, in addition to many already cited, included the Cédula to Admiral Diego Columbus Prohibiting the Overburdening of Indian Carriers, July 21, 1511; Instructions to the Hieronimite Fathers, September 13, 1516; Provision against Capture or Enslavement of Indians, August 2, 1530; Cédula Requiring Stone Houses Be Provided Indians in Encomienda, May 4, 1534; and Cédula on Personal Services of Indians, December 2, 1563. Ibid., passim.

First, I ordain and command that Indian repartimientos be made that are necessary to farm the land and raise flocks, for from their labor comes the common utility of that island. . . . Recognizing the repugnance which the Indians demonstrate toward work, it is not possible to avoid constraining those of the repartimientos not to fall into any or all of the bad habits, as described above, in those places where up to now they have not become accustomed, and if the passage of time and the change of customs might better the nature of the Indians and convert the lazy people of other nations [the Spaniards] to work in such a way that with respect to all of the districts of that region, or at least in some, the problem mentioned above would disappear, there being a sufficient number of natives or foreigners who would come voluntarily to work and at the daily wage of these public jobs.

And at the same time slaves could be used in their places, so you could gradually either do away entirely with the repartimientos where they can be dispensed with or more or less reduce the numbers of Indians or the period of their repartimiento as seems compatible to you for the conservation of the flocks and crops that are truly needed to profit from and maintain the land. . . .

And that therefore in no respect are you to permit it no matter how many Spaniards keep asking for repartimientos, and that they continue to cultivate the soil and increase their flocks in more or less abundance.[14]

But there was another message for the colonists in this same long cédula. In compromising the moral aspects of the Conquest with the expediency of economic exploitation, the king salvaged his conscience by bluntly placing much of the blame for the island's economic problems on the reluctance of the individual Spanish settler to work. Had the colonists made the most efficient use of all resources available to them, and had they been willing to adopt more enlightened labor practices, as the Crown had been demanding for decades, the problem of diminished productivity could have been remedied or at least reduced to manageable proportions. The Crown noted that labor practices of the Spaniards on Española, typified by weakness and disdain for work as if it were vile, served only to advertise the laziness of an idle people.[15] Compared with the more progressive practices followed in other countries, the infamous reputation of the colonists was clearly merited. Nevertheless, the Crown realized that some palliative action other than sharp words was obviously needed. Permission was given to the colonists to procure the additional Negro slaves the needed, with the proviso that work responsibility be more equitably distributed among Indians, Spaniards, Negroes, and *mestizos*.[16]

The strong language in the cédula was augmented by threat of rigorous punishment for failure to observe the law regarding fair and moderate treatment of the Indians as free men and free workers. To make sure that memories would not fail, the Crown repeated royal policy on Indian treatment in unmistakable language. The Church was even warned of possible punishment for burdening the Indians with "injustices."[17]

---

14. Cédula addressed to the president of the royal Audiencia of Santo Domingo, May 26, 1609, *AGI, Audiencia de Santo Domingo, Leg.* 869, *Lib.* G6, quoted in Incháustegui, *Reales cédulas,* 4:1039–48.

15. The king was well aware that the early colonists, regardless of their social origins in the mother country, had rapidly become accustomed to the ready availability of indigenous or slave labor. This way of life created in the colonists an aversion to personal, manual work. If such work were needed, it would usually remain untouched if there were no Indians or Negro slaves to do it. And even if the colonists had been so inclined to work, there were never enough of them to meet the manpower needs of such labor-intensive industries as sugar and mining.

16. As a term generally used in Spanish America, a mestizo is the offspring of a white parent and an Indian parent. As used in this cédula, it probably referred to any slave or worker of mixed blood.

There were several differences between the Crown's Indian labor policy and the labor practices exercised in Española. First, as has been well documented and analyzed elsewhere, the labor system which had developed was inefficient, backward, and certainly inhumane.[18] Second, the colonists were inflexibly committed to a continuation of slave or forced labor, whereas the Crown was thinking more progressively in terms of free labor. Third, typical of every crucial Crown decision of the period taken to resolve a conflict between the moral question of treatment of Indians and the economic and strategic importance of the colony, the latter emerged dominant. In the final analysis, the Crown always perceived a stronger obligation to preserve the material benefits rather than its indigenous subjects.

The Cédula of 1609 had little real effect on the actual working conditions of the Indians. The president of the Audiencia, Governor Diego Gómez de Sandoval, complained to the king in 1617 that despite his having issued the necessary orders, the provincial governors had ignored the Crown's desires to insure fair treatment of the Indians. The greediness of the landowners, if anything, had only increased mistreatment of the remaining Indians, who were required to work continuously and were punished excessively for the slightest infractions. Religious instruction was completely neglected. In what appears to be a relatively mild response, the Crown, in turn, blamed the Audiencia for not having taken the initiative in punishing the delinquent officials and landowners concerned.[19] The king ordered the president to advise the governors in writing that failure to observe and require observance of the law would result in their being removed from office and subjected to appropriate punishment.

The moralizing aspects of the Crown's policy of 1609 had been received with little enthusiasm. Gómez de Sandoval, as well as the provincial governors, must have known long before eight years had passed that the landowners were ignoring the royal instructions. The eight-year delay by Gómez de Sandoval in reporting on the effectiveness of the 1609 Cédula was probably due to the reluctant realization that he simply could not overcome local resistance to royal policy. There is no evidence that the governor himself was a landowner or that he benefited personally from the failure to end mistreatment of the Indians; Gómez de Sandoval died in office on August 10, 1623, a poor man. His estate was unable to pay a personal debt of 2,000 ducats to the king, as well as another debt of 1,000 ducats. He appears to have been an honest man, for his own time as well as later ones.[20]

---

17. "Charging them in my name to punish the teachers of Christian doctrine and other ecclesiastical individuals who mistreat the Indians with oppression and injustices. . . . " Ibid., 1047–48.

18. A number of excellent studies on the encomienda-repartimiento labor systems are available, such as Lesley Byrd Simpson, *The Encomienda in New Spain: Forced Native Labor in the Spanish Colonies, 1492-1550;* Silvio A. Zavala, *La encomienda indiana;* Lewis Hanke, *Aristotle and the American Indians;* and Lewis Hanke, *The Spanish Struggle for Justice in the Conquest of America;* and José María Ots Capdequi, *El estado español en las Indias.*

19. Royal cédula to the president of the royal Audiencia of Santo Domingo, August 10, 1619, *AGI, Audiencia de Santo Domingo, Leg.* 869, *Lib.* G.7, quoted in Incháustegui, *Reales cédulas,* 4: 1114–150. The Crown acknowledged having received Gómez de Sandoval's letter of October 1, 1617, almost two years earlier, and eight years after the cédula had been issued.

20. Oidor Martínez Méndez notified the king in a letter of January 2, 1624, that Gómez de Sandoval had died on the previous August 10 after a week's illness which the doctors could not diagnose. He told the king that the governor had not left sufficient money to pay his debts. Letter of Martínez Méndez, January 2, 1624, *AGI, Audiencia de Santo Domingo, Leg.* 55, quoted in ibid., 4:1123–29.

The labor history of colonial Española has shown that commencing with the Hieronimite Fathers, the authorities periodically advised the Crown of the increasingly serious shortage of Indians and the need to import Negro slaves to maintain a healthy economy. The Crown had responded, but slowly. The first Negro slaves were brought in around 1502 by Ovando,[21] but no significant numbers appeared until after Ferdinand the Catholic began the trade in 1510 in order to keep the mines and sugar mills in full operation. For those colonists who could afford the initial investment, sugar mill ownership offered the surest road to great wealth, although perhaps in a less spectacular manner than gold mining. The early mills of average size each required from 80 to 100 slaves, a herd of 2,000 to 3,000 cattle for food and draft labor, and, most of all, a capital investment of 10,000 to 12,000 ducats. By 1523 there were twenty large sugar mills in operation, the largest worth as much as 50,000 ducats and yielding over 6,000 ducats annually.[22] As more land was placed under cultivation, the manpower requirements of the mills skyrocketed. The two mills of Melchor de Torres, for example, which were located just to the east of the capital, had over 900 slaves; the average size mill used 200 to 300; and there were a great many smaller mills whose work force was between 100 and 150.

Las Casas had suggested the importation of Negro slaves in order to alleviate the treatment of the Indians, as had the Hieronimite Fathers, although the fathers perhaps gave more emphasis to the potential economic benefits than to humanitarian considerations. In response to the increasing demand for more slaves, the Crown established for the Indies a system of *asientos*, or contracts, whereby private contractors would undertake to deliver Negro slaves to destinations on a schedule determined by the Casa de Contratación. Asientos were granted to Spaniards and foreigners alike. By royal Cédula of August 8, 1518, Charles V granted Lorenzo de Gramenot,[23] the governor of Brescia and a court favorite, the privilege of shipping 4,000 slaves to the Indies over a four-year period. The Negroes had either to be Christian or to be baptized upon arrival.

---

21. Ovando brought in Christianized Negro slaves from Spain in small numbers, but found that they would either flee to the mountains or create difficulties with the Indians. Carlos Larrazábal Blanco, *Los negros y la esclavitud en Santo Domingo*, p. 13 (hereafter referred to as *Los negros)*.

22. Gonzalo Fernández de Oviedo y Valdés, *Historia general y natural de las Indias*, 1: 118–124. An approximate idea of the average cost of a sugar mill in 1523 can be obtained by using the following conversion factors:

1 ducat = 375 maravedises
1 peso fuerte (25.563 gms. silver) = 272 maravedises;
Clarence H. Haring "Ledgers of the Royal Treasurers in the Sixteenth Century," *HAHR, 2* (May 1919), 183.
18.5 dollars = 5,000 maravedises;
Incháustegui, *Historia dominicana*, p. 123.

To build a sugar mill, therefore, the average capital investment was 10,900 ducats, the equivalent of 15,000 pesos or 15,123 dollars. Incháustegui, however, does not identify the date of the dollar. A more meaningful indication of the investment involved can be derived from the data on contemporary salaries. Until 1523 the annual salary of an *oidor* in Española was 150,000 maravedises, or slightly over 550 pesos. Ibid., p. 128. The capital required, therefore, was the equivalent of the accumulated salary of an oidor for almost 28 years. Oviedo expressed a comparable thought: "But the truth is that he who is the owner of a sugar mill freely and well provided for, is very well and richly propertied; and such sugar mills are of the greatest use and wealth for the owners." Oviedo, *Historia general*, p. 119.

23. Larrazábal Blanco, *Los negros*, pp. 23–24. The spelling of the governor's name varies. Elliott identifies him as Laurent Gorrevod. J. H. Elliott, *Imperial Spain, 1469–1716*, p. 143. Haring refers to him as Laurent de Gouvenot; *Spanish Empire in America*, p. 204.

Several small asientos were granted later in 1518, and in 1523 a larger one for the entry of 1,500 slaves into Española was also granted. In 1528 two Germans, Einger and Sayller, obtained a concession for 4,000 slaves to be delivered to the Indies over a four-year period; from that year on, the system functioned on a regular basis.[24]

The Crown set minimum selling prices and collected an import tax per head from the contractor after he had delivered the slaves to their destination. Since the Spaniards were not permitted by the Inter-Caetera Bull of 1493 to trade directly at African ports, Spanish holders of asientos made their arrangements through Portuguese ship captains to bring the slaves out of Africa and deliver them.[25] Eventually Dutch, British, and French entrepreneurs were also able to acquire asientos. This local or decentralized system, however, created problems for the Spanish Crown. The foreign slavers tended to use their concessionary rights as a cover for general contraband activity; local asientos also created frequent administrative problems because of quarrels and lawsuits between contractors. The system functioned, but not always smoothly.

By 1569 the scarcity of Indian labor, which had been the subject of reports for over fifty years, finally passed into the critical stage. The Audiencia informed the Crown that for all intents and purposes Indian labor no longer existed and that consequently the prosperity of the island was diminishing by the day.[26] All labor had to be performed by Negroes, and even they were in short supply because of their high death rate. Therefore the economy of the island had decreased in value and would continue to do so if the situation was not remedied. The authorities appealed to the Crown for permission to import more slaves without having to wait for supply by regular fleet schedules. An unfavorable reply came back to the Audiencia in May of the following year. Although admitting the lower cost of direct importation on an as-needed basis, the Crown rejected the idea out of hand, merely saying that to inaugurate a new system would not be desirable. The Crown also rejected as poor business an alternative proposal to import Brazilian Indians. The Crown stated that under the law the Indians thus imported could not leave the island and, after twelve years of service, could purchase their freedom and then form their own settlements. There is no record of the Spaniards on Española ever having imported Brazilian Indians as slaves; Negroes continued to make up the labor force.

The reasons for the Crown's refusal probably lay in the proven evils of the local asiento system. The king could foresee added administrative complications arising from disagree-

---

24. Larrazábal Blanco, *Los negros*, p. 29. Einger and Sayller were Seville merchants.

25. Hubert Herring, *A History of Latin America*, p. 101. Larrazábal Blanco does not make this same observation, but he does mention "intermediaries who had to be paid or who collected payment based on the sale of slaves which they had gone to bring from Africa." Larrazábal Blanco also mentions that the German concessionaires Einger and Sayller subcontracted their asiento to the Portuguese. Larrazábal Blanco, *Los negros*, pp. 26, 29. James F. King also mentions that Spanish slave companies or *asentistas* had to acquire African slaves using Portuguese, Dutch, English, or French ships. "Evolution of the Free Slave Trade Principle in Spanish Colonial Administration," p. 340.

26. Acknowledged by the Crown in *Real respuesta a la Audiencia de Santo Domingo*, May 26, 1570, *AGI, Audiencia de Santo Domingo, Leg.* 899, *Lib.* 2, *fol.* 165v., quoted in Konetzke, *Formación social*, 1: 455–56. In this reply the Crown acknowledged the Audiencia's earlier letter of August 26, 1569, "in which you say that the island is getting worse every day because, since there are no Indians there, the workers who are to support it must be Negro slaves, and these for many days have not gone to that island, and since they die and are taken away, the fruit of the land has gradually diminished and will continue to do so every day if this is not remedied. . . . "

ment between his own contractors and those the Audiencia might hire, and he almost certainly could anticipate that with an asiento under colonial control the contraband traffic would be enlarged. A third, somewhat more remotely possible, explanation was that the Crown simply may have wanted to retain control over the influx of Negroes for security reasons. Española was lightly populated by Spanish colonists, and events in Peru and Panama about 1550 had clearly illustrated the Negro slave's potential for violence and even rebellion.

Nevertheless, a few years later when faced with the choice of either increasing the importation of slaves or accepting the ruin of the island's economy for lack of manpower, the Crown relented. In 1582 the Council of the Indies took note that the authorities on Española had no Indians available and needed more slaves for labor in the cane fields, sugar mills, and on the ranches. The council also noted that the authorities had asked the Crown for permission to import 2,000 Negroes. Because of a lack of local funds the authorities had proposed that the slaves be paid for by the Crown in the form of a loan to be repaid in four years. After due consideration the council recommended that the king grant special license to import 1,000 slaves, 250 a year at 30 ducats each. Those arriving the first year would be paid for within the next two years; those arriving the second year would be paid for within the two years following; and so on. Finding that his Council agreed with the colonists, the king approved the recommendation.[27]

The early Bourbons continued the slave policies of the Hapsburgs without significant change. It remained for Charles III to introduce the innovations that would centralize administrative procedures and minimize the operational problems of the slave trade. Local asientos were withdrawn. In 1764 the Crown put the entire slave enterprise in the hands of a single Spaniard, Miguel Uriarte, subject to direct regulation from Madrid.[28] Under the terms of his asiento the contractor agreed to deliver annually 150 slaves each to Cartagena and Porto Bello, 1,000 to Cuba, and for Cumaná, Santo Domingo, Trinidad, Margarita, and Puerto Rico, all of which were lightly populated, a total of 500 to 600. Because of organizational delays the new asiento did not begin to function until 1768, but it lost money under the profit policy of the Crown. Uriarte, who had agreed to pay a tax of 40 silver pesos on a selling price of 300 pesos for each slave delivered, went bankrupt in 1772. Charles III, therefore, shortly abandoned the profit motive and reorganized the asiento under a policy aimed at providing the cheapest labor possible to the colonies.

The state of war between England and Spain in 1779 created maritime difficulties for the Spanish Crown, forcing it to open the slave trade to allied Frenchmen.[29] By 1780 a much reduced 6 percent import head tax was in effect, along with a minimum selling price of 200 silver pesos per slave, and private asientos were again being granted. Only one further step remained to open wide the importation of slaves—free trade—which was not long delayed.

Influenced by the heavy need for slaves in Santo Domingo, Cuba, and Puerto Rico, the Crown had begun to lean toward free slave trade about 1784. For example, in 1785

---

27. *Consulta del Consejo de Indias,* September 7, 1582, *Archivo General de Simancas, Leg.* 137, *fol.* 259, quoted in Incháustegui, *Reales cédulas,* 3:667. The king approved the recommendation on September 14.

28. James F. King discusses the Uriarte asiento in detail because Uriarte's failure led to the important policy change by the Crown noted above. "Evolution of the Free Slave Trade Principle," pp. 36–44.

29. French slavers were nevertheless required to bring in the slaves under the Spanish flag.

the *cabildo* (or town council) of Panama was authorized to arrange directly for the importation of 2,000 slaves. In 1789 the Spanish monarch officially approved a recommendation by his Council of State to open up Santo Domingo, Cuba, Puerto Rico, and Caracas, where the need for field workers was urgent.[30] All the old restrictions were removed in order for the Spanish sugar islands to compete with Haiti, Jamaica, and Guadeloupe. All import duties were removed; any Spanish subject, either colonist or peninsular, could purchase slaves in foreign markets and transport them in his own ship. During a two-year trial period foreigners could also freely bring in slaves wherever needed, although they were required to use vessels of not over 300 tons. Neither Spaniards nor foreigners could otherwise flout the restrictions of the Crown's mercantile policy. Free importation was limited to slaves only. By 1804 free slave trade had been granted to the rest of the empire.[31]

The full impact of the free slave trade system could never be measured. The French Revolution, the European wars which followed, and, even worse, the Napoleonic Wars—all created a multiplicity of hazards along the sea lanes to the Indies and gradually brought slave traffic to a virtual standstill.

The colonial period in Española, which began with slavery, ended there in the same fashion, with only one major change: the black man had replaced the Indian, who no longer existed as a social entity.

---

30. This was the Cédula of February 28, 1789, "*Real cédula de su magestad concediendo libertad para el comercio de negros con la isla de Cuba, Santo Domingo, Puerto Rico, y provincia de Caracas, a españoles y extrangeros baxo las reglas que se expresan,*" Madrid, 1789. King, "Evolution of the Free Slave Trade Principle," p. 50.

31. Ibid., pp. 52–56. The Rio de la Plata had been opened to free slave trade by royal Cédula of November 24, 1791; by royal order, the Peruvian ports of Callao and Paita were opened to free and direct Negro slave traffic by sea on May 28, 1795. Finally Panama and Guayaquil were given the same privilege in a royal cédula of April 22, 1804.

6

THE DISTRIBUTION OF LAND

As early as 1501 the Crown foresaw that the failure of the colonists to band together for mutual support could lead to failure of settlement, the catastrophe which had overtaken the villa at Navidad in 1493. Accordingly the Crown issued instructions[1] that the settlers not be permitted to scatter and that they be made to live within the communities which were to be established. Here the Crown was falling squarely back on the frontier tactics of the Wars of the Reconquest, the main experience it could draw on for the establishment of settlements. In addition, the Crown prescribed that each settler have on his property a hut or small house to which he could retire when he inspected or worked his land.

In making land available later as settlements began to form in the new colony, the Crown even prescribed the configuration of the population center: "And if the two leagues cannot be laid off as a square along one of the sides as indicated, whatever is lacking you can compensate for on another side as it may seem most suitable and convenient to you. . . . "[2] Thus in 1529 thirty-six square miles were set as the standard area for new villages and their lands, approximately the same dimensions to be used later on the North American frontier. As an added incentive the Crown still later greatly increased the amount of land.

> . . . and if the four leagues cannot be laid off as a square along one of the sides or if it cannot be done without prejudice to the limits of already established settlements, what may be lacking can be fully compensated for by extending or running through, which-

---

1. In their instructions to the governor-designate of Española, Nicolás de Ovando, the Spanish rulers said: "Because our will is that the Christians who now live on the said island of Española, and those who henceforth may leave here to live there, not be scattered, you will prohibit anyone from living outside the settlements which are being made on that island." *AGI, Indiferente* 418, *Lib.* 1, *fol.* 39, quoted in Konetzke, *Formación social*, 1:6.

2. *Real cédula concediendo gracia y mercedes a los que hicieren nuevas poblaciones en la isla Española,* to the president of the royal Audiencia, Santo Domingo, January 15, 1529, *AGI, Patronato Real* 18, *Ramo* 5, quoted in ibid., 1: 123.

ever seems to be most suitable and convenient, because by this cédula we concede and
give them four square leagues for their settlement, as and how you may designate and
give them. . . .[3]

Normally the Crown left the decision of the precise location of the settlements to the
Audiencia, but there was one exception to this general rule. New settlements could not
encompass seaports or other locations which in the opinion of the Audiencia could
prejudice the future interests of either the Crown or the colony. Specific reasons were
not given, at least in the pertinent cédulas, but one can assume that the Crown had in
mind the fact that port areas were vulnerable to invasion and should remain in control
of the state for defense purposes.

By 1560 the Crown began to refine its policy for the establishment of new settlements.
The attorney general of the island, Baltasar García, had included in an earlier official
report[4] a recommendation that the Crown rectify the matter of sparse population and
thus not only improve the royal income and patrimony on Española but also strengthen
and conserve the Crown's position throughout the Indies. García's ideas were well
received. Accordingly, a new policy[5] reflected renewed efforts to facilitate settlement
based on the general emigration procedures established in 1529—that is, responsible
citizens (founders) would be permitted by the Crown to found and populate new towns
on a permanent basis at their own expense, subject to the Crown's granting them certain
political and economic concessions, as well as assigning them certain administrative
responsibilities. The Royal Ordinance of 1560 lowered the minimum distance of new
townsites from the capital from ten to five leagues. It permitted the assignment of four-
league squares (squares twelve miles on a side) for each townsite, so long as it was
located more than five leagues from Santo Domingo. After first assigning common
pasture and crop land to the town ayuntamiento,[6] it gave the founder one-fourth of the
remaining area, the remainder to be divided among the free settlers. It was hoped that
the number of founders would be thirty, but there must be at least ten, whose sons,
daughters, and relatives could qualify as settlers provided they were married and
maintained separate establishments in separate houses. Subject to the authority of the

---

3. *Real ordenanza sobre la población de la isla Española,* to the president of the royal Audiencia,
Santo Domingo, July 9, 1560, *AGI, Santo Domingo, Leg.* 899, *Lib.* 1, *fol.* 173v., quoted in ibid.,
1:378–84.

4. The Royal Ordinance of 1560, cited below, acknowledges receipt of the report made by
Baltasar García "en nombre desa isla" concerning the sparse population. García is identified
as the attorney general *(procurador general)* in another royal letter to the Audiencia concerning
improvement of the port of Santo Domingo. *AGI, Audiencia de Santo Domingo, Leg.* 899, *Lib.* 1,
fol. 49v, March 22, 1557, quoted in Incháustegui, *Reales cédulas,* 2: 399.

5. *Ordenanza sobre la población de la isla Española,* July 9, 1560, quoted in Konetzke, in *Formación
social,* 1:378.

6. Ots Capdequi gives us the typical language used by the Crown in its *capitulaciones,* or
contracts, with founders: "They will be given four leagues of land and territory either in squares
or extended, according to the quality of the land as it may happen to be. The said land will be
distributed in the following form: take out first what may be needed for the village homesites
and for adequate ejidos and pastures in which the cattle can graze freely, which it is ordered to
be given to the settlers, plus an additional amount for the common land of the village. The
remainder of the said territory and land will be divided into four equal parts: one to be selected
by he who is responsible for founding the said town, and the other three will be divided into
thirty parts to be drawn by lot by the thirty settlers of the said place. The pastures of the said
land may be used in common once the crops have been harvested, except for the cattle pastures
owned by the town." Ots Capdequi, *Régimen de la tierra,* pp. 50–51.

Audiencia, the founders would have the responsibility for determining and distributing village lands to the settlers; if the founder could not complete the establishment of his village within the specified ten years, he would not lose his entire investment but would be given an extension in time by the Audiencia. Looking to the future growth of towns around labor-intensive enterprises, the Crown conceded to already established sugar mill owners the same founding rights, privileges, and responsibilities as were given to the leaders of new colonizing groups. As for the Crown itself, for the first ten years after the formation of the settlement, it would collect the royal tenth from the production of gold, silver, other minerals, salt, and pearls, and after the ten years, would collect in perpetuity one-eighth of the production.

No reference was made to royal monopolies of wood, since by 1560 the production of brazilwood and balsam had become insignificant for commercial purposes, but there was specific mention of land for common usage.[7] In the Cédula of 1560 the king not only prescribed that ejidos and pastures be set aside within the new town limits, but he also took the opportunity to restate the principle of common usage for the entire colony. In the city of Santo Domingo, the Crown set aside as communal land all of the fields, slopes, and waters within a radius of ten leagues of the city.

When the king issued the comprehensive Ordinances of 1573, he authorized the *adelantados,* or founders of new settlements, to set aside ejido land, watering places, roads, and trails to be administered by the cabildo; this system has been followed down to the present. The use of common land was reserved exclusively for the settlers, except for privileges specifically given to others. The cabildo supervised common farm land as well as the land assigned the town itself. At times the cabildo would amplify or extend town limits at the expense of ejido land, or at times would lease the land in order to obtain income. Theoretically, all unassigned lands outside the limits of land granted by the Crown either to individual settlers or to the town were *terrenos baldíos* (empty land), whose disposition remained a Crown prerogative. In practice, however, the cabildo itself was often guilty of usurping royal authority over terrenos baldíos. Assuming in many cases that it had, or ought to have, the authority to distribute or sell land, the cabildo would do so without reference to higher authority. Thus as part of the Crown's campaign in the seventeenth century to regain control of the distribution of land, as will be.described below, the viceroys were ordered to revoke all directives giving the cabildos land distribution powers. This order was received with the same notable lack of enthusiasm by the cabildos as were other royal policies intended to correct the illegal land usurpations of individuals (see the next chapter).

During the years following Columbus' pacification of the Indians, the Crown's paramount interest lay in insuring the permanency of settlement. Marginal supplies of food and difficulties in adjusting to the unfamiliar tropical climate were basic problems

7. The ejido idea, introduced in 1498, remained strong in Española throughout the colonial period and beyond. One of the earliest royal orders was given in 1510: "Our desire is to make and for the present we do make the woodlands of wild fruit trees common, so that each one can take from them and carry the plants to his own farm or ranch and thus take advantage of these as a common thing." Royal cédula, June 15, 1510, later repeated in the 1680 *Recopilación de leyes,* Book 4, Title 17, Law 8, quoted in Spain, Ministerio de Trabajo y Previsión, *Selección de las leyes de Indias,* p. 69. Other laws in Book 4 also prescribed that uncleared land and pastures of the village domains be communal, that once the crops had been harvested from cultivated land, the land could be used for common grazing, and that the colonial authorities order cattle removed from watered fields and wheat planted there instead. Ots Capdequi, *El régimen de tierra,* p. 96. See also note 6 above.

which continually tormented the Spaniards. We have seen that by 1516 the Indians were already fast disappearing; that the colonists had less interest in farming and more in searching for gold or adventure in other lands; and that as New Spain and the colonies of Tierra Firme began to assume greater importance to the royal treasury, Española was converted from a principal colony to a mere port of call to and from the newly conquered lands to the west. The king's officials in Española, as well as other responsible citizens, began to appeal to the Crown to take action to stop the drain on the local population and to encourage the emigration of colonists who would till the soil and provide the colony with some economic stability. No one was more zealous in trying to prevent the loss of men to the colony than the president of the Audiencia, Alonso de Fuenmayor—or so he advised the king. As Father Cipriano de Utrera points out,[8] however, there was a world of difference between what the president said and what he did. On the one hand, he was officially doing everything possible to prevent emigration from Española or recruitment of troops for expeditions, in accordance with the Crown's instructions.[9] On the other, he permitted his brother, Diego de Fuenmayor, to take 300 men and 20 horses to Peru to aid Francisco Pizarro, who took all the help he could get—and then asked for more. So the president of the Audiencia sent an additional 150 men and 100 horses, thus creating another example of the Crown's largest administrative difficulty: the divergence between *hecho* and *derecho*, the difference between the execution of royal policy in the colonies and the concepts on which the policy had been formulated in Spain.

By the beginning of the 1530s there was a natural evolution in the Crown's policy. The new objective was growth of settlement rather than permanency of settlement. The capitulaciones and instrucciones to founders of new settlements, as well as the incentives offered to individual emigrants, reflected the Crown's realization that the future of Española depended on agriculture rather than on precious minerals. Gold and silver production had passed their peaks by 1520.[10] Labor in the mines was becoming too costly an investment in terms of lives, and by 1533 the value of the sugar crop produced on the fifty established plantations had exceeded the diminishing value of mine output. By the time the fabulous discoveries had been made at Potosí in Upper Peru, followed by those of Zacatecas, Guanajuato, San Luis Potosí, and Pachuca in New Spain, the Crown had already ordered the mines closed on Española. Although cattle-ranching was a major

---

8. Sánchez Valverde, *Idea,* note, p. 108. De Utrera has annotated this valuable work in an attractive, scholarly style which greatly enhances its usefulness. This observation of Fuenmayor's actual policy is contained in a footnote to Sánchez Valverde's statement that the president of the Audiencia was doing his best to comply with Crown policy. De Utrera would add parenthetically: "except as it applied to his own family."

9. In a royal cédula of November 17, 1526, the Crown directed the oidores, governors, and law authorities to prohibit married settlers in the colonies from abandoning the colonies for the attractions of new discoveries, under pain of death and loss of property. Ots Capdequi, *Régimen de tierra,* p. 46.

10. The production of gold and silver in Española is difficult to estimate accurately. As was the case in New Spain, early records are not reliable; since the gold cycle was so short, perhaps the most that can be said is that the production was disappointing to the Crown. Peter Martyr stated that in 1516 at the height of production, the output of precious metals was valued at 400,000 ducats or 552,000 silver pesos. Arthur P. Newton, *The European Nations in the West Indies, 1493-1688,* p. 31.

Sánchez Valverde says that the annual output of gold was at least 460,000 pesos at peak production, but that this figure did not include gold nuggets or gold illegally withheld from the foundries. Sánchez Valverde, *Idea,* p. 81.

domestic enterprise, sugar was to be the export money crop. As early as 1517, production had exceeded that of Cuba.[11]

By 1558, land was being distributed on a basis of effective occupation—that is, mere desire for ownership was no longer the sole criterion for distribution. Mandatory cultivation within a specified period had become a factor. Settlers were to be given full and clear title, but with the provision that they clear the land and plow and cultivate it within six years after receiving title. Failure to comply with this condition of occupancy would lead to forfeiture. There also appeared another innovation in policy of even greater moment.

These are the words of the Cédula of 1558, directed to the president and oidores of the Audiencia of Española regarding new farmer-settlers:

> To all of the settlers that go there and take their wives, children, and belongings to remain there . . . you may give and sign over in our name one thousand fanegas[12] of land, or less as you see fit, *according to the quality of the individuals,* in the region that seems best suited . . . and that they be obliged to till the soil that is thus given them and convert it into arable farmland within six years or suffer the loss of it which may be given to another. . . .[13]

The significance of the phrase "according to the quality" is most important in the history of land settlement in Española. The Crown had used similar phraseology in a general sense many years earlier in its instructions for the settlement of Tierra Firme and New Spain,[14] but had never applied the distinction to Española. This was the Crown's acknowledgement that the permanent settler possessing greater wealth and therefore a greater potential for production should be given more land. All settlers were to receive some land; yet now the Crown recognized a basic difference among them. Those who were in a position to support a larger concession—the wealthier and usually more influential settlers—could manage, and accordingly were given, more land than the settlers with lesser resources. There was no injustice here, only recognition of an economic fact of life, given the Crown's new emphasis on production. But, as has also happened elsewhere in the history of mankind, the differences in economic status gave birth to excesses which today have become social injustices. Large landholders were to grow larger and more powerful through encroachment, the grant of mayorazgo, inheritance, refusal to put an end to the evils and abuses of the encomienda, and evasion of other royal orders intended to better the lot of the slave or worker, whether Indian or Negro. These were the factors that tended to undermine a royal policy created to increase agricultural production. The socioeconomic implications of the 1558 cédula, as amplified

---

11. Ibid., p. 59.

12. The definition of land area varied from region to region. According to the *Dictionary of the Royal Spanish Academy,* 18th ed., a Castilian fanega of ground area equaled 576 estadades. Since one estadad equaled 11.1756 square meters, the fanega would measure about 6,437 square meters. One thousand fanegas, therefore, would be 6,437,000 square meters, or a square of approximately 2,550 meters on a side. This would equal about 1,600 acres.

13. *AGI, Audiencia de Santo Domingo, Leg.* 899, *Lib. 1, fol.* 121v., quoted in Incháustegui, *Reales cédulas,* 2:406. Author's emphasis.

14. Instructions to Pedro Arias de Avila, August 2, 1513, and to Hernán Cortés, June 16, 1523. The Crown told them to distribute land "according to the quality of the individuals, making sure that to all fall a part of the good and of the average and of the poorer [land]." Ots Capdequi, *Régimen de tierra, p.* 45.

in 1573, would come to dominate the evolution of the agrarian structure not only in Santo Domingo but in many other future Spanish American republics as well.

Essentially the Ordinances of 1573[15] codified all the royal decrees bearing on colonizing activities. The shift in royal policy toward effective occupation was now clearly spelled out. Landless married men would be given preference in the new settlements; a settler would receive homesite, farmlands, and Indians or other workers in proportion to his resources and ability to maintain and provide the means for them to live, work, and subsist. Gentlemen farmers could at their own expense establish tenant arrangements whereby the owner would be required to make land available for the tenant to use. The tenant, in turn, would be required to give from his own harvest to the owner. For the first time since the discovery of Española, the Crown itself specified the amount of land a settler could receive—and here the aspect of economic capability became obvious. All settlers would be given homesites, and most would receive farm and pasture lands to a maximum of five peonías, the equivalent of 233 acres. Some, however, would receive large grants of up to a maximum of three *caballerías*, or twelve peonías, the equivalent of 562.5 acres.[16]

At this point, the history of land relationships in Española begins to show the unhappy influence of political events essentially rooted in other colonies and other countries. The cumulative effects of chronic labor shortage throughout the sixteenth century, coupled with the displacement of the little colony as the administrative center in the New World, brought on a paralysis of development.

---

15. Issued by Philip II to regulate lands newly discovered, conquered, or pacified. *AGI, Indiferente, Leg.* 427, *Lib.* 29, *fol.* 67, quoted in Konetzke, *Formación social*, 1:471.

16. Area definitions varied considerably in the colonies. Those given here were commonly used on Española. Ruiz Tejada, *Estudio, p.* 99. Ots Capdequi mentions that in the Crown's instructions to Pedro Arias de Avila, the first governor of Tierra Firme, a peonía was defined as a site 50 feet by 100 feet, plus 100 fanegas for wheat and barley, 10 for corn, 2 for orchards, 8 for plants and trees, plus pasture land for 10 milk cows, 20 other cattle, 5 horses, 100 sheep, and 20 goats. A caballería would include a site 100 feet by 200 feet, plus 5 peonías—that is, 500 fanegas for wheat and barley, etc. Ots Capdequi, *Régimen de tierra*, p. 63.

7

COLONIAL LAND TITLES

Toward the end of the sixteenth century Española entered a long eclipse that was to endure for over a century and a half. The defeat of the Spanish Armada in 1588, followed by English attacks on Cádiz in 1596 and a series of long and costly wars with Holland, France, and England during the seventeenth century and well into the first quarter of the eighteenth, marked the decline of Spanish sea power. During those years the English achieved maritime dominance as their colonial adventures in the New World expanded. The net effect on Española of these two power shifts was deadly. There was little foreign trade and no emigration to the island; in fact, the population problem of a hundred years earlier had already begun to repeat itself. Francis Drake's raid in 1586 and further depredations by English and Dutch ships caused the Spanish Crown to close all ports except the city of Santo Domingo. The government even destroyed four north and west coastal ports—Puerto Plata, Monte Cristi, Bayahá, and Yaguana—and relocated the inhabitants inland in an effort to stop contraband trade with the enemies of Spain. The trade was reduced but, in the process, agricultural activity in the fertile north was smothered. The English expedition of 1655 under Admiral Sir William Penn and General Robert Venables, although a military failure, hastened the exodus of plantation owners and commoners alike, leaving few to work the land. By 1666 the Indians had disappeared completely. Crops were scanty and poor; the citizens were impoverished. Abandoned farms and homes were a common sight everywhere, especially in the sugar-growing areas, where fear of freebooters stifled any incentive to maintain production.

By 1700 the colony was poverty-stricken; by 1730 the population had been reduced to only 6,000 free Spaniards and their families—in 1519 it had been 53,000. The lack of Indian labor, the scarcity and high cost of importing Negro slaves, the desolation of the land, and the lack of trade—all were factors which operated to prevent the development of an extreme form of latifundismo. Throughout this period land on the island was never in short supply, but elsewhere in other colonies there burned the desire of individual landowners to acquire more land by any means. The first to suffer from the greed for more property were the Indians. The reaction of the Crown was not aimed at the landowners of Española, but they could not avoid becoming involved in the new round of royal edicts.

Continuing reports from the New World of encroachment on Indian land by the Spaniards led the Crown to take more stringent measures to protect Indian rights. An indication of what was to come had been foreshadowed in a cédula of 1583, which, although not addressed to the Audiencia of Santo Domingo,[1] set the policy which was to have a direct impact on them and the colonists there. By 1583 the Crown had accumulated ample evidence that the encomenderos in New Granada were seizing for their own friends and families the best Indian lands and, what was worse, forcing the Indians to work the lands for the benefit of the individuals who were not entitled to encomienda labor. Accordingly, the king asked for a detailed report from the Audiencia, to include the names of the Spaniards involved, which lands had been seized, under what legal title, and specific recommendations as to what action the Crown should take in the interest of justice to the Indians. The Crown thus recognized the practice of encroachment as it had on earlier occasions, but, in addition, now raised the legal question of title.

Shortly afterward the king's concern over land titles sharpened more; he bluntly informed the presidents of all audiencias[2] that individuals (without identifying them) in increasing numbers were attempting to obtain from the Crown the privileges of entail and mayorazgo over their property. Before he would consider such requests, the king demanded to know precisely what these properties and possessions were, their quality and worth, and how many children the petitioners had. He also told his officials that in all such future cases they were to obtain the same information, comment on any possible complications which the granting of a mayorazgo might produce, and forward all the information, along with a specific recommendation, to the Council of the Indies for study and decision.

In moving to protect one of his royal prerogatives, the king, for the second time in two years, at least indirectly had introduced the question of title to land. The tenor of the Cédula of 1585 seemed to be more closely pitched to economic implications than to the legality of land possession, for in it the king did not inquire how the petitioners had obtained the land; he asked only that possession be described and evaluated.

In the sixteenth century the Council of the Indies, like the other high councils of government, was composed mostly of *letrados*, or jurists. The council usually consisted of a president and eight councillors. They were men of middle class background, usually Castilians, graduates of one of the leading traditional universities at Salamanca, Alcalá de Henares, or Valladolid, and qualified by prior experience in provincial courts or municipalities. Their administrative backgrounds, in terms of years of service, were extensive, but in terms of variety, novelty, and scope of problems which the New World generated, their capabilities were limited, narrow, and essentially legalistic.[3]

With reliable evidence of colonial improprieties—that is, of colonists' encroachment on royal land—before it, the Council decided on broad remedial action which found expression in the Cédula of 1591. This document, along with a later cédula to be dis-

---

1. Cédula to the president and oidores of the Audiencia in Santa Fé, November 1, 1583, *AGI, Audiencia de Santa Fé, Leg.* 528, *Lib.* 1, *fol.* 99v., quoted in Konetzke, *Formación social,* 1:522.

2. Cédula, April 21, 1585, *AGI, Indiferente, Leg.* 427, *Lib.* 30, *fol.* 371v., quoted in ibid., 1:557.

3. Harold Livermore, *A History of Spain,* p. 272. Elliott points to another major defect, that of the frequent opportunities for graft and corruption which the Spanish administrative system permitted. The council's advice to the king was not always based on the merits of the particular case. Elliott, *Imperial Spain,* pp. 176–78.

cussed below, became something of a milestone in the history of colonial land ownership because it laid the basis for the *amparo real*.[4] Legal authorities in the Dominican Republic still refer to the 1591 Cédula as the Law of the Amparo Real. A few words in review of the Crown's traditional attitude toward land in the New World might serve to explain this term, which was to become the foundation for claim of title.

The essence of the matter was that all lands discovered, conquered, and pacified in the king's name belonged to the king as an individual. In a papal bull of 1493[5] Pope Alexander VI "gave, ceded, and assigned to the Catholic rulers of Spain personally, their heirs and successors forever, all the dominions, cities, places, and villages, and all rights, jurisdictions, all islands and mainlands found by the rulers' envoys and captains, and to be found and discovered, toward the west and south of a line from the Arctic Pole to the Antarctic Pole and in the direction of India, this line to be distant one hundred leagues toward the west and south of the Azores and Cape Verde islands." Any new lands found or discovered already in the actual possession of any Christian king or prince at the end of 1492 would be excluded from the jurisdiction of the bull. The Pope further appointed and deputized the rulers, their heirs and successors, to be lords of the new lands with full and free power, authority, and jurisdiction of every kind.

From this bull, then, came the authority for the king to claim personal ownership of all the lands of Spanish America as they were discovered. The Spanish term for this proprietary right is *realenga*, which, as Ruiz Tejada has noted,[6] does not mean ownerless property. The word is derived from *realeza* and refers to property belonging to the king. Therefore, as fruits of conquest, all farm lands, fields, rivers, lakes, uncleared land, and mountains belonged to the king by a right sanctioned by the Pope. Through this right the Crown—and only the Crown—had the authority to concede land to the individual settler or to duly constituted local entities such as the cabildo or the Audiencia for use or further distribution as appropriate.

Inherent in the property rights as interpreted above were the prerogatives of *regalia*—that is, such benefits as the privilege of monopoly and rights to subsurface mineral wealth, fish, pearls, and Indian treasure. In most instances the Crown's interest in realenga was financial—that is, the monetary value of gold or pearls. With respect to the land itself, however, political considerations were initially the important ones. These considerations were focused on conquest and pacification. Later, with the settlement and spread of population, economic exploitation became the paramount objective in colonial development. Ownership of land was determined by the economic capability of the individual to exploit his holdings. As generous as the Crown's land grants may have been under the Ordinances of 1573, the terms of the ordinances carried a condition which was in too many cases unfulfilled, that of effective occupation.[7] A distinction must be recognized here between effective ownership and effective occupation. The Crown was only too well informed of the Spaniard's proclivity to seize Indian land and otherwise

---

4. Royal cédula, November 1, 1591, *Colección de documentos inéditos, editada por Pacheco, Cárdenas y Torres de Mendoza*, quoted in Konetzke, *Formación social*, 1:619–20.

5. This was the *Inter Caetera* of May 4, 1493. Balthasar de Tobar, *Compendio bulario índico*, p. 9.

6. Ruiz Tejada, *Estudio*, p. 20.

7. Article 47 of the ordinances specified: "Conforming to the capital which each one might have available, in the same proportion he is to be assigned homesites and land for pastures and farming and for Indians or other workers whom he can support and provide tools for settlement, tilling the soil, and breeding animals." Ibid., p. 98.

usurp property that belonged to the king of Spain. It was not just a question of who owned which land that produced the 1591 Cédula; it was the additional fact that settlers were acquiring land which they then failed to put to productive use. As the wording of the cédula will reveal, economic interests as much as humanitarian ones forced the king's action. In the hands of the Indians land was productive because on it depended the Indians' subsistence; in the hands of land-hungry Spaniards, this was not always so.

The importance of the Cédula of 1591 warrants translation here, not only because of the land tenure implications it was to have but also because it is a clear indication of how the Spanish Crown viewed itself in the matter of land ownership. The king reminded the Audiencia that through inheritance he was still the sole owner of all common land not specifically granted to others. He had been generous in making grants, not only to towns but to both Indian and Spanish inhabitants. But because the errors and abuses of past colonial officials had permitted colonists to occupy the best land without title or just cause, or with false titles, the towns and Indians could not obtain just titles and were being deprived of badly needed land. The king went on:

> All of the above having been studied and considered by my Royal Council of the Indies and in council with me, it seems to be agreed that all land possessed without just and true title should be restored to me . . . to be reserved for all of the things which seem necessary to you for plazas, ejidos, pastures, and common lands in those places which are populated . . . and dividing among the Indians that which is truly needed for them to have to till and plant their crops and raise their flocks, confirming to them what they presently hold and giving them anew what they might need; all of the other land will remain and is free and unencumbered, to grant and dispose of at my will.
>
> And to this end I order you to immediately have presented to you and such men of letters, science, and conscience whom you nominate for this purpose, within the period of time needed for it, the titles that all may hold to land, farms, plantations, and tracts that each one has, and maintaining in possession[8] those which have good titles and security, or lawful continued possession, return and restore to me the remainder to dispose of as I wish, without there being now or in the future any disagreements, and that . . . for the said effect, to you and to them I give and concede sufficient and suitable powers as is required.[9]

The Cédula of 1591 highlighted the continuing struggle between the private interests of the settlers and the interests of the Crown. Or, put another way, this was a conflict which arose because of the differences between the fact of local conditions and the law ordained by a distant government. The Crown could invest the early conquerors with certain specific rights; it could also grant to the settlers the titles to specific lands. But it could not effectively legislate against the excesses of landholders thousands of miles away. Over the years the landholders had too often been tempted by the expanses of the terrenos baldíos of the Crown as well as by the valuable though restricted holdings already under cultivation by the Indians. It was now the Crown's intent that the Spanish settlers legalize their position in order to petition for an amparo real. Any land held in excess of that previously awarded by merced or by purchase was to be returned to the Crown. The amparo real, although a juridical term, did not constitute a clear title; it only presumed the existence of a title. Note the language of the cédula: "those who have good title and security or *lawful continued possession*.[10] The protection afforded by the

---

8. "Amparándolos."
9. See note 4, above.
10. "Los que con buenos títulos y recaudos, o justa prescripción." Emphasis added.

amparo consisted in its certification of present possession, not ownership. As an order or decision emanating from competent authority after due process, the amparo provided the landholder with written evidence of his occupation of the land, thus maintaining him in possession, but not to the prejudice of the rights of a third party who might challenge the first party on grounds of legal title.

Ots Capdequi quotes the following phraseology contained in an amparo real, which will illustrate some of the above points:

> Substantiated as it was in the short and summary procedure in accordance with that prescribed, in view of these documents and the favorable impression they produce, I must render a decision in favor of Tomás Rale, citizen of the villa of San Carlos de Tenerife outside the walls of this city, in possession of a caballería of land located in the section called Las Bueltas de Arroyo Salado. . . .

But to indicate that the amparo real did not constitute legal title, these words were added:

> be it understood, without prejudice to a third party, in order that neither now nor in the future may he be molested or disturbed in his possession by anyone. . . .[11]

Based on the documents the petitioner submitted, the court granted the juridical instrument which served to show that a previous royal merced existed and that the limits of land fit the terms of the merced. Room for challenge of title remained, but Tomás Rale was otherwise assured of continued peaceful possession under existing conditions.

The only way for a settler to acquire an unchallengeable and clear title was for him to request royal confirmation *(real confirmación)* of his current one, even though he may have been in possession of the land by virtue of an original royal cédula or merced signed by the king. The royal confirmation simply meant that the treasury had not been defrauded. This final step was intended by the Crown to uncover abuses, particularly in cases involving Indian titles, but in practice both the Cédula of 1591 and the further procedure utilizing the royal confirmation seem to have produced limited results. The reason can be deduced. Undoubtedly a large number of settlers possessed land under questionable conditions, and while they were prepared to prove possession, they did not want to risk loss of land unsupported by cédula or merced. Local authorities in Española would be more likely to accept a settler's possession without challenge, unless there was a title litigation, whereas the Crown would have no such inclination. Given the prevalence of land usurpation, the landowners simply calculated that the umbrella of local custom was an adequate and surer protection.[12]

---

11. Ots Capdequi, *Régimen de tierra,* p. 75.
12. The terrifying spiritual penalty for careless or exaggerated claims of possession was itself enough to inhibit all but the completely virtuous petitioners and believers. The tribunal receiving the petition warned that in the event of fraudulent claim:
We will order the said priest who, in the said churches, celebrates the important masses on Sundays and religious holidays, as is the custom, carrying a cross covered by a black cloth, a water hyssop, and lighted candles, to anathematize and curse you with the following curses: Cursed be those said excommunicants of God and his Blessed Mother, AMEN! !
May their children be orphans and their wives be widows, AMEN! !
May the sun be hidden from them by day and the moon by night, AMEN! !
May they wander as beggars from door to door and find no one to help them, AMEN! !
May the plagues which God sent the Kingdom of Egypt fall upon them, AMEN! !
May the curse of Sodom, Gomorrah, Hatham, and Avirom, who for their sins were

Dissatisfied with the colonists' reaction to the Cédula of 1591, but recognizing that there were limitations to the effective pressure he could bring to bear, Philip III grudgingly compromised. His Cédula of 1631, the so-called Law of Land Composition, recognized that many of the colonists had occupied lands in excess of those to which they were entitled. The Crown did not insist that this excess (lands occupied without any title and lands exceeding the limits authorized by cédula or amparo) be returned to the Crown. Philip desired to leave all present owners in peaceful possession, but he also wanted to be sure that the royal treasury received all monies due it from those who had usurped the Crown's land. Therefore he was willing for his viceroys and governors to arrange with those landowners the following adjustment: a moderate (the adjective was not defined by the Crown) proportion of the lands in excess would be considered to be the legal property of the landowner, and new titles to include this proportion would be issued. The remainder of the excess land would be put up for auction by the state and sold to the highest bidder, whose quit-rent purchase would then be an acceptable basis upon which to petition for the amparo real. The Crown, in effect, was delegating to the local authorities the power to establish the basis for consolidating and legalizing an essentially illegal situation. In many cases the Crown was giving the usurping landholder the opportunity to purchase the excess land he was already occupying, thus the term *composición*, or adjustment.

The Cédula of Land Composition also noted that many officials who did not possess the legal authority had granted titles to land, titles which subsequently had received the royal confirmation. To the owners of such land the Crown now was willing to grant the amparo real, subject to the provisions of the Law of Land Composition. Note that this law, as the Law of Amparo Real, did not guarantee title, only possession.

The 1631 Cédula was well conceived. The settlers could keep a reasonable amount of their illegally occupied land, the amount to be determined locally, and the royal treasury would salvage payment for land which the Crown had not been using anyway. But on the whole, the Crown was no more successful in rectifying land abuses with the 1631 Cédula than it had been with the 1591 Cédula, and for the same reason—reluctance on the part of many landowners to gamble on losing land for the sake of acquiring the amparo real. One can only conjecture on the extent to which the king's lands had been illegally occupied at the expense of the Indians or of towns which needed additional land for expansion.

The Crown made another major effort to straighten out the matter of land titles in the Royal Instruction of 1754.[13] The financially pressed Charles III was willing to recognize private possession of terrenos realengos if the land had been acquired by sale or composición, and not necessarily by occupation, prior to 1700, even though possession had not been confirmed by the Crown, a viceroy, or president of the Audiencia. In short, the Crown finally accepted the fact of occupation and moved to support it by royal authority. Here again the interest was primarily fiscal. Also, for individuals who occupied land prior to 1700 even without any title or document of ownership, the Crown would accept application for the amparo real, but not for legal title, on the basis of

---

swallowed alive by the earth, fall upon them, AMEN! !

And once the said curses are pronounced, he will throw water on the candles, saying in this manner: As these candles die in this water, so may die the souls of the said excommunicants, and may they descend into Hell with that of Judas Apostate! ! ! !

Ibid., p. 76.

13. Ibid., p. 104.

actual, long-term occupation alone. In cases of land not cultivated, however, the owners would have three months in which to commence working the soil or they would lose the land to someone else who was willing to meet this requirement. Thus for the man who had some sort of title, the 1754 law established absolute protection; to those owners without title but who could prove lengthy occupation, the law would give equal protection provided that the occupation was effective or became effective within three months.

For lands duly acquired by sale or composición after 1700, the owners were not to be disturbed, provided that they had obtained royal confirmation from the Crown, viceroy, or president of the audiencia. But those in possession of land without the necessary documents would have to obtain them from the appropriate audiencia.

Judging from the Crown's action, which followed within a few years, one concludes that colonial landholders remained unbudged. To the passive resistance of the colonists there remained only complete royal capitulation, and Charles III took this step in 1780.[14] The colonies were advised that any honest basis for ownership would receive the Crown's protection. Purchase, composición, private contract, occupation, or any other act which would dissolve any suspicion of fraud would suffice. Initially generous though jealous in his land policies, the king thus retired from the struggle over land usurpation, leaving the matter to local authorities to resolve on a basis of local considerations.

Almost two hundred years of effort on the part of the king to protect Crown land terminated in victory for the stubborn colonists. The 1591 Cédula was based in law, but it was law which had no real effect. Back of the 1631 Cédula was recognition of the colonial attitude by the Crown; this particular decree represented a compromise between the legalists in Spain and the realists in the New World. Fiscal considerations in a long era of frequent wars began to emerge as important. With the 1754 instruction, the Crown, in effect, abandoned ownership by merced as a basis for royal protection and accepted instead the mere fact of possession. Finally, in 1780 the Crown settled on honesty as the sole criterion. From narrow legalism to fiscal interest to practical morality, the Crown conducted a steady retreat. There was no other choice.

The matter of absentee ownership of land had been brought to the attention of the Crown as early as 1517 with the first report of the Hieronimite Fathers. In this document the fathers advised that they had stripped all absentee landowners of the Indians they held in encomienda, in accordance with the regent's orders.[15] This action was taken for the good of the people and the colony but only after consultation with the oidores and other officials in the capital. The latter concurred unanimously in the proposed action without knowing that the fathers already possessed specific orders to this effect. Informed later of the orders, local officials demonstrated considerable pleasure with the regent's action, to which must be added the observation that the Hieronimites appear to have been bountifully blessed with qualities of tactfulness and diplomatic finesse.

A later cédula prohibited any encomendero from leaving his land during the first ten years of his tenure to go to another island or province without royal permission. Should he go anyway, he could not there be given a new assignment of Indians in encomienda, nor could he receive any other special benefit. This decree[16] was applicable to all the

---

14. This was the royal cédula of August 2, 1780, ibid., p. 119.

15. Instructions given to the fathers of the order of San Hierónimo, September 13, 1516, quoted in Konetzke, *Formación social*, 1:63.

16. Royal order, April 18, 1534, *AGI, Indiferente, Leg.* 422, *Lib.* 16, *fol.* 88, quoted in ibid., 1:159.

possessions in the New World, but was specifically repeated in the Additions to the New Laws of 1542 as a warning to absentee landowners and encomenderos in New Spain where owners of land in distant provinces too frequently resided in Mexico.

Complaints about the troublesome "Spanish vagabond" were sprinkled through the correspondence of the times, both from officials in Española[17] and from the Crown itself, which repeatedly deplored itinerancy in the colony. The most notorious evils produced by the owners' absence from farm lands were twofold. First, there was no incentive to make the soil productive at a time when the colony possessed a marginal capability for self-subsistence, and, second, the Indians held in encomienda by the absentee did not receive the continuing attention which the Crown desired be given them. Despite the fact that the Crown began to impose time limits within which settlers had to give satisfactory evidence that they were working the land ceded to them, reports trickled back to Spain that the law was not being observed. In 1564, in response to a complaint registered by the attorney general of Española, the Council of the Indies took another hard look at the practice of absentee ownership and secured the Crown's approval to issue the following strong warning to the Audiencia in Santo Domingo:

> Many important and rich settlers . . . petitioned the cabildo and Land Administration for lands in which to sow wheat and plant grapes and build sugar mills and county homes, and these requests were granted and they were given titles thereto, which they neither sowed, nor planted, nor built sugar mills nor homes as they had been given permission to do, and if any have done so, they have since left the land, *and thus the land lies without being worked. And the workers and other persons who would do the work do not venture to do so because afterwards the owners would throw them off, displaying their titles and concessions, saying that the land was theirs, because of which the aforesaid island and citizens thereof, especially the poor, common people, are badly hurt*; [emphasis added] and begged me to have the situation corrected, ordering the persons to whom these lands have been conceded to sow and plant them within a short period of time and to perform on them the work which they asked to do and which was granted to them to do, and if they have not done so by the end of the specified period, the lands can be given to whoever will do so willingly.
>
> And in this manner many fraudulent practices will be stopped and the people of the island will be greatly helped as is my desire. . . . I order you, after you read this, to find out and identify which of the lands given to the citizens of that city need to be worked, and to these citizens you will indicate the time by which they must have worked and sown as they had requested and been given permission to do, and failing to do this, the time you indicated having passed, *you will take the land and redistribute it among the persons as seem best to you who are citizens of that city, so that they can cultivate and work the soil,* [emphasis added] under the same conditions, and from this time on, you will give orders to observe and obey these same conditions on any newly granted land, thus by our wish as by order of the cabildo of that city.[18]

What a perfect example of the twentieth-century problems of absentee ownership, peasant invasion of unoccupied or undeveloped land, redistribution of land, and the subsequent legal complications which may arise! Given the date of the cédula, one can only conclude that the Crown's well-intentioned orders were not being fully incorporated into the land tenure structure of the colony. The mere fact that it was necessary for the

---

17. Governor Alonso de Fuenmayor urged the Crown to issue orders giving landowners a three-month period in which to start to work their land or lose it. The Crown complied by issuing the Cédula of November 20, 1536. Mejía Ricart, *Historia de Santo Domingo*, p. 72.

18. Royal cédula on lands distributed on the island of Española, November 13, 1564, to the president of the royal Audiencia of Santo Domingo, *AGI, Audiencia de Santo Domingo, Leg.* 899, *Lib.* 1, *fol.* 361, quoted in Konetzke, *Formación social*, 1:413.

attorney general to appeal ultimately to the Crown in 1564 indicates that the landowning hierarchy of Santo Domingo was already so strongly entrenched or represented in the Audiencia that local appeal was useless. The Audiencia did not lack the authority, but (not uncommon for the times) the members lacked the will or the social conscience to correct an obvious evasion of the law, to the detriment of the common good. Parenthetically, from this example one might also appreciate today why the Crown took pains to develop parallel administrative lines of communication to the colonies. Granted that such a practice was not efficient by modern administrative standards, it did provide the peninsular authorities with perhaps the only means to obtain a better insight into colonial problems and the zeal, or lack of it, with which their policies were observed.

Absentee ownership in Española probably reached a peak in the late seventeenth and early eighteenth centuries as the colony struck the bottom of the economic depression which did not end until well into the Bourbon era. Absent landlords were the rule rather than the exception, but in fairness to them it must be admitted that their absence was caused by unprecedented domestic conditions and not necessarily by unwillingness or disinterest in working the land. What point was there in trying to make the land productive if labor was scarce and the land subject to virtually unopposed raids and attacks by foreign corsairs? And even if there were products for export, where were the ships to carry them? Lack of evidence to the contrary leads to the conclusion that as a causal factor the absentee landlord did not constitute a continuing, major defect in the agrarian structure during the remainder of the colonial period.

This is not to say, however, that absentee ownership did not exist at the end of the eighteenth century when the economy had regained much of its health. Under Charles IV the Spanish government carried on the Bourbon family effort to increase the flow of income from the colonies by registering a strong complaint in 1789 about the economic loss to the state caused by abandonment of entailed homes and lands.[19] But by the terms of the merced granting a mayorazgo, such land could not be subjected to seizure or be subdivided, sold, or otherwise disposed of by the heirs or successors except in case of grave crimes against the Crown. The king, therefore, had to recognize that since the mayorazgos were "sacred cows," those owners who could not or would not put the land to use were legally protected against action to force them to cultivate. Even in cases of economic necessity, owners were inhibited from breaking up the estate or selling parcels of it in order to raise money. Those owners who abandoned their lands under the safeguards of the mayorazgo were, in fact, less to be criticized than was the original authority which tied up the property in perpetuity. In addition to the evils of noncultivation, there were other even greater evils which stemmed from smaller mayorazgos which were producing only too well. Where the land was reasonably good, even a small estate employing slave labor could support a large, extended colonial family. As a result, there was little incentive for the members of the family to seek a livelihood elsewhere or to take a serious interest in any matter which did not touch the family establishement. From the Crown's point of view, the tropical slothfulness and arrogance of the colonists, their children, and their relatives were reprehensible and were depriving the army, the navy, commercial and farming institutions, the arts, and public administrative bodies of much needed manpower and talent. The king could hardly use the phrase, but what he was complaining about was a lack of the Protestant ethic in Española.

After summing up his indictment of the social, political, and economic evils of the

---

19. Royal cédula, May 14, 1789, *AGI, Indiferente, Leg.* 1609, quoted in ibid., 3:642.

mayorazgo, Charles IV concluded the 1789 Cédula by emphatically forbidding the granting of any further mayorazgos without his personal permission or that of his royal successors. Although special exceptions might be made, the Crown intended to reduce drastically the amount of land in the colonies which could not be made to produce. There is no record of just how much land Charles IV was able to rescue from idleness, but the amount may have been quite limited. By 1801, in what appeared to be a more profitable operation, he was charging 20,000 reales[20] for his permission to found a mayorazgo and 20,000 more for royal confirmation. And for a mere 1,400 reales an encomendero could obtain the Crown's permission to reside in Spain.[21] This last speaks volumes about the royal policy toward absentee ownership at the end of the colonial period.

---

20. One real equals 1/8 of a peso fuerte (25.563 grams of silver). One real equals 34 maravedises. "Pieces of eight" were pesos of 8 reales.

21. *AGI, Ultramar, Leg.* 733, quoted in Ots Capdequi, *Régimen de tierra*, p. 59.

8

THE CHURCH AS LANDHOLDER

A historical study of landholding in the Dominican Republic would be incomplete without appropriate reference to the Catholic Church, which has exerted such a powerful influence in Spanish America.

In a long report to Cardinal Jiménez de Cisneros, one of the three Hieronimite Fathers had observed that none of the colony's ecclesiastics should possess Indians in encomienda, but, rather, should have only free Indians to serve them, since bishops, clerics, and friars should not engage in such material matters.[1] Furthermore, the diezmos and other perquisites of the Church ought to be sufficient for the clergy. The fathers feared that the assignment of encomiendas to the numerous clergy alone would probably absorb most of the available manpower. Father Bernardino de Manzanedo, the writer, did state, however, that solely from the point of view of the Indians' welfare, the Indians would be better cared for by the Church than by others. Nevertheless, the early Church seems to have been commendably absorbed in its missionary purposes of propagating the Christian faith to the exclusion of more worldly matters.

The Spanish Crown never slackened its policy of maintaining close control over the material wealth of the Church in Española. As the Crown was to emphasize repeatedly, the Church in the New World was committed to an existence of frugality and austerity, and any action which would alter this way of life would be scrutinized closely by the king. The ecclesiastical organization in Española conformed for the most part to royal decrees, perhaps influenced by the fact that many of the early governors and presidents of the Audiencia were churchmen. It appears, too, that the colonial authorities did not always respect the caliber of churchmen whom they found there and therefore were disposed to insist on strict compliance with the Crown's law.[2]

---

1. Memorial of Fray Bernardino de Manzanedo, 1518, *AGI, Patronato Real, Leg.* 177, *Ramo* 2, *fol.* 1, quoted in Incháustegui, *Reales cédulas,* 1:42.

2. "In that city there is a great Church, strong and very austere. There is a dean, Doctor Ribera, a theologian. He's a notorious shopkeeper. Verdeci is the treasurer. These and all the rest, except for two others whom the archbishop of the city has with him and who they say

There is good evidence that during the early part of the sixteenth century at least some of the representatives of the Church were indeed living under trying conditions. The prior and friars of San Benito de Alcántara in Santo Domingo, in justifying their claim to a share of certain houses and real estate, complained bitterly of the lack of money to feed and clothe themselves. The property had belonged to Nicolás de Ovando, the early governor of Santo Domingo, who had been a comendador in this military order. Ovando had willed some of his estate to the order in Santo Domingo, but under their own law the bequests could not be received without permission from the king, who was the perpetual administrator of the order. The visitador general of the order inspected conditions in the monastery in 1553 and concurred that there were just legal grounds for the Crown to approve the prior's claim.[3] Convinced that the inhabitants of the monastery in Santo Domingo suffered from a lack of basic creature comforts, the Crown approved the terms of the will.

The decision in this case not only improved living conditions for the prior and friars of the order but provided them with a continuing rental income from the property. The record does not show the extent or value of the real estate involved, but the Crown's decision reveals a tardy willingness to approve reasonable requests.

Possibly a more substantial example of acquisition of property by the Church was that of María de Arana, a rich widow of Santo Domingo who donated to the Church several large houses in the capital, a country estate with seven Negro slaves, farmlands along the bank of Soco River in the eastern province of El Seibo, and a pasture full of cattle—all for the construction of a convent for the sisters of the order of Santo Domingo. The nuns would live in the town houses, supported by the produce and income of the farms and estates. The offer was made to Augstín de Campuzano, prior of Santo Domingo, who submitted an official request through the Audiencia for approval of the project by the Crown. The prior also asked permission to bring several nuns to Spain so the king could be further convinced of the necessity to build additional convents in a land where there was an excess of widows and unmarried women of high social standing. Both the prior and the president of the Audiencia certified that there was a shortage of marriageable males in Española, which made the convents a necessity if these females were to remain on the island. The president conducted a searching investigation of the situation, however, before concurring in the basic request.[4]

Here was a case where the acquisition of valuable property by the Church rendered

---

are learned, who are a schoolteacher and an archdeacon-canon—all the rest are idiots, except for a canonical scholar who is a good man, of good quality, and the best ecclesiastic of all. A post of this sort pays more than a thousand pesos of bad money, which in good money is 250 ducats, and the deanship more than twice as much, and similarly even more for the other dignitaries. The one who has the doctoral post is crazy. The bishop of San Juan is located in the city of Santo Domingo; because he is very old and very rich from the inheritances of his parents, he can remain there. . . . " Emilio Rodríguez Demorizi, ed., *Relaciones históricas de Santo Domingo*, 1:137 (hereafter referred to as *Relaciones históricas*). These comments are quoted from the report on the island of Española, submitted to the Crown in 1568 by Oidor Echagoia.

3. *Archivo Histórico Nacional, Sección Ordenes Militares, Archivo de Toledo*, 33, 489, quoted in Incháustegui, *Reales cédulas*, 2:373.

4. Report dated 1556, *AGI, Audiencia de Santo Domingo, Leg.* 95, Incháustegui, *Reales cédulas*, 2:381. This rather ponderous procedure was an outgrowth of the tight control over ecclesiastical activity in the New World maintained by the Crown to protect its *patronato real*. Although the request to form the new convent did not necessarily involve the assignment of additional regular clergy, the administrative procedures followed here by the prior and the Audiencia were nevertheless required. See Mecham, *Church and State in Latin America*, pp. 24–25.

a social service to the colony and at the same time contributed to the Crown's purpose of not permitting the local population to dwindle.

The Crown's methods for controlling Church efforts to obtain outside financial aid were by no means slipshod. A very extensive and detailed investigation involving the testimony of many witnesses was invariably required. For example, before forwarding the one-time request of the nuns of the Queen of Angels Convent, order of Santo Domingo, for royal alms of 6,700 silver pesos, the bishop of Santo Domingo and the president of the Audiencia followed an investigative procedure almost as formal as for a *residencia*.[5] Similar preliminary action was required before a request could be forwarded for money to repair hurricane damage to church buildings. The king's permission was even needed before an order could beg for public alms for whatever purpose, be it to repair a church or for the benefit of a captive held by the Moors in Africa.

With the passing of years, however, the Crown became aware that despite royal policy, the Church was steadily acquiring extensive real estate and other worldly goods, and the Crown may well have suspected that some of the orders were overly active in this respect. In a series of cédulas issued between 1570 and 1577[6] the Crown specifically pointed out that the orders of Santo Domingo and San Agustín had been established in the New World on the principles of poverty and disregard of worldly goods. On this basis they had existed for many years, setting exemplary models of frugality for the Indians. But in recent years, the Crown went on to say, the orders had begun to accept legacies and inheritances and had acquired worldly goods such as farms, businesses, pastures, and cattle. To the Crown, such a development was a discredit to the orders, since they now appeared to be avid for wealth and had lost the original apostolic perfection. Furthermore, being so occupied with the acquisition of worldly goods, they were paying more attention to their farms and cattle than to their primary religious responsibilities. In fact, it appeared that in a few years the orders might acquire so much of the land that there would be none left for the Indians or for the colonists or their descendants. And without income from land, how could the colonists contribute to the support of the Church itself, to monasteries, hospitals, and other public works?

It was the Crown's wish that such lands be converted from sources of Church income to more pious purposes and that the orders revert to their earlier ways of poverty and simplicity. As a means of controlling the increase of Church wealth, the respective presidents of audiencias, viceroys, and governors were required to submit immediately a complete report containing the following information: a list of all the monasteries and convents in both Spanish and Indian centers of population; a list of all the properties, income, wealth, and businesses of each; a description of these worldly goods, including an estimate of what the income from each was and might be; those properties which were purchased and those which were inherited, received as legacies, or by any other

---

5. A judicial process of review of the administration of a public official at the end of his term. The proceedings included the calling of witnesses and examination of records and accounts. Theoretically the investigation was a detailed one, usually conducted by a judge, *juez de residencia*, in the cases of lesser officials. In the case of Crown-appointed officials, such as the viceroys, the Council of the Indies appointed the judge. Occasionally the newly appointed official would be ordered to conduct the residencia. The judge submitted his final report, with recommendations for appropriate action, to the Audiencia or to the Crown in the cases of Crown appointees.

6. Royal cédula, *Cédulas de Quito*, 1:184, quoted in Konetzke, *Formación social*, 1:453; Royal cédula, October 24, 1576, and Royal cédula, December 17, 1577, quoted in ibid., 1:495–98 and 1:507–8.

means; their capital value; and the minimum needs to sustain each convent or monastery. The president of the Audiencia was to forward the report by the first available ship; in the meantime all monsteries and convents would be forbidden to acquire, buy, or receive under any circumstances more property, income, lands, or profits from those already possessed.

From the wording of these cédulas, it appears that the Crown was more concerned over the loss of royal revenue from these lands and properties which Church ownership would imply than over any other factor. From the fiscal point of view, the Crown would have preferred to see taxable property in the hands of taxpayers. At this stage in Spanish history Philip II's expenses, especially in Europe, were mountainous, and the empire was heavily dependent on income from the New World. Although the potential for acquisition of vast estates in tiny Española was insignificant compared with that in either Peru or New Spain, ecclesiastical authorities in Santo Domingo were nevertheless bound by royal policy.

There were no further complaints by the Crown about the Church in Española. On the contrary, a reverse situation began to develop. As the little colony continued to wither away, the routine reports became a handy vehicle for the Church officials to use to let the Crown know of their financial difficulties. For example, an official report submitted in 1650 by Canónigo Luis Jerónimo Alcocer[7] gives a fair indication of the depressed economic conditions. Alcocer reported that the Church was very poor. Income amounted to less than 2,000 ducats, including the real merced of two-ninths of the diezmo. If it were not for the merced and the inheritances of some of the bishops in years past, plus some alms, the Church could not have survived. The canónigo took the opportunity to complain of local prices, pointing out that a pound of wax cost sixteen to twenty-four reales of silver, and that this price, as well as that of most other products on the market, was three times higher than in Spain.

Alcocer reported eighteen clerics on the payroll. The dean of the cathedral received from all rents and emoluments 3,000 reales, more or less, and the others from 2,200 to 2,700. The emoluments of all these officials had been gradually reduced over the preceding years,[8] but with continually diminishing income from the local economy, Alcocer predicted that the Church would soon be in need of more royal assistance. The Crown, however, developed other alternatives over the next few decades.

As happened so frequently when colonial practice failed to match the Crown's policy, instructions had to be repeated. In 1687 Charles II and his Council of the Indies found it necessary to reissue[9] the warnings of the previous century concerning acquisition of property by the Church. This time the instructions were more detailed. In addition to the business and property inventory, viceroys and governors were ordered to submit their individual plans by which priests and nuns would be prevented from obtaining real estate by any means whatsoever. The Crown again forbade the clergy from receiving benefits of inheritance, titles to property, or any other source of income including tithes

---

7. *La relación de Alcocer, canónigo de la catedral, 1650.* This is a long report to the Crown, containing demographic data, descriptions of the economy and living conditions, climate, crops, geography, and notable events, quoted in Rodríguez Demorizi, *Relaciones históricas,* 1:198–267.

8. At 8 reales to the peso of silver and 1.38 pesos to the ducat, the dean's emolument was 273 ducats, down over fifty percent from 1568; the salary of the canonicate was 218 ducats, down about fifteen percent during the same period.

9. *AGI, Indiferente, Leg.* 431, *Lib.* 43, *folios* 47 and 49, quoted in Antonio Muro Orejón, ed., *Cedulario americano del siglo XVIII,* pp. 299–300.

or royal income. Dowries could not accrue to convents. The objective of the Crown was to allow the Church the bare means to maintain itself. The language of this cédula emphasized a point raised indirectly in the case noted earlier, of the donation by María de Arana to the sisters of the order of Santo Domingo. Many unmarried daughters of wealthy Dominican colonists were entering the convents, which thereupon received the dowries. Other nuns, as well as priests, eventually inherited valuable property and goods which also became part of the Church's wealth. Church tax immunity privileges in these cases deprived the Crown of inheritance taxes and later of the taxes which might have been derived from the property.

In response to the above directive, the archbishop of Santo Domingo, Fernando de Carvajal y Rivera, reported[10] that the annual diezmo income of his organization had dropped from 628,563 maravedises (about 2,300 silver pesos) in 1666 to 104,120 (about 380 silver pesos) in 1690—no small loss. Since he had to pay the salaries of the heads of his religious communities, church choirs, musicians, sub-chanter, altar boys, organists, and the mace bearers, as well as the costs of bread and wax, he was forced to acknowledge that his finances were in a miserable state. The archbishop did not report the local scale of wages.

The various religious communities were also having financial problems, according to the report. The order of La Virgen de las Mercedes possessed four monasteries. In and around Santo Domingo City the order had lost cattle ranches, fruit orchards, and slaves worth 30,000 pesos. There remained only an income of 700 pesos from fruit, a third of which was lost in the marketing process. There were now only twenty-five priests and one lay brother in the Santo Domingo monastery, where for over thirty years sixty had been maintained. In Santo Cerro, near La Vega, French freebooters had run off 20,000 head of cattle and 120 slaves and had burned all the houses and ranches owned by the order, leaving no property whatsoever. Present income was 44 pesos, and there were now only two priests where before there had been ten or twelve. In Azua, income had dropped from 80 pesos to 50. The French had burned the church in 1680 and looted the town. There were now only three priests in the monastery. The only information available on the fourth monastery at Santiago concerned the population. There were three priests and a lay brother[11]; in earlier years there had always been at least twelve to fourteen clerics.

Similar data were included for the order of Santo Domingo (Predicadores), which owned one convent and one monastery, and the order of San Francisco,[12] which owned one monastery in the capital and derived an income from a capital investment of 17,472 pesos. As of 1690 there were eleven priests and four lay brothers in the Franciscan monastery. In total personnel figures, the archbishop could count thirty-nine secular and thirty-six regular clergy in the colony, a reduction of well over fifty percent during the preceding seventy years. The archbishop himself had a working fund of 500,000 maravedises, but according to him this was pitifully inadequate for a church receiving neither

---

10. "Noticias de la isla Española," August 10, 1690, Archbishop Fernando de Carvajal y Rivera, quoted in Rodríguez Demorizi, *Relaciones históricas*, 3:67–88.

11. Archbishop Domingo Fernández Navarrete had earlier reported (1680) that the French had twice destroyed the cathedral at Santiago and once the cathedral at La Vega. The intruders had ruined farms and ranches, robbed and killed the defenseless inhabitants. Quoted in ibid., 3:24.

12. There was no Jesuit monastery.

emoluments nor alms. He pointed out that an oidor could not support himself on 600,000 maravedises; so how could an archbishop get along on 500,000?

Two years later Archbishop de Carvajal y Rivera again wrote, emphasizing the poor quality of the regular clerics assigned him.[13] Some were ill; some were blind; two were so old that they could not function; and all spent their time complaining of local conditions. The church in Santo Domingo, which was the first to be established in the Indies and which deserved better treatment, was in the worst shape of any the archbishop had ever seen. The country was poor; the best citizens were leaving, and the remainder had no money. Houses could not be maintained properly; haciendas were being lost or abandoned because there was no money to operate them. There were neither settlers nor slaves left on the land. The mines were not producing, and the French controlled the mountains and upland regions. The inevitable result of all these calamities was that the Church had no income. There were two recommendations, both simply stated: open the colony to commerce and trade, and drive out the French. One line near the end of the letter was an unusual one, and it must have grated on the monarch's conception of true ecclesiastical humility. If conditions did not improve, wrote the spiritual leader of the colony, he thought he should take all the Church personnel out of Santo Domingo and relocate them in a more pleasant, more prosperous environment. Carvajal y Rivera clearly did not concur with the king's opinion that the orders should revert to their earlier ways of poverty and simplicity. Or rather, having been forced by circumstances to accept austerity, he found it so unpalatable that he considered abandoning his religious responsibilities to the citizens of Santo Domingo.

Local conditions in the colony throughout the seventeenth century forced the Church to reduce radically the number of clergy. Materially the Church suffered serious losses at the hands of foreign invaders and from the economic depression. The history of relations between the Church and the Bourbon Crown during the eighteenth century leaves little room for a supposition that ecclesiastical fortunes in Española improved. Certainly there was no additional construction of monasteries or convents in the capital. In 1783 the archbishop's report showed the same three monasteries and two convents which Oidor Echagoia had reported in 1564.

The above details would support the conclusion that while the Church in Santo Domingo did acquire property, the restrictions on ownership imposed by the Crown were usually obeyed. These and other external factors inhibited excessive massing of wealth during the colonial period and minimized Church influence derived from landholdings. Never exerting a significant political influence, the Church retained an essentially ecclesiastical role. Perhaps the point to be made here reinforces the widsom of the Crown's policy regarding the Church in the New World: conformance to a policy of austerity, whether willing or unwilling, led to fewer abuses.

---

13. Letter, archbishop of Santo Domingo to the king, August 27, 1692, quoted in ibid., 3:99.

9

AGRICULTURAL DEVELOPMENT
UNDER THE BOURBONS

Its Caribbean possessions threatened with almost complete isolation by British maritime supremacy, the Spanish government in 1740 threw open the ports in Santo Domingo to neutral trade, and the long economic misery began to dissipate slowly. Foreign demand for sugar, tobacco, and other export crops brought money to the little colony, stimulated agriculture, and induced a steady growth in population. Although conditions shortly after the mid-century mark could hardly be described as prosperous, the more liberal attitude of the later Bourbons toward foreign trade and commerce had removed the principal cause of the economic doldrums. The opening to West Indian trade of a number of ports from Barcelona around the entire Spanish coast to Gijón and Santander was a particular blessing to the Dominican economy. In 1773 the estimated population of Santo Domingo was about 125,000[1]; by 1780 a Church census showed that the population had reached over 133,000, and by 1785 it was 152,640. Nevertheless, the full agricultural potential of the country had not been realized during these years. The density of population was still only 8.1 inhabitants per square mile.

Based on the recommendations of the colonial officials themselves, Charles III took the first enlightened step to create an active program to improve the economy in Santo Domingo. In 1769 he ordered Governor José Solano y Bote to form a junta (Sociedad de Hacendados)[2] to develop a plan for agricultural development. Given the opportunity to renew longstanding efforts to improve the island's economy, Solano complied with his instructions with a reasonable amount of energy, and in a letter of October 24, 1772, requested the Crown to act on a number of recommendations which he and the junta considered essential. With the usual bureaucratic delay in Madrid, the king finally in 1786 made several concessions, including the following:

The colonists would be free to bring in Negro slaves in unlimited numbers; meanwhile,

---

1. Sánchez Valverde, *Idea*, p. 146.
2. Ibid., pp. 145–46. Father Cipriano de Utrera observes that the junta was probably the Sociedad de Hacendados, a landowning group founded about this time.

the Crown was ordering the Council of State to prepare a special slave code similar to the Code Noire adopted by the French in 1784.

The colonists would be granted exemption from payment of the diezmo and certain other taxes.

The Crown would provide the colony with agricultural tools.

The Crown would authorize, under regulated conditions, cattle trade with Saint Domingue.[3]

In waiting 14 years for a reply to his 1772 letter, Solano could do little to stimulate new policy. In 1778, however, he did at least manage to obtain from the Crown a fifty percent reduction of the *alcabala*, the local sales tax, for a period of five years.

Other voices were beginning to be heard. One of the more articulate polemicists of the day was a Jesuit *criollo* named Antonio Sánchez Valverde who had throughly studied his native land, particularly its geography and economic potential as well as its problems.[4] In 1785 he completed a book best described by the title Sánchez Valverde gave it: *Idea del valor de la isla Española* (*A Conception of the Worth of the Island of Española*). Convinced that the Crown was neglecting the welfare of Santo Domingo, the author's stated purpose was to awaken Spanish authorities to the true potential of the colony. Most of the work is a description of the terrain, ports, rivers, climate, villages, cities, and economy of Santo Domingo. The final chapters, however, assume a tone which is loyally nativistic yet impatient and almost outraged at the state of the economy. Sánchez Valverde was highly irritated at the condescending, if not belittling, statements which were being made by French writers of the period as they compared the wealth and luxury of Saint Domingue with the poverty and stagnation of its Spanish counterpart. French figures of agricultural production in 1773 showed that the younger, much smaller Saint Domingue was appreciably outproducing the Spanish two-thirds of the island.[5] The reasons were clear.

First, the French had been importing African slaves to Saint Domingue at a rate of 30,000 a year. In 1785 there were over 700,000 slaves there, compared to 12,000 to 14,000 on the Spanish side; this one factor alone would account for most of the disparity in production.

Second, the Spaniards celebrated many national and religious holidays; as a consequence, slaves were not working a full quarter of the year. The French, on the other

---

3. Royal cédula, April 12, 1786, ibid., p. 146.

4. Sánchez Valverde was born in 1734 in Bayaguana, which was founded in 1602 by some of the displaced inhabitants of the four coastal towns destroyed by the Spanish government to eliminate contraband activity. He was only too familiar with the history of the long economic depression of the seventeenth and eighteenth centuries. He acquired a degree in theology at the age of 21, followed by a law degree at the University of Santo Domingo in 1758. He became a *racionero* in the cabildo of the cathedral in 1765. (In this sense, "cabildo" is the collective term for the body or community of the members of the ecclesiastical chapters of the cathedral.) He lived in Spain from 1763 to 1765, qualifying himself to practice law before the royal councils. After returning to Santo Domingo he became a staunch defender of the poor, got into trouble with the Audiencia for having publicly criticized a judgment in favor of a priest against a penniless worker, and was apprehended trying to leave the country. The Church authorities found him guilty, prohibited him from speaking publicly, and ordered him confined. He was later pardoned by the king. Father Cipriano de Utrera, in his annotations of *Idea del valor de la isla Española*, has included a long biographical sketch of the author. Ibid., pp. 7–32.

5. Ibid., pp. 159–60. Production ratios, all favorable to the French, were as follows: sugar, 2.4 to 1.5; coffee, 8.4 to 3.0; indigo, 15 to 2.1; and cotton, 4 to 3.7.

hand, were less compassionate and drove their slaves harshly and continuously, with no time off.[6]

Third, the Spanish free workers would remain on their jobs only long enough to earn a little money for temporary subsistence. For every day they worked, they rested two. Steady labor had no attraction for them.

Fourth, the Spanish laboring-class women "earned money with their bodies; their men, therefore, would not work and were suited only for robbery."

An eighteenth-century land reform in the areas of productivity and land usage was needed to lift Santo Domingo out of the economic rut. A quantum increase in productivity was indicated, and above all, the Crown must be made to see that the manpower shortage was the critical factor. All the slaves who could be purchased should be brought into the country. Without them sugar could not be produced, and without increased sugar production, the colonists could make no satisfying economic improvements.

Sánchez Valverde also attacked the customary installation of one sugar mill for every square league of cane field, that is, one mill per nine square miles. With such fertile soil, production should be sufficient to require four mills to the square league instead of one. The only proviso, a marketing consideration, was that the mills should be located no further than twelve to fifteen miles from navigable waters in order to minimize transportation costs. Furthermore, much more land could be planted in sugar. For example, by increasing the amount of land under cultivation in the Barahona area and improving mill efficiency, Sánchez Valverde calculated that an additional 151 mills would be needed, bringing the total to 320.[7] These new mills would all lie within a strip of four leagues from the sea and would occupy three-sevenths of all the arable land on the strip. The remainder of the strip would be devoted to coffee, indigo, tobacco, and cotton, each in a specified quantity. He also proposed to plant 100,000 or more additional trees on the larger cacao plantations so as to utilize the land more fully and provide an important export crop, instead of just enough for local consumption.

As an additional step, he calculated for each distinct region a special agricultural production plan based on climate and terrain peculiarities. For example, planning for the eastern region contemplated the increased use of river transportation in the extreme eastern provinces where there were a number of good-sized streams terminating in ports on the Caribbean Sea. In this region there should be greatly increased cane plantings, an increase of 400 or 500 in the number of sugar mills, and increased plantings of coffee, cotton, and indigo, with labor to be provided by a sufficient number of Negro slaves.

On the Samaná Peninsula, Sánchez Valverde wanted to install over the next ten years some 200 or 300 new sugar mills, along with new plantings, so that each mill with an annual production of 125 to 150 tons of sugar would bring in a total of 45,000 tons of new sugar production. Concurrently with the increase in sugar, less emphasis would be given the traditional production of indigo in order to maximize profits from the more valuable sugar.

To support the increased plantings and production throughout the country this eighteenth-century agricultural economist had perceived the need to install irrigation

---

6. Ibid., p. 169. Utrera cites a letter of March 12, 1784, written by a Dominican official, Ignacio Pérez Caro, in which the latter complains of the excessive number of holidays. According to Pérez Caro, slaves did not work on ninety-three days during the year.

7. These figures obviously refer to the very small mills, or trapiches, which were operated by individual landowners. The author calculated an annual output of between 125 and 150 tons from each mill.

facilities in the arid regions and to launch a general increase in the use of fertilizers. The overall production objective was to double the output of sugar within the shortest time possible and to triple or even increase sixfold the outputs of coffee and cotton.

The above program was calculated not to prejudice the raising of cattle, which also needed modernizing.[8] In the first place, nearly all the agricultural expansion would take place within 25 miles of the coasts. On this land there was little or no livestock. In the second place, the cattle ranchers had more land than they needed for the size of their herds. Every large ranch still had on it wild, uncleared land (los montes) which became an almost impenetrable refuge for freely drifting cattle. Sánchez Valverde recommended the following action with respect to cattle lands:

Increase the number of pastures by clearing away wild lands.
Corral the stock at night instead of allowing them to run free and wander away. This would protect the newborn and would prevent theft.
Decrease the meadows to a minimum size so that more herds could be accommodated on a fixed ratio of one bull per set number of cows.
Eliminate the low-breeders.

And, finally, he turned his analytical eye to pigs. The widespread custom of raising pigs and letting them run wild to forage for themselves was one of the greatest causes of agricultural decadence. As an unidentified but shrewd observer was to remark later of this continued custom: "Pigs and revolutions were the two greatest enemies of the country." The ever present threat of herds of uncontrolled, voracious wild pigs was enough to inhibit the expansion of agriculture even where additional land might have been available. No conuco could stand up against the rooting of foraging pig herds. Hence, pig owners were even more in need of reconstruction than cattle owners.[9] Pigs should not be allowed to roam freely; they should be raised in herds, fed by the owner, and locked up at night. Thus they would become domesticated, and the threat to the farmer's fields would be removed.

On the whole, Sánchez Valverde's ideas were good; his background facts were accurate. His targets, even if overly ambitious, were certainly the correct ones. There was

---

8. With regard to land use, raising of livestock was a highly profitable and the most widespread industry of this period, and remained so until the founding of the great sugar companies after 1870. The loss of Indian labor, the scarcity of manpower toward the end of the sixteenth century, and the relatively large expanses of natural pastures and grassy, watered savannas contributed to increasing the economic attractiveness of land-intensive cattle-raising. In the absence of an inland transportation network, cattle and swine could be walked to more distant markets to which other products could not be shipped. The Dominican *hato* of the remote, eastern provinces was a small-scale version of the self-sufficient Mexican *hacienda* or the Brazilian *fazenda*. Here the rancher bred his cattle for food, sale, and draft labor in the small sugar mill. The workers' *conucos* (an Indian term for the little plot of subsistence farmland; by legal definition, a conuco is an area of slightly over thirty-six square meters) provided the necessary additional subsistence.

9. The threat to agriculture posed by free grazing continued into this century. Complaints were registered publicly. The leading newspaper in Santo Domingo said: "The campesino has two enemies: common land and free cattle in farming zones." *Listín Diario*, June 8, 1899. It was not until 1911 that the Dominican government prohibited the free grazing of animals within four kilometers of capital cities and seats of the comunes. Free ranges were also prohibited in zones declared to be agricultural by the executive branch of the government, that is, where exportable or consumable crops were grown on parcels of two or more caballerías (370 acres or more). Alcibíades Alburquerque, *Títulos de los terrenos comuneros de la República Dominicana*, p. 13 (hereafter referred to as *Títulos*).

only one major flaw in his production objectives: from the cost-of-manpower point of view, the investment capital was simply not available. Nowhere in his work does the author fully calculate the number of slaves which would be needed to perform the increased labor, the attrition of slaves due to sickness and disease, the costs of slave importation, nor even the cost of additional free labor, provided that these men could be made to work industriously. In light of the author's frequent use of cold numbers, the omission of personnel and cost implications borders on the glaring side. It is quite likely that Sánchez Valverde's calculations of increased production were based on the carefree assumption that there would be a never ending availability of slaves. Had he computed the cost, however, he would have seen that even assuming a modest goal of 100,000 additional slaves, there would be required approximately thirty million pesos for capital investment for labor alone.[10] Such a sum even amortized over a ten-year period would have been far out of reach of the weak local economy and the strained treasury of Charles III. The growth that Saint Domingue had achieved in seventy-five years could not be duplicated in ten, twenty, or fifty years in Santo Domingo.

As for the king's long overdue measures to revive and strengthen the still shaky economy in Santo Domingo, they had come too late. The inertia of almost three hundred years of slow and corrupt administrative practices essentially could not be overcome by the Bourbon reforms. In fact, the Bourbon tendency to centralize authority served only to suppress initiative on the part of local authorities and private individuals alike who, as the record shows, had been warning the Crown for centuries of the defects in the colony's economic and agricultural structure. The Royal Cédula of 1786 mentioned earlier gave evidence that the Crown fully intended to modify its commercial and economic policies throughout the New World. With time and under the new policies, Santo Domingo might have achieved a degree of prosperity even greater than that of Saint Domingue. But there was no time. The enlightened Charles III died in 1788, to be succeeded by an incompetent Charles IV, and in rapid succession thereafter came the French Revolution, the slave revolts in Saint Domingue, the cession of Santo Domingo to France by the 1795 Treaty of Basel, and in 1801 the appearance of the Haitians at the gates of the city of Santo Domingo.

---

10. Based on the selling price specified in the *asiento* of 1764 granted to Miguel Uriarte, 300 pesos.

The Middle Period

10

THE HAITIANS

The main features of Dominican history in the nineteenth and early twentieth centuries were widespread civil unrest and violence. Legally joined to the French colony of Saint Domingue, but culturally divided by over one hundred years of separate identity, Spanish Santo Domingo after 1795 could only endure the repercussions of the earlier slave revolts in the western third of the island. Spaniards who could (and there were thousands) fled the colony, believing that the only alternative was massacre at the hands of the black troops of Toussaint L'Ouverture. The exodus in the late sixteenth century was repeating itself, this time in the face of a more immediate and concentrated threat. One Dominican historian estimates that well over ten thousand Spaniards with their families abandoned their possessions and sought asylum in Puerto Rico, Cuba, Mexico, and Venezuela. Within twenty years the population of Santo Domingo had dropped to about sixty thousand.[1]

Toussaint did indeed take possession of Santo Domingo City in January 1801 after easily defeating local resistance in the Cibao and along the western approaches to the capital. The expected slaughter did not materialize, but when Toussaint returned to Saint Domingue six months later he left behind him a thoroughly terrified populace. He installed his brother Paul in Santo Domingo as governor of the southern section of the former Spanish colony, and at Santiago established a northern government under General Philippe Clerveaux.[2] Rule of Haitian law was dictatorially instituted over the entire island under a new Haitian constitution of August 1801, which named Toussaint "Governor for Life and Commander-in-Chief of the Armies." Toussaint's rule over Santo Domingo was brief, but in a period of about a year and a half he issued a number of decrees, two of which were to affect the ownership of land in Santo Domingo for

---

1. Pedro Henríquez Ureña, *La cultura y las letras coloniales en Santo Domingo*, pp. 107–10.
2. García, *Compendio*, 1:287–91. In describing the Haitian government of this period García points out that both Clerveaux and Paul L'Ouverture opened up active trade with Saint Domingue, which offered commercial advantages previously denied the Spanish colonists. This Haitian invasion was not a complete disaster for the latter.

generations. He abolished slavery and ordered all property of Spaniards in exile to be confiscated and turned over to his government.[3] These two actions brought agricultural activity to a standstill and upset the traditional norms of ownership. Land records were lost or destroyed during the confiscatory process as the old Spanish colonial administrative structure was dismantled.

Toussaint's objective of independence hardly fitted the plans of Napoleon, who, as soon as his European commitments allowed, took positive steps to reinstitute French rule. A large force under his brother-in-law, General Charles Victor Emmanuel Leclerc, arrived in Samaná in early 1802 to reestablish control of the colony. Leclerc's strategy included the direct invasion of Saint Domingue, concurrently with the engagement and defeat of Toussaint's forces in the Cibao and, of course, the recapture of the capital. The last two objectives were achieved under Generals Marie Louis Ferrand and Antoine Nicolas Kerverseau. Ferrand landed at Monte Cristi and took the Cibao with little difficulty; Kerverseau, aided by a Spanish revolt in the capital, took the city but only after some very bloody fighting. In the north and the south the defeated black armies laid waste the countryside as they retreated to Saint Domingue. Here, in mid-1802, the French captured Toussaint and defeated the main elements of the organized rebellion.[4]

The whole history not only of Santo Domingo but perhaps of the United States might have been radically changed if at this point Leclerc, and with him Napoleon's plans for America, had not been destroyed by a new enemy—yellow fever. Details of the French catastrophe and the birth of the Haitian Republic need not be given here.[5] For our purposes it will be sufficient to note that on January 1, 1804, the illiterate but capable Jean Jacques Dessalines proclaimed the independence of Haiti and was in turn named governor-general for life. These developments in the western part of the island persuaded Kerverseau, who was no hero, to consider surrendering his command in Santo Domingo. Ferrand, on the other hand, was a fighter and was determined to hold on to the colony.

---

3. Toussaint, as well as the Haitian leaders who followed him, was less than gentle with the Church. All Church property passed to the municipalities for its "conservation, fructification, and administration." The national treasury took over monastery and convent properties, and payment of the diezmo was suppressed. The consequence of this confiscatory law, later wrote an archbishop of Santo Domingo, was the stringent inhibition of the Church's economic activities. Insofar as sustaining the Faith and its ministers, the Church was reduced to such a state of poverty that it could hardly meet its most urgent necessities, nor could it help, as it had earlier, those unhappy, embarrassed families who were forced to live on the alms which Church charity distributed secretly to them. Carlos Nouel, *La historia eclesiástica de la arquidiócesis de Santo Domingo*, 2:63. The reference here is to the remaining families and relatives of Spaniards who had gone into voluntary exile and whose lands and properties had been seized by the Haitian government. Those left behind had no established means of support. The British consul in Port-au-Prince later reported that Haitian President Boyer was following a similar policy.

4. James G. Leyburn has an especially fine description of the defeat of Toussaint in *The Haitian People*, pp. 22–29.

5. An excellent account of the final defeat of the French forces can be found in J.B. Lemonnier Delafosse, *Segunda campaña de Santo Domingo*. Lemonnier Delafosse, a French army officer, provides a competent eyewitness report of the French withdrawal. Out of a total original expeditionary force of 58,545, only 150 officers of all branches and 320 enlisted men sailed from Santo Domingo on July 15, 1809. These survivors were to return to France via Jamaica and Philadelphia. The officers were paroled and eventually reached their homeland after a seven-week stay in Philadelphia. All the enlisted men were confined to British prison ships, and by 1814 all had perished. Years later, Lemonnier Delafosse was able to reconstruct an essentially complete list of survivors. Ibid., pp. 232–35.

He proceeded to Santo Domingo City and shipped the wavering Kerverseau back to France. On January 1, 1804, on the same day that Dessalines was ordering the extermination of the remaining whites in Haiti,[6] Ferrand declared himself governor of Santo Domingo.

One of Ferrand's earliest administrative projects was the revitalization of agriculture, which had been hampered not only by the back-and-forth fighting of the first Haitian invasion but also by Toussaint's freeing of the slaves. The French governor issued an important decree which permitted the resumption of the slave trade and the enslavement of all Haitians, including children, taken on Dominican territory.[7] Dessalines apparently decided to use the slave decree as immediate justification for invading the eastern part of the island. As his first move in a campaign to restore Haitian domination over the Spanish part of the island, he sent a moderate force in a tentative effort to overrun the Cibao. The alert Ferrand quickly repelled the invasion. Dessalines' next

---

6. Otto Schoenrich, *Santo Domingo: A Country with a Future*, p. 36. There is ample evidence of Haitian racist policies. Dessalines left no doubt concerning the future of race relations in Haiti. His proclamation of April 28, 1804, established as a fundamental basis for the Haitian Constitution the prohibition against any European setting foot on Haitian territory as a proprietor or landowner. This debarment was reflected in Article 12 of the Constitution of 1805, Article 27 of the Constitution of 1806, and Article 38 of the Constitution of 1816, all of which stated that as an immutable principle of public law of Haiti, no white man, whatever his nationality, could enter Haiti to become owner or proprietor, nor would he ever be able to acquire any property in Haiti.

After 1822 President Boyer had to compromise in the Haitian Constitution to recognize the racial mixtures that existed in the former Spanish colony. He declared that Dominicans could be admitted and considered as Haitians, whether or not they were land proprietors, provided that they swore allegiance to the Haitian Republic and Constitution as descendants of Indians, who were accepted as a privileged race along with Africans. Nouel, *La historia eclesiástica*, pp. 326–28; and Consul General Charles MacKenzie in Great Britain, Foreign Office, *Communications Received at the Foreign Office Relative to Hayti*, pp. 23, 133, 149 (hereafter referred to as *Communications*). MacKenzie forwarded copies of the Haitian Constitutions of 1805, 1806, and 1816. Article 12 of the Constitution of 1805 reads: "Aucun blanc, quelle que soit sa nation, ne mettra le pied sur ce territoire, à titre de maître ou de propriétaire; et ne pourra à l'avenir y acquérir aucune propriété."

Cultural historians should be intrigued by such legislative resourcefulness whereby a white man could acquire the rights of a black man by calling himself a red man.

7. Haitian resentment of the decree is understandable. The following is a partial summary of Ferrand's order of January 6, 1805:

Article 1. Inhabitants of the Ozama and Cibao frontiers, as well as troops in the outlying protective garrisons, are authorized to operate into territory occupied by Haitians and take prisoners of either sex up to fourteen years of age.

Article 2. Prisoners will become the property of their captors.

Article 3. Male child captives under ten years of age and females under twelve must remain in the colony and may not be exported. Captors may either leave them on their plantations or sell them to inhabitants of the departments of the Ozama and Cibao.

Article 4. Those captives who cannot be exported will not be considered as property of their captors and cannot be sold until the captors obtain a certificate from the appropriate local authorities that the negroes were captured on territory occupied by the rebellious Haitians.

Article 5. Males ten to fourteen years of age and females twelve to fourteen may be sold for export.

Article 6. Slaves may be exported only through the port of Santo Domingo so that the government may be able to collect the five percent export tax on the sales price.

The decree of thirteen articles is quoted in full in Emilio Rodríguez Demorizi, ed., *Invasiones haitianas de 1801, 1805, y 1822*, pp. 304–5.

move was a more aggressive one which brought death and destruction to the Spanish settlements standing between Haitian columns and Santo Domingo City.[8]

On February 16, 1805, Dessalines launched a two-pronged, 25,000-man attack. One force under Henri Christophe swept into the Cibao to sack Santiago and then move south to the capital; the second force under Dessalines himself cut across the southern region directly for Santo Domingo City. Both Haitian forces met at the besieged capital early in March, having pillaged and laid waste the border towns, the Cibao, and the southern provinces. Santiago had been devastated. Only the arrival of a French naval force prevented the Haitian siege from overwhelming the garrison of 2,000 men. Dessalines withdrew on March 29 along the same route by which he had entered, slaughtering many who had escaped him earlier. He spared no one: women, children, the aged, priests. Santiago was now almost completely destroyed, as were Azua, Monte Plata, Cotuí, San Francisco de Macorís, Moca, La Vega, and Monte Cristi.[9]

The Haitian invasion left Ferrand with a ruined colony to administer, but the stouthearted Frenchman, who probably deserved better treatment at the hands of the Dominicans than he was to receive, set about the work of reconstruction. One of his first decrees[10] as governor was issued to stem any further exodus of Spanish citizens, to penalize those who had fled, and to lighten the economic and defense burdens of those who had stayed behind. Many who had stayed behind simply lacked the means to escape, but there were also large numbers who for patriotic motives were willing to bear the suffering. Ferrand warned the inhabitants that flight would be considered a crime against the nation, since the numbers available for defense would be reduced thereby. To compensate for their absence, the land of any Spanish citizen who had left or who might leave Santo Domingo without a passport would automatically be forfeited. Urging those

---

8. Dominican, French, and Haitian historians have written extensively on the Haitian invasions of Santo Domingo. Emilio Rodríguez Demorizi's *Invasiones haitianas* is an edited collection of interesting original documents including campaign and battle reports, as well as legislative acts of the Haitian government. Lemonnier Delafosse in his *Segunda campaña de Santo Domingo* and Antonio Del Monte y Tejada in his *Historia de Santo Domingo* both report in detail on military operations. Ramón Marrero Aristy's *La República Dominicana* includes an excellent general account of the invasions, with both military and political details. James Leyburn's *The Haitian People* contains excellent material on Haitian culture and society of the period. Archbishop of Santo Domingo, Carlos Nouel, in his *La historia eclesiástica*, devotes considerable attention to the ravages of the Haitians, especially where the clergy and Church property were affected. José Gabriel García, the Dominican national historian of the nineteenth century, in his *Compendio de la historia de Santo Domingo* also gives careful attention to the Haitian invasions, especially in connection with the marauding in the Cibao. The outstanding Haitian author whose scholarly work covers the whole history of Haitian-Dominican relations is Jean price-Mars in his *La République d'Haiti et la République Dominicaine.*

9. Price-Mars points out that one of the reasons the Haitians failed to take Santo Domingo was that Dessalines had no artillery, nor did he have any naval forces to blockade the city from seaward. As for the retreat to Haiti: "And the retreat of the Haitian army was one of the most dramatic and bloody episodes of a dramatic and bloody history. Burning of farms, destruction of livestock, shooting of hostages, the capture of women and children and their brutal passage westward in the army's trail—nothing was lacking in this sad picture of useless horrors." Ibid., 1:69. Of Dessalines he adds: "The whites were Dessalines' enemy; he was revenge personified." Dessalines later admitted the cruelty of the retreat, but said: "What difference to me does the judgment of posterity make of this event which was made necessary by politics, so long as I save my country?"

10. Taken from an original government handbill printed in Santo Domingo on January 22, 1804, in the printing establishment of A. J. Blocquerst, reprinted in Rodríguez Demorizi, ed., *Invasiones haitianas*, pp. 94–95.

already in exile to return, Ferrand granted a moratorium of forty days for those in Puerto Rico, two months for those in New Spain, three months for those in Cuba, and a proportionate time for those in the other places, depending on the distance involved. Meanwhile he ordered his officials to proceed with an inventory of abandoned possessions and to plan how these might best be utilized for the benefit of the state. Income from the sequestered property was to be used to support the costs of military operations.

Some of the exiles did come home, but the memories of Toussaint and the continuous threat of invasion throughout 1804, followed by the actual event in 1805, effectively dampened the willingness of most of the more affluent ones to risk further persecution. Many successfully reestablished themselves in their new surroundings, especially in Cuba, and never returned.

With the main Haitian threat removed, Ferrand accelerated his comprehensive program of reconstruction.[11] Conscious of cultural differences, he took several measures to increase mutual understanding between the Spanish Dominicans and the French. Some of the garrison forces were organized on a mixed binational basis; French soldiers were warned to respect local customs, especially those of religion; Ferrand obtained Napoleon's permission to maintain the Spanish legal code; and he established courts in which Spanish judges would hear cases involving Spanish citizens and French judges would hear those involving French citizens.

Under Ferrand the Church regained much of its prestige, although the Frenchman did not go so far as to return property to the previous ecclesiastical owners. With the help of the clergy, he was able to reestablish his authority in the Cibao where the demoralized citizens were still vulnerable to Haitian raids. Ferrand took steps to stimulate trade, particularly with the United States. He sought business credits; he continued his earlier efforts to increase agricultural production, especially export crops. He lowered taxes, built an aqueduct for the city of Santo Domingo, and encouraged other badly needed public works projects. He initiated the establishment and construction of schools, and even began the development of a major port to be named Port Napoleon, in the vicinity of Puerto Escondido on the southeastern shore of Samaná Bay.[12]

Ferrand was personally popular with Dominicans, especially the wealthier class, who began to enjoy a peaceful national existence for the first time since the early Haitian revolts. But as an administrator he made one serious mistake; he relied too heavily on his commissioner of police, a talented but pitiless Spaniard named Gallardo, whose cruelties to the poor of Santo Domingo somehow escaped Ferrand's attention.[13] Thus, although in no way condoning Gallardo's activities, Ferrand's administration earned the dislike if not the hatred of the oppressed poor, who three years later watched his downfall without concern.

---

11. A concise but complete sketch of Ferrand's administration is contained in García, *Compendio*, 1:305–9, 321–22.

12. A reprint of the harbor development plan for Port Napoleon is contained in [Emilio Rodríguez Demorizi], *Samaná: pasado y porvenir*, p. 19. Copies of the original plans are in the National Archives, Washington, D. C.

13. Troncoso de la Concha devotes a chapter to Gallardo, whom he describes as the black splotch on Ferrand's administrative record. Gallardo, a Spanish lawyer, capable but possessing a heart as hard as rock and the soul of a serpent, was "weak against the powerful and powerful against the weak." After Ferrand's defeat at Palo Hincado, Gallardo retired to an impecunious solitary life in his house on the Calle de los Mártires in Santo Domingo, to pass his remaining years isolated and thoroughly hated by the masses of Dominicans. Manuel de Jesús Troncoso de la Concha, *Narraciones dominicanas*, pp. 84–88.

Despite Ferrand's sturdy efforts to build a prosperous economy, Dominican refusal to live indefinitely under foreign rule began to emerge as a more powerful force than the attractions of material progress. The story of Ferrand's governorship might have been studied with more care by those Americans 115 years later who could not understand Dominican objections to the continued rule of the American Military Government of Occupation.[14]

Bitterly opposing the cession of Santo Domingo to France in 1795, the Dominicans had at the time lamented the diplomacy which had sold and handed them over like so many animals. By 1808 the old desire to remain a part of the Spanish empire would not be repressed despite[15] Napoleon's invasion of Spain and the accompanying revelation to the world of the weakness of the Spanish Crown. At a time when the seeds of revolution were sprouting over most of Spanish America, Dominican leaders took the decision to overthrow the Ferrand government and return Santo Domingo to her former status as a Spanish colony. The apparent inconsistencies of such an action have been noted by historians.[16] Perhaps loyalty to the Spanish Crown was less diluted in this colony; perhaps the Spanish colonists preferred the risk of another Haitian invasion to French domination; or perhaps they may have felt that with the French out of the island the Haitians would remain behind their own frontiers. At any rate, the Spanish flag of revolution was raised in October 1808. After early successes in the field, Ferrand was defeated on November 7, 1808, at Palo Hincado, whereupon he shot himself. By mid-1809, with the help of a British force from Jamaica, the revolutionaries ejected the last French forces from Dominican territory. These events were well received by the Spanish junta at Seville, where a government in opposition to the French had been organized. Santo Domingo was restored to colonial status and its citizens promised protection and special benefits by the mother country.[17] Some of the most important provisions are noted here:

---

14. Rear Admiral Samuel S. Robison, the last military governor, wrote somewhat plaintively: "Soon after I arrived, I was directed to issue a proclamation containing the plan for electing a Dominican government and our consequent withdrawal, all to be done within a period of eight months. Since the people here through their press and other methods object to everything we do, they naturally objected to this plan, and have been objecting daily up to the present time. But we are proceeding to do all our part of the plan, and we hope that they will eventually carry out their part, which is to elect their electors in the different communes." República Dominicana, *Archivo de la Nación, Records of the Military Government of Occupation*, personal files of Rear Admiral S. S. Robison, Santo Domingo, D.R. (hereafter referred to as *Records of Military Government*), letter, Rear Admiral S. S. Robison to Captain Elliot Snow, Navy Yard, Boston, July 10, 1921. Robison is referring to his proclamation of June 14, 1921, to which the Dominicans violently objected as being an unwarranted interference in their political affairs, especially since it prescribed the procedures for their presidential election.

15. Marrero Aristy flatly states that Ferrand's progressive regime was overthrown because of Dominican reaction against Napoleon's seizure of the Spanish throne—an act of "unpardonable treason against the Spanish people." The return to Spanish colonial status was as an emotional, nostalgic gesture not wisely thought out. Marrero Aristy, *La República Dominicana*, 1:236, 243.

16. José Gabriel García points this out in his *Compendio*, 4:9. Otto Schoenrich on p. 40 of *Santo Domingo* and Ramón Marrero Aristy in *La República Dominicana*, 1:255–58, have also commented on this quixotic Dominican decision. Sumner Welles describes the Dominican decision as "astonishing." *Naboth's Vineyard*, 1:46.

17. In decrees of January 12 and April 29, 1810, the junta committed itself to measures that would facilitate the repopulating of the "always faithful colony" as well as its agriculture, industry, and commerce. These would include the assignment of garrison troops to defend

For administrative purposes the colony was subordinated to the Audiencia at Caracas.[18] Ferrand's confiscation of the lands of exiled Spaniards was declared void, and French owners were ordered to restore these properties immediately to the former owners without appeal or compensation. For a period of fifteen years trade was authorized between Dominican ports and Spain and Spanish ports in America free of all royal taxes except a one percent import tax and a one percent export tax, ad valorem. Commerce was also opened up between Santo Domingo and Spanish possessions anywhere in the world, as well as with those of Great Britain and her allies, subject only to a one percent export tax and a six percent import tax. Goods imported from Spain or Spanish American ports could be reexported upon payment of a one percent cargo tax; goods imported from foreign countries could be reexported to other Spanish colonies upon payment of a one percent export tax from Santo Domingo and a seven percent import tax on arrival at port of destination. Payment of the diezmo on industrial and agricultural production was eliminated for a period of ten years, and the Church regained its former stature.[19]

In 1811 the Spanish Cortes now seated at Cádiz began to decree new and important changes affecting the colony which, had they remained in effect for a longer period of time, might have bound Santo Domingo more securely to the Spanish Crown. The colony was granted representation in the Cortes commensurate with that of the peninsular provinces. Unlimited freedom to develop industry was conceded. Rights equal to those of European Spaniards were granted for employment in all classes of work and duties. Negro subjects were declared eligible to enter the university, the seminaries, and the Church orders. The Inquisition was abolished, and on January 23, 1812, a political constitution was approved. Unfortunately the return of Ferdinand VII to the throne in 1814 effectively wiped these progressive measures from the records. The acts of the Cortes were annulled.[20] The Crown almost immediately became more occupied with events in Europe and South America, and the colony soon found itself in the same neglected status that had prevailed during the long years of the Hapsburg decline. Labor was scarce; except for tobacco, agriculture slumped; and there was little or no industry or trade except from modest transactions with the United States in cattle, hides, mahogany, and rum. With the Spanish-American empire crumbling, Santo Domingo was

---

against invasion and free transportation and other financial assistance to Dominicans who had fled the country from the French and who now wished to return. García, *Compendio*, 2:14–15.

18. Ibid., p. 15. The records of the Audiencia of Santo Domingo had been transferred to Havana, Cuba, in 1799, where they remained in the custody of Francisco Figueras, an oidor of the Audiencia of Caracas. The Audiencia of Santo Domingo was reconstituted in Havana, by July 31, 1800. Ibid., 1:279–80. Also see Javier Barceló Malagón, *El distrito de la audiencia de Santo Domingo en los siglos XVI a XIX*, p. 6.

19. A more complete résumé of the special benefits and concessions granted by the junta in the name of Ferdinand VII can be found in García, *Compendio*, 2:14–24.

20. Rafael Altamira, *A History of Spain*, p. 538. Regarding this return to absolutism, Altamira says: " . . . the new enactments had many enemies, beginning with King Ferdinand, who saw with displeasure that they trimmed down his absolutist faculties. All the social classes and organisms whose ancient privileges were sacrificed on the altars of juridical equality (and especially many of the clergy) stirred up public opinion against the political and social reforms. The masses, indifferent in the matter because they failed to understand the new ideas, could be inclined much more easily toward familiar tradition than toward things new and strange. Thus it was possible, on Ferdinand VII's return to Spain (March 22, 1814), to abolish—lock, stock and barrel—all the work of the Cortes. . . . "

again relegated to a state of poverty and limbo which lasted eight years. Well named was this period: *"España Boba."*[21]

Into this abandoned arena, however, there filtered some of the philosophic ideals that had pervaded the colonies elsewhere in America. Santo Domingo was no less vulnerable. Ferdinand VII suppressed the liberal Constitution of Cádiz. In reverting to the tradition of absolute monarchy he created a reactionary political climate in the little colony which fostered discontent and inflated the attractions of independence.

There being no strong Spanish garrison to prevent it, a successful uprising took place in the capital on November 30, 1821. Under the leadership of José Núñez de Cáceres, a lawyer who dreamed less of complete independence and—vainly—more of association with Bolívar's Gran Colombia, the birth of Spanish Haiti was proclaimed.[22] The new state "El estado independiente de Haiti Español," endured for nine weeks, the precise time from Núñez de Cáceres' request to the president of Haiti for a treaty of amity, commerce, and mutual defense, to the consequent appearance on February 9, 1822, of Jean Pierre Boyer and 12,000 Haitians at the gates of Santo Domingo City. There was no resistance.[23] The third Haitian invasion was relatively bloodless, and this time the Haitians stayed.

Jean Pierre Boyer seized the opportunity to unite the island under the Haitian flag and to consolidate a Haitian rule of military control, racial antagonism, and continued

---

21. Literally, "silly Spain." Incháustegui says the term is derived from the fact that all of the governors sent from Spain during this period were inept. Incháustegui, *Historia dominicana,* p. 235. On the other hand, José Gabriel García attributes the expression to the fact that between 1810 and 1821 the entire colony was impoverished because of a lack of exterior trade. There was no social life, no theater, and no imported luxury. During this era of simple living, no one even had the opportunity to misspend his money in gambling casinos or houses of prostitution. García, *Compendio,* 2:25.

22. García gives a good description of the brief but successful revolt in ibid., pp. 71–75. Of considerable interest is the mission of Doctor Antonio María Pineda, de Cáceres' emissary to Bolívar. Pineda was to arrange in Caracas for the adherence of Spanish Haiti to Gran Colombia, but, unfortunately for de Cáceres, Bolívar was in Guayaquil, and no one else in his government wished to take up the matter with Pineda. The mission failed, as did de Cáceres' plans for a friendly association with Haiti. Pineda is given credit for the establishment in early 1821 of the first newspaper in Santo Domingo—*El Telégrafo Constitucional de Santo Domingo. El Telégrafo* was essentially a chronicle of governmental activities and decisions; its existence was brief.

23. Dominican historians tend to criticize de Cáceres more for a lack of political perceptiveness than for possibly unpatriotic motives. The opinions of García, Lepervanche Parparcen, and Luᵤo, generally expressed, paint de Cáceres as an irresolute, naive, legalistic half-apostle, a patriot without enthusiasm, character, or heroism. One of the most favorable evaluations is that of Antonio Martínez Ramírez, who says: "We can conclude principally and definitively therefore, that Dr. José Núñez de Cáceres, creator of the independent state in the year 1821, deserves to be officially recognized as the Liberator, not only for his brilliant intellectual gifts with which he was blessed and which motivated him to produce the very fact of independence, but in addition, for the seldom appreciated vision which guided him, since without his heroic action having taken place, the invading Haitian army would have fallen on a Spanish colony, which inevitably was to produce in the year 1844 a true independence with respect to the black state of Haiti." *El Dr. José Núñez de Cáceres y la verdadera independencia dominicana,* p. 166. The weakness in Martínez Ramírez' conclusion is that he assumes that Boyer would have invaded a Spanish colony with the same feeling of impunity as he displayed in attacking the defenseless, independent state of Spanish Haiti. Boyer might well have decided that he lacked the strength to confront a European power. Nevertheless, de Cáceres, despite any criticism of his political perspicuity, merits credit as the first Dominican to crystallize the as yet unvoiced aspirations of his people for independence.

economic retrogression.[24] During the preceding ten or twelve years there had been some travel back and forth from Santo Domingo by Dominican exiles established in other countries. Some had reclaimed their lands during the España Boba period. Completely abandoned lands had of course been seized by the Haitian government, or, as the case might be, by the Ferrand administration. But before going into exile a number of Spaniards had signed over their powers to relatives, friends, attorneys, or, the Church for management of their property.[25] The exiles lived abroad on the income thus produced. Some even sent their children back to the University of Santo Domingo for their education. Boyer's arrival was the signal for most of the best and oldest remaining Dominican families to abandon the country en masse and irrevocably.[26] What immediately followed the 1822 invasion is described in the first public pronouncement made by the Dominican leaders when they finally drove the Haitians out twenty-two years later. In the "Manifesto of the Peoples of the Eastern Part of the Island Previously Known as Española or Santo Domingo on the Causes of its Separation from the Haitian Republic," the Junta Central Gubernativa rhetorically listed a bill of particulars against Boyer and the Haitians:

> By means of his disorganizing and Machiavellian system, he forced the principal and richest families to emigrate, and with them the talent, the wealth, the commerce, and the agriculture. He removed from the country's councils and high posts those men who might have been able to speak for the rights of their fellow citizens, to ask for the correction of evils and to make manifest the real needs of the country. Disclaiming all principles of public and common law, Boyer reduced these families to poverty, taking from them their land to put it with that of the republic, giving it to Haitians, selling it at low prices. He desolated farms, destroyed agriculture and commerce, despoiled the churches of their wealth, abused the clergy, taking from them their income and fees, and left public buildings to fall, abandoned, sacked, and despoiled, into utter ruin.
>
> Later, to give his acts an appearance of legality, he decreed that the property of those Spaniards who had fled was forfeited to the state. On July 8, 1824, he prohibited the communal ownership of land, which by agreement, and use and family necessity had existed since earliest colonial days. In so doing, Boyer did irreparable damage to the herds of livestock which had used communal lands for grazing. Unable to continue this practice, many farmers were forced to abandon the raising of livestock.

24. MacKenzie, the British consul general in Port-au-Prince, draws a depressing sketch of the Boyer administration. He reported that the government was completely military and that in 1826 there was not a single civilian charged with extensive political authority. The population of the Spanish part of the island, according to his best estimate, had dropped from around 100,000 to 71,000, including former slaves. The Haitian treasury was empty; back pay was due soldiers and other government employees. Trade had dropped off by at least one-third and perhaps by one-half. Boyer had broken up all the formerly magnificent plantations. In 1789, 47,516,531 pounds of clayed sugar and 93,573,300 pounds of brown sugar were exported; in 1825, the entire sugar exports from Haiti were a mere 2,020 pounds. The abolition of slavery was a fundamental state law, and Boyer's Code Rural reduced agriculture in the countryside to a simple subsistence operation. Great Britain, *Communications*, pp. 17–24.

25. Henríquez Ureña, *La cultura y las letras coloniales en Santo Domingo*, p. 115. Nouel also mentions this transfer of their legal powers by departing exiles. *La historia eclesiástica*, 2:337.

26. Henríquez Ureña, *La cultura y las letras coloniales en Santo Domingo*, p. 110. Henríquez Ureña mentions by name a number of exiled Dominicans who became prominent citizens in Cuba, Puerto Rico, and Venezuela. Schoenrich also mentions the exodus, stating that most of the voluntary exiles were white or light colored and consisted of the more prominent families. The Haitians encouraged the whites to leave and thereafter embarked on a rule of economic neglect and opposition to Spanish culture. Schoenrich, *Santo Domingo*, p. 42.

The manifesto[27] appears to have been written primarily in defense of two special groups, the wealthy landowners and the Church, but there is little doubt that among the higher-class Dominicans who went into permanent exile there must have been many whose abilities could well have served the young republic after 1844. Boyer did attack the system of large landholdings. He abhorred the plantation as a symbol of the French colonial agricultural economy of the eighteenth century and, as had Toussaint, emancipated all slaves as the most effective first step in attacking the plantation system. He also seized the abandoned land of the exiles.[28]

With regard to confiscation, Boyer did at least maintain an external appearance of legality in his treatment of the Dominican land system. After the initial shock of the invasion had worn off, a number of Dominicans sought to reclaim their confiscated lands. To investigate and hear these cases, Boyer on August 26, 1822, appointed a six-man commission of five Haitians and one Dominican.[29] By October he had received the commission's recommendations, which were based on land conditions in Spanish Haiti, political status of the owners, and the causes and circumstances under which they had left the country. The commission agreed unanimously with Boyer that the land belonged to the state.[30]

Boyer also assigned the commission the task of investigating Church-owned property. By 1822 Church fortunes, first under Ferrand and then under Spanish rule, had improved since the second Haitian invasion. The cathedral in Santo Domingo had been restored to full cabildo staff and was operating normally, although in relatively poor economic condition.[31] Some lands had been restored during the years under Spanish rule and some additionally acquired; these were the properties which Boyer's commission was investigating. The commission ruled that the monasteries, convents, and Church farms

---

27. Dated January 16, 1844, quoted in República Dominicana, *Colección de leyes, decretos, y resoluciones, 1844–1847*, pp. 8–15 (hereafter referred to as *Colección, 1844–1847*). The manifesto is also found in Gregorio Luperón, *Notas autobiográficas y apuntes históricos*, 1:39–40 (hereafter referred to as *Notas autobiográficas*).

28. For an excellent, detailed account of Boyer's activities see García, *Compendio*, 2:89–185. García has devoted almost 100 pages to the Haitian era, which includes events both in Haiti and in Santo Domingo. Price-Mars, *La République d'Haiti*, writes of the same period, but with most of the emphasis on events in Haiti. Leyburn, in *The Haitian People*, pp. 32–87, analyzes in detail the oppressive agricultural system Boyer imposed in the belief that the small landholding would produce effectively. Boyer failed to provide the landholder with the security and incentive to produce above the subsistence level.

29. Nouel, *La historia eclesiástica*, 2:339.

30. Article 3 of the report declared to be state property all the possessions, chattel and fixed, in Santo Domingo belonging to individuals who were then absent from the territory and who had not returned by June 10, 1823, or which belonged to those who refused to swear allegiance to the republic of Haiti. Price-Mars, *La République d'Haiti*, 1:143. Evidently the Dominicans who had returned in 1822 refused allegiance to Haiti.

31. Verification of Church wealth is difficult. The Church history of the archdiocese of Santo Domingo reveals that the ecclesiastical archives were in such a state of abandon in 1790 because of the indifference of the capitulars, people taking papers from the files for private uses and not returning them, and the loss of many of the records, that the cabildo of the cathedral restricted entry to the archives to one priest, except by special permission of the cabildo itself. By 1816 the archives were disordered, termite-ridden, and partially missing. Nouel, *La historia eclesiástica*, 1:397, and 2:175. Nevertheless, there are good indications that the Church had its financial problems. A Father Regalado in 1820 had to sell the land owned by the Church in Puerto Plata which had been leased but was bringing in practically no revenue in order to raise money to repair the church which had been almost destroyed by Dessalines fifteen years earlier. Ibid., 2:263.

which produced revenue for Church causes and works, including education, should be stripped of such property as houses, lots, pastures, and heavy equipment and all should be turned over to the state.[32] The state would also take the mortgages on the convents themselves, in addition to the various mortgages on the cathedral.[33]

Boyer took the commission's recommendations, with his concurrence therein, to his legislative House and obtained unanimous approval and praise for his wise concepts and patriotic actions in behalf of the public good.[34] The Haitians did not, however, forbid the Church to operate, but they did insist on tolerance for all faiths.[35]

To exploit some of this good land which was reverting to the state, Boyer established Haitian colonies on the Samaná Peninsula, in the western provinces, and in Puerto Plata. He even successfully encouraged numbers of Negroes from the United States to settle in the country[36] to help build an African state. There is little question that the framework existed for such an enterprise. The entire population of the former Spanish colony at this time was probably no more than seventy thousand.

Boyer's efforts to unite the island under one flag and the Haitian Constitution of 1816 brought the Dominicans under tight military control. Boyer appointed Haitian army officers to command all important political or administrative posts. General Gerónimo Maximiliano Borgellá became commander of the Department of Santo Domingo, assisted by General Placide Lebrun in La Vega, General Prophète Daniel in Santiago, and

32. Ibid., p. 342. Also see Price-Mars, *La République d'Haiti*, 1:141–43.

33. The Church today does not possess title to the land occupied by the cathedral of Santo Domingo; the state holds title.

34. The British consul general in Port-au-Prince confirmed Boyer's having stripped the Church of its property. In his lengthy letter dated September 9, 1826, he reported that the clergy were entirely dependent for subsistence on the government; that the government had appropriated all the Church property to its own use; that two-thirds of the clergy's fees had to be paid into the treasury; and, not surprisingly, that these acts had called forth hostile feelings from the Spanish part of the island. He added that education was at a very low ebb—in point of fact, almost entirely neglected. Most of the rural areas had no schools at all. Great Britain, *Communications*, p. 23. Consul General Mackenzie also reported that government records were rudely kept and even if procured must be considered defective; under Boyer they were at best extremely defective. In the Spanish portion of the island no records of any kind existed for the period prior to 1817, every official document having been removed to Cuba.

35. Nouel, *La historia eclesiástica*, p. 342. The author's language is understandably bitter, but an objective analysis of Boyer's attitude toward the Church as a landowner and source of revenue shows that the Haitian policy was only slightly more stringent than that desired by the Spanish Crown in colonial times.

36. Testimony of Jacob James in Benjamin F. Wade, Andrew D. White, and Samuel G. Howe, *Report of the Commission of Inquiry to Santo Domingo*, p. 230 (hereafter referred to as *Report of Commission*). James stated that Boyer promised and gave to each immigrant five carreaux, or about sixteen acres, of land on the Samaná Peninsula so that they could become property owners and citizens immediately. By 1871 the descendants of these immigrants numbered about 2,000.

Boyer wanted to encourage the immigration of at least 6,000 persons of African ancestry, distributing them as follows: 300 to the San Cristóbal area to grow coffee and fruit; 1,000 to the Cibao to grow coffee, tobacco, and cotton; 200 to Samaná; and the remainder among the other coffee-,cacao-,and sugar-producing areas in the country. The first settlers from the United States arrived in October 1824 and the remainder soon after. The total never exceeded 3,000; large numbers died of typhus or returned to the United States voluntarily, finding themselves unable to adjust.

Those who emigrated to the Samaná Peninsula found conditions more agreeable, and remained to form a respectable minority of the local population. By 1851 the total population of the Samaná Peninsula was 1,721, of which 300 were descendants of the earlier U.S. Negro families. García, *Compendio*, 2:119.

General Jacques Simon in Puerto Plata as his principal subordinates. Haitian colonels were sent to command the former provinces of Azua, El Seibo, Baní, San Juan, and Las Matas. Haitian armed forces were stationed at various strategic points throughout Santo Domingo. Boyer conceded the right to the Dominicans to elect one deputy from each of the fourteen *comunes*[37] to represent the comunes in the Haitian legislature at Port-au-Prince. There would be one senator elected to the Haitian Senate for a term of nine years. These elections were duly held by the común primary assemblies on February 27 and July 6, 1822, respectively.

The generally depressed conditions in Haiti during the 1820s have already been described.[38] The economy of Spanish Haiti was even further handicapped by decrees which prohibited foreign trade from Spanish Haiti ports and instead instituted a cabotage system. The net effect was to increase the tax burden and the cost of imports in Spanish Haiti. Boyer also tried to bolster his economy by issuing paper money, which, since the currency was worthless, only weakened the fiscal structure more. Fretting under the military rule of the Haitians, Spanish Haiti began to reflect the added discontent generated by an obvious lack of economic progress.

Against this depressing background Juan Pablo Duarte founded La Trinitaria, a secret revolutionary society dedicated to achieving national independence.[39] In 1842 and 1843 two developments accelerated the activities of La Trinitaria. In 1842 a series of earthquakes destroyed La Vega, Santiago,[40] and a number of towns along the north coast of Haiti and Santo Domingo. Reversing the impact of a similar occurrence in Venezuela in 1812, the conspirators seized on the panic which swept the countryside as a positive psychological lever for political change. The second development was the overthrow of Boyer himself on March 13, 1843.

Revolt broke out openly on March 24, 1843. Although the Haitian authorities were able to repress the movement for independence throughout the remainder of the year, its momentum could not be stopped permanently. On February 27, 1844, a band of Dominicans overpowered the military garrison of Santo Domingo at the Baluarte (Bastion) del Conde, and within two days had ousted the Haitians. The "Era of Independence" had begun. Duarte, exiled in Curaçao for his political activity, returned in triumph to his homeland on March 14 and today is revered as the father of Dominican independence.[41]

---

37. Santo Domingo, Las Matas de Farfán, San Juan, Neiva, Azua, Baní, Seibo, Higüey, Samaná, Cotuí, La Vega, Santiago, Puerto Plata and Monte Cristi. The común was and still is roughly equivalent to an American county. Each province consisted of a number of comunes, each común with its principal city or town.

38. See note 24 above.

39. Duarte, born on January 26, 1813, founded La Trinitaria in Santo Domingo on July 16, 1838. He was the son of a businessman, was educated in France and returned to Santo Domingo at the age of 22. Including Duarte, there were nine young founders in the original group, whose motto was "God, Fatherland, and Freedom." Theirs was the struggle "of the idea which frees, against the force which represses." Their secret oath bound them to work for a separation from the Haitian state and the implantation of a free, sovereign, and independent republic, independent of all foreign domination, which would be named the Dominican Republic. Bernardo Pichardo, *Resumen de historia patria*, p. 86.

40. This was the second time these towns had been destroyed by earthquake. On November 2, 1564, a powerful quake leveled Santiago and La Vega.

41. A complete biography of Duarte, including the history of his unfortunate political career after March 1844, is to be found in Pedro L. Verges Vidal, *Duarte*. Duarte died in exile in Caracas on July 15, 1876. On February 25, 1884, his remains were brought to Santo Domingo

Within ten days the Haitian government took steps to reconquer the eastern portion of the island.[42] Two invading armies, following the historic routes across the southern provinces and down through the Cibao, commenced the approach to the capital. Both were thrown back by poorly equipped and organized but determined Dominican forces. On this retreat across the frontier the Haitians again sacked and burned the countryside. During the next three years, the Haitians made repeated invasion efforts, the most serious under the leadership of President Soulouque in 1849. Soulouque was decisively defeated by Dominican forces under General Pedro Santana in the vicinity of Azua, seventy miles west of Santo Domingo City, on April 21, 1849. For three years thereafter there were no major invasions, but the Haitians did continue a border guerrilla warfare which kept the western and northern provinces of Santo Domingo in state of unrest. Soulouque made one last effort to retake Santo Domingo at the end of 1855, again driving through the Cibao and across the south. Again he was defeated—for the last time— and again the towns and villages of the Cibao and the southwest suffered the depredations of the retreating Haitians.

The threat of further invasion from the west, however, was never far from the minds of Dominican leaders of the period.

---

and buried in the Capilla de Nuestra Señora de Altagracia in the cathedral. On February 27, 1944, on the centennial of the birth of the Dominican Republic, his remains, along with those of Francisco del Rosario Sánchez and Matías Ramón Mella, were buried in the Baluarte del Conde. A continuous military honor guard is maintained at this national shrine.

42. Marrero Aristy, *La República Dominicana*, 1: 283–319, 389–96; and García, *Compendio*, 2:232–46, 287–99, 3:15–33, 161–74, both describe these campaigns in detail. García (1834– 1910) fought as an artillery officer during a number of these engagements.

11

INDEPENDENCE AND THE ESTABLISHMENT OF POLITICAL TRADITION

The Dominicans fought, bled, and suffered through most of the forty-nine years of successive French, Haitian, again French, Spanish, and again Haitian rule. During these long years, except for the brief interlude under Ferrand, there could be little thought of development. Under the frequently changing but always alien or unsympathetic regimes, the thinly populated colony was unable to forge a viable economy. Even if by some sort of magic this had been possible, many of the Dominicans best qualified to administer public affairs had been driven away during the pre-independence turbulence. After 1844 authority was concentrated in the hands of the generals, who, if they lacked the ruthlessness of Argentina's Juan Facundo Quiroga or the brutality of the Bolivian Mariano Melgarejo, retained in common a characteristic unwillingness to sacrifice personal interest for the long-range benefit of the state. By 1855 the Dominican Republic had repelled several Haitian invasions, but internally the picture was one of political immaturity.

The provisional central junta, which had proudly arranged for the return of patriot Duarte, almost immediately encountered strong political opposition from a number of regional caudillos, including two, Pedro Santana and Buenaventura Baez, who were to figure prominently during the political vicissitudes of the next thirty-five years. By force of arms, or threat of it, Santana, *La Pantera del Seibo,* declared himself dictator less than five months after the country had achieved independence. By so doing, this harsh, arrogant, and unpolished fighter-hero of the Haitian wars set the general pattern of Dominican politics for the following twenty years, until his death in 1864.[1] Baez was more cultured, more devious, much less the military figure, but no less dictatorial. Santana and then Baez dominated national politics until 1878, when for the fifth time (four by force) Baez was removed from office and forced into permanent exile. By their frequent

---

1. For an excellent character study of Santana and appreciation of the problems of early independence in the Dominican Republic, see Rodríguez Demorizi, *Santana y los poetas de su tiempo* (hereafter referred to as *Santana*).

arbitrary actions these two leaders established an unhappy political tradition based on personalism which made a mockery of Dominican democratic constitutional law and order.[2] Perhaps Santana is less to be criticized for his actions than Baez, because on Santana's broad shoulders repeatedly fell the responsibility for the military defense of the young and weak republic. Santana, who promised his people liberty, order, and progress—but above all, order—resorted to repressive tactics to achieve order. Thereby he created enemies among the more liberal Dominicans, who found in the cosmopolitan Baez a leader more to their liking. Thus was born the either/or politics of *Santanismo* and *Baecismo*—the Blues versus the Reds. Lamentably, there was no middle ground between the two parties, no moderating element or catalyst to serve as a regulating wheel to the violence and passion of the opposing extremes. Those on the outside, whether Red or Blue, continued to plot revolution in order to regain power; neither group saw beyond the figure of its own leader what should have been the true concern of all—the welfare of the country as a whole.

The two party chiefs did not limit the scope of their manipulations to the domestic arena. Santana's fiercely criticized, ill-conceived plans to annex the Dominican Republic to Spain in 1861 brought on vicious warfare from 1863 to 1865 between Dominican forces and Spanish garrison troops, which left some sections of the country devastated. Santana's role in the 1861 reannexation can be evaluated as one either of high treason or of excusable treason. On December 25, 1863, the Provisional Government of the Restoration condemned him to death as a fugitive from the law, guilty of high treason. He had, according to the Dominicans who were fighting to restore their country's freedom, alienated the republic in favor of the Spanish Crown without the free and legal will of the people and against the express terms of the fundamental law of the land.

Although not forgiving him for the surrender of his country's sovereignty, Santana's defenders have reminded his critics that fear of additional Haitian attacks and the knowledge that the weak little republic needed a powerful friend caused him to adopt the policies he did. They claim that his original idea was to seek only a protectorate relationship whereby the Dominican Republic would retain full independence but could rely on outside assistance in a military emergency. Further, as Rufino Martínez says, Santana was moral, honest, serious, and proud; his weakness lay in his inability to accept a fall from personal power. Martínez adds that the majority of the people frankly supported the projected annexation. On this point he meets violent opposition, and the argument continues to the present.[3] The opinions of two of Santana's contemporaries are worth noting here. Although Luperón fought against Santana during the *Revolución Restauradora*, he took one of the moderate views. In his autobiography years later,[4] Luperón wrote that the magnificent services rendered earlier by Santana during the war

---

2. Schoenrich, *Santo Domingo*, pp. 45–75, contains a complete, concise review of the political disorders which plagued the country from 1845 to 1887.

3. For the reader desiring to explore this still live issue further, I suggest that in addition to Luperón and García he consult Rufino Martínez, *Hombres dominicanos*, vol. 2, *Santana y Baez*, which is pro-Santana; Hugo Tolentino Dipp, *La traición de Pedro Santana*, a brief anti-Santana essay written by the eminent former vice rector for academic affairs at the University of Santo Domingo; Rodríguez Demorizi, *Santana*, a more balanced study; and Vetilio Alfau Durán's illuminating, annotated *Controversia histórica: polémica de Santana*. Alfau Durán has reprinted an account of a literary duel fought in the Santo Domingo press from 1889 to 1892. The duelists were the two leading writers of the day, José Gabriel García and Manuel J. Galván. The book also contains a useful bibliography.

4. Luperón, *Notas autobiográficas*, 1:236–37.

for independence from Haiti could perhaps excuse his tyranny but never his treason in handing over his country to a foreign power. Santana's crime was not his venality but, rather, his stupidity in believing that the Spanish governors would be just, honest and law-abiding.

José Gabriel García also recognized the old warrior's merits and his sins:

> So ended the days of the man who, from the time he appeared on the public scene, played important roles in the political vicissitudes of the country; who three times took power as supreme commander and another three as president of the republic; who in his service record counted two glorious battles: Azua and Las Carreras; who had as rivals Duarte, Jiménez, and Baez, and who conquered all three; who had made and destroyed constitutions; who had headed three clamorous revolutions and had won over the Revolution of July 7 [started in 1857 against Baez]; who spent sixteen years imposing himself on the country whose destiny he trifled with capriciously; who did, in short, whatever he felt like doing, even destroying the nation . . . to convert it into a Spanish colony and leave it wrapped in a fratricidal war . . . . But let us permit his venerable remains to rest in peace.[5]

When the Dominicans needed a fighting leader in 1843, Santana filled that role admirably. One might even go further and admit that his forceful hand was needed all through the first ten or twelve years of independence. But the efforts that he made prior to 1856 to preserve the independence of his country were rudely counterbalanced by his willingness in 1861 to turn over the republic to Spain. He did not consult his people prior to the annexation, except for a few sycophants and confidants. Regardless of his motives, whether they were patriotic or selfish, or of the fact that he was supported later by his own partisans, it was an individual power play, and it led to a bloody civil war. Santana had been called on to complete the overthrow of Baez in 1858. Thereafter, had he been able to relinquish the practice of personal politics, his memory would probably be as thoroughly respected today in the Dominican Republic as is that of Gregorio Luperón. The lure was too tempting, however, and Santana's weakness drained the young nation of resources it could ill afford to lose.

The total cost of the Revolución Restauradora in lives, money, and property was never known accurately. The cost to Spain alone was 21,000 men killed or wounded[6] and thirty-five million pesos. High-handedly exercising his presidential initiative eight years later,[7] Baez tried to alienate Dominican territory and territorial waters in favor of the

---

5. García, *Compendio*, 3:479. This evaluation is not nearly as succinct as an epitaph of Santana written anonymously in 1864:

> Here lies a great jackass
> More despotic than anyone,
> Who never knew his role
> And died like a pig
> Having accomplished no good.

Rodríguez Demorizi, *Santana*, p. 341.

6. Marrero Aristy, *La República Dominicana*, 2:98. Pichardo puts the Spanish losses at 10,888, not counting the casualties sustained by reserved and volunteer forces which accompanied the Spanish army during the campaign. There are no Dominican casualty figures. Pichardo, *Resumen de historia patria*, p. 187. García, who lived during this period and fought against the Spaniards throughout the War of the Restoration, provides excellent coverage, especially on the military operations, in his *Compendio*, 3:325–506.

7. The story of Baez' negotiations in 1869 with agents of the U.S. has attracted the attention of a number of historians. Schoenrich, in *Santo Domingo*, and especially Charles Callan Tansill, in *The United States and Santo Domingo, 1798–1873*, give full accounts. Dominican historians,

United States in order to replenish his empty treasury. Compared to Santana's, this was a limited transaction, but both men acted arbitrarily in these ventures, ignoring the machinery of government and, from the bulk of the evidence, the will of the Dominican people. In both cases their actions led to destructive civil war. Reflecting the precedent of such administrations as these, civil unrest, political conspiracy, and public irresponsibility became the norm of Dominican public life. The peak of instability was reached in 1878, a year which saw six presidencies, not to mention a brief, separate government-in-opposition proclaimed in the Cibao.[8]

No further direct commentary on Dominican national government need be made here, except to point out that at the three-quarter mark of the century, after almost forty years of independence, the Dominican people had been afforded scant opportunity to develop progressive, stabilized, working political institutions. Party leadership would not compromise party goals, which in themselves were only a reflection of the desires of an individual leader. The personal politics of the regional leaders not only hampered the development of national policy based on true national interests but also prevented the growth of rational political institutions in the rural areas. In the provinces, and especially in the more remote districts such as Samaná, Monte Cristi, and the Cibao, the main symbols of power were the local governors, who possessed full military and civil authority in their regions. The unscrupulous and belligerent ones could and did commit political abuses, mismanage funds, inject themselves personally into the machinery of justice, and dominate every aspect of political life in the municipalities and comunes.[9] Even among the wealthier classes, life in the small towns was punctuated by frequent calls to arms or to actual fighting. The existence of these Dominicans was disjointed, isolated, and without any real faith in government. There was no community feeling and little incentive to progress. Provincial society, unable to correct its lack of unity, was stratified both socially and economically.[10]

---

all of whom condemn Baez, attack not only him but also the report submitted by the Commission of Inquiry which President Grant sent to the Dominican Republic in 1871 to determine public opinion on the proposed annexation. These historians feel that the commission talked almost exclusively with pro-Baez Dominicans. See José G. García, *A Brief Refutal of the Report of the Santo Domingo Commissioners;* Luperón, *Notas autobiográficas;* and Emilio Rodríguez Demorizi, *Informe de la comisión de investigación de los E.U.A. en Santo Domingo en 1871,* annotated Spanish-language version of the commission's report. It might be noted here that historically all the official proposals for the lease or sale of the Bay of Samaná or for the annexation of Dominican territory to the United States have been created as a result of Dominican initiatives and not by American governments.

8. These were the administrations of: Buenaventura Baez, constitutional president to February 24, 1878; Cesareo Guillermo, provisional president, February 24–April 13; Cesareo Guillermo, constitutional president April 13–July 6; Ignacio María González, constitutional president July 6–September 2; Jacinto de Castro, acting president, September 2–September 29; and Cesareo Guillermo, provisional president, September 29–February 27, 1879.

9. Pedro Troncoso Sánchez, *Ramón Cáceres,* p. 296. Troncoso Sánchez' term for this kind of independent administration is "regional caciquism," which reached its peak of prevalence during the dictatorship of Ulises Heureaux, 1887–99. Heureaux did not restrain the local governors, all of whom he had appointed, so long as they were loyal to him. What distinguished him from his predecessors in office was his ability to detect and ruthlessly crush incipient opposition. In this respect he served as the model for Trujillo 30 years later. See Martínez, *Hombres dominicanos,* vol. 3, *Trujillo y Heureaux,* for an interesting comparison of these two dictators.

10. José Ramón Abad, ed., *La República Dominicana: reseña general,* p. 153. This book is an excellent comprehensive, factual report on the geography, demography, political history, and economy of the late nineteenth century. It was prepared in 1888 at the request of the

To understand how local authority was maintained in the rural areas, one must retrace Dominican history as it was affected by the conditions that existed in 1844: a sparse population and a political vacuum created by the sudden disappearance of Haitian military administration from the provinces. Both weaknesses would have to be corrected if the new republic was to register internal growth. There was little that could be done to stimulate the return of exiles, most of whom were now well established, and, certainly the country offered no special attraction to potential European immigrants seeking a more peaceful way of life.[11] Of more immediate relevance here, however, is the manner in which the central government organized provincial and local governments on a constitutional basis and how martial law was imposed on this legitimate superstructure. The eventual result of these measures, much of which must be attributed to Pedro Santana, was the tradition of military preeminence in rural government—*es el capitán quien manda*—which still exists today.[12]

Santana had emerged from the 1843–44 war for independence as the undisputed military leader and hero of the nation. With the loyal support of the majority of army troops, he seized the opportunity presented by internal dissension over party leadership among the liberal Trinitarians to proclaim himself "Supreme Chief of the Republic with dictatorial powers, in the name of the Army and the people" until a constitutional government could be established and elections held.[13] The date was July 16, 1844. In the style so typical in Latin America, *caudillismo* smothered *liberalismo* and thereafter, except for an occasional brief period or two, dominated political life in the Dominican Republic for over a hundred years.

Santana and the constitutional Congress which met on September 21, 1844, at San Cristóbal disagreed on several legal dispositions, at one point so violently that the dictator branded the Congress as traitorous. The Congress, in turn, hastily moved to pass a resolution conferring immunity on the members for their votes or expressed opinions. Not surprisingly, Santana rejected the first liberal draft constitution which was modeled largely on the Constitution of Cádiz of 1812 and the Constitution of the United States. Maintaining that in the prevailing circumstances dictatorship was vitally needed to save the republic, he refused to accept any constitutional limitation on the chief executive's authority. By threatening to resign and by ordering the movement of troops openly in and around San Cristóbal,[14] Santana was able to "persuade" the Congress to include the notorious Article 210[15] in the draft constitution:

During actual war and while peace is not firmly established, the President of the Re-

---

minister of development and public works, Pedro Tomás Garrido. Abad gives the land ownership system more than adequate attention, and he also devotes considerable space to the economic future of the country. He unfortunately could not predict the financial misadventures which lay immediately ahead.

11. Santana did issue an immigration law in 1847 for the purpose of promoting immigration. Under this law the chief executive was authorized to grant fifty acres of land to each immigrant family, with the sole condition that it be cultivated. Colonists would be exempt from military service.

12. I use the term "military" loosely, to mean men under arms, more or less organized in a military command structure and responsive to authority, often local. The term does not necessarily apply to duly constituted, national armed forces.

13. Santana, described as the hope of the nation, was proclaimed *jefe supremo militar, presidente de la junta central gubernativa*.

14. Marrero Aristy, *La República Dominicana*, 1:304–5.

15. Liberal Dominicans soon began to protest Santana's arbitrary and often repressive use

public may freely organize the Army and Navy, mobilize the national guard forces and take the measures he believes needed for the defense and the security of the Nation, being empowered as a consequence to give the orders, dispositions and decrees he considers necessary, without being subject to any authority.[16]

As thus modified, the Constitution of San Cristóbal was promulgated on November 6, 1844. The government quickly organized its political administration based on constitutional provisions, reestablishing the provinces, comunes, and ayuntamientos.[17] Decrees 32 and 40, the Laws for the Ayuntamientos and for Provincial Administration, were detailed and lengthy. They remain in effect today, basically unchanged. Only those portions concerning political organization will be discussed here.

The Dominican común was the basic political unit of the province. The five cacicatos of the Tainos had become the first provinces of Española; as their population increased they were divided into comunes. By the beginning of the nineteenth century all the provinces had been subdivided, each común growing up around a principal town. Sparsely populated provinces might have only one or two comunes. Each principal town had its ayuntamiento whose jurisdiction extended only to the minicipal limits. Outside the limits the remainder of the común was divided into small *secciones*, or sections. These arrangements were disrupted by the Haitian reorganizations in 1805 and 1822, when the country was divided into six departments: those of the North, West, South, and Artibonito, all generally in the western half, and the Cibao and Ozama, which comprised the eastern half of what had been Española. The latter two departments contained the bulk of the Spanish-Dominican population and were further subdivided into cantons and comunes as follows: Santiago and Puerto Plata in the north, with six and one comunes, respectively; Azua and Santo Domingo in the south, with three and seven comunes, respectively.[18]

Now, in 1845, the government referred back to the pre-Haitian organization and decreed that in all comunes where in 1821 an ayuntamiento had been seated, and in all comunes formed since, an ayuntamiento consisting of a constitutional *alcalde,* three *regidores* and a *procurador síndico*[19] would be established, with the concurrence of the provin-

---

of this article which was eventually eliminated in the constitutional revision of 1854.

16. Manuel Arturo Peña Batlle, ed., *Colección Trujillo*, vols. 1 and 2, *Constitución política y reformas constitucionales, 1844–1942*, 1:161 (hereafter referred to as *Constitución política*).

17. Part 1 of Article 159, *Constitución de 1844*, ibid. The ayuntamiento was the municipal council. The term is still used in the Dominican Republic and generally elsewhere in Latin America.

18. Haitian decree of July 11, 1823, Rodríguez Demorizi, *Invasiones haitianas*, p. 315.

19. The functions of alcalde and regidor were generally similar to those of mayor/magistrate and councilman, respectively. The alcalde was the president of the ayuntamiento. The síndico functioned more or less as a combination district attorney, ombudsman, and city manager. He insured the execution of municipal laws, defended the rights of the public, promoted the well-being and prosperity of the común, and inspected public markets, butcher shops, bakeries, and food stores. His authority extended to inspections of public accounts and weights and measures. He could remove or suspend licenses and could prosecute offenders of municipal law. He could be ordered to respond officially to the provincial legislature when that body judged it necessary. He was a member of the ayuntamiento and he was almost always the jefe político of the común.

In addition to his municipal duties, the alcalde served also as justice of the peace in those cases brought forward by the section commanders. As the population in the común grew, the alcalde normally designated an alcalde *pedaneo*, or petty mayor, to represent him in the section. The section commander, however, retained the effective political authority.

cial assembly. In provincial capitals the ayuntamiento consisted of two constitutional alcaldes, five regidores and a procurador síndico, all with equal votes. In those cases where the population of the común did not exceed 1,000, the administration was to consist of only one constitutional alcalde and the procurador síndico. All these offices were to be honorific and gratuitous; no citizen could refuse to accept the nomination. Members of the ayuntamientos would be elected by primary assemblies, and thereafter each ayuntamiento would determine which of its members would hold the municipal offices. Under later constitutions and regimes the president of the republic reserved the power to appoint constitutional alcaldes and the síndicos as well, since the latter doubled as jefes políticos, or local political bosses, of the comunes.

The constitutional alcalde exercised some civil jurisdiction over the común outside the municipality, but the senior political power holder in the común was the jefe político, to whom the alcalde was subordinate except for strictly municipal matters in which by law the ayuntamiento was autonomous.[20] The president of the republic always appointed the senior political official in the province, the provincial governor.

The central government soon perceived that police supervision in the rural areas was inadequate and that agricultural production was not receiving the attention its importance merited. In 1846 came the first of several sets of regulations intended to remedy this double weakness.[21] The government organized and assigned to every section a company of civil guards[22] whose captain was designated section commander (jefe de sección). The section commander had as assistants a lieutenant and a sub-lieutenant. The size of the company was not prescribed, since that depended on the population of the section, but the usual strength was 50 to 100 men.

Briefly, these were some of the duties of the section commander and his company: patrol the section, denouncing all crimes, infractions, and law-breaking; maintain order and tranquility, arresting anyone who on first demand does not obey the orders given him and sending him without delay before the alcalde; stop all gambling, except for cock-fighting on Sundays and feast days; stop all amusements, except on Sunday evenings and on national and religious holidays when work is prohibited; prevent anyone from en-

20. As an example of the constitutional language used to establish this authority, Article 71 of the Constitution of 1907 says: "The ayuntamientos, with regard to the exercise of their normal administrative authority, are independent and are required only to render an accounting of their collections and disbursements of funds in accordance with the law." República Dominicana, *Colección de leyes, decretos, y resoluciones, 1905–1907*, p. 550 (hereafter referred to as *Colección, 1905–1907*).

21. Decree number 95, Rural Regulations for the Común of Santo Domingo, October 15, 1846, signed by Santana, quoted in República Dominicana, *Colección, 1844–1847*, pp. 471–74.

22. The regulations did not identify the civil guards. They were members of a national militia which, according to the constitution, came under the direct orders of the governor. In 1905 Vice-President Ramón Cáceres signed the law creating the rural guard (*guardia rural*) which was organized on military lines, but whose function was stated to be "essentially civil." The rural guard had as its principal objectives the conserving public order, protecting property, and giving assistance to local authorities as needed to repress crime. As a body, the guard was the responsibility of the minister of interior and police. In the provinces the guard detachments came under the jurisdiction of the governors, and in their respective comunes, the jefes políticos. The guard was composed of 940 men organized into a regiment of four cavalry squadrons and four infantry companies. There were about 100 men in each of these subunits, which were further divided into squads of about 10 to 12 men each. República Dominicana, *Colección, 1905–1907*, pp. 106–9. This was the law of June 10, 1905. According to the law, candidates for the guard had to be able to read and write.

tering the section on any pretext unless that person had written authority to enter and establish himself there or had a passport to travel; oblige landowners to keep their land in a good and full state of cultivation; check on the production and exportation of agricultural products; force workers to comply with any contract they may have made with landowners; and require landowners to pay agreed wages to workers. Any person who had no useful profession or who could not demonstrate that he possessed an honest means of self-support could be forced to work as an agricultural laborer.

The section commander appeared every three months before the jefe político of the común to report fully on conditions within the section, with special notes on the state of agriculture. In turn, the jefe político made periodic reports to the provincial governor.

In addition to the presidentially appointed jefe político, there was in each común a *comandante de armas*, a military officer appointed by the governor. The comandante de armas was the military superior of the section commanders, but he was theoretically subordinate to the jefe político. In practice he usually commanded more respect because he controlled the military elements.

To recapitulate the civil and military relationships in the provinces: the provincial governor, who possessed both civil and military powers, was the appointee and direct representative of the president. He exercised civil authority down through the jefe político of each común, who in turn was the political superior of the section commanders and, for certain purposes, of the alcalde of the ayuntamiento. The governor exercised his military authority through the comandante de armas in each común, who in turn was the military superior of the same section commanders.

The regulations for the various comunes were generally very similar, although there were interesting variations. The laws for El Seibo and Higüey, for instance, placed even more emphasis on agricultural production. In these comunes the section commanders had the authority to force the inhabitants within their jurisdiction to place their unused land under cultivation in export crops such as coffee, cotton, tobacco, or cacao, the crop to be chosen by the farmer. Failure to comply within a three-month period could result in the offender's having to appear before the alcalde, who could condemn him as a vagabond and assign him to public works projects for three months. The law also designated the jefes políticos and the alcaldes as truant officers; these two officials were enjoined to require heads of families to place at least one of their children in public schools.[23]

Although the desire to stimulate agricultural production was well founded, Santana's government selected a cure which over the years created far more evil than good. There was a tendency for civil and military lines to blur at lower levels of authority; in the process the military usually gained ascendancy. This tendency toward armed authority was continually aggravated by the frequent military operations against the Haitians up to 1855, by the War of the Restoration in 1863 and 1864, and by the recurring revolutions and counterrevolutions thereafter. The result was a permanent condition of near martial law in rural areas; the government simply put weapons in the hands of untrained militia troops and looked to them to maintain order.

Perhaps there was no other alternative in the early years of independence. The country was being invaded periodically; whatever manpower resources existed were needed for military service, and even if conditions of internal security had permitted and the necessary manpower had been available, there was neither the money, a democratic tra-

---

23. Decree number 98, January 21, 1847, signed by President Santana, quoted in República Dominicana, *Colección, 1844–1847*, pp. 480–82.

dition, nor the administrative experience in the country to organize a rural police force on any basis except the one that was adopted. Unfortunately the system gave the jefes excessive arbitrary power, which made it easy for them to take frequent advantage of the ignorant and authority-ridden poor farmer. It was a simple matter for an unscrupulous landowner to cheat on a work contract, or for a conniving lawyer to falsify a land title, knowing that the campesino rarely had documents of ownership and could not read anyway. And since he was being drafted by the alcalde for forced labor on the latter's own farm, to whom could the prisoner appeal? To the officer who had arrested him in the first place at the hint of the alcalde or the latter's *compadre*[24] the jefe político?

Throughout the years the abuses stemming from the expedients devised in 1846 and 1847 successively became custom, then tradition, and finally, by the end of the century, unwritten law. In the isolated provinces the effective source of rural political power came to lie less with the president of the republic and more with the jefe político, and still more with the comandante de armas and his section commanders. With justification, José Ramón Abad wrote in 1888:

> The masses live in the country, obedient to the jefe comunal who is the sole representative of authority to them. So they are indifferent to the actions of the Popular Assembly where real national sovereignty lies. Therefore, this sovereignty does not always carry the authority which it represents, and the governments wishing to remain in power have had to resort to opportunism.[25]

Abad's point was a telling one: the guardia with a gun was the usual authority with whom the campesino came into contact. It was the gun which earned the respect of the campesino, not the law.

One should not infer that although the campesinos were ignorant and illiterate, they always submitted willingly to exploitation. Even when the lack of public funds forced the provincial authorities to draft men to work without pay on legitimate public works projects such as roads and bridges, there was frequent violence. Reluctant draftees in the vicinity of Bonao suddenly decided to cooperate with the authorities when one of their number was arbitrarily hanged for refusing to work on a local project.[26]

Even into the twentieth century it was still customary in the Cibao for the local alcalde to draft rural workers for labor on his land or on that of an influential landowner who needed an extra labor force temporarily. For the campesino, the idea of resisting this modern version of the repartimiento was tempered by the weight of past custom and the

---

24. Strictly defined, compadre is derived from the godfather-godson relationship. It is the word by which the godfather and godmother address the father of their godson or daughter, and by which the father and mother address the godfather and godmother. The godparents and real parents are compadres. In the Dominican Republic, as elsewhere in Spanish America, compadre is also used to describe a friendly relationship even though godchildren may not be involved. The word "crony" in English is an approximation. The feminine counterpart is of course *comadre*.

25. Abad, *La República Dominicana*, p. 152.

26. Interview with a former minister of agriculture and governor of the province of La Vega, La Vega, November 6, 1969. Perhaps even more illustrative of this point is the little story that many Dominicans attribute to "that cold-blooded devil" Lilís (Dictator Ulises Heureaux). The governor of Samaná had begged Lilís to find fifty workers for some badly needed projects on the Samaná Peninsula. With characteristic callousness, Lilís ordered fifty workers trussed up and shipped to Samaná, with the following message to the governor: "Estoy mandándole los cincuenta voluntarios; devuélvame las sogas." ("I am sending you the fifty volunteers; return the ropes to me.")

armed superiority of the guardia. As for the latter, he had no strong feelings one way or another. He was merely carrying out the orders of the jefe. The usual labor detachments consisted of groups of ten men who rotated in performing one day's work a week, or perhaps five days a month, without pay. Even when a wage was paid, the landowner frequently resorted to almost any illegal tactic in order to impose a substantial fine on the ignorant workers.[27] This was the sort of exploitation which a very perceptive Santiago writer hoped to eliminate through a double reform process. In the discerning study cited below, López appealed to Dominicans at all economic and social levels to unite in an effort to bring progress and economic stability to their country. The progress would come through rural education, the economic stability through improved agricultural research, modern marketing methods, and technical and financial assistance for the farmers.

The Dominican Republic was young, insecure, and underdeveloped. It was supported by a backward agricultural economy on which a majority of the inhabitants were dependent for subsistence and a meager income. Future development lay in the ability of the national government to strengthen the economy and to prepare the rural majority for the responsibilities of citizenship. A broad attack on national illiteracy was indicated as the logical beginning step, one which would be fundamental for the needed economic, social, and cultural endeavors.

What, then, is the history of education, especially primary rural education, in the nineteenth-century Dominican Republic?

27. José R. López, *La paz en la República Dominicana*, p. 37. This work is small in size but large and thoughtful in the concepts it offers for land reform and economic progress at the beginning of the twentieth century.

12

PUBLIC INSTRUCTION AND
THE CAMPESINO

No serious attention was given public instruction until after independence had been achieved. The Spanish colonial inheritance of disregard for the general education of the lower classes, especially in the rural areas, focused what little desultory educational effort there was on a minority, the sons of the well-to-do.[1] It made little difference to these families if public schools were inadequate or nonexistent, because private tutors were usually available, if not preferred. Furthermore, many wealthy parents preferred to educate their children abroad. The sons of middle-class families, which were fewer in number and almost always urban, might or might not obtain a primary education, depending on whether the family lived in one of the principal towns. A few of these families might be willing to pay a private tutor if there was no Church-supported school available. The sons of the urban poor received little or no education, because public schools, if there were any available, required a modest tuition payment which was still beyond the reach of these families. In rare cases scholarships were offered to the deserving poor. The son of the rural poor man—the campesino working his small subsistence plot as owner, lessee, or tenant farmer—received no public education whatsoever. The campesino could not afford to put his children into the nearest town school, nor could he spare them from the labors of the land. Living passively in relative isolation, the vast majority of rural fathers, themselves illiterate, could not be expected to appreciate the value or need for their numerous children to be educated.[2] The fact that well over three-quarters of the population lived in rural areas, some of them extremely remote, therefore becomes a culturally significant determinant.[3]

---

1. There was little interest in general public education, but, as Haring points out, this attitude had existed in continental Europe as a whole. There is no reason to expect that popular education would have been established in Española or any other Spanish colony when this institution did not exist in Spain itself. Haring, *Spanish Empire in America*, pp. 208–9.

2. Abad, *La República Dominicana*, pp. 157–74. Abad was reform-minded; these pages not only describe existing school conditions but also include ideas for expanding and improving public education. Abad saw the close relationship between education and progressive agriculture.

Judging solely from the applicable legislation, one would conclude that after 1844 the early national governments prescribed commendably effective educational measures for their young people. Early decrees of the junta central gubernativa included a Law of the Ayuntamientos[4] and a Law on Public Instruction.[5] The former include a clause which placed the responsibility for establishing and supervising schools and other municipal agencies of public instruction on the ayuntamientos. The latter was a complete law, relatively enlightened in its provisions. The Dominican system of education was founded on the recognition that the establishment of public schools was highly necessary to the prosperity of the state, to the cultural, moral, and social advancement of the individual, and to the securing of an honest and useful existence.

The law called for the installation of one primary school in each común[6] and two in each provincial capital. The number of students to be enrolled in each school would be determined on a basis of total population by the respective ayuntamientos. No higher-level schools would be established immediately. When considered necessary by the provincial legislature, one of the two schools in the capital could be converted to the more advanced level.

Religion, writing, arithmetic, grammar, and principles of good behavior would be taught in all primary schools, to which children of all Dominican parents could be admitted free.[7] The government would provide paper, ink, and primers for poor children in quantities decided by the alcalde.

---

3. There are no dependable census figures for this entire period. An unreliable Church census of 1863 placed the population at 207,700. A similar census of 1888 showed 382,321 inhabitants, but the Church records became more unreliable as the population increased and spread into distant areas. In 1885 there were probably no more than four or five towns in the entire country with populations over 3,000. As late as 1917 rough estimates showed that the province of La Vega had 90,000 inhabitants, of which only 5,000 lived in the provincial capital and only sizeable town, La Vega. Similar figures for other provinces were: Santiago, 110,000 and 14,000; Santo Domingo, 115,000 and 21,000; San Pedro de Macorís, 28,000 and 5,000; and Puerto Plata, 50,000 and 7,000. In these provinces, which were the most heavily populated, rural inhabitants constituted from 82 to 94 percent of the provincial population. Schoenrich, *Santo Domingo*, pp. 166–67. Referring to the Church census of 1888, Abad points out that the Church figures did not include foreigners in transit, non-Catholics, and unbaptized children, all of whom probably totaled no less than 25,000. He therefore uses a population figure of 415,000 for 1888. Abad, *La República Dominicana*, p. 92.

4. Decree number 32, 1845, quoted in República Dominicana, *Colección, 1844–1847*, pp. 111–16.

5. Decree number 33, May 7, 1845, quoted in ibid., pp. 117–23.

6. At this time the government had just decreed that the republic would consist of five provinces, divided into 27 comunes as follows:

Compostela de Azua	9
Santo Domingo	7
Santa Cruz del Seybo	3
Concepción de La Vega	4
Santiago de los Caballeros	4

Decree number 40, Law of Provincial Administration, quoted in ibid., p. 199.

7. This provision was eventually disregarded at the local level, probably as shortcomings in pubic finances became apparent. To finance the war effort against the Haitians from 1845 to 1855, the central government ordered all local governments to place their cash assets at the disposal of the executive power without restrictions. The state promised to reimburse communal treasuries after hostilities had ceased. This drain of money out of the provinces, which, judging from later evidence, was probably never repaid, radically reduced the local ability to support public instruction. Decree number 107, 1847, quoted in ibid., p. 512. By 1867 Minister of

The admission age was set at six years, and parents were to submit documentary evidence of date of children's birth as well as a certificate of vaccination against small-pox. Parents were encouraged to send their children to school.

Additional provisions of the Law of Public Instruction covered in general terms the selection,[8] duties, and instruction of teachers; monthly school inspections by the members of the ayuntamiento to inquire into disciplinary and health conditions; and salaries. The annual salary of an urban primary teacher was 840 pesos, and that of a rural teacher, 600 pesos.[9]

An 1846 modification of this first law of public instruction provided for a general council of public instruction to direct and supervise all public and private schools in the nation and to make a comprehensive report semi-annually to the minister of public education. A system of provincial and communal sub-inspectors whose offices would be located in the provincial capitals and in the various comunes was also devised as part of the national educational administrative structure.

The new modification made provision for public secondary schools, new curricula, and even prescribed that on admission lists preference would be given to orphans and to children of poverty-stricken parents. Obviously the drafters of the law considered that children of all economic classes without exception should be permitted to obtain an education.

For reasons which Dominican records do not show—perhaps a general mistrust of centralized education—the 1846 modification was annulled a year later, thus removing the legal foundation for a national school system.[10] Four years later the Congress again

---

Education Pedro F. Bonó noted that apart from the capital itself, no común in Santo Domingo province offered free public education. Quoted in Emilio Rodríguez Demorizi, *Papeles de Pedro F. Bonó*, p. 145.

8. Criteria for selection were essentially those of character and reputation. There was no normal school in the country; accordingly, the law indicated no professional training quali-fications. It was not unusual for a civic-minded lady to volunteer to teach on a part-time or intermittent basis, or perhaps she might be a widow in need of a tiny income. Her only quali-fication might be that she could read and write.

9. These were probably either Spanish or Mexican silver pesos fuertes, since the first national coin was not established until 1848. Law 145 of June 15, 1848, established the Dominican peso at 400 grains of silver. The legal silver used was measured by the pound Troy, of 5,760 grains, and consisted of 11 1/10 ounces of pure silver and 9/10 ounce of copper. The legal gold, or *oro de ley* pound Troy, consisted of 11 ounces of pure gold and one ounce of copper. On March 9, 1858, in Decree number 531, the government prescribed the peso fuerte de plata as the standard coin. Banco Central de la Repúbilca Dominicana, *Compilación de las disposiciones legales dictadas sobre la moneda metálica en la República Dominicana con anterioridad a la ley monetaria no. 1528, de fecha 6 de Octubre de 1947*, pp. 13, 30 (hereafter referred to as *Compilación*).

10. The Law of May 15, 1846 was annulled by the Law of June 26, 1847, which is quoted in República Dominicana, *Colección, 1844–1847*, p. 518. Educational records for the latter part of the century are sparse enough; practically no data are available for the years prior to 1870. One of the main reasons was the independent attitude of the municipalities toward higher authority. During the 1851–53 congressional sessions, the president of the Congress pressed for legislation that would permit centralized school funding from the national treasury rather than from the municipalities. In his experience the ayuntamientos had frequently mismanaged funds and had never rendered a satisfactory accounting of monies received, much less spent. Manuel Arturo Peña Batlle, ed., *Colección Trujillo*, vol. 4, *Congreso nacional, 1851–1853*, p. 37.

Almost twenty years later this administrative defect still had not been remedied. The minister of public instruction informed the provincial governors that he was preparing a publication for which he needed the following data: number of schools in the provinces; number of higher

addressed itself to problems of education which, if anything, had become even more serious during the troubled intervening years.

The record of the proceedings of the National Congress of 1851 throws some interesting, albeit somewhat pitiful, light on the condition of public education in the Dominican Republic at mid-nineteenth century. After long plenary discussions of the need for school support and unanimous approval of a proposal to require the ayuntamientos to earmark certain local taxes[11] for public primary schools, the representative from Santiago, Gaspar Hernández, made a motion for additional legislation, the nature of which could alone serve to describe the state of education in the country. Based on his certain knowledge that nine-year-olds had been taken out of school to perform provincial military service, Hernández called for a law prohibiting the conscription of school children for the *guardia cívica* (the provincial militia). Even though the conscription law had set the minimum age at fifteen years, such violations as Hernández denounced had been frequent, as the president of the Congress and serveral representatives testified. The law was passed on May 3, 1851.[12] Neither the Constitution of 1844, which established free public instruction, nor the national school laws of 1851 and 1852 made school attendance mandatory.[13]

Although the revised Constitution of 1854, as well as later constitutions, placed on the executive or legislative branches the responsibility for establishing schools of all classes, including schools of agriculture, little was achieved in this field, usually because of a lack of funds. By 1858 this responsibility had been passed to the provinces. With all due respect to enlightened representatives such as Gaspar Hernández and his associates, who in 1851 had believed so strongly in education for their children, one must conclude that their ability to pass legislation was far superior to their capacity to insure execution of the law. As minister of public instruction, Pedro Bonó attacked the Congress on this very point

---

level schools supported by the government; number of teachers and assistants; number of students enrolled; number of primary schools in each común and enrollment; salaries of teachers and dates of establishment of schools. In other words, the government did not possess even such basic information as the number and location of schools. Small wonder there are no accurate data on the illiteracy rate for this period. Minister of public instruction letter to all provincial governors and provincial commissions of education, published in *El Monitor* (the official government gazette), number 112, October 26, 1867, quoted in Rodríguez Demoriz , *Papeles de Pedro F. Bonó*, p. 151.

11. These were the full amount of license fees collected by the municipal governments and half the *derechos de comiso*, similar to a local income tax. Dedicating the license fee tax to support of education was an important element in the educational reforms established almost seventy years later by the American Military Government of Occupation.

12. Peña Batlle, *Colección Trujillo*, vol. 4, *Congreso nacional, 1851–1853*, p. 37. A year later, in its session of May 3, 1852, the Congress passed a comprehensive school law requiring the establishment of primary schools in each city or común, to be supported by funds collected in the municipalities but sent directly to the national treasury for disbursement; a central commission of public instruction similar to the defunct general council of public instruction; school curricula; school hours; and monthly visits by specified provincial officials. Article 15 of the law specifically exempted all enrolled students in primary and secondary schools from military service.

13. The first mention of obligatory education appears in Article 10, Clause 17 of the Constitution of 1874, which placed on the legislative branch the responsibility to decree, when judged opportune, that primary education be obligatory. This clause was repeated in the Constitutions of 1875 and 1877, in the constitutional revision of 1878, again in the constitutional revision of 1879 as a joint responsibility of the bicameral Congress, and in the constitutional revision of 1880. Peña Batlle, *Colección Trujillo*, vol. 1, *Constitución política*, p. 389.

in 1867. Pointing to a legislative history full of words but lacking in action and to a government which passed many laws providing for public instruction but which did not pay its teachers, Bonó issued a fact-loaded statement[14] which merits summarizing here because its data offer the best available description of the public school system at the time.

Bonó noted that the proposed Congressional budget for education included 13,176 pesos for primary education and 3,960 pesos for secondary education, and that of the total, the capital alone would receive 7,656 pesos, or almost forty-five percent. He commented that too much money was allocated for the capital and not enough for the rest of the country; that Santiago had an almost equal population, was a wealthy, useful, and progressive city, yet it would get only 2,800 pesos; and that La Vega, El Seibo, Puerto Plata, and Azua *combined* would receive only 3,120 pesos. He noted that a total of thirty-four out of forty-two comunes, poor but with a large rural population and mostly lacking in educational facilities which the ayuntamientos could not provide, were allotted only 3,000 pesos. These thirty-four comunes comprised well over half the nation's area.[15]

Bonó listed a total of only eleven primary schools in the country outside of Santo Domingo City: two in Santo Domingo province, three in Santiago City, one each in the cities of Puerto Plata, La Vega, and Azua, two in El Seibo, and one in Higüey. There were no rural public schools anywhere; there was only one secondary public school, and that was in the capital. Of the forty-two comunes in the country, at most only fourteen had public schools. Bonó calculated that out of a total national population of approximately 300,000, there were about 600 children in private schools and about 700 in public schools of all categories.[16] Thus one child out of 430 inhabitants was receiving public education. He concluded that those citizens who were educated were either Dominican adults who learned prior to independence, foreigners, children of Santo Domingo City residents, young people who had been educated abroad, or children whose parents could not pay school tuition costs and therefore taught their children at home.

This was a dreary picture, and Bonó requested 10,500 pesos to correct budget deficiencies in order to achieve a general, acceptable level of education. The money would be used to create a chair of natural sciences and classroom facilities in the Seminary of Santo Tomás;[17] to assist or expand the higher primary schools throughout the country; to increase the sum already proposed by the Congress for a higher primary school for

14. Published in *El Monitor*, No. 115, November 16, 1867. Rodríguez Demorizi, *Papeles de Pedro F. Bonó*, pp. 145–49.

15. As an educator, Bonó could well be disturbed. With an expected income in 1868 of 487,571 pesos, only 3.5 percent was being budgeted for primary and secondary education. República Dominicana, Junta Nacional de Planificación y Coordinación, *Informaciones estadísticas dominicanas*, Table 92 (hereafter referred to as Junta Nacional, *Informaciones*).

16. There were three types of public school during this stage of Dominican history: urban primary, offering the first five grade levels; higher urban primary, the next three grade levels; and the lone secondary school, the rough equivalent of a United States high school. When rural schools were finally established, they usually offered no more than the first three grades. Of the eleven primary schools listed above, outside the capital, four were higher urban, one each in La Vega, Azua, El Seibo, and Puerto Plata. La Vega had no public urban primary school, according to Bonó's data, but there was a private school.

17. The Spanish Regency Council had decreed in 1810 that as one of the benefits granted Santo Domingo for returning to colonial status voluntarily, Spain would construct a seminary which, in addition to training young men for the priesthood, could also be used as a public technical school. Marrero Aristy, *La República Dominicana*, 1:58.

boys in Santiago; 4,000 pesos to augment the 3,000 already voted for rural primary education; and to buy books, desks, and instruments for primary schools. Both the Congress and the ministry of public instruction were now trying to rectify the lack of rural education, but despite the best intentions of the former and the valiant efforts of the latter, there is fairly reliable evidence that little change was immediately forthcoming. Later on, Bonó protested publicly that the school facilities were inequitably distributed despite a need for more rural education that had been foreseen decades earlier. He observed that the farmers and cattlemen were paying for nearly all of the schools, but they were receiving the fewest benefits and needed the education the most. Quite correctly he concluded that the state would derive greater advantages if there were more free, rural primary schools, and that until all citizens could read, write, and know Christian doctrine, the government would not be meeting its primary obligation.[18]

The scarcity of educational facilities in the cities and towns and the almost complete lack of schools in rural areas up to 1875 lead to the inescapable conclusion that the nationwide illiteracy rate was extremely high, probably over 90 percent. It was undoubtedly even higher in rural areas.

As a cultural or social achievement the literacy of a people has significance only to the extent that effective means of written communication are available to them. Even the individual who learns to read and write in school will lose most or all of these capabilities if he is never thereafter given the opportunity to use them. A short summary of the development of written media in the Dominican Republic to 1870 reveals that few newspapers and periodicals were available to the public during this period. The lack of written matter in rural areas tends to confirm the existence of an almost entirely illiterate rural population.

During the first ten years of the republic's existence, the only press to make its appearance was a number of small, irregularly issued papers, most of which rarely lasted for a year.[19] As a rule, they were partisan papers such as *El Correo de Santo Domingo,* which was first issued in 1860 to promote the projected reannexation with Spain and which, obviously, faded away about 1864 as the War of the Restoration drew to a climax. Starting with the Restoration in 1865, a number of anti-Baez periodicals such as *La Regeneración* and *El Patriota* appeared from time to time, but during Baez' five years in office, beginning in 1868, they ceased publication. There were also a number of embryo literary periodicals which also suffered from the perils of very limited circulation and unexpected political developments. For example, the highly respected literary society Amantes de las Letras issued a new publication in 1854 called *El Oasis* which unfortunately had to suspend operations a year later when General Santana had its patron, General Antonio Duvergé, shot for treason.

Twenty-five years after independence there was only one small printing establishment in the country, in the capital. There two small weekly newspapers were published, plus a third, even smaller one, which was issued only occasionally. Each weekly paper had a circulation of about six hundred, of which twenty-five copies were sent to Puerto Plata, twenty-five to Santiago, and a few to other places. Each had about seventy paying subscribers in the capital. No newspapers were printed in La Vega, Santiago, or Puerto

18. These comments were contained in a long article entitled "Opiniones de un Dominicano," published in *El Eco del Pueblo,* Santiago, January 13, 1884, quoted in Rodríguez Demorizi, *Papeles de Pedró F. Bono,* p. 291.

19. Luis F. Mejía, *De Lilís a Trujillo,* pp. 261–62.

Plata (nor, for that matter, was there a bookstore or library in any of these towns).

It will be easily understood, therefore, why the following paragraphs reveal such a dismal state of education around 1870. The rough composite picture is based mostly on the recorded testimony of a large number of witnesses who appeared before the United States Commission of Inquiry in 1871. The history of the commission goes back to President Buenaventura Baez' attempts in 1869 to promote the annexation of the Dominican Republic to the United States. A proposed treaty had been signed by Baez' foreign minister and the United States commercial agent in Santo Domingo, and was awaiting approval by the United States Senate when violent opposition to the plan broke out in the Dominican Republic. Senate doubts that the treaty reflected the true desires of the Dominican people were probably not quieted by the results of the plebescite arranged by Baez: 16,000 votes in favor and 11 against. Led by Senator Charles Sumner, chairman of the Senate Foreign Relations Committee, anti-administration forces defeated the treaty in late 1870, but agreed to a resolution authorizing President Grant to send a commission to the Dominican Republic to determine the true state of affairs there. Further details of this interesting chapter in U.S.-Dominican relations need not be recounted here except to note that the commission[20] did travel around the country and hear testimony concerning political, social, cultural, and economic conditions. The commission report was duly submitted to President Grant who transmitted it to the Senate on April 5, 1871. Sumner's continued opposition, however, killed further action on the project.

In 1871 this was the school situation in the provinces, beginning with the most favorable:

In the capital, with an estimated population of 6,000, the limited resources of the ayuntamiento had restricted the establishing of schools to five primary institutions, two for girls, and three for boys. There was no lack of desire by the citizens for educational institutions, only a lack of money. The local authorities recognized that many more schools were needed. There were several private elementary schools supervised by the Church, but none was of the quality of a private school of the times in the southern United States. The president of the Dominican Supreme Court stated that although the law provided for public schools in the principal towns and districts, it had been impossible to carry out the law in this respect except in a few places. He added that if a general school system were established all over the republic, the schools would be well attended because the people were desirous of seeing their children educated.

Santiago de los Caballeros, the second city of the country, was not so well off. There were three primary schools, one public, and two private. Neither of the latter was a Church school. There were no secondary schools. There were no rural schools because of a lack of public funds, yet the rural children were judged fully capable of absorbing instruction.

---

20. The commissioners themselves were, in President Grant's words, men of high character and capacity, assisted by other citizens of eminence, including an assistant professor of modern languages at Cornell University. The witnesses included Dominican citizens from all regions. In addition to native-born Dominicans, there were earlier immigrants, or their decendants, from the United States, Germany, France, Haiti, Jamaica, Bermuda, and Puerto Rico. Witnesses ranged from farmers, businessmen, teachers, bank cashiers, surveyors, Church officials, and physicians to cabinet ministers, governors, the president of the ayuntamiento of Santo Domingo, and the president of the Supreme Court. Wade, White, and Howe, *Report of Commission*, pp. 209–85, passim.

La Vega, located in the heart of the Cibao some twenty-five miles southeast of Santiago, had one Church-operated elementary school. Enrollment in the parish school was about 80. There were about 18,000 inhabitants in the parish, including the rural area surrounding La Vega. There was a great lack of teachers, but the government had no money to pay for education. There were no rural schools, but there were several ladies in La Vega who could teach; they visited the homes of the more affluent rural inhabitants as private tutors.

In the rural province of Samaná, where during Boyer's regime some Negroes from the United States had settled, there was a stronger desire on the part of parents for education. The Baptist Church maintained an elementary school in the small village of Samaná for twenty-five pupils taught by the young son of an American Baptist missionary. Three of his pupils were grown girls. Students paid a tuition fee of one dollar a month. There was also a second private elementary school run by a Dominican who had been educated in England. He had gone from England to Haiti in 1861, had become an army brigade commander, but had fled after a political revolution. The consensus of these two schoolteachers, and other residents of the peninsula, was that educational facilities in the province, apart from the two schools, did not exist; that the Negro Americans or their descendants were far more anxious for education than the indifferent native Dominicans; and that there was no organized means of general education in the country but that a school system, enforced by law, would be well received and supported. The young Baptist teacher stated that a number of persons had begged him to open a night school for adults, which he intended to do.

There was also a Methodist preacher in Samaná whose testimony provided an excellent example of the consequences of the frequent revolutions and wars. The Methodist Church had a good schoolhouse under construction in 1863, but the Spaniards burned it down, as well as the adjacent church and mission house, in one of their periodic raids. On the Samaná Peninsula, then, there were no public schools of any sort. The descendants and families of American settlers, reflecting the traditions of a different culture, were using their own meager resources as best they could to educate their children. As for the native-born Dominicans, the government did little, and they did even less for themselves.

Finally, the alcalde of Maniela (today called San José de Ocoa, in Peravia province), located thirty-five miles west of the capital, who was born in France but had been a resident of the Dominican Republic for fifty years, stated that in his town there was no school at all. There had been a small class of ten pupils taught by the alcalde's secretary, but the secretary left his job and with him went the town's educational system. The population of Maniela was 3,000, which, in addition to being without a school or teacher, had no priest.

The United States commission was only incidentally interested in education; nevertheless, the above testimony which they recorded more than amply indicates the inadequacies of the system, especially in the rural areas, and tends to confirm the conclusion that the rural illiteracy rate nationwide was around ninety-eight percent.

To round out the description of rural education in the Dominican Republic in the 1870s, a letter from a priest in Higüey to newly elected President Ulises F. Espaillat is quoted in part:

Public instruction expects much of the generosity and recognized understanding of the new chief of state. It urges, then, that you grant it your high protection. When for the third time I came here as priest, there was not a single school in all of the común and I, ignoring the fact that I already had more than enough obligations to keep me busy, undertook the laborious task of providing *free* instruction for all of the children of the común, proof of which I attach hereto the vote of thanks which the ayuntamiento then awarded me. Later there was someone to take charge of the school, and it is now going on three years that Sr. Alfredo Goico has it under his exclusive direction.

It is only right to say that Sr. Goico does everything possible to deserve the confidence which the parents have placed in him. For my part, I recommend him to the attention of the government. I am certain that of the thirty-five students who attend school, only fifteen pay Sr. Goico.

In Los Palitos there is a school taught by a young man from the capital, but he receives no pay; they give him plantain, rice, etc. Here there is a notable lack of an Aesculapius; there is no one even to let blood or to pull a tooth. A DOCTOR, Illustrious President, a doctor would be a precious, inestimable gift which you could offer the inhabitants of Salvaleón de Higüey.[21]

The evidence indicates that municipal tax money for education was being collected during this period and submitted to the national government,[22] but certainly had it been used for the purposes intended originally, the money would have permitted the establishment of a more substantial educational structure. In 1871 there was no effective school system in existence; whatever progress had been made during the twenty-seven years of national existence obviously did not extend into the rural areas. An example of the weakness of the system is provided by the inaccuracies in the section on public education contained in the official memorandum given the U. S. commissioners in Santo Domingo.[23] The Dominican government stated that the municipalities supported twenty-one

---

21. Letter from Father Moreno del Cristo, May 20, 1876, quoted in Rodríguez Demorizi, *Papeles de Espaillat*, pp. 201–2.

22. In 1870, for example, government income from license fee taxes was $12,721. Wade, White, and Howe, *Report of Commission*, p. 26. The amount shown is in dollars. The Dominican peso and the United States dollar coins of this period were nearly equivalent. The Dominican government's Resolution no. 1767 of May 14, 1879, for the first time in Dominican banking history established an official foreign exchange rate for domestic purposes. Some of the equivalents are shown:

Foreign coin	Dominican pesos
U.S. $20 gold piece	21
U.S. $5 gold piece	5.25
U.S. silver	at face value
Spain, gold ounce	17.00
Spain, silver	at face value
Mexico, silver peso	1.00
Venezuela, 5 bolívar piece	5.00
Colombia, Peru, Chile, and Mexico gold ounce (onza)	16.50
Great Britain, pound sterling	5.00
France, 20 francs, gold	4.00
Germany, 20 Reichmarks	5.00

The monetary system at the end of the Heureaux administration was completely unsettled (at one time Heureaux had even been using the French franc as the monetary base), but by 1905 U.S.-minted gold was established as the monetary base (Resolution 4579 of June 21, 1905). Thereafter the Dominican peso was equal to the United States dollar at the official rate of exchange. Banco central, *Compilación*, pp. 37, 118–33.

23. Manuel María Gautier, minister of foreign affairs, memorandum of February 20, 1871, to the U.S. commissioners, translated and quoted in Wade, White, and Howe, *Report of Commission*, p. 173. The memorandum was one of several included in a covering note which transmitted certain demographic, commercial, and financial data which the commission had

public schools, seventeen for boys, and five for girls, at an annual expense of $8,686. The list, in fact, showed a total of twenty-eight schools, not twenty-one or twenty-two, and revealed additional discrepancies. The memorandum indicated the existence of eight public elementary schools in the capital; but later, in his testimony before the commission, the president of the ayuntamiento, with the concurrence of all of his fellow members, stated that there were five. The government claimed there were eight schools in Santiago, whereas the testimony of educated witnesses showed only three; and the government claimed one public school in La Vega, although witnesses stated there were none. Confusing data such as these reveal the inability or unwillingness of national and local governments to meet their legal and philosophic commitments to education. If the authorities in Santo Domingo had no accurate idea of the number of public schools in the country, how could they be certain whether or for what actual purposes the municipalities were expending the money allocated for education? Perhaps one should first inquire as to whether the central government ever released the money to the municipalities.

The usual explanation for the lack of schools was the shortage of money, which may well have been a valid reason. During the 1851–71 period there were revolutions in 1857, 1864, three in 1865, one in 1866, and one in 1867. Apart from these internal disturbances, the cost of the Haitian invasions up to 1855 and the devastations of the 1863–65 War of the Restoration heavily damaged the economy. Precise figures on national agricultural production are not available. The Dominican government has no records showing total annual production, nor are the export figures reliable.[24] There is partial evidence, however, which shows that the destruction of property caused by war and revolution and the drafting of farmers for forced military service were accompanied by a radical decrease in foreign trade[25] and a reduction of agricultural activity at the subsistence

---

requested from the Dominican government. Gautier signed the note and each memorandum.

24. Schoenrich discovered that accurate trade figures were maintained only from the time the U.S. general receiver of customs commenced operations on April 8,1905. Before 1891 no statistics were kept. One of the reasons for the inaccuracies of figures was the corruption prevalent in the Dominican customs administration, especially in the customs offices in north coast ports. Schoenrich also points out that prior to World War I the United States took between 50 and 60 percent of all Dominican foreign trade. Schoenrich, *Santo Domingo*, pp. 234–35.

25. An examination of United States import trade statistics shows the following trade with the Dominican Republic, in American dollars:

Year	Duty-free imports	Dutiable imports	Total imports
1861	$ 5,675	$ 171,084	$ 176,759
1867	49,870	13,823	63,693
1868	56,503	28,860	83,363
1873	220,070	189,780	409,850
1874	152,607	129,581	282,188
1878	151,582	234,653	386,235
1880	164,979	495,514	660,493
1885	96,217	1,365,202	1,461,419

United States, Secretary of the Treasury, *A Report of the Commerce and Navigation of the United States*, 1861, 1867, 1868, 1872, 1873, 1874, 1878, 1880, 1885.

It appears that Dominican foreign trade may have been cut by as much as two-thirds during the War of the Restoration, which generally coincided with the Civil War in the United States. The large increase in Dominican exports in 1873 was due to sugar, which by this year had replaced mahogany and fine woods as the money export crop. Exports during the years shown invariably consisted of coffee, gums, hides, honey, woods, guano, sugar and sugar products, and very little tobacco.

level in many areas. The testimony given by a number of witnesses before the U.S. Commission of Inquiry in 1871 clearly shows that the production of food on small farms was frequently and seriously disturbed, that barter was resorted to because paper money was worthless, that the government and revolutionary forces customarily commandeered livestock for their commissaries, and that food crops were often left to rot for lack of market or manpower to harvest them.[26] Although no one starved, excessive portions of the national budget went for military supplies and for support of the military establishment. Accordingly, normal peacetime expenditures for public works and education suffered.[27] Small wonder, then, that in an era dominated by military leaders and military requirements there was little school construction.

The last quarter of the nineteenth century saw some progress in the field of education, but hardly enough to correct the deficiencies of the past and at the same time meet the needs of an expanding population. Had the enlightened Ulises Espaillat remained in office for any length of time, it seems fairly certain he would have tried to accelerate the growth of the school system. But to the everlasting misfortune of the Dominican people, his administration was overthrown almost as soon as it was organized. There is a strong temptation to devote more attention to Espaillat than his short term in office merits. Espaillat was a man far, far ahead of his times. Cosmopolitan, liberal, and progressive even by modern standards, he has been compared to Benjamin Franklin by his own Latin American contemporaries. He was no impractical dreamer cut of the mold of Mexico's Francisco Madero. Here are some of his recorded thoughts,[28] which show a firm and practical appreciation of the needs of a modern democracy:

On immigration of rural manpower to his troubled country:

> We have our immigration right here. Let us teach our farmers to work. We ought not try to govern 400,000 citizens when we don't know how to govern the 200,000 of our present population.

On the role of the press in a democracy:

> If I were to announce to you that the country cannot progress without newspapers, I would be telling you nothing new.

On "men on white horses":

> I believe that the greatest calamity that can happen to a nation is the need to be saved by a genius. I prefer that each citizen be one in his own sphere.

On the subjection of private interests to the general good:

> It appeared to me that the country would have to pass through more destructive changes before the political parties would see the need to sacrifice their respective interests. . . . The political parties do not believe they should abandon their interests to the hands of a third party or make any sort of sacrifice.

On law and order:

> As you see, this administration, whose program is the *uniting of liberty with justice,* does

---

26. Wade, White, and Howe, *Report of Commission,* pp. 214, 217, 223, 232, 240, 253, 269.

27. The national budget for July 1, 1845, to June 30, 1846, reveals the scope of the defense problem. The entire budget was 1,179,889 pesos, of which the ministries of war and navy were allotted 1,000,000 pesos. República Dominicana, *Colección, 1844–1847,* p. 236. Public education was allotted 2,720 pesos, 2,000 for books, furniture, and equipment, and 720 for the annual salary of one teacher.

28. Rodríguez Demorizi, *Papeles de Espaillat,* pp. 19–50, passim.

not desire to grant amnesty to the colonels and generals who are fugitives or are under arms, and proposes to order the measures leading to their capture and punishment according to the law.

On politics:

Let us form a party—the Constitutional party. Let us teach this party, which will be a true political party, that its duties can be reduced to the practice of a single concept: that of respecting and requiring respect for the Constitution of the state.

On the pen and the sword:

Thank you, Juan de Jesús [General Juan de J. Salcedo, who later helped overthrow Espaillat], but I will not need generals. My strength will be the schoolteacher.

These expressions, which accurately reflected the ideals of the man, reveal the wide gap between his understanding of democracy and good government and that of such destructive patriots as "Great Citizen" Baez and General Ignacio María González.

Espaillat was overwhelmingly elected to the presidency on April 15, 1876. By July 15 a revolution had started in the Cibao by agents of Buenaventura Baez, exiled at the time in Curaçao. Within a month a second uprising broke out in Azua, sparked from Mayagüez, Puerto Rico, by Espaillat's predecessor, General González, who supported Baez. During the weeks that followed, Espaillat tried but could not reason with the malcontents whose only motive for revolt was the irresponsible desire to see their party in power at any cost. Rather than cause further bloodshed, Espaillat resigned in a crisis of arms on October 5, 1876. He was out of office within six months after his election, never having had a real chance to serve.

He was not rejected by the masses of Dominicans. He simply surrendered out of humanitarian motives to the ultimate selfishness of two shallow revolutionaries. Espaillat died in 1878, disillusioned and weary. Gregorio Luperón, who became president the year Espaillat died and whose memory is deeply respected throughout the republic, attributed Espaillat's downfall to legislators who gave the nation good laws but failed to instruct the masses in an understanding of their rights and duties. From this failure arose the evils of tyranny, treason, and exploitation of the state. Bitterly, Luperón says: "Espaillat was not a good president because he was loyal, honest, and moral, and was not a thief or a traitor. This is the hard and severe truth, but it is the truth."[29]

Espaillat had wanted to be tolerant without being weak, to establish order without being arbitrary, to put an end to corruption without being cruel, and to prove that the law was stronger than any tyrant. Perhaps more than anything else he looked to open, democratic political processes and an educated citizenry for the regeneration of his country. Lamentably, he achieved none of these measures. A majority of Dominicans respected him as an individual, for his beliefs, and for his objectives. Perhaps his awareness of this sentiment prompted him to comment later, "The seed has been sown, and sooner or later it will bear its fruit."[30]

The months following the downfall of the Espaillat government were full of internal political upset and disarray, but within a few years there was to be some improvement in Dominican public education. Between 1880 and 1885 a measure of stability was achieved under the rising influence on the national scene of Ulises Heureaux. In the successive

---

29. Luperón, *Notas autobiográficas*, 2:328.
30. Letter, Espaillat to A. Galván, February 11, 1877, Rodríguez Demorizi, *Papeles de Espaillat*, p. 29.

administrations of Luperón, Father Fernando A. Meriño, Heureaux (first term), and Francisco G. Billini, all four of whom had been friends or political associates of Espaillat,[31] a modest educational program began to make headway. The 1884 General School Law was fashioned after the long-neglected 1852 legislation. Municipal responsibility for primary instruction was reemphasized; the central government now assumed sponsorship of secondary instruction. A central board of education, directly under the minister of justice and public instruction, began to exert influence on a truly national scale as it operated through its school inspectors in the provinces. In addition, provincial boards of education presided over by the respective governors were formed, as well as communal school boards.[32] Putting flesh on this skeleton, however, was quite another matter.

By 1885, in the forty-seven comunes of the country, there were 271 teachers for 6,535 primary school students enrolled in 173 schools. A lone high school was established in the capital by Eugenio de Hostos[33] in 1880 with an enrollment of 52 pupils. Thus any youngster desiring to pursue his public education past the primary level had to await a vacancy in the school and in any event had to live in Santo Domingo. From these figures it is apparent that most of the schools, which were located in established towns and villages, had only one teacher. Rural educational facilities were even more limited. One can only imagine how effective were the few *maestros ambulantes*, the visiting teachers who served the remote countryside. The total annual disbursement for public school facilities, supplies, and salaries during 1885 was 64,166 pesos, which was 5.4 percent of the national budget, a slight increase over earlier years.[34] The picture had improved considerably over the past, but the school financial support structure retained the same defects. There were no systematic reporting procedures in effect whereby the central

---

31. Luperón's autobiography reveals a very warm personal relationship between himself and Espaillat. Luperón describes the latter as "his companion, his friend, his counselor, his doctor." Luperón was Espaillat's minister of war and navy. Heureaux, a major military commander during this administration, crushed an early attempt to overthrow Espaillat by force. Luperón, *Notas autobiográficas*, 2:291–328, 354. The autobiography also shows a continuing cooperation among Billini, Heureaux, Meriño, and Luperón, at least to 1882. Ibid., 3:17–123. José Gabriel García, who was Espaillat's minister of education, refers also to the loyalty of Luperón, Billini, and Heureaux to President Espaillat. García, *Compendio*, 4:253–69, passim. Meriño, Luperón, and Espaillat were all *Azules*, or Blues, the political party of which Luperón became the titular head when Espaillat left politics. Marrero Aristy, *La República Dominicana*, 2:200.

32. Gregorio B. Palacín Iglesias, "Cien años de educación nacional," *Educación*, 76 (Oct.–Dec. 1944), p. 42. See also Hipolito Billini, *Present Condition of the Dominican Republic*, p. 41.

33. De Hostos' school replaced the Seminary of Santo Tomás as the secondary public school in the capital. Eugenio de Hostos was born in 1839 in Puerto Rico; he studied philosophy, law, and literature in Spain, and became something of a literary revolutionary. He dreamed of a free Antillean confederation composed of Puerto Rico, Cuba, and the Dominican Republic. He wandered through South America—Peru, Chile, and Argentina—to New York and back to Venezuela. In 1879 he arrived in Santo Domingo, where, under the sponsorship of President Luperón, he founded the first high school in the country. Shunning the dead classics and ecclesiastical philosophy, de Hostos developed a teaching tradition of rational, objective thought. Biology, natural history, physical geography, mathematics, constitutional law, and sociology were emphasized. One of the members of the first graduating class, 1884, was a future lawyer of whom much more will be written in this book—Francisco J. Peynado. De Hostos ran afoul of Dictator Heureaux in 1888 and fled the country. He returned in 1900 and resumed teaching until his death in 1903. He is still revered in the Dominican Republic as the precursor of modern education.

34. Billini, ibid., p. 42. Abad confirms the general conditions described by Billini. He also

government would always know exactly how much money the local governments were receiving and how much they were spending for educational purposes. The ayuntamientos imposed the local taxes, collected the money, but did not always allocate the funds to schools as required by law. As a result, there was renewed clamor—to no avail—to centralize the financial structure by placing the disbursement of school funds in the hands of the central government.[35]

By 1888 the number of schools had increased to 200, but the school-age population, six to fourteen years, reached 62,000. Thus each school should have been of sufficient average size to accommodate 310 students, assuming that they were all in school. In fact, the average school could barely hold forty students, which meant that about only one-eighth of the school-age population was receiving an education.

The ruinous financial maneuverings of Ulises Heureaux, dictator from 1887 until his assassination in 1899, left a legacy of $5 million in unredeemable paper money in circulation, a national debt of $33 million, a customs collection service under foreign control, and no international credit.[36] In a period when the annual income of the government averaged 1 to 1.5 million pesos, these conditions were not substantially checked until the administration of Ramón Cáceres from 1906 to 1911. Financial problems bred educational problems; the slow expansion of school facilities was outpaced by the population growth, and the illiteracy rate well into the twentieth century remained at over 90 percent. Fortunate were children living in sparsely populated areas who once a week might see a priest or a visiting teacher to teach them the letters of the alphabet.

---

provides the following educational budget figures for 1887:

from ayuntamientos (*patentes y registro*)	58,832.05	pesos
direct support from state	7,526.00	pesos
profits on investments by central board of education	6,898.38	pesos
Subtotal	73,256.43	pesos
direct support for normal school	4,188.00	pesos
for instituto profesional	4,623.05	pesos
Total	82,067.48	pesos

Abad, *La República Dominicana*, p. 163. The 1887 educational budget was 5.5 percent of the national budget of 1,484,434 pesos. The national budget for 1885 was 1,196,461 pesos. Junta Nacional, *Informaciones*, Table 92.

35. Abad, *La República Dominicana*, p. 169. The school system was not changed basically until the U.S. Military Government of Occupation passed a comprehensive school law in 1918.

36. The real architect of Dominican financial troubles around the turn of the twentieth century was not Baez but Heureaux. His dealings with European, American, and even private Dominican businessmen and bankers such as Marchena and Juan B. Vicini brought no benefit to the Dominican people, led to foreign control of Dominican customs collection first by Europeans and later by Americans, and plunged the nation into a near-permanent state of bankruptcy for decades to follow. The sordid history is outlined in detail in Jacob H. Hollander, *Santo Domingo Debt*; Schoenrich, *Santo Domingo*; Welles, *Naboth's Vineyard*; and from the Dominican viewpoint in a small but extremely useful book by Manuel de Jesús Troncoso de la Concha, *La génesis de la convención domínico-americana* (hereafter referred to as *Génesis*). The Haitian writer Antonio de la Rosa [Alexandre Poujols] also writes about Heureaux in *Les finances de Saint Domingue et le contrôl Américain*. Schoenrich's comment on Heureaux' extravagant irresponsibility is worth noting:

"The enormous foreign and internal debt left by the Heureaux administration had been constantly increased by ruinous loans to which the succeeding governments were obliged to resort during the years of civil warfare, until the country was in a condition of hopeless bankruptcy. In the beginning of 1904 every item of the debt had been in default for months." Schoenrich, *Santo Domingo*, p. 81.

In the remote countryside, where the majority of the population lived, the little subsistence farmer was only just beginning to emerge from a state of social immaturity. Pedro Bonó, a farsighted, progressive farmer-economist-educator, described this metamorphosis:

> Before . . . the slave or tenant only needed two pens, one to enclose the pigs and the other to live in, a conuco of two to four *tareas* for plantain and the other garden ingredients for his *sancocho* [country stew], a single change of work clothes, a machete, knife and flint, and tobacco to chew or smoke; that is, the life of a Kaffir or Hottentot. Today, this is not so. Civilization has, little by little, infiltrated into him because of the close contact with farmers who have emigrated to those places, because of the travels and long stays which the wars obliged him to make to the cities and farming areas, and because of the continual and direct communication with educated men which these same wars imposed.[37]

Had anyone pondered the future of the children of these campesinos, he might well have asked about the still unbuilt rural schools which the school laws had promised or about the agricultural schools so necessary in a country dependent upon effective exploitation of the land, which had not been established. The ignorance of the farmers not only constituted a major obstacle to increased agricultural production but also exposed them to exploitation by unprincipled officials and large landowners.

These points were raised publicly. One citizen in particular, José Ramón López, mentioned earlier in connection with official exploitation of campesino labor, was born and raised in an agricultural community, and his became one of the more articulate voices to appeal for progress in the rural areas. Calling for major reforms which would closely link education to agriculture, López argued strongly for the long-overdue school construction program to be put into effect, for the establishment of special agricultural schools, also long overdue, for an increase in agricultural research, for the establishment of cooperatives for production and for farm credit, and for the organization of an agricultural credit bank. In his proposal for a farm cooperative system, he even included plans for an office to coordinate foreign sales of Dominican products. His book[38] was, in effect, a planning document, for it also included a draft national law for an agricultural cooperative society, with articles for the organization of the central authority, the establishment of the bank and the manner of arranging loans and deposits. His basic thesis was that the farmer was not lazy, only uninformed and technically backward. With more cooperation at ministerial levels within the central government and between the central government and the local governments, the small farmer or farm tenant could be taught modern agricultural methods. The ancient abuses of illiterate campesinos would be corrected, and the economy of the whole country would prosper accordingly. López'

---

37. Rodríguez Demorizi, *Papeles de Pedro F. Bonó*, p. 221. These words are taken from the same long newspaper article Bonó wrote for the Santiago *El Eco del Pueblo*, cited earlier. One acre = approximately 6.5 tareas.

38. *La paz en la República Dominicana*. López (1866–1922) was a competent observer. He was born in Monte Cristi and later lived in Puerto Plata. As a young journalist he was jailed for writing anti-Heureaux articles and later exiled to Puerto Rico. He worked as a news editor there and in Caracas, returning to the Dominican Republic in 1897. He continued his journalistic career with *Listín Diario* and other periodicals and in 1909 became chief editor of *Pluma y Espada*. He also taught school and help a succession of public offices as senator, director of statistics, and in the ministry of agriculture. He wrote prolifically on a variety of subjects, including nutrition, geography, and statistics. His last published work was a manual on agriculture in 1920.

ideas were solid ones, due within a few years to be translated into action by a series of events he never anticipated.

Political irresponsibility and instability during the nineteenth century hampered the development of the republic from the point of view of the majority of individual Dominicans. Their labors were continually being interrupted by calls for military service. They never knew whether they might be forced into the army just at harvest time or whether, after a harvest, their crops and cattle might be "requisitioned" by revolutionaries. Educational facilities, at best only limited in large cities and towns, were almost nonexistent for their children as they had been for them. There had been little encouragement to labor and almost none to accumulate an agricultural surplus for local markets. So reduced was the incentive that at times many farmers refused to introduce new or modern equipment for fear it would be destroyed by marauding soldiers.[39] Espaillat had planned to make increased agricultural production the theme of all of his national policies. He had wanted to develop and expand an informed scientific farming industry as a substitute for revolutions,[40] but to do this he needed the one element that was denied him—time.

By the end of the century, as the population began to expand more rapidly, a new threat to rural development began to take shape. The threat was a deep one, because it tended to undermine the small farmer's confidence in the land tenure system and eventually in the government itself. The problem involved the security of landownership.

39. Wade, White, and Howe, *Report of Commission*, p. 40.

40. Letter, July 3, 1876, Espaillat to Pedro F. Bonó, quoted in Rodríguez Demorizi, *Papeles de Espaillat*, p. 24. Espaillat issued a Law on the Free Concession of State Lands, which was intended to put unused state land into production. The preamble and body of this law of July 8, 1876, contain considerable philosophy on the value and role of agriculture, on the security of ownership as an incentive to higher production and the maintenance of order, peace, and justice, and on the need for judicious offers by the government to guarantee stability in order to attract foreign investment capital. Espaillat considered agriculture to be the origin and development of industry and commerce. Quoted in ibid., pp. 194–98.

13

LANDOWNERSHIP

The colonial origins of the assignment of communal lands to villages and towns were explained in Chapter 3. One of the purposes for which the Crown had intended communal lands was the raising of livestock. Accordingly, the principle of free pasture (pastos comunes) had been well established in earliest colonial times. Similarly, the Crown assigned common land for water, threshing, and other municipal activities (ejido) and for woodcutting (montes). Under such a system there was no need, nor would it have been an easy task, to divide the common land into separate holdings; community rights in the pastures and woodlands served the settlers adequately. The original guardian of the common land, whose exterior limits were more or less known, was the village ayuntamiento which might later sell or lease unused common land (*propios*) if local conditions warranted, but otherwise would retain full control. Thus there was an element of inalienability associated with common lands. The settlers became mere possessors because their rights to common land had not been granted in fee, that is, without limitation or restrictions. In addition to his communal rights, each settler of course had private rights to a homesite.

Three Haitian invasions, the periodic confiscation and redistribution of abandoned land, the burning of public buildings and the disruptions in public administration raised havoc with the Dominican system of landownership during the pre-independence years. Communal land did not exist in Haiti; furthermore, Jean Pierre Boyer was committed there to a land system of small farms operated by single, independent owners.[1] Compounding the confusion caused by his prohibition of the traditional form of ownership, Boyer assigned these lands to the state, then under Haitian titles redistributed portions to landless farm workers, to Haitians who occupied farms, or to sponsored immigrants who came in later. The consequences of this policy, aggravated by the loss or destruction

---

1. This was his Code Rural, which eventually failed because of the independence of the owners, who refused to work their land intensively. See Great Britain, *Communications, 1829,* Annex, Articles 17, 27, 28, 30, 174, 175, 184.

of earlier land records, were important because they led to a defective land title system, illegal occupation of land, an inadequate land tax system, and widespread fraud in connection with ownership of rural land.

After Dominican independence, several articles relating to land were written into the Constitution of San Cristóbal, but, as appropriate in such a document, the articles went no further than the establishment of certain principles, such as the division of the country into five provinces, the further division of provinces into comunes where number and distribution could be set by law, and the security of private property from expropriation, except when justified by the public good and then only after just indemnification.

All land was owned either by the state, by private citizens, or by the Church. Private lands could be grouped into three categories: urban, rural communal land, and rural noncommunal land. The fact is that owing to causes outlined above, no one in the newly established republic knew precisely how much land the state owned, because of the number of cases where the precise boundaries between rural communal lands and state lands had never been determined. Efforts to clarify this rather unusual legal situation were complicated later by the difficulties involved in the partitioning of rural communal land. Partition, an action relatively rare in colonial times, was ordered and carried out under Haitian rule, countermanded and ignored after independence, ordered and ignored in 1911, and ordered again by the American Military Government of Occupation in 1920.

So turbulent were the early years of the nineteenth century that as of 1845 there was no land law in effect and no public office charged with direct or indirect intervention or supervision of acts involving the transmission of property rights. Public notaries in all parts of the country performed limited formalities in recording written documents, but as will be described later, these acts were legally inadequate if not defective. On July 2, 1845, President Santana decreed the Law of National Property, to the effect that:

All property without a recognized owner, located in the territory of the republic, belonged to the state.

All property, chattel and landed, capital, and rent which belonged to previous governments, to religious convents[2] of both sexes, no longer existing, to other classes of orders, brotherhoods, and communities which no longer existed, belonged to the state.

Land, property, and chattel goods which may have belonged to former Haitians who refused to become Dominicans, or to anyone who had fled the country without taking the oath of loyalty to the new republic, or to anyone who had aided the enemy, would become state property.[3]

These were all reasonable terms, but even so the authorities had considerable difficulty deciding just what had been the property of earlier governments, which were the no longer existing institutions, and who were the individuals who had aided the enemy. With the purpose of avoiding injustices, the new government announced a period of three months during which all landholders must present their titles for confirmation to a national or a provincial commission. The five-man national commission, located in the capital, was composed of the presidents of the three courts,[4] a representative of the

---

2. The word "convento" may mean either a convent or a monastery.

3. República Dominicana, *Colección, 1844–1847*, p. 251.

4. *Suprema corte de justicia, tribunal de apelación, juzgado de primer instancia.* See F. Tavares hijo, *Elementos de derecho procesal civil Dominicano*, 1:43.

provincial chamber of deputies, and the inspector of the treasury. In each of the five provinces the commissions were composed of the president of the provincial court, a member of the provincial chamber of deputies, the alcalde of the provincial capital, and the provincial administrator of the treasury. Pending the decisions of the various commissions, all property remained in trust, that is, there could be no transfer of property rights. The law made specific provision for the Church.

The Church was not to be deprived of its property. The state could not logically place the Church in the category of an earlier government, nor could it consider the Church to be nonexistent. There was no desire on the part of the legislators to hamper the Church, nor was there any need. Not overly rich at the end of the colonial period, the Church as a landowner had suffered as much as any other Dominican institution at the hands of the Haitians.[5] Furthermore, a careful reading of the 1844 Constitution quickly reveals the subordinate position of the Church. Even though apostolic Roman Catholicism was designated as the state religion, the drafters of the constitution had immediately seen the need for a prompt reconciliation between the independence of the Church and the supremacy of civil authority. To the dismay of the clergy, the constitutional convention did not hesitate to intervene in matters of ecclesiastical discipline. Foreseeing the desirability of a concordat with the Holy See, and also anticipating long delays in achieving one, the convention fully empowered the president to negotiate the agreement.[6]

Following the example of the colonial patronato real of the Spanish Crown, the same article also authorized the president to seek the right of presentation over all bishops and ecclesiastical benefices. Another direct blow at an ancient Church privilege was the responsibility assigned to the Congress of decreeing out of existence forever the feudal vestiges of annuities for more than one life: mayorazgos, entailed estates, property, or rights; and *capellanías,* or foundations of capital, the interest of which over the years had been assigned to the support of an ecclesiastic or a religious purpose, such as the construction of a church or altar or the celebration of a fixed number of Masses. As if the mere listing of the responsibility were not sufficiently aggressive, the Constitution further prescribed that the necessary enabling legislation be passed in the first legislative session.[7]

The legislation was passed as Decree number 39 on May 30, 1845. The first article stated:

---

5. One of the witnesses who testified before the U.S. Commission of Inquiry in 1871 was the curate of La Vega, Teodisio Ramírez Ariedo. The priest stated that the churches had been despoiled considerably in the times of Boyer, and that his own curacy at the time of the interview possessed *only* [my emphasis] 100,000 pesos worth of land, which had been willed and was therefore held in trust by the Church. It is impossible to calculate just how much land this was, since the priest did not identify it by location or say whether it was improved land. Land in 1871 was exceedingly cheap, as low as pennies an unimproved acre in remote undeveloped areas, and as high as 10 to 12 pesos an acre within a mile and a half of the capital. Even with the not unrealistic assumption that the lands referred to by Father Ramírez lay somewhere in the rich Cibao, one could easily conclude that the La Vega church holdings were relatively extensive and that the good father was exaggerating the impoverishment of his church. Despite this testimony, I have uncovered no evidence leading to conclusions other than those which follow immediately concerning the overall position of the Church as a landholding institution in the Dominican Republic.

6. República Dominicana, Constitution of 1844, Art. 208, Peña Batlle, ed., *Colección Trujillo,* vol. 1, *Constitución política,* p. 46.

7. Art. 94; Peña Batlle, ibid., p. 24.

There are hereby declared extinguished and terminated permanently the capital and income of pension annuities or other impositions or entailments under whatever higher authority they may have been made, which applied to the communal rural landholdings located in former Española; and that no matter how originated or related to the state or any communities [meaning religious communities] these said properties will be free of all lien or mortgage without any other formality, since the Constitution has the force of law.[8]

Succeeding articles dealt similarly with capellanías, annuities, and entailments affecting private landholdings, holdings of the government, and holdings of religious communities that no longer existed. Those with valid title to capellanías were required to negotiate with the existing owners of the burdened property to arrive at an agreed upon sum as final settlement, the sum not to exceed one-third of the capital value and to be paid to the erstwhile holder of the capellanía in convenient payments as mutually arranged.

At the Diocesan Synod of 1851 the Dominican clergy strongly reaffirmed their objections to the above articles, but were unable to influence the Church-state relationship that had been established.[9] Succeeding constitutions retained all of the same articles. Ever since the first days of independence, the founders of the republic were determined to eliminate any possibility of the Church's achieving undue political influence through the accumulation of wealth derived from the entailed labors of others. The owning of property by the Church would not be illegal, but benefits generated from earlier colonial privileges vested in the land would henceforth be denied. The government's attitude toward the Church was more generous than that of Haiti, but under the law and in practice the Church was nevertheless categorically subordinated to civil authority.[10] Church-state relations in the Dominican Republic, therefore, have followed a pattern distinct from that in several other Latin American countries. Accordingly, for the remainder of the nineteenth century and until after the death of Trujillo, the Church may be ignored as a significant institution in matters affecting land relationships. Quite a different picture was to develop in the post-Trujillo period.

Santana's government realized that strengthening the agricultural economy should not be impeded by legal difficulties in determining land ownership. To repopulate abandoned state lands and place them under cultivation, he authorized the ayuntamientos to lease rural communal lands to any individual willing to farm them.[11] A concurrent objective in opening up public lands was rewarding those soldiers who after 1844 found themselves poverty-stricken from having neglected their normal pursuits to fight in the

---

8. República Dominicana, *Colección, 1844–1847*, pp. 196–97.

9. Peña Batlle, ed., *Colección Trujillo*, vol. 1, *Constitución política*, p. 67.

10. In 1851 the Church, having no capellanías or diezmos to support the ordination of twelve young men, had to ask for public funds for this purpose. Ibid., p. 18 .

Samuel Guy Inman traveled through the Dominican Republic in 1919 and observed that the Church had little prestige. The citizens did not seem to regard the Church as having any relevance to current conditions or problems. There was no hostility, only an ignoring of clerical existence except for strictly religious ceremonies. The priesthood had a generally unsavory moral reputation. At this time there were reported to be 66 secular priests, 12 regular priests, 32 Sisters of Charity, 68 churches, 103 chapels, and one seminary in the country. There had been an attempt to nationalize Church property, but opposition by ecclesiastical authorities had prevented a final decision. Samuel Guy Inman, *Through Santo Domingo and Haiti*, p. 48.

11. Law of Lease of Common Land by Ayuntamientos, June 17, 1847. República Dominicana, *Colección, 1844–1847*, pp. 504–5.

Revolution. A sergeant first class or below, without property and unable to obtain any, was permitted to establish himself on government land at no cost, under the sole condition that he devote himself to farming. This was a reversion to the old colonial policy of free land and effective occupation. Other settlers could purchase land or could acquire leases[12] for periods from one to nine years at the discretion of the ayuntamiento. Subleasing was prohibited. Tenants would be required to pay rent annually. The jefe político, the alcalde, and the local treasury administrator, acting as a body, fixed the amount of any taxes to be levied.

Since these were common lands, a lease did not authorize the cutting of wood for export or construction unless needed for the construction of homes and farm structures of the settlers themselves.[13] Communal lands could not be sold, alienated, or given away without the authority and approval by the national Congress of a petition submitted by the ayuntamiento with the recommendation of the provincial legislature. However, the ayuntamiento could waive lease payments in cases of truly poverty-stricken citizens, widows of those patriots who had died fighting for independence, minor or orphan children, and war invalids. Leaseholds of common lands were to be accomplished so as to guarantee owners and their heirs the enjoyment and use of the improvements they had made or might make, without disturbing them so long as they complied with the lease conditions and so long as they occupied the land.

The government urged ayuntamientos to use moderation and equity in granting leases, taking into consideration the wealth of the prospective lessees, whether they already owned urban or rural land, and in what quantities. Leases would not be given to an individual if he represented the interests of a group.

The 1845 Law of National Property and the 1847 laws governing the lease of public rural common lands in a large measure identified and preserved the state's patrimony over public land. Still not resolved, however, was the ownership of public lands which had been occupied without title, or the serious problems of defective titles, partition of communal lands, and fraud. These matters will be dealt with separately and in sufficient detail for an understanding of the problems which triggered legislative action in the early twentieth century.

One of the most confusing and disorganized aspects of Dominican public administration throughout this period concerned the documentation of landownership, even of private noncommunal land. As has been mentioned frequently, public records in many towns had been destroyed or were not available. Nor was there a central office which maintained the record of titles, transfers of property, or any other legal act involving land. Particularly vexing was the existence of extensive communal lands and the traditional manner in which these lands were occupied without title or were inherited and passed on. The flaws in the system were an open invitation to fraud.[14] Despite the fact

---

12. *Actos de arrendamientos.*

13. *Bienes comunales,* or common lands, were defined as lands known under the name of ejidos which were included within the limits assigned to eacl village from its first establishment and erection, or by public acts or by private concession, which might or might not be under cultivation, and which were for use as homesites, streets, plazas and other common purposes. Excluded from the above definition were farmlands and urban sites whose titles could be traced to exceptions in the original assignment or grant to the ayuntamiento; land acquired by gift or purchase made by earlier governments in conformance to national law; and those lands within the común whose titles were in due form and legally beyond question.

14. Two contemporary Dominican land law authorities, Manuel Ramón Ruiz Tejada and Alcibíades Alburquerque have made these observations. Their views can be found in Ruiz

that the government passed corrective legislation in 1885 and again in 1907, 1911, 1912, and 1916, the system retained its defects until 1920.

Prescription of land may be defined as the establishment of a claim of title based on use and enjoyment during a time fixed by law.[15] With respect to land, the term "squatter's rights" conveys a similar meaning. The precedent for rights by prescription in Santo Domingo had appeared at the end of the long history of the Spanish Crown's efforts to force the settlers to legalize landholdings, and thereby afford a basis for collecting more royal revenue. Charles III had recognized these rights so long as they were not fraudulent.[16] Later, in the absence of a firmly established government over long periods of time and a lack of records, there is no doubt that rural inhabitants seized good lands wherever they saw them, under almost any pretext, and continued to hold them as their own.[17] These persons, by long peaceful possession either in their own hands or in those of their predecessors, were able to acquire prescriptive rights. Traditionally, a period of thirty years of possession would give a clear title,[18] but possession had to be undisputed, as the Widow Echavarría of Santiago discovered. She applied to the ayuntamiento of Santiago for title to land she had peacefully occupied for forty years. The investigation by the ayuntamiento showed that the tax collector had been trying during those same forty years to collect her annual lease payments but that she had never let him set foot on the property. Although no legal action in consequence had ever been instituted, the ayuntamiento rejected her request, ruling that her occupation had not been "peaceful," for in fact the collector had been trying to interrupt her possession for forty years. His presence voided the definition of "peaceful" and, therefore, any claim to prescriptive rights.[19]

Despite the long history of prescriptive rights, no applicable written law was incorporated into the land law system until 1912. The easy availability of land and the under populated condition of the country throughout most of the nineteenth century made such recourse unnecessary. As will be explained later, the urgent necessity to survey and register titles to rural lands placed prescriptive rights under a spotlight.

One of the weakest links in the land registration system was the notary, who had his immediate origins in the Spanish colonial administrative system. The colonial *escribano*

Tejada, *Estudio,* pp. 45–47, and in Alburquerque, *Títulos,* pp. 126–27, 130–34. Almost a century ago, however, when the problem was beginning to become apparent, Pedro Francisco Bonó, by then retired from public life, published a long, open letter to his old friend, President Fernando Arturo de Meriño, in the Santo Domingo periodical, *El Mensajero.* Bonó included a lengthy commentary on the confused land title situation. The specific problems he outlined were a lack of reliable records, poor administrative procedures, and encroachment. "Carta al Presidente de la República," *El Mensajero*(Santo Domingo, Nos. 17, 18, and 19, June–August 1882), quoted in Rodríguez Demorizi, *Papeles de Pedro F. Bonó,* pp. 265–66. Bonó was qualified to comment on the land title situation and on agricultural matters in general. He was the preeminent "farmer-economist" of San Pedro de Macorís and one of the prominent national figures of his day. He had served as senator and in various other political capacities, including minister of justice and public instruction and, under Espaillat, special commissioner for agriculture. In 1883 he was offered the presidential nomination, but turned it down, not wishing to reenter politics. Bonó lived in Philadelphia in 1858–59 and in Europe in 1875–76.

15. Ruiz Tejada, *Estudio,* p. 259.
16. See Chapter 7.
17. Alburquerque, *Títulos,* p. 126.
18. Ruiz Tejada, *Estudio,* p. 259. Ruiz Tejada cites Article 2262 of the Civil Code. The thirty-year prescriptive period was also mentioned in the testimony given before the U.S. Commission of Inquiry in 1871. Wade, White, and Howe, *Report of Commission,* p. 234.
19. República Dominicana, Santiago de los Caballeros, *Honorable Ayuntamiento de Santiago, Boletín oficial No. 1124,* July 10–20, 1923, p. 5.

was a minor public official whose primary function was to put into legal form or to authenticate agreements between parties, as well as wills, testaments, and other documents. The staff of the first audiencia in Española included an escribano. Later others served as clerks or secretaries at meetings of provincial bodies and local cabildos. Starting early in the seventeenth century the office of escribano, as well as all other saleable offices, was granted for lifetime by the Crown. This clerical or secretarial function extended into the post-colonial period and found its way into the first constitution of the republic as well as later ones.[20] During the nineteenth century the title "notario" replaced that of "escribano."

Dominican notaries were appointed by the supreme court and given life tenure.[21] The numbers of appointments were determined by the size of the population of the común served, one appointment for every 4,000 inhabitants or fraction over 2,000. Except for Santo Domingo, Santiago, and La Vega, most comunes had but one notary. A candidate had to be a lawyer, at least twenty-five years old, of good character, and in full enjoyment of his civil and political rights. He had to be a resident of the común he served. Once appointed, he was obliged to render his services, which were deemed incompatible with any other public function. Notaries were forbidden to function in cases to which they or any relative to the fourth generation were parties. The office clearly was not an unimportant one, especially in rural areas where courts were not seated. In general, the notary performed many acts of legal substance far beyond those normally imputed to a notary public in the United States.

In a real estate transaction the parties concerned were required to appear before the notary, who would draw an act of transaction, the original of which he retained in his files. For a small fee, the notary would draw, certify, and hand over a first copy to the owner. In the case of transfer of property, this first copy became the title to the land. The only records of the transaction were the notary's; because of carelessness, destruction, or even theft, it was frequently impossible to track down specific information on land transfer. A notary who kept accurate records was a rarity. There was no requirement that a transaction be registered with the nearest notary; in order to be reasonably confident of his findings, an interested party might have to conduct a title search in all the notarial offices of several provinces. A further inconvenience could be caused by the fact that while the notaries were public officials, their records were not public. No one could examine the records unless he had acquired or was about to acquire an interest in the

---

20. The Constitution of 1844, Article 127, under "Administration of Justice," prescribed that all executive acts of *escribanos públicos* must be given and executed "In the name of the Dominican Republic."

21. The information which follows is contained in the early Law of Notaries of 1847, contained in República Dominicana, *Colección, 1844–1847*, pp. 524–28.

As a matter of historical interest, the charges for notarial acts or services were originally fixed by law as follows:

To record a will or a wedding, 8 pesos, 4 pesos per copy;
To record an act of sale, mortgage, or donation, 4 pesos, 2 pesos per copy;
To draw up a special or general power or contract, 4 pesos, 2 pesos per copy;
For a copy of any other act, 2 pesos;
For a protest, 5 pesos.

For notarial services rendered at night, defined as between the hours of seven o'clock in the evening and five in the morning, the above charges were doubled. If the notary was called away from his village to render official services, he could collect 4 pesos for transportation, or up to 6 pesos for the first league and 3 for each league thereafter. Ibid., p. 527.

property. Under such a title registration system, the owner of land newly acquired in a private transaction—for example, an immigrant or an unsuspecting campesino—might be challenged later in court and find that his apparently legal title was defective. Furthermore, the lack of any central repository of land transaction data encouraged fraud by collusion between notary and interested parties.[22]

For the purchase of government land, the prospective buyer had only to prove that the land belonged to the government and then pay the fee. Frequently the difficulty with this apparently simple procedure related to the absence of title documentation derived from adequate land surveys. A geological surveyor estimated in 1871 that, based solely on the possession of clear titles, the government possessed from two-thirds to three-fourths of the territory of the republic, but that if a spirit of liberality was exercised and some questionable titles as well as preemptive rights were recognized, then probably only fifty to sixty percent of the land was public domain.[23] These figures mean that as of 1871 possibly as much as twenty-five percent of Dominican land was held under questionable title or with no written title at all.

Terrenos comuneros, or communal lands, were defined as undivided tracts of land owned or claimed to be owned by two or more persons, the interest of each being represented by shares (*acciones*) or pesos or other units which had reference to value or proportionate rights, rather than to area of land owned or claimed by them. The common expression "peso title" was universally understood to mean title to communal land. The origin of peso titles is obscure, but all of the several possible explanations relate in some way to the vagueness of land boundaries and lack of accurate surveys.[24] One explanation is related to the descriptive language used by the Spanish Crown or its representative to define land granted to an individual by merced. The property, usually extensive, was defined in terms of natural limits without indicating area, for the practical reason that cadastral surveys as we know them today did not exist. Owners marked their property

---

22. Quoted below as a matter relevant to the role of the notary in land transactions is the preamble to the 1907 Notarial Law of the Dominican government. The law itself will be discussed later. The preamble is given here because it confirms the need for the reform:

Considering: that the undivided state in which is found the major part of the lands of the republic lends itself to the commission of endless frauds which are the constant cause of discord between co-owners of common land;

Considering: that the undivided state noticeably prejudices the development of agriculture;

Considering: that it is the duty of the state to seek through the means within its reach to put an end to that state of affairs in order to guarantee the property and the tranquillity of the associates, . . .

Land Law of June 29, 1907, República Dominicana, *Colección, 1905–1907,* pp. 440–42.

23. Testimony of William M. Gabb of Philadelphia, geologist-surveyor for the Santo Domingo Company. Wade, White, and Howe, *Report of Commission,* p. 237. Gabb spent three years (1869–71) completing a survey of the Dominican Republic, except for the portion west of Azua to the Haitian border. The Santo Domingo Company (not to be confused with the San Domingo Improvement Company of the Heureaux era) had contracted for this work at the request of the Dominican government, which needed factual information on the nation's mineral resources. Gabb, a geologist, was in charge of the team of surveyors and draftsmen. After his return to Philadelphia, he presented a paper to the American Philosophical Society on October 18, 1872, giving a complete geological description of the Dominican Republic. His was the first professional survey, and was especially detailed in the Cibao, the Northwest, Constanza Valley, and Samaná Peninsula. William M. Gabb, "On the Topography and Geology of Santo Domingo."

24. Ruiz Tejada, *Estudio,* pp. 53–55. Also see Alburquerque, *Títulos,* pp. 20–23.

lines from hilltops, along roads, rivers, or ravines, and other landmarks. The area enclosed by these imprecise limits was never measured. When a landowner wanted to sell a part of the land, he put a value of the whole and sold a fraction in terms of that value. For example, possessing land worth 1,000 pesos, he might sell a parcel corresponding in value to 100 pesos. The buyer would not know precisely how much area he was purchasing, but he could have in his possession a title to 100 pesos of value in the land. The peso title making him a shareholder was exclusively his, but in time this process might create a number of other shareholders. Some might have peso titles of less value or more value than his, but all would own the land in common.

A second explanation for the origin of peso titles (mentioned at the beginning of this chapter) concerns communal lands granted to a colonial settlement, either of Spaniards or of Indians. Whereas in the first case the land was originally granted to an individual and later became communal when he sold a share of it, in the second case the possession of land in common within an individual tract was specified from the beginning of settlement. Eventually the transmission of any right to or on this tract required some convenient medium of exchange which, according to this second explanation, became known as the peso title. For example, a woodcutting right of so many pesos gave a man the right to cut that much wood, but he would not have that right to the land once the wood was cut. This custom endured into this century.

In the town of Maniela the right to cut mahogany on common land was kept distinct from the right to common land. The ayuntamiento of Maniela sold a mahogany right in the común to a Santo Domingo merchant for 2,000 pesos and later sold the same man land rights for 50 pesos.[25] The 2,000 pesos gave him the mahogany, and the 50 pesos gave him a title to the land in the común, that is, in any unoccupied part of it, to farm it or use it as he needed. According to the alcalde the land was not measured because the survey would be more expensive than the selling price of the land. There was a strict requirement, however, that although the buyer could take the land he wanted for his needs, he must justify the need by the act of occupying and using the land. The same reasoning applied to the colonial cattle lands, or hatos. These were grazing lands which lost their usefulness if physically subdivided. Hence individual rights were stated in terms of pesos or shares in order to preserve the integrity of the common land.

A third possible explanation of the origin of peso titles was the process which in modern terminology would be called incorporation. A landowner possessing extensive private land which had not been surveyed might organize a group of associates to agree on the value of the land and purchase shares, thus avoiding the need to subdivide the land or have it surveyed.

Another common derivation of the peso title is explained by the legal procedures involved in inheritance of land. Under Dominican law the widow of the landowner inherited half the property, and his legitimate children the other half. In the case of a title or right to communal land which could not be subdivided, or of privately owned land which by common consent or agreement could not be suitably subdivided among a large number of heirs—for example, a small city lot or rural grazing land—the heirs usually received as their inheritance titles to fractions of the value of the land. The peso values of these fractions were usually assigned by a competent court or notary, based on an official evaluation of the property.[26] This does not mean that inherited

---

25. Testimony of the alcalde of Maniela before the U.S. commission of 1871, Wade, White, and Howe, *Report of Commission,* p. 278.

lands were never partitioned. Article 185 of the Dominican Civil Code provided that no citizen was obliged to keep property in an undivided state, and if he so desired, he could petition for partition; or in the case of inheritance, if all heirs were present they could submit a petition in the form and as documented by mutual agreement. Utilizing the services of a public surveyor, the notary would then award peso titles based on a specific survey. Frequently, however, these proceedings, although fair, might not be legal or binding because not all co-owners had in fact been present, or the rights of minors had not been properly represented.

Regardless of the origin of custom, the effect of transmitting land rights by peso title rather than by partitioning the land created an indeterminate and frequently anonymous number of co-proprietors, each not knowing precisely what proportion of the area he owned in the common land. Nor could he be sure of the portion on which he could locate his private property. Each heir could retain or dispose of his title as he saw fit. So long as the land remained in the possession of a single family there was some measure of control over the land and a reasonably fair chance of avoiding litigation, problems of false titles, and fraud. But as owners of small fractions began to sell their titles outside the family, control was diluted and there grew up the anonymous form of comunero property noted above. It should be pointed out here that as a result of the distribution and redistribution of land inheritance and subsequent sale of inheritance, many individuals became owners of peso titles without actually occupying or using the land. Other holders of peso titles simply failed to improve the land, holding it as an investment. It was not until land values began to rise that the government took action against the nonusing, nonpossessing owner, not because of burning social issues but in order to reduce land frauds.

By the second half of the nineteenth century the difficulties encountered in title search procedures, the fact that a complete, accurate survey of national territory had never been made, and the existence of undivided, unused, and unoccupied communal land began to expose the public to the unprincipled use of false titles. Some of the fraudulent methods used were extremely difficult to challenge or even detect until considerable time—perhaps generations—had elapsed. Years earlier an individual might have gone before a notary, or a judge, or even an alcalde and declared he was the owner of a number of pesos in such a place where all the titles had been lost. He would have witnesses to swear in his behalf and would receive a document in his favor. The document did not constitute title but, with the passage of time, might be difficult to challenge. Some notaries, through ignorance or connivance with a cheat, accepted documents to the effect that a peso title had been sold, duly authorized by the owner. The document might be forged or the owner might even be nonexistent, but the cheat came away with a peso title. The notary's seal was thus used to legalize a fraud.

Peso owners also created difficulties by selling their shares simply by endorsing the back of a title without having the signature legalized. Years later it would not be possible for the buyer or his heirs to prove that the signature was a true one. The courts would have to decide, if they could.

The widespread illegal operations of some lawyers, notaries, and surveyors jammed the courts with litigation. An American official later stated that there were falsely manufactured titles to more lands than the republic contained, and more were being

---

26. An example of the manner in which property was bequeathed and distributed is contained in the Notarial Act shown in Appendix 1.

manufactured. This statement may have been an exaggeration, but it indicates how commonplace were the violations of the law. Unfortunately many of those responsible were influential citizens too well entrenched in the government to be prosecuted.[27] As the number of false peso titles grew, lack of public confidence in the land system began to hinder land development and cause problems in the rural areas.[28]

The earliest legislation in land reform appeared in 1895 when the government of Heureaux passed the Land Registry Law[29] which, although intended to be chiefly a revenue-raising measure, might have brought some order to the system of title registration. The law required all land transactions to be registered, and imposed a mandatory tax of one percent of the amount named as a cost of transfer. The size of the tax, however, frequently induced the parties to the transaction to evade the law. Instead of having a notary record the sale, the principals recorded the transaction under private signature, but never registered it unless by chance it might be needed later for legal evidence. In some cases the principals made transaction under private signature and deposited the deed with the notary, who would then issue an act of deposit stating that an act of private signature had been deposited in the archives. For a fee of one peso, a major economy for the parties concerned, the act could be duly registered. As a land registration document, therefore, the act was of little value because the notary had to record only the names of the parties, the date, and the amount of his fee. There was no description of the property, nor was there even a summary of the content of the act.

The first law aimed directly at communal land abuse was that of June 29, 1907, intended to correct the countless frauds which were producing continuous disagreement between co-owners of common land. There were two main provisions. First, all notaries were prohibited from executing acts of sale if the land had not previously been measured by a public surveyor; second, no registrar[30] anywhere could enter documents which under private signature referred to land sales, unless an official plat of the land was presented, together with the deed. The intention of the law was to cancel and render void all peso titles by requiring the owner to have his land surveyed (a legal act) or to prove some act of possession or occupation. False peso titles of owners not in possession would then be exposed. Failure of officials to comply with the law would result in a fine of 200 pesos for the first offense and removal from office if repeated. Well intentioned, the law had a serious defect. It required the survey of a given peso portion of communal land when there was no way of knowing exactly how much land by area belonged to each shareholder. Since no law had previously set up the procedures for partitioning common land, the exact perimeter, extension, and number of titles or shares of the whole were unknown. How, then, could the component shares be determined? Because of this defect, some parties limited themselves to surveying what they possessed. Others, greedier,

---

27. United States, Department of State, *Records Relating to Internal Affairs of the Dominican Republic 1910–1929* (hereafter referred to as *Internal Affairs of the D.R.*), letter serial 2W, September 12, 1917, Minister William W. Russell to State Department.

28. This is a major theme of the novel by Manuel A. Amiama based on life in San Pedro de Macorís around 1916. The legal problem in the novel occurs between two Dominicans, one a peso titleholder living in the capital who has never occupied his family's property, and the other an influential local sugar operator who claims to hold title to the same property, valuable sugar land. Manuel A. Amiama, *El terrateniente*.

29. Law of May 20, 1895, published in *Gaceta Oficial*, No. 2184.

30. The official in charge of the registry of judicial and extrajudicial acts. In the provincial capitals the provincial registries were maintained by the custodians (*conservadores*) of mortgages. In the comunes the secretary of the ayuntamiento performed this function.

had surveyed what they wanted to possess, to the prejudice of other shareholders. The law caused a large number of irresponsible surveys, and was superseded by the 1911 Law of the Division of Common Lands.[31]

The existence of communal lands in their peculiar Dominican context was a major problem. Neither the evils of minifundismo nor of uneconomical latifundismo were in evidence. The country was lightly populated in 1908 with about 605,000 inhabitants. This figure gives a population density of only about 31 inhabitants per square mile. Land was fertile and still inexpensive. A man who needed land to feed his family could acquire what he needed, or was able to manage, with relative ease. Only a limited, though increasing, portion of the country was under cultivation.

There had existed, of course, several large family landholdings, such as the Domingo de la Rocha cattle estates in El Seibo, the Baez sugar estates west of Azua, and one or two others in the Cibao. But even these did not exceed 10,000 acres.[32] By far the majority of landholdings in the country were by tradition small ones, about 10 to 15 acres, frequently only a part of which was under cultivation. If an individual wanted more land, it was available.[33] Shortly after he took office in 1879, President Gregorio Luperón, who himself was a Puerto Plata farmer-exporter, made a strong effort to increase agricultural production, especially in sugar, cacao, coffee, and tobacco—the export money crops. One of the results of his program was an influx of foreign businessmen, many of them technically competent Cubans, to revive the sugar industry in what today are the provinces of Puerto Plata, Azua, Samaná, San Pedro de Macorís, Peravia, San Cristóbal, La Romana, and the National District.[34] The growth of the sugar industry caused land values to rise, and increased the number of false titles, thus contributing to the

31. Ruiz Tejada, *Estudio*, p. 32, and República Dominicana, *Ley sobre división de terrenos comuneros*, passed by the senate, April 17, 1909, by the chamber of deputies, April 17, 1911, and signed into law by President Ramón Cáceres on April 21, 1911. Published in the *Gazeta Oficial*, No. 2187.

32. Wade, White, and Howe, *Report of Commission*, p. 234.

33. The testimony given by a number of farmers before the U.S. Commission of Inquiry in 1871 is very revealing in this respect. Some of their statements, which confirm the richness of farmland and describe the manner in which it was worked, are quoted;

I have myself leased 10 or 12 acres. . . . I find the soil very rich. . . . any little piece of ground will give a family food enough, and they can have it ready for growing and eating in forty days from landing. . . .

A great many [heads of family] own lands of their own and lease it from the government. . . . The farms average about five carreaux or sixteen acres. About four or five are under cultivation, depending on the size of the family. They can support themselves from that much. . . .

The land around here is generally held in small farms. A great many own their own lands, though perhaps almost as many rent. The part the family cultivate and live on is generally only three or four acres, which is enough. . . . Land within two miles of here, back on the hills, is worth perhaps $4 or $5 per acre.

. . . in some of the more distant regions on the north side of the island, you can buy half a dozen acres for $1, of land that would be considered a most magnificent farm in your state (Ohio) or mine. . . . I have bought a whole caballería (187 acres) within rifle-shot of the church on the hill . . . which you see from here [Santo Domingo], and for it I gave $200.

. . . I do not think there is one-fourteenth part of the island in cultivation. . . . Ibid., pp. 218–39, passim.

34. The first steam-powered sugar mill was "La Esperanza," which had been founded in 1874 near Santo Domingo by the Cuban, Joaquín M. Delgado. "La Caridad" and "La Angelina" were founded by Cubans a few years later near San Carlos and San Pedro de Macorís, respectively. Most of the other thirty mills established by the early 1890s were owned by Cuban, Dominican, Puerto Rican, or Spanish companies or individuals, with a light sprinkling of

universal complication of ownership in unpartitioned rural communal land.[35] Peso title-holders over the years had sold and resold shares worth as little as ten pesos or as much as one hundred or more until, in districts of from a thousand to several thousand acres there might be as many as two hundred proprietors, some with legal titles, some with false titles, and some with no titles at all. With respect to each other, their claims had never been adjusted. Individually they were small landowners; collectively they were owners of a large tract.[36]

The 1911 law was the first positive legislation prescribing systematic partition of communal land. Although its life was relatively short, a number of the provisions of this law found their way into the basic Land Registry Law of 1920 and into succeeding laws down to the present day. The 1911 law was called forth in the interests of public utility, as the first article attested: surveys, boundary determination, and partition of communal lands were declared to be in the public interest. Of the remaining articles only the most important need be summarized here.

On receipt of a request by one or more co-owners of common land (defined as land whose property was held in shares belonging to two or more persons) along with their land titles, the court would order a survey and partition of the land. To receive the titles the court designated a notary who, together with a court-appointed surveyor, made the actual judgments. These two officials based their decisions on the titles, the quality of the land, the shares of each owner, and the location of the improvements made by each owner, with the understanding that the individual boundaries need not be continuous. This last clause would cover those cases where a landowner was entitled to more land than he actually possessed and was using.

The decision of the court to proceed with the partition had to be given wide public notice throughout the country so that possible objections could be heard by the court before it ordered the final step. If no litigation developed within three months, the surveyor could begin his operations. If a conflict did arise during the three-month period, the surveyor would await the court's decision before proceeding.

Once the surveyor had completed his exterior measurements of the common lands, he prepared the general plan and then, with the notary, worked out the partition. Essentially this action involved the mathematical dividing of the number of tareas[37] of land by the number of pesos in the titles previously deposited. Knowing the number of tareas per peso and the number of pesos per title, the two officials then allotted the land corresponding to each owner. This was the legal step not provided for in the 1907

French, German, Italian, American, and British. By 1893, through mismanagement or lack of technical knowledge, the total number had been reduced to 25. These produced 35,547 tons of sugar that year, an insignificant amount compared to the world production of 6,297,547 tons. Cuba alone produced 900,000 tons and Puerto Rico 65,000. Juan J. Sánchez Guerrero, *La caña en Santo Domingo*, pp. 22, 56–57. As the mills began to expand their production capabilities they either acquired more adjoining land or arranged with *colonos*, or growers, to grind the cane grown on the colonos' land. Legal problems arose from the fact that these lands newly placed under cultivation had never been surveyed.

35. Harmannus Hoetink, "*Materiales para el estudio de la República Dominicana en la segunda mitad del siglo XIX*" (Parte primera), *Caribbean Studies*, vol. 5, no. 3 (October 1965), 7.

36. Wade, White, and Howe, *Report of Commission*, p. 234.

37. The following conversion factors have been used in this book: one acre equals 6.48 tareas or 40.47 areas or .4047 hectares. The tarea is the standard rural land area unit universally used in the Dominican Republic. One peonía equals 300 tareas equals 18.866 hectares. One tarea also equals 100 square varas (vara de conuco). One vara equals 6.29 meters.

law. A cadastral survey of the individual holdings then followed the office distribution. Based on the results of the official partition the notary would then certify the respective subdivisions awarded each co-owner.

Any co-owner found to be occupying more than the share justified by his title was required to buy the excess from the rightful owner or to sell his improvements to the latter.[38] In case buyer and seller could not agree on a price, a board of three court-appointed experts set a value on the excess land and the improvements. If the parties still failed to agree, the disputed property was put up for sale at public auction and the proceeds distributed proportionately to the interested parties. The law made no provision for cases in which a buyer could not be found.

The surveyor was required to file with the secretary of the court a copy of all of his records, decisions, and expenses, all to be approved by the court and prosecuting attorney or modified by them as appropriate.

The 1911 law placed considerable power in the hands of the notaries and surveyors. Short of evidence of collusion involving the surveyor, the notary or the board of appraisers, the court would be hard pressed to overrule any partition based on existing improvements and pesos of title. There was, however, a weakness in the law. It was based on voluntary action of the owners. The court could not force a partition, although once one had been requested the partitioning decisions were final and irrevocable. Furthermore, the voluntary feature, combined with the supersession of the 1907 law, removed the inhibitions on the manufacture of false titles, which continued at an alarming rate. It has been claimed that no partition was ever legally completed in accordance with the terms of the 1911 law because of so many court litigations. Here is how one eminent Dominican legal authority described the situation:

> The capricious assignment of value to communal areas; the lack of proof in some cases of title . . .the continual transmission of land rights . . . without existence of a law requiring the inscription of the titles in a fixed register; the lack of scruples of some shareholders who would sell the same title more than once; the lack of control of the partitioning operation in common land . . . the increasing expansion of the sugar industry which took place in the eastern part of the country, which was precisely where there were more communal lands; and the period of doubts and uncertainties and of disorganization which we lived in during our past civil wars, permitted individuals of turbid conscience to devise a new business which rapidly increased: the fabrication of false titles. They would, for example, fake a transaction made in the past by some unknown campesino to a known person; in the current sales document the latter would now state that "he was selling so many pesos of title of such and such communal land, which had been acquired by inheritance or by sale, etc., etc.," and would fix the date of the earlier document serving as a basis for the sale so far in the past that an investigation would be impossible, or taking advantage of some fortuitous incident . . . dating the contrived document that gave origin to the sale one day before that fortuitous incident. Thus, when one tried to find the original document it couldn't be located because the files had all burned. . . . And in this manner the buyer would be handed an apparently valid title, whose history it was difficult to prove and where, because of a lack of title inscription law, no reference could be made to an earlier registry or inscription since this formality did not exist. The counterfeiters and makers of titles never faltered; places that originally were worth 200 to 300 pesos were suddenly at the moment of partition worth thousands, thus reducing the quantity due the holder of a good title. The acquisitions of lands that were taken for the sugar industry led to increased greediness, and the business flourished.[39]

---

38. A familiar solution; see the old Spanish Law of Composición, Chapter 7.
39. Ruiz Tejada, *Estudio*, pp. 74–75.

It was small wonder, then, that the government began to act more vigorously. The 1911 Law of Partition was followed in 1912 by the Law of Inscription of Rural Titles.[40] There were no options in this legislation; it was general, obligatory, and directed toward the creation of a land registry system. For the first time in Dominican history the law also contained certain administrative provisions which would facilitate a complete cadastral survey of rural land.

Owners of rural lands were given a grace period of one year in which to inscribe their titles. The owner of any rural land acquired after the end of the grace period had to inscribe his title within sixty days. Data to be entered in the land registry included the name, domicile, and profession of the current owner and the previous owner; date and nature of the title document, indicating the name of the functionary who drew it up; and the number of shares or extent and condition of the land being inscribed. The land registry book was to be maintained by the provincial custodian of mortgages, who was now also required to maintain two additional books of indices. The first was an alphabetical index of the names of places, that is, homesites, farms, or ranches, together with such supplementary information as the name of the común and province where each place was located; the name of the person who had acquired the land; the person from whom acquired; and the file or folio containing the inscription. The second book contained similar data, except that it was an alphabetical index of the names of owners. Thus the two lists, one of places and one of owners' names, formed the basic source of information on which to begin future survey operations.

Notaries were forbidden to execute any document relative to land titles if the titles had not been previously registered, and they were obliged to make specific reference to previous registry in executing these documents. Possessors of unregistered titles also found their freedom of action circumscribed. The owner of an unregistered title could not use the title for legal purposes, for example, to demand a partition or to oppose one. No transfer of rural property would be valid until the seller had inscribed his property. There was also an important innovation in the law—formal recognition of claims based on prescriptive rights. Owners in long possession but without title were given the right to claim title by so inscribing their land in the land registry book. Prescriptive claims had to include the full name of the owner, his profession and domicile; the quantity of land possessed; the crops which were being grown; date of initial possession; location of land with names of owners and limits of contiguous properties; and a statement as to whether the claimed land was communal. Two witnesses, preferably neighboring landowners, had to confirm the prescriptive declaration. The act of inscription did not give a clear title; it could be challenged by third parties.

A new feature of the law, the creation of a central office for land registry operations to be known as the General Land Registry Administration,[41] could have been an extremely important provision. From the reports of all inscriptions made in the provinces, the central office would set up a control system which would have converted the frustrating title search process into a relatively simple matter. Unfortunately, the new office never functioned, possibly because of the turbulent political situation between 1912 and 1916.

The 1912 law was in theory a strong step in the direction of correcting the deep confusion over rural land titles. Nonregistered titles would have been forced onto the books;

---

40. República Dominicana, *Ley sobre inscripción de títulos de terrenos rurales.* The law was passed on May 25 and published on May 29 in the *Gaceta Oficial,* No. 2301.

41. Article 16, 1912 Law of Inscription.

thereafter, any shareholder legally entitled to question the validity of the title could invoke the earlier 1911 law and petition an official survey and partition. The law gave full legal status to prescriptive claims which in prior years might not have withstood the claims of co-owners possessing documented rights, even though the latter may not have been in occupation of the land. Finally, the centralizing of land registry operations, had it been carried out, would have reduced fraud and the inadequacies of the system and would sooner or later have led to a complete national land survey based on the data provided the central land registry office.

Adequate for registration, the 1912 law was not satisfactory for transcription purposes, since it did not require a complete cadastral description of the property involved. Still, the main shortcoming associated with the law lay in quite another direction: it was never effectively enforced. The period from late 1911 to 1916 was a tumultuous one. President Ramón Cáceres was assassinated in November 1911; in early 1912 the exiled Cibaeño caudillo, Horacio Vásquez, returned, and almost instantly revolution broke out to overthrow Cáceres' more or less duly elected successor, Eladio Victoria. The civil war which lasted almost all of 1912 was followed by the weak and agitated administrations of Archbishop Adolfo A. Nouel, José Bordas, Ramón Baez, Juan Isidro Jimenes, and Francisco Henríquez y Carvajal.[42] Even in normal, or more accurately, less chaotic times, the campesino was likely to ignore the formalities required by law. Reflecting long bitter experience, his reaction to a legal requirement to present his documents of ownership at any given public office was the conviction that someone planned to take his land. As a result, many titles had not been inscribed when the legal grace period of one year expired, and the beleaguered government could not divert the financial resources to enforce the law. Over the next several years and for the same reason, the government extended the grace period from time to time until the law was finally overtaken by the major land reform of the American occupation.

As a direct result of the 1911 Law of Partition there was one more legal effort to tighten the administration of the land system, which need be mentioned only for purposes of the record. As already described, notaries in executing or authenticating dcouments would normally perform such acts as affixing dates, placing documents in safekeeping, and making official copies. The law of 1911, however, outlined special notarial responsibilities, which in turn necessitated some amplification and clarification of the regulations governing the notaries. In 1916, legislation was approved to meet this need.[43] Most of the provisions of the law dealt with procedural details for the handling of titles and deeds, preparation of reports and files, and publishing of the necessary public notices.

Between 1895 and 1916 it appeared that the government had at least recognized the outlines of most of the major legal problems associated with landownership, especially communal lands, and had taken some corrective action at least in the national legislative chambers. Had all the relevant legislation passed during this period been enforced, or at least written more in consonance with government objectives, these would have been the welcome results: all lands, including rural communal lands, would have been duly registered; communal lands would have been partitioned and the individual land holdings would have been made to coincide with the description in the land titles; false peso titles and other land frauds would have been identified; and all public lands would have been identified.

---

42. This period will be described in more detail in the next chapter.
43. Law of October 6, 1916, Ruiz Tejada, *Estudio*, pp. 88–99.

The government's intentions were commendable, but inherent inadequacies of the individual laws, an antiquated, inadequate land registry system, the inability or reluctance of authorities to enforce the laws which did exist, the unwillingness of many landholders to cooperate with the authorities, the ignorance and suspicion of the campesinos, the unchecked, widespread fraudulent land practices, and the not unusual collusion between notary and surveyor—all combined to give results which fell well short of the reform that was wanted and badly needed. The early colonial gap between *hecho* and *derecho* had been reincarnated, and, as many had been saying for years, the best titles were still those of the early Spaniards, the French, and the Haitian Boyer. On the eve of military occupation by the United States, land litigations choked the courts, land records were in a state of extreme confusion, land values were rising, and many small landowners had no confidence in their titles. As a result they were reluctant to improve their land, fearing dispossession. One of the country's leading lawyers and future president of the land court was to write: "I have never been happy with the 1912 Law because it was ineffective in preventing the manufacture of illegal titles. In fact there has been an increase in this activity which has inundated the country with false papers."[44] The title system was admittedy obsolete, deficient, and sadly in need of major reconstruction.

---

44. Letter, Manuel de J. Troncoso de la Concha to Colonel Rufus H. Lane, May 25,1918, U.S., *Military Government*.

The Modern Period

14

THE DOMINICAN DEBT AND
THE DISORDERS OF 1912-16

The aftermath of the Heureaux era was misfortune compounded. Mired in a multitude of costly foreign loans, the governments which immediately succeeded him were disunified, weak, and crippled by the selfish party politics which superseded Heureaux' dictatorship. Laboring under this double handicap, the Dominicans earned an unfortunate reputation for political and financial chicanery among their French, Belgian, Italian, British, Spanish, German, American, and Dutch creditors. Their treasury was described as a financial carnival and their government as having practiced every form of bankruptcy known to the history of finance.[1] As one respected political figure and analytical writer stated later, in lamenting the United States intervention in Dominican fiscal affairs and his countrymen's hypersensitivity to the sanctity of their national

---

1. The best example of short-sighted politics was the action of the opposition parties in the Congress during the first presidency of Juan Isidro Jimenes from 1899 to 1902 (see note 30 below). Faced with increasing pressure by creditors insisting on loan payments, Jimenes in 1901 sent the capable Dr. Francisco Henríquez y Carvajal to Europe and to the United States to try to arrange with creditors a less onerous solution to the foreign debt problem. Henríquez y Carvajal was able to persuade the international creditors to accept an equitable plan which would have permitted the Dominicans to work their way out from under their burden of debts, some of which had actually existed for twenty years, and still be able to maintain a viable government.

The opposition parties, staunch supporters, respectively, of Horacio Vásquez and the defunct Heureaux, blocked the plan in Congress on the grounds that acceptance of it would lend too much personal prestige to Henríquez y Carvajal who was a potential candidate for either the presidency or the vice-presidency in the 1902 elections! As a result, more loans had to be negotiated in order for the government to pay for urgent expenses. Concurrently, contraband activity with the complicity of customs officials lowered the income of the government. The public debt could not be served, and Jimenes was overthrown by Vásquez early in 1902. Vásquez, in turn, was overthrown within a year, and this cycle of revolution and increasing counterrevolutionary expenses to maintain government continued. Insofar as the Dominican treasury was concerned, the debt increased as old obligations were not serviced and new ones were incurred. Troncoso de la Concha, *Génesis*, pp. 14–16, 55–59.

sovereignty: "It was not with literature that we were going to stop this conflict. Legal allegations, furthermore, are worth little when they are not supported by a reality which inspires confidence, a necessary basic quality if one is to defend himself with moral authority."[2]

The Dominican crises of 1903–4 have been recorded elsewhere, as has the history of the Convention of 1905 and the "modus vivendi" arrived at between President Theodore Roosevelt and President Luis Morales Languasco.[3] Under this arrangement, born of the application of the Roosevelt Corollary to the threat of armed intervention in the Dominican Republic by Italian and French forces,[4] the United States assumed the administration of Dominican customs collections.[5] Forty five percent of the collections were handed over to the Dominican government and 55 percent to creditors. In accordance with the demand of the Dominicans, none of the officials of the San Domingo Improvement Company was permitted a part in the administration of the customs as fiscal agent. The initiatives leading to both the Convention of 1905 and the modus vivendi came from the United States, although Morales appears to have made official requests for United States assistance. There is, however, no evidence that American Minister Dawson, in conferring with Morales and his minister of finance, in any way failed to carry out to the letter his instructions not to press the Dominicans.[6]

---

2. Ibid., p. 55.

3. See Chapter 12, note 36.

4. Because of complaints by European creditors, the Italian and French governments had warships in adjacent Caribbean waters; a German cruiser was also in the area. Ibid., p. 31. Spain and England, both with private citizen creditors, formulated no threats against the tiny republic. The San Domingo Improvement Company, the principal American creditor, had made earlier representations in 1901 to the United States government when it appeared that the Dominicans were not going to make full payment on their foreign debts. Since the Jimenes government was practically bankrupt at the time, this action of "the Improvement" served mainly to increase dislike for it in the Dominican Republic.

5. There were two agreements involved—the formal treaty of January 20, 1905, and the modus vivendi, which went into effect on April, 20, 1905. The U.S. Senate refused to approve the formal treaty after it had been signed by both governments because it contained several clauses which the Senate believed would give the United States authority to intervene in internal Dominican affairs. President Roosevelt, determined to avoid a repetition of foreign intervention such as had occurred in Venezuela in 1902, then simply put the plan in effect by means of an executive agreement with Morales. The American receivership was officially created on March 31, 1905, by a decree of Morales, who followed the protocol of the modus vivendi. The Convention of 1907 formally recognized receivership, and the Trujillo-Hull Convention of September 24, 1940 ended it after some thirty-five years of operation. U.S. Department of State, *Papers Relating to the Foreign Relations of The United States 1899–1945* (hereafter cited as *Foreign Relations*), 1940, pp. 789–829. See also United States, Department of State, Treaty Series No.965.

6. Dawson was told to find out in a discreet, serious, and perfectly friendly manner whether the Dominican government, in view of existing unsettled conditions and pressures from other governments, would be disposed to ask the United States to take charge of Dominican customs houses. Secretary of State Hay said: "We have grounds to think that such an arrangement would satisfy the other powers, besides serving as a practical guarantee of the peace of Santo Domingo from external influences or internal disturbances." Hay to Dawson, December 30, 1904, quoted in Troncoso de la Concha, *Génesis*, p. 33. For the American source see "Instructions, Dominican Republic, vol. 1," quoted in J. Fred Rippy, "The Initiation of the Customs Receivership in the Dominican Republic." Troncoso de la Concha makes no claim that Morales was coerced. In fact, in describing a later meeting between Dawson and Morales to discuss the possibility of a "modus vivendi," Troncoso de la Concha cites Morales as having responded to Dawson's suggestion as follows: "Morales not only accepted the idea but said: 'That has been my very thought.'" *Génesis*, p. 42.

With the creation of the modus vivendi the fiscal situation of the Dominican government radically changed as it began to benefit from a regular, undisturbed income. Creditors received payments on the loans, domestic business took an upward turn, and the salaries of government employees were paid on time.

In the United States, the Senate and a large segment of public opinion had displayed a distinct aversion to the possibility of imperialistic adventures at the expense of the Dominicans even as the Senate had in 1871 and 1872. Others saw the Convention of 1905 as a simple imposition of humanitarian acts on a small, poor, and disorderly nation. In the Dominican Republic opinion was also split. In general, the supporters of the government defended Morales, while his opposition attacked him. But all considered the agreement a disgrace in the sense that it was the disastrous consequence of the unfortunate acts committed by earlier Dominican governments. *Listín Diario* said: "The convention focused attention on the peak of Dominican adventures. The imperialistic ambition of the colossus of North America has collided with a series of unhappy and irreparable Dominican errors to produce an effect which could not be stopped."[7]

Morales was unable to overcome the political opposition to his policies.[8] By August 1905 open warfare had broken out between him and the most influential leaders of the country. By the end of the year he had lost all control of the government. The stage was set for Ramón Cáceres, who on June 20, 1904 had been inaugurated as Morales' vice-president. Cáceres, the most dominant figure to enter the presidency after the turn of the century, was to bring order to the country. Destined to provide the firm leadership Ulises Espaillat had hoped for decades earlier, Cáceres took office upon Morales' departure with this idea: "I propose to be the last machete-wielding president."[9] In his determination to form a government of national projects rather than of party or individuals, he led the Dominican Republic out of a long period of financial bankruptcy, governmental instability, and economic crisis and into one which gave promise of

---

7. Editorial, "We Have Reached the End," *Listín Diario,* January 21, 1905.

8. A former priest, Morales was honest and progressive. During the early years of his presidency he constructed a number of public works, improved communications between the Cibao and the capital, and increased the national educational effort. But he was not a strong administrator. In trying to formulate financial policies for payment of debts he pleased none of the political leaders and antagonized many with his acceptance of American control of the disbursement of customs revenues. He was accused of forming a private political party from which he selected a majority of his cabinet. After surviving two attempts on his life, he launched an effort to form a revolutionary government on December 24, 1905, failed, broke a leg trying to escape arrest and spent the next ten days in hiding. He resigned on January 12, 1906 after having secured from Minister Dawson a guarantee of his personal safety. The USS *Dubuque* carried him to exile in Puerto Rico.

9. "Me propongo ser el último presidente machetero." Pedro Troncoso Sánchez, *Ramón Cáceres,* p. 14. Cáceres, one of the two slayers of Dictator Ulises Heureaux in Moca, held offices as minister of war and navy and governor of Santiago province before being elected vice-president in 1904. He had made a late entry into politics, for which he had had no special preparation or experience. Up until 1900 he was a moderately well-to-do cacao farmer in the Moca-La Vega-Santiago area. He and his cousin, Horacio Vásquez, were the two most influential individuals in the Cibao, especially after the death of Heureaux. Cáceres possessed the personal qualities, the force, and the charisma of the typical caudillo, but his political philosophy was entirely democratic. He believed in civil supremacy over the military, in rigorous fiscal responsibility, and in strong government built on a broad political, economic, and administrative base. Except for the element of "strength," these ideals were the antithesis of Heureaux' form of government.

prosperity. He was assisted by a talented group of principal advisors, the most influential of whom was the minister of finance, Federico Velásquez y Hernández.[10]

For at least the first four years of his administration Cáceres was able to control—and what was more important, unify—national politics. Perhaps his most difficult problem arose over Dominican ratification of the 1907 Convention with the United States[11] by which the U.S. assumed responsibility for collecting the Dominican customs revenues and amortizing more than thirty million dollars' worth of internal and foreign debts and claims. The modus vivendi had proven to be so effective a fiscal arrangement that by 1907 there appeared to be sufficient support in the U.S. Senate and the Dominican Republic for a formal treaty arrangement. Roosevelt made a second effort. The proposed 1907 Convention differed from the 1905 plan in two major respects. Under the new version the United States would not deal directly with the Dominican creditors, but would appoint an individual who would become general receiver of Dominican customs. This official would collect and disburse customs revenues in accordance with the proposed agreement. The second major difference was the debt adjustment and amortization scheme of the new plan. The arrangement included a fresh twenty million-dollar Dominican bond issue, financed by Kuhn, Loeb, and Company, the proceeds of which would be applied toward the thirty million dollar debt, as adjusted.[12] The customs revenues would be used as required for the administrative and collection expenses of the customs receivership, the payment of interest on the bonds, the payment of annual sums provided for amortization of the bonds, the purchase, cancellation, or retirement of any of the bonds as directed by the Dominican government, and finally, the remainder to the Dominican government. U.S. participation was the key to the plan. The role of the U.S. in the Dominican Republic was derived from the title and preamble of the convention itself[13]: to assist the Dominican Republic in the collection of customs revenues and to apply the money collected in accordance with the agreed terms of the convention. In other words, the United States' role was to be an active one in the plan to liquidate

---

10. Velásquez, who was also Morales' minister of finance, was the outstanding personality in the cabinet. He was intelligent, cultured, energetic, and indomitable. His private life was austere, and his public policies were similar. He was a graduate of the normal school and had taught in Puerto Rico in exile during the Heureaux period. Velásquez' knowledge and respect for constitutional law inculcated in him a respect for American institutions and a wish to implant them in the Dominican Republic. Mejía, *De Lilís a Trujillo*, pp. 43–44. Knight describes Velásquez as "one of those occasional men whose intelligence commands the respect of a whole country but who lack the theatrical quality to fire the popular imagination. . . . He was the one Dominican who came nearest to knowing exactly what he was doing." Melvin M. Knight, *The Americans in Santo Domingo*, pp. 40–41.

11. Convention Providing for the Assistance of the United States with the Collection and Application of the Customs Revenues of the Dominican Republic, concluded February 8, 1907, ratifications exchanged July 8, 1907, William M. Malloy, comp., *Treaties, Conventions, International Acts, Protocols, and Agreements, 1776–1909*, 1: 418–20 (hereafter referred to as *Treaties*).

12. With the help of Professor Jacob H. Hollander, Theodore Roosevelt's special commissioner, Minister Velásquez was able to persuade creditors to settle for $17 million. The details of Hollander's mission are contained in his 250–page report to the president, *Santo Domingo Debt*. Troncoso de la Concha calculates that with the interest, the external Dominican debt prior to adjustment reached $40 million. *Génesis*, p. 52.

13. The preamble stated: ". . . .And whereas the whole of said plan is conditioned and dependent upon the assistance of the United States in the collection of customs revenues of the Dominican Republic and the applications thereof. . . . " Malloy, *Treaties*, 1:418–19. The general receiver had no executive or policy-making authority except as prescribed in the convention.

Dominican debts. The preamble also noted that disturbed political conditions in the Dominican Republic had in the past prevented the peaceable and continuous collection and application of national revenues for payment of interest or principal of debts and claims, some of which had been created by revolutionary governments. The convention was signed in Santo Domingo on February 8, 1907, and ratified by the United States on February 25. The next step was up to the Dominicans.

Article III of the convention should be noted here, for it figured prominently in the events which culminated in the military occupation of Santo Domingo by United States forces in 1916. The article stated that "until the Dominican Republic has paid the whole amount of the bonds of debt, its public debt shall not be increased except by previous agreement between the Dominican government and the United States."[14] At no time during the signing or ratifying processes did either government define "public debt" or make provision for settlement of disputes over definitions.

Cáceres, of course, had made enemies of a number of politicians out of office for his adherence to a single standard of honesty.[15] There had been many of these cases of disgruntled figures and would-be profiteers whom he had denied the usual privileges of falsifying revenue stamps, illegal manufacture of alcohol, control of customs offices, and contraband for their personal gain. Now he was strongly attacked by political opponents and by nationalists for "unpatriotically" supporting ratification of the 1907 Convention. Opposition to the convention centered on the question of national sovereignty. G. Alfredo Morales spoke in the chamber of deputies against ratification, pointing out that treaties creating protectorates and vassalage had often had as their sole objective the peaceful conquest of weak or barbaric states. He focused his objections with this sentence: "Once the Congress ratifies the convention which we have before us, the secret diplomacy of the Cabinet in Washington will undertake to complete the suspended annexation of Santo Domingo."[16]

---

14. The entire article is quoted: "Until the Dominican Republic has paid the whole amount of the bonds of the debt, its public debt shall not be increased except by previous agreement between the Dominican Government and the United States. A like agreement shall be necessary to modify the import duties, it being an indispensable condition for the modification of such duties that the Dominican Executive demonstrate and that the President of the United States recognize that, on the basis of exportations and importations to the like amount and the like character during the two years preceding that in which it is desired to make such modification, the total net customs receipts would at such altered rates of duties have been for each of such two years in excess of the sum of $2,000,000 United States gold." Ibid., 1:420.

15. Troncoso Sánchez, *Cáceres*, pp. 315-25, passim. Reporting generally on conditions in the republic, the American legation noted that Cáceres had these problems: first, people of substance and property owners favored reform in the country but were pessimistic because of the past and therefore were indifferent to political events. Second, political revolutionaries, having lost their entree to the customs houses, were trying to urge the ignorant classes to resist the government forcibly; and third, the politicians out of office did not want to see a strong government lest their political retirement become permanent. U.S., *Foreign Relations, 1907,* p. 333.

16. Quoted in Peña Batlle, ed., *Colección Trujillo,* vol. 15: *Reconstrucción financiera de la República Dominicana, 1903-1930,* pp. 192-93 (hereafter referred to as *Reconstrucción financiera*). Morales was not referring here only to the historic efforts of Buenaventura Baez and President Ulysses S. Grant to annex the Dominican Republic to the United States in 1869. U.S. Senator Welden B. Heyburn, Republican from Idaho, was quoted in the Santo Domingo *Listín Diario* of March 30, 1907, as stating that he favored the 1907 Convention because he considered it a step in the direction of annexation, and that the United States needed the island as a picket post, "lying as it does in front of the isthmian canal and in line of travel between the Atlantic seaboard and the Panama Canal." The American minister reported that the article had created

Cáceres was a realist, however, as was Velásquez, and perceived nothing in Dominican history[17] that justified the rejection of a plan that would strengthen the Dominican economy and financial structure. Both felt that the country would be safe and bound to prosper under the convention which would assure these important objectives without imposing impossible political conditions. Cáceres sought peace, progress, and an honorable solution to the horrible situation created by past international debts. He did not coerce the Congress. No patriotic Dominican could be expected to like the solution, but no other road was open. The logic of the arrangement was inescapable. Onerous as they were, these debts were just ones that had to be honorably discharged.[18] To the indignant nationalist who protested that the country's sovereignty was being trampled on, his less emotional opponent could point out that the trampling had been going on ever since 1888 when Heureaux put the collection of customs in the hands of the Westendorp agency of Amsterdam. Under that arrangement customs collections were made by a foreign organization operated by foreigners and subject to foreign-made policy decisions. The loss of sovereignty blamed on the convention had existed years before it was adopted.

In the Dominican legislature opponents of the 1907 Convention limited themselves to criticizing the agreement from the point of view of its incompatibility with the rights of Dominican sovereignty. Those who defended it, as they had in 1905, considered it a disgrace, a near fatality, but nonetheless needed to prevent a greater evil in the future. Alternatives to the proposed convention, the terms of which had been openly announced on February 23, 1907, were put forward publicly in letters to the press. One such suggestion was that the government could raise $1.2 million annual interest by arranging a reciprocal trade agreement, combined with a national lottery and increases in tobacco, alcohol, and salt taxes. The excess raised over the interest payment would be used to

---

a tremendous sensation in the Dominican Republic and led the Dominicans to believe that any treaty would have this strategic political objective. Minister H.G. Knowles to Department of State, "Report on Political Conditions," April 4, 1910, U.S., *Internal Affairs of the D.R.*

17. Referring to past revolts, rebellions, and wars, Troncoso Sánchez asks this question: "How could Cáceres and Velásquez and Tejera [Emiliano Tejera, Cáceres' Minister of Foreign Relations] be too nationalistic in the face of all that had happened? What was there in the history of revolts and *cuartelazos* [barracks revolts] that promised anything different to France, Belgium, the United States, Italy, and Germany?" *Cáceres*, p. 272.

18. Cáceres submitted the signed convention to the Congress for ratification with a long message which included the following statements. ". . . It was the unanimous hope of the country to remove the Improvement Company forever from Dominican territory . . . to free the public revenues from the inhuman assaults of those fortune hunters who incited or fomented civil war . . . to honor the Dominican name, before so respected and until very recently in an abyss, by paying just and unjust, but legal, debts which weighed upon the nation; to cement the peace so that progress would be effective and continuous, and that a useful immigration would bring us the new sap of life and of civilization. . . . All those great desires of the country, all those aspirations of patriotism will be or can be realized with the execution of the agreements that I submit to you. . . . The country will be saved and the very ones who today in error, ignorance, or passion fight against the convention and deny the immense and beneficial change it will bring to the national life, will be the first to enjoy its advantages because once made legal, they will have peace, opportunities to work, complete personal independence, and legal access to the opportunities to serve their country effectively. . . . The ever increasing orbit of our growing blunders has brought us within the radius of action of the powerful reach of the interests of the great American power, and if we insist in continuing along that path of international danger, we will be absorbed and cut into bits. The return to order, the fulfilling of contracted obligations, to the life of a civilized people impels us with irresistible charge. We either proceed as civilized beings or we disappear." *Listín Diario*, April 6, 1907.

improve roads and agricultural techniques. It was also pointed out by the author of the proposal that the United States was no longer the major market for Dominican exports since so much tobacco was sent to Germany, cacao to various European ports, and sugar prices in England were higher than in North America.[19] A second letter referred to the proposed limitations on the public debt. The writer of the letter wanted to add reservations that would permit the government to withdraw from the agreement whenever it wanted, thus ending U.S. financial intervention in the customs houses. Then, he said, the Dominicans should make a political treaty based on the Monroe Doctrine, in consonance with mutual interests and the sovereignties of the two countries. He would also make provision for the resolution of difficulties by the Hague Tribunal.[20] Neither letter gained much support in the Congress.

The debate was furious, but the Congress ratified the convention on May 3, 1907, by a vote of 17 to 7. Although virtually all Dominicans regarded the act as a national tragedy, it was entered into freely by due democratic process.

One other point merits attention here. Article II of the convention stated:

> The Dominican government will provide by law for the payment of all customs duties to the General Receiver and his assistants, and will give to them all needful aid and assistance and full protection to the extent of its powers. *The Government of the United States will give to the General Receiver and his assistants such protection as it may find to be requisite for the performance of their duties.*[21]

With reference to the article the Dominican Congress, in ratifying the convention, placed on the record a "clarification" which said: "The protection of the American[22] government for the general receiver and his assistants will only take place in case the Dominican government finds it impossible to do so." The convention was not ratified subject to this clarification, nor did either government ever incorporate it in the convention document.[23]

Cáceres' achievements included the completion of the railroad from Santiago to Moca; extensive public works improvements in Santo Domingo, such as roads, streets, and sanitation projects; liberation of the country from the "free range" curse introduced by Santana by requiring stockmen to fence their ranges;[24] reorganization of the courts and introduction of constitutional reforms intended to limit the political power of the regional caudillos; creation of a general directory of agriculture to develop modern agricultural techniques; inauguration of two agricultural experimental farms; reorganization of the army to place it more firmly under civilian control; and the increased support of institutions and projects in the field of natural sciences.

His firm administration of fiscal affairs unquestionably permitted the Dominicans to reduce their external debt and to increase the general solvency of their finances, but the country by no means enjoyed full domestic prosperity. Wages were low, local business

---

19. José R. López, *Listín Diario*, April 6, 1907.
20. Mariano Antonio Cestero, ibid., April 19, 1907.
21. Malloy, *Treaties*, 1:420. Author's emphasis.
22. I am aware that in a number of Latin American countries the adjective "North American" is commonly used to refer to the United States of America, since, strictly speaking, "American" is applicable to all countries of the North and South American continents. Dominicans, however, have frequently used "American" rather than "North American."
23. Marrero Aristy, *La República Dominicana*, 2:323. There were four clarifications in all, but only one referred to Article II.
24. Communal lands could not be fenced.

was sluggish, agricultural techniques were still backward, and immigration was needed to stimulate agriculture and industry. Crops, especially the valuable cacao, were often exported in poor condition and, consequently, with high wastage. Although Cáceres himself was popular with most Dominicans, there were a number of political leaders of all persuasions who felt that his minister of the treasury had become too much of a "grey eminence."[25] Velásquez' policies of retrenchment and fiscal integrity were viewed with hostility by regional politicians who still criticized both Cáceres and Velásquez for surrendering national sovereignty with the ratification of the convention. In 1911 a clear warning of political plots reached Cáceres.[26] Luis Tejera, the son of Cáceres' old friend and cabinet minister, Emiliano Tejera, was deeply involved, but the president chose not to act on the reports, partly because he felt confident the army could smother any insurrection. Strongly influenced by a sense of personal loyalty, he was also reluctant to break with his old friend by taking precipitate action against the son. But Cáceres did not realize that the objective of the plot was not rebellion but his own assassination.[27] He was shot on November 19, 1911, as he rode in his carriage down the Avenida Independencia. His estate consisted of some small rural properties inherited from his father, which he himself had farmed and improved, and a life insurance policy for ten thousand pesos. When he died, the country had seven million dollars in its New York bank account, earmarked for public works projects, and the external and internal debts were being paid on time.

Ramón Cáceres was personally and politically so influential that had he lived beyond 1911 he might well have changed the entire modern history of the Dominican Republic. He made enemies because he was strong, not because he was unjust. Mejía sums up the Cáceres years in language few Dominicans would challenge today:

> He created an atmosphere of security and confidence; the impartial press criticized his economic measures, the opposition press his political ones. We have never enjoyed a regime of such honest, efficient and progressive administration. . . .

And of his death:

---

25. "Comments on General Political and Economic Conditions in Santo Domingo," February 4, 1910, signed A.W. Lithgow, American Consul, Puerto Plata, U.S., *Internal Affairs of the D.R.* Lithgow added that commercially the country was in a terrible state and that the government needed an able advisor on investment of its money and other economic questions. Shortly afterward, U.S. minister Horace G. Knowles also reported to the Department of State that the main political opposition was to Velásquez, not Cáceres himself, and "that periodic visits by warships would have a very salutary effect on political conditions here. Would act as a deterrent to revolutionary scheming." U.S. Minister to Dept. of State, March 12, 1910, ibid.

26. Troncoso Sánchez and Mejía both describe in detail the events which led up to Cáceres' death. Troncoso Sánchez, *Cáceres*, pp. 370–86; Mejía, *De Lilís a Trujillo*, pp. 73–78.

27. This point has been debated. Mejía claims that the original idea of the plotters was to kidnap Cáceres and force him to resign; that to murder him would be to leave the presidency in the hands of either Velásquez or army chief Alfredo Victoria, both of whom they hated more than Cáceres. This was a political plot, not a personal one. According to Mejía, Cáceres was killed as the result of an unpremeditated, impulsive order given by Luis Tejera. Mejía, *De Lilís a Trujillo*, p. 75. Troncoso Sánchez disagrees, stating that Tejera planned to kill Cáceres since he could not defeat him politically. Troncoso Sánchez, *Cáceres*, p. 372. American Minister Russell agreed with Troncoso Sánchez' version. According to Russell's information, Tejera planned to kill Cáceres, start an uprising, and take the capital. Tejera and his accomplices had almost $50,000 in their possession and had made elaborate preparations for horses and equipment. Russell to Department of State, message no. 107, December 6, 1911, U.S., *Internal Affairs of the D.R.*

Armed revolutions, bold *golpes*, civil war, these would bring with them, as happened, complete disorganization, recession, the appearance of new military caudillos, new assassins, the involuntary increase in internal debt and, finally, foreign intervention. And this was the panorama which Dominicans contemplated during the five years initiated by that sad event.[28]

The American general receiver provided the following evaluation of the Cáceres regime:

Santo Domingo was never in such good condition as before the assassination of President Cáceres. The favorable reports were entirely warranted. The country was actually progressing. It was on the road to that development which was attracting merited attention from the outside. Now the entire complexion of things has changed, and from all sides, particularly Dominican, the views expressed are very pessimistic.[29]

The history of the five years following Cáceres' death is a painful one. During this short span, the two main warring political parties, neither of which had a distinguishable political platform,[30] refused to concede to the other a reasonable opportunity to stabilize the country or, if in power, slipped back into the weak or corrupt administrative habits of pre-Cáceres times. In late 1911 and through November 1912 the elected government of Eladio Victoria was challenged in a widespread, debilitating civil war by revolutionary forces of Horacio Vásquez, who feared that the legal government would become a military dictatorship.[31] By October 1912 not only had the cost of military operations exhausted the surplus Cáceres had left in the treasury but, according to reports received in the U.S. State Department, President Victoria had unilaterally increased the public debt by $300,000 to $400,000 and was trying to arrange still another loan by pledging customs revenues. The State Department viewed Victoria's borrowing as contrary to Dominican obligations assumed under Article III of the Convention of 1907. Minister

---

28. Mejía, *De Lilís a Trujillo*, p. 77.

29. Letter, General Receiver to Brig. Gen. Clarence R. Edwards, Chief of the Bureau of Insular Affairs, Dec. 15, 1911, signed Pulliam, U.S., *Internal Affairs of the D.R.*

30. Santana and Baez formed around themselves the important parties of the pre-Heureaux period. Party objectives were derived from the personal objectives of these leaders, usually to regain power, and this tradition persisted thereafter. In 1912 there were two parties: *Jimenistas* and *Horacistas*. The former were followers of Juan Isidro Jimenes, constitutional president from 1899 to 1902. Jimenes' father had been president in 1848. The son was a wealthy businessman of Monte Cristi and a constant conspirator against the tyranny of Heureaux. As president, Jimenes was not very effective, but he was very influential, especially in the northwestern provinces. The Horacistas were partisans of the rural caudillo of the Cibao, Horacio Vásquez, who, with his cousin Ramón Cáceres, went into hiding in 1899 after the latter killed Heureaux in Moca. Vásquez was a chronic revolutionary, cultured, good-hearted even to the point of sentimentality, but not as politically apt as those about him. Neither Jimenes nor Vásquez ever formulated specific, constructive political goals that would identify or distinguish between their parties. Both were believers in the spoils system of public administration. Both had large, devoted followings, and both were men of high personal character. Vásquez had been provisional president in 1899, again from 1902 to 1903; he would figure prominently as president from 1924 to 1930 when the Trujillo era was about to be launched.

31. The tough commander of army forces in Santo Domingo City, General Alfredo Victoria, twenty-six years old, had been responsible for the somewhat hasty installation of his uncle as provisional president after Cáceres' death. (Under the new Constitution of 1908 there was no office of vice-president.) Eladio Victoria, even after his election two months later as constitutional president, left much of the political responsibility of office to his nephew. Vásquez did not trust the motives of the latter. Mejía, *De Lilís a Trujillo*, p. 85. Eladio Victoria had been a senator from Santiago. He was a man of good intentions, but without much administrative strength or ability. Report from General Receiver to Chief, Bureau of Insular Affairs, War Department, December 5, 1911, signed Pulliam, U.S., *Internal Affairs of the D.R.*

W.W. Russell had also kept the State Department fully informed on the revolutionary disturbances created by Desiderio Arias and others along the Haitian border. During the first twenty-eight months of the receivership a total of eighteen American customs officials were killed or wounded in gun battles with contraband gangs, and now Russell advised again that customs collectors on the frontier had been unable to collect the duties and that on several occasions customs money intended for the general receivership had been seized by the revolutionaries.[32] Frontier customs houses had been abandoned because of the inability of the Dominican government to suppress revolution. In Russell's opinion the Victoria government could not maintain order; he recommended that the United States take steps to occupy the customs houses temporarily to insure collection of customs and the security of receivership personnel and to block off aid to the revolutionaries from Haitian territory. Occupation of the frontier customs houses by United States forces might inhibit revolutionary activity on the frontier and allow the government to concentrate forces in other regions, thus collapsing the main force of the revolution. Russell based the recommendation on the United States' rights under Article II of the convention, but in this September 19 communication he also suggested that effective control of the Dominican Republic by the United States, either by persuasion or by force, would be the only long-term solution to establish a policy beneficial to the country and put an end to the evils of court subservience, forced recruiting by the army, wholesale imprisonment without trial, and peculation of public funds.[33]

The events of 1912 brought into focus the two points in the 1907 Convention which led to the decision by the United States to intervene in the Dominican Republic four years later: unilateral increase in the Dominican public debt and the failure of the Dominican government to protect the collection of customs by the general receiver. In response to Russell's recommendation, President Taft sent two commissioners to investi-

---

32. Minister Russell to Department of State, report of September 19, 1912, ibid. Revolutionaries had actually assaulted and captured the customs houses and towns of Dajabón, Tierra Nueva, and Comendador. The temporary collector at Monte Cristi, who had been forced to abandon Dajabón a few days earlier, reported in writing: "The Dominican government officials do not furnish any protection whatsoever to the frontier customs service. THIS FACT MIGHT AS WELL BE UNDERSTOOD ONCE AND FOR ALL. We have ample proof to back up such a statement." General Receiver to American Minister, Santo Domingo, September 2, 1912, ibid. The refugee Dajabón collector reported frontier conditions in full detail to his superiors. He had been entirely cut off from communications; his customs functions could not be carried out; anarchy existed among both the revolutionary and the government officers, none of whom paid any attention to the orders of their chiefs; and no protection was furnished the customs collectors, nor was any likely to be forthcoming. The Dominicans have never denied their inability to protect these customs houses. Marrero Aristy generally confirms Russell's statements in La República Dominicana, 2:335. Arias had been heavily involved in revolutionary activities since early 1911 or even before. He had succeeded in gaining the cooperation of Haitian revolutionaries and outlaws who supplied him with sanctuary and material support on the Haitian side of the border. Arias, Zenón Toribio, and other anti-government leaders were able to keep government forces occupied all along the northwest frontier in an effort to protect towns and customs houses. W. W. Russell to Secretary of State, January, 1912; U.S. Consular Agent, Monte Cristi to American Consul, Puerto Plata, February 13, 1912, signed I. T. Petit, U.S., Internal Affairs of the D.R. Petit added that Arias did not seem to be popular; the people in Monte Cristi wanted peace and security. They were essentially indifferent to the central government, provided that their property and interests were protected against the raids of the revolutionaries. Businessmen in particular hated the revolutionaries, whose favorite practice in order to raise money was to impose a "voluntary" contribution on local merchants.

33. Russell was the United States minister from 1911 until early 1913 when the first Wilson

gate internal conditions in the Dominican Republic.[34] Arriving early in October they shortly afterward reported that the government was in debt by $1.2 million; that back salaries were owed government employees; that $400,000 obtained under the 1907 Convention for public works projects had been diverted to pay military expenses; and that there was a lack of military protection for the general receivership. They did not think prolonged intervention should be attempted, recommending that any action taken should be within treaty rights, with due regard to the laws and constitution of the Dominican Republic.[35] The commissioners tried but were unable to reconcile President Victoria and the revolutionaries, the most important being Horacio Vásquez, José Bordas, and Desiderio Arias. Nor were they able to persuade Victoria to agree to the appointment of an American financial advisor to audit the disbursement of the funds of a loan which the United States would be willing to consider making. The United States wanted to assist Victoria with the debts his government had incurred, but wanted as-

administration began. President Wilson reappointed him in September 1915. Thus Russell was to play a key role in many of the major decisions leading to the military intervention in 1916. His general approach toward the solution of Dominican problems and, accordingly, the diplomacy he recommended, were largely conditioned by his experiences during 1911, 1912, and 1913. Familiar with Vásquez, Arias, Vidal, and others, as well as the activities of government forces, Russell reported on July 3, 1912, that the prisons were full of political suspects, the government was disbursing enormous sums for military operations, and that government military chiefs were reported to be deliberately prolonging the revolution in order to appropriate for their personal use the money destined for the troops. (This practice was known as *filtración*.) Government salaries were two months in arrears, there would probably be a budget deficit of $600,000, and conditions due to the civil war were still chaotic. One month later, Russell reported that revolutionists were ravaging and plundering at will. The corruption of military chiefs was generally admitted. On August 19, 1912, Russell reported "the well known fact" that the government was now in arrears one million dollars, including a shortage of $150,000 from the funds Cáceres had left on deposit in New York to be used only for public works. Misappropriation had created a general shortage of funds and had led the government to use this money for purposes other than that intended. Government troops in the northwest region were abusing the campesinos and robbing them of goats and pigs—the few left after nine months of war. Officers could not restrain their men in the field. None had been paid nor was there any subsistence for them.

Thus Russell was led to write: "Only complete control by the United States of affairs in this country will bring about permanent conditions of justice and order. Any lesser control must necessarily be beneficial; one administration here would be just as good as another without our effective control." Russell to State Department, September 19, 1912, ibid.

34. William T. Doyle, Chief of the Latin American Division of the State Department, and Brig. Gen. Frank McIntyre, U.S. Army, Bureau of Insular Affairs, War Department. The commissioners were given wide authority. Their instructions from President Taft generally followed State Department recommendations to the president that the commissioners be empowered to advise the Dominican government on measures to restore and maintain peace, or, failing this, to consider the handing of a strong note to the Dominicans protesting violations of the 1907 Convention and expressing certain demands, primarily the resignation of the "unscrupulous and brutal" Alfredo Victoria, now minister of war and marine and minister of interior. Alfredo Victoria had placed his brother in direct control of the army; with his weak uncle at the head of civil government he was in a position to control all civil and military authority in the country. The State Department recommended taking all measures short of war which could be justified under the 1907 Convention if a strong note failed to achieve the desired results. It should be noted that the commissioners traveled to the Dominican Republic aboard the USS *Prairie*, which also carried 750 marines. Memorandum, Assistant Secretary of State Huntington Wilson to President Taft, Sept. 19, 1912; H. Wilson to W.W. Russell, September 24, 1912, ibid. The latter reference informed Russell of the detailed instructions given the commissioners.

35. Memorandum from McIntyre to Department of State, Oct. 8, 1912, ibid. The report of

surances that the money would be spent for the agreed-upon purposes, as well as some provision against maladministration and illegal loans. In view of the continued civil war,[36] the commissioners then applied extreme pressure on Victoria, who resigned November 26, 1912. This was the first in a series of efforts by the United States, based on the American interpretation of the Convention of 1907, to insist that the Dominican government meet its treaty obligations.[37]

Proposed by the American commissioners as a compromise candidate in the elections which followed Victoria's resignation, Archbishop Adolfo Nouel was unanimously elected to the provisional presidency by the Dominican legislature, with the approval of all of the revolutionaries except Arias. That Jimenista revolutionary continued his own war in the northwest against the Horacistas as well as the government. Nouel, who believed Arias was far more hostile to the Horacistas than to the government because they threatened his political and military influence, quickly ran into difficulties with the Jimenista element in his cabinet. At the same time, the Horacistas, placated earlier by the

---

the General Receiver on this period highlights conditions in the Dominican customs organization and the collection problems of the Receivership. U.S., *Foreign Relations, 1907,* pp. 324–30. A mounted and armed customs and frontier guard service was organized by the general receiver on September 1, 1905, to prevent smuggling along the Haitian frontier and to assist in the collection of customs at the three entry points where customs houses were maintained: Dajabón, Comendador, and Tierra Nueva. On July 1, 1908, the Dominican government undertook the operation of this service and in 1912 incorporated it into the Dominican army. In 1913 the receivership, with the approval of the Dominicans, established a new organization, the Frontier Customs Service, to assist with customs collection. In 1915 the number of mounted inspectors had to be increased greatly in order to stop the traffic in arms across the frontier. After the establishment of the U.S. military government of 1916 the Frontier Customs Service was incorporated into the Dominican National Guard on May 1, 1918.

36. Casualties in the fighting around La Vega were heavy. The American consul at Puerto Plata estimated that at least 3,000 had been killled or wounded. The same percentage of the population in the United States would reach 450,000. In the vicinity of Sánchez, La Vega, Santiago, San Pedro de Macorís, Puerto Plata, and Monte Cristi mail was disrupted; robberies and thefts were commonplace. Farmers refused to market their produce, and, accordingly, food prices were doubling. Revolutionaries were levying heavy cash contributions on merchants. Monte Cristi had no water supply. Arias' men had captured the water tanks, and the nearest water was the Yaque del Norte, two miles away. The town was blockaded on all sides. Reports of American Consul, Puerto Plata and American Consular Agent, Monte Cristi, Sept. 21, 1912, U.S., *Internal Affairs of the D.R.*

To make matters worse, a nefarious business grew up out of the misfortune of the unpaid government employees. High officials of the government, acting through other officials, became money sharks, fattening on the financial embarrassment of schoolteachers and other government employees without influence. These had to discount heavily their meager pay in order to borrow money for basic necessities. Report by General Receiver, Sept. 19, 1912, signed Pulliam, ibid. Pulliam's report was based on his interviews with Dominican officials, including the minister of finance and commerce, Francisco A. Córdova.

37. Welles, *Naboth's Vineyard,* 2:697–99. Reduced to simple terms, Victoria was given the choice of continuing in office but losing all payments from the American-controlled customs receivership, or resigning in favor of an elected government which would be protected by the United States. Vásquez was advised of these terms, which also included a warning to him that the United States would not recognize any revolutionary government and, further, that the commissioners would propose to all Dominican political leaders that they elect the archbishop of Santo Domingo as provisional president to fill out the remainder of Victoria's term. Since this solution would achieve Vásquez' objective of driving the Victorias from government, he agreed. Victoria accepted the proposal to elect Nouel, realizing that his own government must fall in any event.

election of Nouel, now returned to the political wars. Caught between the two forces and unable to control either, and victimized by Arias as well, Nouel resigned on March 31, 1913, and left the country.[38] He returned later to participate actively in his country's affairs during the military occupation from 1916 to 1924.

The years 1914, 1915, and the first half of 1916 were filled with crises, political upsets, and local insurrections created by the personal politics of Horacista and Jimenista leaders alike.[39] There was loss of private property caused by revolutionary and counterrevolutionary activity; crops were not being marketed for lack of transportation facilities; and government funds were exhausted. Central political authority, especially that of the Jimenes government in late 1915 and early 1916, was nearly impotent.[40]

38. Nouel had been sworn in on December 1, 1912. On December 4 Russell accurately predicted that the archbishop would be forced out of office early because of pressures being placed on him. On December 10, in office barely a week, Nouel told Russell he was going to resign, whereupon the United States government made every effort to encourage and support Nouel, including the dispatching of the battleship *New Hampshire* to Dominican waters. With U.S. concurrence Nouel and the Dominican Congress authorized a loan of $1.5 million, but the language of the U.S. concurrence was intended to blanket any further revolutionary activity by Vásquez: no government which was nonconstitutional or not recognized by the United States could receive any of the money. As will be seen, the U.S. government applied this same caveat to the government of Henríquez y Carvajal in the summer of 1916. U.S., *Internal Affairs of the D. R.* for December 1912.

39. Bernardo Pichardo offers a summary description of conditions in the country: the rebellion and siege of Puerto Plata in 1914, accompanied by epidemics of typhoid fever, beriberi, and dysentery; revolution in El Seibo; a bankrupt government in mid-1914; two brief uprisings in Santiago and San Cristóbal in July 1915; and the armed uprising in the capital by Desiderio Arias in May 1916. Pichardo, *Resumen de la historia patria*, pp. 356–87. The two most influential leaders in the republic were now earning political reputations in the old Dominican tradition: "Horacio Vásquez, although . . . Sumner Welles has tried to present him as a political figure of advanced ideas and great social conceptions, was not even remotely a man of the principles his supporters attributed to him. . . . Neither was Juan Isidro Jimenes, the other principal caudillo of the moment, a person in whom predominated the brilliant qualities of leadership of the Dominican people, as were attributed to him. But both put together and used for their own political purposes the great harvest of the desires of anti-Lilismo, and this was the main reason for the rapid growth of these two new and mediocre caudillos." Marrero Aristy, *La República Dominicana,* 2:269. Surviving members of the Vásquez family describe him as a big, hearty, well-liked, and honest farmer, ambitious but not especially qualified to unify and lead the nation.

40. "The overflowing ambitions and the appetites of the caudillos grew larger in direct relation to the misery which their own battles had created for the people and the State." Ibid., 2:351. Marrero Aristy attributes Jimenes' incapacity and inability to command to his age (71) and frail health.

15

THE CONVENTION OF 1907:
INTERPRETATION AND
CONFRONTATION

Shortly after taking office Woodrow Wilson announced a new policy toward Latin America which substituted sympathetic understanding and full respect for national sovereignty for the old "dollar diplomacy."[1] Eminently progressive in concept, the new policy as it was applied to relations with the Dominican Republic was in the end reduced to no more than the unilateral American interpretation of the Convention of 1907. Animated by his own high moral standards and ideals, Wilson sincerely wanted the Dominicans to put an end to revolution and establish through their own institutions a responsible, constitutional government which could and would earn their respect. He thought these conditions would logically flow from free and fair elections, bolstered by public announcements of support of the winner by the United States. In this manner the Dominicans would no longer be hindered from meeting their obligations under the Convention of 1907. Wilson's well-intentioned efforts to bring about peace in the Dominican Republic were continually frustrated not only by the weaknesses of Dominican governments but by his own failure to understand that order could not be brought about merely by his demanding free and honest elections. In all their history the Dominicans had never really participated in the institutions of representative and democratic government envisaged by their constitutions. This was an essential ingredient which Wilson and his policy advisors consistently seemed not to understand in demanding that the Dominicans cease all revolution, reconstitute regular and constitutional political authority, and hold free and fair elections to enable the people to express their real choice. When Wilson finally realized that the Dominicans could not establish stable government even with the full moral support of the United States and some open military support, he abandoned the policy of comprehending, disinterested friendship for a policy of more forceful interference in internal Dominican affairs. Some of these actions by the

---

1. Speech before the Southern Commerical Congress, Mobile, Alabama, October 27, 1913. Text in Ray S. Baker and William E. Dodd, eds., *The Public Papers of Woodrow Wilson,* vol. 1, *The New Democracy,* pp. 64–69.

United States government prior to 1915 should be reviewed. The first concerns the financial advisor and reaches back to March 20, 1914.

At the insistence of Secretary of State William Jennings Bryan, the Bordas government, which had followed that of Nouel, acceded under pressure to the appointment of an American financial expert "to aid the Dominican government to settle its debts, devise a system of public accountability, and take other measures which would assure financial order and avoid future deficits."[2] General Receiver Walker Whiting Vick, who had arrived in Santo Domingo on July 5, 1913, had all along been submitting pessimistic reports of Dominican financial affairs which reinforced similar reports Washington had been receiving since 1905. Vick wrote that an auditor was needed to keep an eye on the government's accounts. According to him, the best method of bringing about good government "is the recognition by the Dominican government of their actual condition financially, and [the U.S.] retaining control and auditorship of their receipts and expenditures. We can then assist them to pay their just debts in a reasonable and intelligent manner. The Dominican people have many excellent qualities, but they lack business and financial perspective in government affairs."[3] Vick also referred to the Dominican loan sharks who were discounting civil salaries to about twenty cents on the dollar; that is, they would loan twenty cents now and collect a dollar later when the employee was paid.

Charles M. Johnston, the man appointed to advise Bordas, was employed by virtue of the terms of the 1907 Convention, but he was not an officer of the receivership. He functioned throughout 1914, but his presence created a political crisis early in 1915.[4]

President Wilson had a direct hand in the next diplomatic move. State Department files for 1913 and early 1914 had shown that Arias was still blackmailing the government and actively disturbing the peace. Arias was a fearless guerrilla leader of the northwest frontier region, of limited culture and even less education. He trusted no one, least of all men of reputedly high political morality. Arias was neither cruel nor tyrannical, but his political objectives centered on the creation of a personal following rather than the well-being of the state. He had no principles and scruples when money was involved. Ill-advised by those around him, he was not capable of efficient or fair public administration.[5] Arias had been successful in blackmailing President Nouel in 1913. His price for cooperation included appointment of his nominees to all official posts in Monte Cristi, Puerto Plata, Santiago, La Vega, and San Francisco de Macorís; recognition by the

---

2. Bordas was told to request the financial expert if he expected to receive any financial help from the United States. Welles, *Naboth's Vineyard*, 2:729. It should be noted that the expert was to be an advisor; he was to make no fiscal decisions.

3. Letter, W.W. Vick to Boaz W. Long, Chief of the Bureau of Latin American Affairs, State Department, December 21, 1913, U.S., *Internal Affairs of the D.R.*

4. Johnston was a shrewd observer whose reports were read with interest and appreciation in the Department of State. He spent a great deal of time in Puerto Plata, then a major seaport for foreign trade. A typical report of 1914 read as follows; "Business opinion throughout the island unanimously in favor of comptrollership scheme. Politicians unanimously against it. . . . Business situation universally bad, labor unemployed; contracts repudiated; mail and telephone communications suspended; foreign commerce paralyzed; customs receipts suffering more than $100,000 monthly on account of Puerto Plata blockade. . . . These perennial revolutions will continue so long as there is a stake to be played for; they will cease when control of Santo Domingo funds passes from the hands of professional politicians who are now manipulating them. . . . Johnston." Letter, Johnston to Secretary of State, July 17, 1914, ibid.

5. Mejía, *De Lilís a Trujillo*, pp. 113, 115.

government that Monte Cristi was a fortified town under a garrison responsive only to Arias; that Arias be named government delegate in the Cibao and as such have the authority to appoint half the civil employees under his jurisdiction and all the military; that he name two of the cabinet ministers and be provided with $50,000 in gold for distribution among his followers in revolt who had been away from their homes for thirteen months; and that the garrison troops of the capital be replaced by a Monte Cristi detachment subservient personally to Arias, who would also name the comandante de armas. Arias got essentially all that he demanded from the weak archbishop; he continued to practice the same brand of patriotic blackmail on Nouel's successors with considerable success.[6] Vásquez was in revolt at this time because the Bordas government had taken the patronage-laden Dominican Central Railway concession (Puerto Plata–Santiago–Moca) away from him and given it to Arias,[7] customs collections on the frontier were being impeded, and the north coast towns were being blockaded by revolutionaries, thus cutting off both export and import trade and government revenue.[8] On March 12, 1913, Secretary of State Bryan had sent the following policy memorandum to all diplomatic officers in Latin America. It was President Wilson's declaration of policy regarding the United States attitude toward the legally constituted authorities in Latin American republics:

> Cooperation is possible only when supported at every turn by the orderly processes of just government based upon law, not upon arbitrary or regular force. . . .
> The United States has nothing to seek in Central and South America except the lasting interests of the peoples of the two continents, the security of governments intended for the people, and for no special group or interest, and the development o

6. See Report from American Legation to Department of State, December 22, 1912, signed Russell; and Russell's report January 31, 1913, of meeting between Arias and Nouel at Santiago toward the end of January when Nouel met Arias's demands, U.S., *Internal Affairs of the D.R.*

Most modern Dominican historians view Arias as a poorly educated revolutionary, a personal friend of Jimenes so politically immature that he failed to see that his so-called patriotism was damaging the nation as a whole. They see little moral distinction between Arias' open blackmail of Nouel, Bordas, and Jimenes and the "patriotic" bankers who loaned their unstable governments money at annual interest rates of twenty-five percent. Consequently there is a tendency to describe Arias today not as a blackhearted villain but rather as a revolutionary, a frontier cacique who really never did anyone any harm—*no mató a nadie*.

The American legation, the U.S. Department of State, and Jimenes himself would hardly have concurred in this time-softened description. Nevertheless, after a very interesting political conversation with Arias, the American consul at Puerto Plata whose reports indicate a shrewd knowledge of Dominican affairs, said of Arias: "The man impresses me . . . not as a bad man, deliberately doing wrong, but as a man of narrow ideals, and intensely suspicious who, even if—as may be the case—he is acting up to his light, is not likely to be of advantage to the country." Cable No. 154, American Consul to Department of State, subject: General Arias in Puerto Plata, signed Hathaway, dated November 13, 1913, ibid.

Desiderio Arias' luck ran out on June 20, 1931. He had resorted to his customary tactics against Trujillo, but this time his poor judgment literally cost him his head.

7. Vásquez was not only furious over the loss of railway patronage but was also disappointed that Bordas had not abolished the electoral college and instituted a system of direct elections under a revised constitution, as Bordas had agreed. But most alarming of all, he saw as a threat to his supremacy in the Cibao the continuing presence there of the government delegate, Desiderio Arias, who was his bitter political enemy. The sum of all these circumstances indicated to Vásquez that Bordas intended to crush him. American Consul, Puerto Plata, to Legation, Oct. 6, 1913, ibid.

8. "Political and Financial History of the Dominican Republic, 1905–1925," Latin American Division, Department of State, ibid., pp. 13–17.

personal and trade relationships between the two continents which shall redound to the profit and advantage of both and interfere with the rights and liberties of neither.

. . . I may, I hope, be permitted with as much confidence as earnestness to extend to the governments of all the republics of America the hand of genuine disinterest and friendship, and to pledge my own honor and the honor of my colleagues to every enterprise of peace and amity that a fortunate future may disclose. . . . We can have no sympathy with those who seek to seize the power of government to advance their own personal interest or ambition. . . .[9]

This United States policy toward local revolution in Latin America provided the framework for U.S. diplomacy in the Dominican Republic for the decade to follow. Bryan had then specifically warned the Dominican revolutionaries in September 1913 that the United States government would employ all legitimate means to restore order and avoid new revolutions.[10] A second pointed message contained an indication of the events still three years in the future:

Make it known to those revolutionists and those who foment revolution that as the Dominican Republic under the Convention of 1907 cannot increase its debt without the consent of the United States of America, that this government will not consent that the Dominican government increase its debts for the purpose of paying revolutionary expenses and claims; also, this Administration would look with disfavor on any administrative act that would have for its object the increasing of the taxes, thereby imposing a burden on the people, for the purpose of satisfying revolutionists; and that in view of the President's Declaration of Policy, this government shall, should the revolution succeed, withhold recognition to the *de facto* government and withhold, consequently, the portion of the customs collection belonging to Santo Domingo, so long as an unrecognized *de facto* government shall exist. Communicate the above to proper authorities. Bryan.[11]

But as 1913 wore on, internal conditions in the Dominican Republic did not improve. Revolutionary and other illegal activities of Arias cropped up repeatedly in the legation reports. By February 1914 Arias had been branded within the U.S. Department of State as a smuggler, brigand, and professional revolutionist. He was labeled as the chief menace to peace and betterment of economic conditions. "Until he is eliminated either by agreement or by being taken in some way from the scene of his activities, the Republic of Santo Domingo may not enjoy that peace and quiet which is desired by the better classes."[12] Banditry as well as the civil war against the Bordas government continued in

---

9. Ibid. Bryan was to refer to this policy frequently, not only in communications with the Dominican government and Dominican leaders, but also to avoid making commitments to American businessmen seeking protection for their Dominican interests.

10. Memorandum, Bryan to Legation, Sept. 9, 1913, ibid.

11. Bryan to American Minister, Santo Domingo, Sept. 11, 1913, ibid.

12. State Department study, "Political Conditions in the Dominican Republic Prior to and Following the Convention of 1907 between the United States and That Republic," Feb. 18, 1914, signed Jordan H. Stabler, ibid. Stabler had two recommendations of interest here. He said: "It is in the province of the American government under the terms of the Convention to arrest and imprison Arias as a malefactor who is taking the laws of the Republic in his own hands and interfering with the collection of the customs." In referring to other measures which might be taken to help the country—education, immigration, measures to improve agricultural products, interior communications—he considered education of the lower classes one of the most important. Secretary Bryan repeated Stabler's description of Arias in a later measage to Santo Domingo saying that Arias' activities must be definitely stopped because, "they are hampering the government of the United States in the fulfillment of its obligations under the Convention of 1907." Bryan to Minister Sullivan, April 4, 1914, ibid.

and around Santiago, La Vega, Monte Cristi, Puerto Plata, and other populated areas, including the Haitian frontier customs houses. Neither the lives nor the property of private citizens, Dominican as well as foreign, was safe, and the government was helpless to act.[13]

These unfortunate and apparently incurable conditions only sharpened Wilson's determination to create the machinery for reform. Accordingly, in August 1914 he personally drafted a new statement of demands for compliance by Dominican political leaders. He warned the opposing factions to cease hostilities, disperse, and reconstitute a responsible political authority. Failure by the Dominicans to organize a government acceptable to the United States would cause the U.S. to name a provisional president, sustain him in office, and support him in the exercise of his temporary authority. Wilson also demanded that elections be held thereafter, with the understanding that the United States would send observers of its own choosing. Then, if the United States government was satisfied that the elections had been free and represented the choice of the Dominican people, the United States would recognize the new president and Congress. If elections of the "right kind" had not been held, another election would be held, in which the earlier mistakes observed would be corrected. Thereafter, the United States government would feel at liberty to insist that revolutionary movements cease.

This was the so-called Wilson Plan, and Wilson's long message to the Dominicans ended with this statement of purpose of the U.S. policy: "By no other course can the government of the United States fulfill its treaty obligation with Santo Domingo or *its tacitly conceded obligation* [emphasis added] as the nearest friend of Santo Domingo in her relations with the rest of the world."[14] With this statement Wilson affirmed the right to intervene in Dominican affairs as the obligation of a friend. Under Wilson's plan, which was immediately accepted by all factions, Dr. Ramón Baez was unanimously elected provisional president on August 27.[15] Recognized by the United States, he quickly arranged for a constitutional president to be elected, which occurred on October 25, 1914. On December 5, 1914, Juan Isidro Jimenes, aging and not in good health, was for the second time inaugurated as president of the Dominican Republic.

Jimenes did not securely control his administration. He was indebted politically to

13. Memorandum from War Department to Long, State Department, dated May 20, 1914, signed Calcutt; letter ser. BIA–389(a) from Deputy General Receiver to Brig. Gen. Frank MacIntyre, May 18, 1914; and telegram, American Consul to Secretary of State, July 16, 1914, ibid.

14. Presidential draft, August 1914 (marked "Wilson Plan"), ibid.

15. Dominican writers credit the plan with bringing about peace, if only temporarily, but do not comment on Wilson's final statement concerning the United States "obligation." Public reaction to the Wilson Plan was muted. With cautious optimism *Listín Diario* expressed the hope that the United States was acting in good faith, and observed that its only legitimate role was that of advising and helping the Dominicans to learn how to govern themselves in accordance with the practices of free peoples. The paper urged Dominicans to reject anything outside these lines of action. *Listín Diario.* August 20, 1914.

Wilson's note was widely disseminated. Dominican leaders accepted it at full face value. Wilson's references to "legitimate means" of restoring order and to the theories of democracy and a republican form of government fitted their own theoretical norms and seemed to pose no threat to their sovereignty. Furthermore, the country had been subjected to a long and costly civil war which had severely damaged the economy and had posed a constant threat to the security of most of the citizens. The republic seized Wilson's ideas with no hesitation and sought out Baez, a highly respected, prominent physcian, educated in France. His personal reputation evoked the confidence and cooperation of virtually all Dominicans.

Arias and Federico Velásquez, whom he accordingly appointed to his cabinet as minister of war and navy and minister of finance, respectively. Both controlled congressional groups, although Arias was more influential. In addition there was a large Horacista segment in the Congress. When Secretary Bryan suggested in January 1915 that Jimenes recognize the American financial advisor as comptroller of Dominican finances,[16] the suggestion was roundly rejected by the Dominican cabinet and senate, particularly by the Horacista and Arias factions. Throughout the spring and into the summer of 1915 Bryan continued to battle with Jimenes over the assignment of an American comptroller.[17] After Bryan resigned in June the new secretary of state, Robert Lansing, temporarily abandoned the fight.

Meanwhile Jimenes had been unable to unite the country. His Cabinet was split and a guerrilla form of civil war continued to smolder in San Cristóbal, Puerto Plata, and the eastern provinces, especially in the vicinity of the sugar estates. Again the Dominican government was forced into financial difficulties in order to maintain military forces in the field, and again the American legation warned[18] revolutionary leaders to desist. This time, however, the landing of U.S. troops was mentioned as a possibility. The government appeared unable to control the bandits.[19] In September 1915 Wilson ap-

---

16. Marrero Aristy, *La República Dominicana*, 2:352–53. Johnston was to have responsibility, so the Dominicans were told, to prepare the national budget, which would be rigorously adhered to, and to approve and countersign all government expenditures. No expenditure would be legal without his signature.

17. Jimenes, "perhaps the only friend the Americans had in Santo Domingo," wanted to reach some sort of arrangement for American fiscal supervision, but was blocked by the overwhelming opposition of the public and Congress. Ibid., 2:355. An exchange of personal correspondence between Jimenes and Woodrow Wilson in the fall of 1915 indicated warmth and understanding on the part of each for the other's problems. Jimenes' letter could easily be interpreted (as did Secretary of State Lansing) as personal acceptance of the need to revise the Convention of 1907 to conform to the American interpretation. Jimenes, however, was reluctant to launch such a project publicly at the time, for fear of triggering a full-scale civil war. Personal letter, President Juan Isidro Jimenes to President Woodrow Wilson, October 19, 1915, U.S., *Internal Affairs of the D.R.* Bryan had also been determined to see an end to Dominican revolutions, as his earlier messages had indicated. On February 13, 1915 he told the legation: "Make it clear to them [Arias, Vidal, et al.] that this government will not permit any interference whatever with the Jimenes government . . . this government will furnish whatever force may be necessary to suppress insurrection and preserve orderly government. Any attempt to use force against the government will be dealt with immediately and firmly. The sooner this is understood by everybody in Santo Domingo the better. Bryan." Telegram, Secretary of State, to Legation, Feb. 13, 1915, ibid. Then slightly over two months later: "You will see those leaders also and notify them that this government will hold them personally responsible for any attempt which they make to interfere with government, whether that attempt is made by them directly or through their supporters. This government meant what it said when it declared that it would tolerate no more insurrections in Santo Domingo and it will furnish whatever force may be necessary to put down insurrections and to punish those guilty of exciting or supporting insurrection." Secretary of State, to American Legation, April 20, 1915, ibid.

18. This was Chargé d'Affaires Stewart Johnson's open letter to the revolutionary leaders, published in the Dominican press July 21, 1915. It brought a scorching reply from Horacio Vásquez, which, in effect, was a statement of his right to revolution.

19. José Ramón López, cited earlier for his vision and comprehension of the nation's educational and economic problems, now came forth with a warning to the Dominican people to establish peace: "Where there is guarantee for neither life nor property, we cannot look for the benefits which come from international law. . . . There are two groups in this country, one small and the other large. Both equally love the sovereignty of the Dominican Republic,

pointed William W. Russell as minister to the Dominican Republic.[20] Russell was instructed to make known immediately to the Dominican government certain circumstances which the United States viewed seriously.

On November 19,[21] Russell told the Dominicans that in the opinion of the United States government the Dominicans had consistently violated Article III of the 1907 Convention and that the United States government had the right to insist that the Dominican government observe its obligations under this article. Further, the United States government had determined that the violation of these obligations, freely assumed, must cease. Russell's note, which among other things was an American interpretation of the 1907 Convention, also referred to the increasing public debt, reliable reports of embezzlement of customs revenues, the Dominican government's failure to pay its employees, the money being paid General Arias as tribute for his cooperation with the government,[22] and the probability of complete bankruptcy should the government continue to function in this fashion.[23] To compel observance of Article III, Russell again

but while the former believes that the only force capable of supporting them and promoting growth is the force of an earnest civilization, the latter, blind and misguided and with more muscle than nerve, trusts in noise and blows to make secure the edifice.

"I am of the opinion that the national Dominican personality in its present form can endure but a few more years. . . . It is sad to confess this, but either we regulate ourselves or we will be regulated, and in the latter case, we run the danger that the regulation will destroy us." *Listín Diario*, August 11, 1915. The warning was picked up. The Puerto Plata *Boletín de Noticias* said in an August 30 editorial: "The recent warning of the American Minister to the opposition and the insistent demand that the government pacify the country are not just vain words but a serious matter that must be resolved in a short time."

20. Russell left the Dominican Republic in 1913 at the end of the Taft administration. He is not remembered with affection in the Dominican Republic because of his insistence on intervention as a solution to political difficulties. He viewed the frequent revolutions with distaste which grew stronger as succeeding administrations demonstrated the inability to govern honestly, firmly, and responsibly. Yet he was not anti-Dominican. How many Dominicans are aware that it was Russell who brought to the American military governor's attention early in 1917 the fact that exiled President Juan Isidro Jimenes was living in almost abject poverty in Puerto Rico? Russell asked the military governor to assign Jimenes a monthly pension of $200. The military governor, Captain Harry S. Knapp, heartily concurred, as did the U.S. Department of State, in approving the request. Telegram, State Department Counselor Polk to Legation, Jan. 4, 1917, United States, *Internal Affairs of the D.R.*

21. Note No. 14, ibid.

22. Arias, still Jimenes' minister of war and navy, was the government's worst enemy, who not only posed a constant military threat but also frustrated every effort of the president to get the support of Congress. At the same time, Arias forced the president "to supply him with money and more money for uses that would best suit his [Arias's] political convenience." Marrero Aristy, *La República Dominicana*, 2:358.

23. Charles M. Johnston, in several thoughtful personal letters written to Boaz Long in the State Department about the time Russell returned to the Dominican Republic, described the Jimenes administration as a divided, discordant failure. Only the fear of American intervention had kept the cabinet members from each others' throats. Jimenes was heavily criticized by his colleagues for nepotism; misappropriation of funds; lax, if not illegal, use of the executive franking privilege; abuse of customs regulations; suspension of constitutional guarantees without due authority from the Congress; unjustified and excessive political repression; increasing the public debt by over $600,000 in nine months; and failure to audit internal revenues. Filtración absorbed half of the government collections. Johnston recommended intervention with about a thousand marines to take control of the seven principal seaports, compulsory disarming of Dominicans, installation of an efficient comptrollership having authority to supervise every disbursement and to approve the annual budget, disbanding of the army and the republican guard, and creation of a constabulary under American officers. "With finances and police

advanced the plan for an American finanical advisor to the Dominican government with specific powers, as well as an American-commanded national constabulary. Under this arrangement, permitted although not specified by Article II, the defects in the financial administration of the government could be corrected and the constabulary could preserve the domestic peace, including protection of the customs houses.

The Dominican minister of foreign affairs rejected the Russell note, repeating earlier objections to American terms for the financial expert and the establishment of the constabulary. The proposed police force, according to Pichardo, would be seen by Dominicans as an abdication of national sovereignty and a continuing source of friction within the country. Pichardo went on:

> The question is not one of those which can be settled by increasing or abolishing the armed forces of the republic. The most important aspect of the matter is the economic side, and with the reestablishment of the productive vitality of the country, social and political phenomena which are presently a source of alarm both to our citizens and to foreigners will be easily and advantageously modified.
> This is the constant aim of the government, and the foreign aid which it might need and which on a number of occasions the American government has offered and which will be accepted with thanks, must be of that nature which does not wound the sensitivities of the Dominican people, since everything which upsets peace of mind must, accordingly, produce an effect contrary to the whole social life of the Dominican Republic.[24]

The last paragraph is one of the most significant in all the correspondence between the two governments during this period. The implications were broad, much broader than any of the specific points of disagreement. To the United States government, which sought peace and fiscal responsibility in the Dominican Republic even at the necessary expense of Dominican sovereignty, the Dominicans were stubbornly saying that the preservation of their national values intact was a prerequisite to any paternal, working solution, however well meaning or badly needed it might be. They would accept American aid, but only under their own terms and without authoritative American supervision.

American concepts of orderly and legal processes could not be accommodated to Dominican political realities which were being defined in near-Lockean terms by Américo Lugo:

---

under U.S. supervision, our Dominican friends could be left to play the game of self-government to their hearts' delight. They would progress rapidly, I predict, for they are an apt people, a lovable people; to know them intimately as I know them is to discover in them many admirable qualities, but the ability to administer public funds is not among their present qualifications. . . . " Letter of September 9.

Johnston described the political situation as absolutely chaotic with no effective government and disorder and confusion rampant in the capital. He had been engaged for three weeks in an audit of the books of the Dominican government. On this point he said: "Inasmuch as books have been kept for the purpose of concealing the true conditions of Dominican finances, I have a man-sized job on my hands. To do the work properly will require six months with a corps of a dozen chartered accountants. Once the work is done, some system of supervision should be insisted upon, or it will be love's labor lost." Letter of November 8, 1915; U.S., *Internal Affairs of the D.R.* Johnston also commented on a number of specific instances of contraband activity, naming the prominent individuals apprehended by customs officials.

24. Dominican Note of December 8, 1915, no. 582, to American Minister Russell, signed Pichardo, quoted in Peña Batlle, *Reconstrucción financiera*, pp. 423–27. Pichardo also quotes part of the note in his *Resumen de la historia patria*, pp. 380–81.

Revolution is the natural and necessary means for free men to employ as an ultimate resource against tyranny or despotism of their governments. It is a live and spontaneous manifestation of the inherent sovereignty that is never totally delegated; the brake which controls the impulses of the political ambitions of personal character; the only voice, finally, of heaven, expressed by the people. The United States has no moral or legal right to intervene even if the revolutionary governments continued.[25]

A letter written by the eminent poet, Fabio Fiallo, revealed a different sense of political responsibility. Fiallo attacked the Jimenes government, calling for its resignation en masse:

The obligations created by the convention remain unfulfilled, not because the republic has insufficient revenues to meet them but because those revenues have been spent on unforeseen expenses and in shameful filtraciones. This is the plain and unvarnished truth . . . . Our weakness, then, is moral and perhaps more the fault of the government than of the republic. . . . In any event, we are up against Washington and up against ourselves in a sad condition of fraudulent bankruptcy which we cannot ascribe to bad times, bad business, or to the consequences of the European war.[26]

Fiallo was no less perturbed over political conditions than Lugo (both were highly nationalistic), but he rightfully saw the cure in agitation, not revolution.

The imposition of unwanted election observers, the forced assignment of an unwanted financial advisor whose mission it was to insure observance of the convention according to the American interpretation, blunt recommendations to the Dominicans as to the manner of nominating presidential candidates, holding elections, and organizing their governments, and the enforced creation of a constabulary to be organized and commanded by Americans—all were interpreted by most Dominicans as interference in their internal affairs. As a result, the rare leader who might have seriously considered the merits of the United States' suggestions would have been almost certain to lose influence among his own followers. Yet, handicapped by a disrupted economy, no administration, unaided, could muster the political and material support to stabilize internal conditions permanently. Without the necessary financial resources to meet the costs of counterrevolutionary military operations which the government did not foresee in 1907, both the Bordas government of 1914 and the Jimenes government of 1916, with exhausted treasuries, sought approval by the United States to seek foreign loans. But prior to approving further advances of funds needed to establish order, the United States insisted on conditions which in turn were not compatible with the Dominican interpretation of the Convention of 1907 or with Dominican concepts of national sovereignty.[27] Here was a vicious circle which apparently could not be broken. To preserve their political establishment the Dominican governments needed more money;

25. *Listín Diario*, January 28, 1914.
26. Ibid., December 13, 1915.
27. Sumner Welles attributes much of this failure of communication to the poor quality of American diplomacy displayed by Secretary of State Bryan and the United States' representatives in the Dominican Republic during this trying period. Welles, *Naboth's Vineyard*, 2:716–22, passim. The repressive nature of the Victoria administration, the weakness of Nouel, and the enervating, seemingly endless revolutionary activities of Vásquez, Arias, Vidal, and others would have seriously challenged even the very highest quality of diplomacy. One hesitates to accept Welles' implication that a more professional team in 1914 and 1915 could have changed the course of events whose roots lay so deep in the distant past. Part of the problem, of course, was the preeminence of the war in Europe. It was only later that the increased attention to Latin American affairs as a result of the occupation of Santo Domingo brought a commensurate in-

the United States would provide the money, but only on terms unacceptable to the Dominican governments.

The climax occurred in May 1916, when President Jimenes tried to clip the growing ambition of Minister Arias. Arias ignited a military revolt in Santo Domingo in the presentiment of his own arrest for treason. The events which then took place between May 1 and May 6 in Santo Domingo were exciting ones and, later, controversial. Arias' forces had gained control of the capital but on May 1 were under siege by Jimenes. That same day the chamber of deputies, intimidated by Arias, impeached the president for "unconstitutional acts." Jimenes claimed the impeachment procedures were illegal, and Minister Russell himself reported that according to the Constitution the president was not incapacitated in the absence of conviction by the Senate. The Senate approved the House action on May 2 and set May 5 as the date for the president to answer to the proceedings. Meanwhile the fighting between the Arias and Jimenes forces had become serious enough to provoke the landing of U.S. forces.[28] President Jimenes may or may not have requested assistance from the United States forces which had just arrived from Haiti to support his government. Prior to May 3, U.S. naval forces en route to or in Dominican waters were advised of the situation ashore and told to take such steps as deemed necessary. Captain W.S. Crosley, U.S.N., commanding officer of the USS *Prairie* and also the senior naval officer at Santo Domingo, had gone ashore on May 2. He personally viewed the military situation and decided that it would be necessary to land troops to protect the American legation. On May 3 he issued a newspaper warning alerting all Dominicans to the certainty of rapid counteractions should they commit any hostile acts in case of a landing by U.S. forces. (This was the warning that alarmed Henríquez y Carvajal.) Crosley could not obtain permission to proceed with the landing until May 5. When more fighting broke out ashore Minister Russell requested that Crosley land his entire force of embarked marines and march them to the legation.

---

crease in the number of personnel assigned to the Latin American Affairs Division in the Department of State. By 1924 there were seven assigned; ten years earlier there had been only three or four.

28. Federico Henríquez y Carvajal, president of the Supreme Court, and whose brother Francisco was shortly to become provisional president, records his last-minute effort to prevent the landing of U.S. forces. On May 4, after receiving word that such a landing was imminent, he sought out Desiderio Arias, who admitted that there was a need for concerted action. Arias added that he was prepared to make any sacrifice, even that of voluntary exile, to prevent the Americans from landing on Dominican soil. Asked if he would consider the nomination for the presidency, Henríquez y Carvajal told Arias that he would not leave the Supreme Court. Arias then said that he would agree in advance to any arrangement which the Supreme Court president could work out personally with President Jimenes. An hour later Henríquez y Carvajal met with Jimenes and his advisors. The latter either could not agree on a course of action or were dazed and rendered ineffective at the imminence of failure. Thus no positive action to forestall the landing was taken by Jimenes, who it must be noted in all fairness, was sick in body and spirit. Federico Henríquez y Carvajal, *Nacionalismo*, pp. 4–5. Arias' offer of self-sacrifice for the good of his country came years too late and was never accepted. Jimenes said later in the year in a newspaper interview that Arias was personally responsible for the overthrow of his government and thus "for the occupation of the Dominican Republic by forces of the United States. Arias was responsible for all of the misfortunes which have happened in the Dominican Republic and for the loss of lives which has accompanied the American intervention. . . . He was my Secretary of War, and when I fell ill and absented myself from the Capital, he took advantage of the first opportunity to launch a revolution. If Arias had not revolted, there would have been peace in the Republic, and the American intervention would never have taken place." *New York Herald-Tribune*, Sept. 4, 1916, carried in *Listín Diario*, Sept. 5, 1916.

Both U.S. Secretary of the Navy Josephus Daniels and Secretary of State Robert Lansing were aware of the impending landing. An initial force of almost five hundred sailors and marines landed at Fort San Jerónimo, four miles west of the capital, on May 5, 1916. The decision to land was made by authorities on the scene, not in Washington. The stated purpose of the landing was to protect the American legation located in the residential section of Gascue in the western part of the capital. Thus the marines could land and march to the legation without becoming actively involved in the fighting farther east. They reached the legation at 4 P.M. without casualties, and the Dominicans continued to fight.

On May 6, Russell advised the State Department that "the President is out of ammunition and cannot win and has requested us to take the city. And if we do this, it would be for ultimate occupation and not for Jimenes, as it is a question whether we can hold it against the claim of Congress [Dominican] that no matter what the President was by commission, he has been incapacitated by the House passage of the impeachment bill." Faced with betrayal by Arias, on one hand, and unwilling to force a bloody confrontation with the Americans or accept intervention, on the other, Jimenes announced his resignation on May 7, leaving the government in the hands of the council of ministers. During a supreme crisis he simply abandoned the field.[29] The controversy usually raised by Dominicans concerns the landing of troops, which the Dominicans have claimed had never been requested by their government. Russell and Welles say that Jimenes asked for troop assistance but later retracted. Pichardo violently denies that his government consented.[30] It is a matter of historical regret that there is no written record of Jimenes' words.

Protection of the general receivership and foreigners in the city was also considered necessary. Some sixty women and children sought refuge aboard the *Prairie*. Among the incidents reported by the ship was the deliberate bombardment of the American legation by an armed Dominican ferryboat; it scored several hits while the American flag was flying.[31]

With the arrival of Rear Admiral William B. Caperton and more American marines from Haiti on May 13, however, the mission of the landing force took on broader dimensions. Caperton took command of all United States forces in the Dominican Re-

---

29. On May 7 Lansing queried Russell concerning a Navy report from Santo Domingo that Jimenes had canceled the request for occupation of the city and had the evening before placed his resignation in Russell's hands. Russell confirmed the report and strongly advised that the landing force and all protective naval forces be kept in place, including destroyers then off the ports of Sánchez, Puerto Plata, and San Pedro de Macorís.

By May 8 the Dominican government was in the hands of four cabinet ministers; the capital and the country at large were quiet, and a landing force of almost 600 U.S. sailors and marines was ashore, but not in occupation. Minister Russell wanted a full regiment of marines instead of the 370 he had available. Lansing approved the idea and told Russell to request more troops through the senior naval officer present. Letter, Secretary of the Navy to Secretary of State, serial 27818–24–152, May 3, signed Josephus Daniels; message, Russell to Secretary of State, 6:00 A.M., May 6; message, Department of State to American Legation, S.D., May 7, 2:00 A.M., signed Lansing; message, American Legation, S.D. to Department of State, May 7, 7:00 A.M., signed Russell; message, American Legation S.D. to Department of State, May 10, 11:00 A.M., signed Russell. U.S., *Internal Affairs of the D.R.*

30. Pichardo, *Resumen de historia patria*, p. 386.

31. Message, C.O. *Prairie* to Secretary of the Navy, FD–1755, May 6, 1916, U.S., *Internal Affairs of the D.R.* The files reflect no confirmation of the report or give any indication of the actual damage, if any, sustained.

public. He and Russell signed and delivered an ultimatum to Arias and two of his principal associates to surrender and turn over their arms and ammunition by 6 A.M on the 15th or be disarmed by force.[32] With about 200 men Arias discretely abandoned the capital without a fight.[33] His force was later broken up by U.S. marines in the Cibao. On the morning of May 15, 1916, the marines peacefully occupied Santo Domingo, marking the first American military occupation in the Dominican Republic. Small detachments were quickly stationed near Puerto Plata, Monte Cristi, and other strategic locations throughout the country for the purpose of "supporting the constitutional government, preserving peace and order, and protecting lives and property of American citizens and other foreigners."[34]

The government remained in the hands of the Dominicans, who continued to ignore the American insistence for modification of the 1907 Convention.[35] Another political demand was even more aggressive. Minister Russell, contemplating the leverage offered by the presence of U.S. forces during any election in the near future, recommended that the United States move to have the financial advisor to the Dominican Republic appointed and that whoever became the next president be informed that the United States would stay in the Dominican Republic until the reforms proposed were well under way.[36] The immediate reply from the State Department to Russell contained policy which prepared the ground for the establishment of military government by the United States:

> Inasmuch as the United States will not tolerate revolutions, and will if necessary enforce the peace in Santo Domingo, the government cannot countenance the election of Arias or any of his friends. . .because this will lead to revolution and bloodshed. The Department believes that the present *status quo* should be maintained until peace is restored, but if the Senate insists upon elections, no candidate should be chosen who is not acceptable to this country and who will not be in sympathy with the policy of the United States. . . .[37]

---

32. The Spanish version is contained in Mejía, *De Lilís a Trujillo*, pp. 125–26.

33. Arias freed the military prisoners; then he and his forces fled northward with all the arms and ammunition they could carry. He compromised the capital and then abandoned it without striking a blow. Arias' original force consisted of about 500 men. Several diplomatic reports based on personal interviews with Arias from 1914 through 1916 indicate that the American landing may have taken Arias by surprise. He had expressed contempt for Americans, convinced that they might talk but would never act.

34. Orders of Commander, Cruiser Squadron to C.O. *Salem*, serial 5181–15, May 23, U.S., *Internal Affairs of the D.R.* Senior naval officers invariably used this phraseology in orders issued to subordinate units.

35. President Wilson approved instructions for Russell by which Russell was to try to obtain agreement on the financial advisor, the constabulary, a protocol for settlement by arbitration of all pecuniary claims, a survey of the republic for tax purposes, and the right to intervene in the Dominican Republic for the maintenance of a government adequate to protect life, property, and individual liberty. Memorandum to Counselor Polk, June 3, 1916, signed by Woodrow Wilson, ibid. Russell was also told to request further instructions if he could not obtain these rights. Russell took the matter up with Foreign Minister Bernardo Pichardo, who refused to accede. According to a memorandum for record, Latin American Division of the State Department, the U.S. took no further action because President Wilson was not prepared to press the matter. It should be noted that the modifications included those contained in Russell's note of November 19 of the preceding year.

36. Message, June 2, 1916, Russell to Secretary of State, ibid.

37. Telegram, June 3, 1916, State Department to Legation, Santo Domingo, signed Polk, Counselor, ibid. The department's instructions did not provide guidance in case the Dominicans ignored the U.S. conditions.

In other words, before any presidential candidate could receive the United States' stamp of approval, he must first make a pre-election commitment to concede to the United States the powers which the United States had not been able to obtain through diplomatic channels. Acquiescence in the United States' interpretation of the Convention of 1907—that is, Dominican violations of Article III gave the United States the right to control all Dominican finances and the proposed constabulary, as well as certain other measures of control, were to be made prior conditions for election.

Rear Admiral Caperton reported a meeting with Archbishop Nouel toward the end of June 1916 which revealed the deep disillusion the respected ex-president still felt. He had no hope that any diplomatic solution short of one imposed by the United States would produce a change in Dominican politics. Nouel did not elaborate on the nature of such a contingency, but the report must have given Secretaries Lansing and Daniels every reason to continue to press the American demands for reform. Nouel told Caperton that the Dominican people would be glad to have the help of the United States and that he too would do everything within his control to help the United States in what it was trying to do.[38] Lansing reacted positively to Caperton's report. In a confidential memorandum to Counselor Polk shortly afterward, Lansing said:

> I think that constant pressure should be exerted to bring about the necessary reforms to prevent the Treasury being plundered by government officials. That, and a Constabulary system, will ensure peace in the Republic. We should endeavor to secure a treaty or amendment of the present treaty so that it will be similar to our own treaty with Haiti. The peace of the whole island depends upon similar financial control in the two republics. Otherwise, revolutionary movements are fostered across the international boundary.[39]

The Dominicans, however, not only resisted the American diplomatic pressures but promptly took a step that circumvented the American demands for a pre-election commitment. On July 25 the Congress, in accordance with constitutional procedures, elected as provisional president, Francisco Henríquez y Carvajal who at the time was living in seclusion in Santiago, Cuba. No American official had anticipated this turn of events; time and space factors did not permit consultation prior to the inauguration. The new provisional president took the oath of office on July 31, 1916.

---

38. Caperton's long message is quoted in part: "Nouel says that he loves his people but has no faith in them because he knows them so well; and that they will make many promises but will keep none of them; that the Senators and Deputies cannot get together and select a neutral, one unaffiliated with revolutionary parties, because each faction is determined upon selecting its own candidate and will agree to no compromise, no matter how the interests of the country may suffer; that the reasons actuating these Senators and Deputies are simply a desire to make money and to have power for the purpose of making money for themselves. He states that the whole lot are nothing but selfish grafters; he also states that the Secretaries of State (the Cabinet Ministers) who are in opposition to these Deputies and Senators are even worse than the Deputies and Senators and that he has no hope of any good coming out of this crowd.

"He says that the only hope for good order, prosperity and decency in the Republic of Santo Domingo is that the United States should force these things on Santo Domingo; that the sentiment of the Dominican people is not against what the United States wants to do, and that the people themselves would be glad to have the help of the United States; that he, the Archbishop, would use every power within his control, and with the help of the clergy of his Church, to help the United States in what it is trying to do." Commander, Cruiser Squadron to Secretary of the Navy, message dated June 27, 1916, ibid. This conversation should be compared with that between Nouel and Captain Harry S. Knapp, USN, on November 27, 1916.

39. Memorandum, Lansing to Polk, July 3, 1916, ibid.

The State Department pressed the same demands as before, this time as the price for diplomatic recognition. Henríquez y Carvajal was willing to compromise within the limits of the Dominican Constitution, but none of his suggestions was acceptable to the Americans because they restricted the U.S. strictly to advisory roles. Past experience had demonstrated to the State Department that nothing less than active American control could bring about the necessary reforms. Francisco J. Peynado, then the minister of the treasury, encouraged the Dominican president to hold his ground: "In the serene light of an impartial conscience it will become evident that acceptance by the Dominican government of the previous demands would constitute the absolute loss of all attributes of sovereignty."[40]

Diplomatically there was deadlock. On the economic side there now developed a new and heavier pressure produced by Russell's instructions to the general receiver of customs to suspend all disbursements of Dominican funds to the government, which the United States had not recognized.[41] Withholding the funds plunged the Dominican governmenti nto deeper financial crises and even prevented payment of salaries to public employees.[42]

In the Congress political leaders seemed unable to formulate a national, coordinated course of action. There was no general plan for armed resistance, nor was there a willingness to accept American control. Did the continued failure of the majority of the people's representatives to act confirm the criticism of their selfish, narrow leadership, criticism voiced by Archbishop Nouel, Charles M. Johnston, José Ramón López, and Fabio Fiallo, among others? Did their stubborn insistence reflect the true desire of the majority of Dominicans, most of whom could not even spell the word "sovereignty," but who had suffered so inordinately from the effects of the almost continuous personal revolutions sponsored by their leaders?

The relationship between the two countries was not improved by the increasing number of arrests made by American military patrols, shooting and street crime incidents charged to American military personnel, by the overbearing attitude of some marine officers, and by a number of cases of mistreatment of citizens by American troops who would never have dared to conduct themselves in a similar fashion in their own country. In the general circumstances which existed at the time the natural reaction of the Dominicans, aided by a propensity for exaggeration and rumor—*el comadreo*— would be to inflate both the number and seriousness of incidents. They could also be expected to commit provocative acts as serious as the bold, premeditated murder of an American marine officer aboard ship in San Pedro de Macorís. The murderer was a sixteen-year-old boy, Gregorio Gilbert, who killed one officer and wounded others, "with a certain insolence very typical of his age."[43]

40. Troncoso de la Concha, *Génesis*, p. 69.

41. When Russell advised the Dominican government that the United States would proceed to take control of all Dominican finances, he cited his earlier note of November 19, 1915, and the rights accorded the United States under the terms of Article III of the 1907 Convention. Note 57, Russell to Bernardo Pichardo, June 5, 1916, U.S., *Internal Affairs of the D.R.* Pichardo replied on June 6 that Article III gave the United States no such right. Russell ignored the Dominican reply and gave the suspension order on June 16.

42. The Dominican press carried almost daily editorials and special articles protesting American demands and denying that the Dominican government had violated the 1907 Convention. Only occasionally did a letter appear urging Dominicans to solve this problem soon or else expect to lose their autonomy. One writer asked the question: "Those who say the country will not concede—how do they know if the country or even two thirds of it are disposed to fight?"

43. Mejía, *De Lilís a Trujillo*, p. 130.

With respect to the occupation forces, there is no evidence to indicate that they, at least at this time, had received special training or instruction which might render their presence as representatives of the United States more palatable. They were invaders, and they had landed prepared for battle. Among them were officers and men from southern states who would treat the Dominicans as a racially inferior, conquered people. No greater insult could have been devised. There were proven cases of abuse by marines and of crimes not excused even by the exigencies of guerrilla warfare in the eastern provinces. Yet all these acts were contrary to the policies of the American authorities and were not condoned by them. The acts should be considered for what they were: offenses no less repugnant to the vast majority of Americans in the Dominican Republic and in the United States than to the Dominicans themselves. Unfortunately, the memory of the acts could not be obliterated. Marrero, who notes also that language problems caused some of the difficulties, has recognized the essential justice of the above observations when he comments on these cases:

> Nevertheless, one cannot in all fairness pretend that the American people were responsible in any way for the excesses committed by ignorant soldiers, at times exasperated by fear of a guerrilla warfare that delivered death to them from the jungle of an unfamiliar country, but such events serve to demonstrate once again that the policy of a powerful nation to intervene by force in the internal affairs of another smaller one to impose "democracy" or administrative norms considered better by the oppressor nation, only leads to the discredit of the one who commits such acts and to widen for a long period of time the gap of misunderstanding which might separate the oppressor and the oppressed.[44]

On the Dominican side there were sporadic attacks on American marine detachments, sniping,[45] and the ever active Arias, who, with his armed band, was doing considerable damage to property in Puerto Plata, especially American property. Arias had violated an agreement with Caperton to disarm his men.

The first official mention of a U.S.-controlled government appeared in a report from Russell in September.[46] He had heard a rumor that Henríquez y Carvajal might resign, and if this were true, chaos would follow. He was certain that only a recognized de facto

---

44. Marrero Aristy, *La República Dominicana*, 2:382.

45. Most of the incidents took place in the eastern provinces and in the capital. Elsewhere, relations between marines and Dominicans were more amicable, especially in the Cibao. *Listín Diario,* October 23, November 13, 1916. As a result of their personal experiences many Veganos remember the Americans as tough but fair. *Listín* also carried a report on November 7, 1916, of a meeting between the attorney general of Santo Domingo, Nicolás Pichardo, and the marine officer commanding forces ashore. Pichardo was upset over the atrocities which were being reported, whereupon Colonel J.H. Pendleton told him that as chief of occupation forces and as a citizen of a civilized country he, Pendleton, was vitally interested in not letting a single marine-committed crime go unpunished, where proof was clearly established. Pendleton asked to be advised immediately of any crime allegedly committed by an American marine so that military investigators could parallel those of the court.

46. Telegram, Russell to State Department, September 5, 1916, U.S., *Internal Affairs of the D.R.* Both State and Navy Departments concurred with Russell. On October 27, Russell again discussed the matter of a U.S.-controlled government in a long memorandum to the State Department. He believed there were two alternatives: a junta of the best Dominican elements under U.S. control, or military control by an American governor. The latter option would probably be too extreme a solution, would require full-scale martial law, would probably involve more U.S. forces, and would be criticized by other Latin American republics.

government or a government controlled by the United States could succeed. By the end of October the State Department had become worried about sporadic incidents of armed violence, one of which claimed the lives of a marine officer and a sergeant. It appeared to the department that a declaration of martial law throughout the country might be necessary.[47] Within the department there was also considerable concern over the responsibility of the United States for the deteriorating economic conditions in the Dominican Republic due to the suspension of payments from the general receivership.

On October 31, 1916, officers in the State and Navy Departments came to the conclusion that because of the continued political impasse with the Henríquez y Carvajal government, violence in the country, and the continued transgressions of the disreputable Arias, the United States would either have to remove the occupation forces or institutionalize their presence, up to this point intended as a temporary measure. The preference determined after lengthy conference[48] was to declare martial law, leave the government in the hands of the Dominicans but under U.S. military government control, retain the function of collecting the revenues, resume distribution of funds, and proceed to establish the constabulary. The group agreed that "the landing of our forces was for the purpose of upholding the then constituted government and of putting down revolution in accordance with our interpretation of the Convention and our statements in this regard, and keeping order in the country."[49] There was no mention of Caribbean military strategy or of American economic interests in the Dominican Republic. The group also drafted a proclamation for a prospective military governor, placing the Dominican Republic in a state of military occupation. This was preparatory planning only; no authority had been granted to declare martial law or take any of the other measures contemplated.

On November 20 a legation message reported the probable election of a pro-Arias majority of senators and deputies.[50] The effect was momentous. Lansing immediately reviewed the Dominican situation with Stabler and asked him to put their conclusions in a memorandum. Stabler recommended martial law and military occupation based on the 1907 Convention, as interpreted by the United States, because of: first, probable control of the Dominican government by Arias; second, the refusal of the Henríquez y Carvajal government to meet the views of the United States; and third, the economic crisis in the Dominican Republic brought on by nonrecognition and the withholding of

---

47. Memorandum, J. H. Stabler, Latin American Division, to Secretary of State, October 30, 1916, ibid. Russell and the Navy Department agreed with Stabler's conclusion.

Stabler was no stranger to Dominican affairs or to Russell personally. He had served in the Latin American Division until mid-1914 and returned as chief exactly two years later. Most important, he and Russell understood each other's attitudes and problems, a critical factor in the development of the department's policy toward the Dominican Republic.

48. State Department Counselor Frank Polk presided. Present were: Admiral W.B. Benson, Chief of Naval Operations; Captain Harry S. Knapp, Navy Department; W.W. Russell, State Department; and Jordan H. Stabler, Chief of the Latin American Division, State Department. Memorandum of meeting, October 31, 1916, signed Stabler, ibid.

49. Ibid.

50. Cable, Legation to State Department, November 20, 1916, signed Brewer, ibid. Brewer (Chargé d'Affaires John Brewer) predicted that if presidential elections were held as contemplated, the majority of the Congress would be for Arias, and since Henríquez y Carvajal was an Arias man, Arias would then have full control of the government. It should be noted that Brewer's cable was essentially a prediction, but the prospect it offered was enough to trigger the plan for intervention.

funds, a crisis for which the U.S. government would not like to bear responsibility.[51] Stabler also pointed out that Captain Knapp was arriving that same day at Santo Domingo in his flagship, the cruiser *Olympia,* and should be instructed to execute the plan.[52]

Lansing concurred with Stabler's recommendations on November 22 and sent them to President Wilson, saying that the United States should determine a course of action immediately; otherwise revolution and economic disaster in the Dominican Republic were imminent.[53] The moment of truth had arrived.

President Wilson's reply to Lansing on November 26, 1916, was to approve the draft proclamation, with one minor change, and to authorize the occupation. His memorandum to Lansing began with these words: "It is with the deepest reluctance that I approve and authorize the course here proposed, but I am convinced that it is the least of evils in sight in this very perplexing situation."[54] With Wilson's approval, the plan for occupation was put in effect.

---

51. Memorandum to Secretary of State, November 21, 1916, signed Stabler, ibid.

52. Knapp had just been ordered to sea duty as Commander, Cruiser Squadron, Atlantic Fleet.

53. Letter, Secretary of State to the President, November 22, 1916, signed Lansing, ibid. Lansing added some words of praise for Knapp's judgment and discretion, saying that he knew Knapp well and that he had just been given command of the naval squadron in Dominican waters. Knapp had been a Navy Department representative on the Joint State and Navy Neutrality Board established by Lansing in mid-August 1914.

54. Memorandum, President Wilson to Secretary of State, November 26, 1916, ibid.

16

CONFLICT OF NATIONAL INTERESTS

These chapters are primarily concerned with the fact of intervention and how effectively the United States military government in the Dominican Republic exercised certain of its powers after November 1916. A debate over the morality or legality of President Wilson's decisions will not change the conclusions relevant to this book. Still, having set forth the pertinent historical facts, I would be remiss in not reviewing and appraising the American president's action.

Protection of American economic interests in the Dominican Republic did not form a part of Secretary Lansing's recommendations to the president in November 1916. There is no evidence that Wilson was influenced by the scope of American investments in deciding to order the intervention. The State Department had received a number of letters from U.S. sugar companies from 1912 on, pointing to the turbulent conditions in the Dominican Republic and asking the U.S. government to use its friendly offices to secure peace and a stable government there,[1] for fear the turbulence would spread to the sugar estates. The department, nevertheless, refused to make specific commitments as to what action, if any, it would take. Even when repeated appeals indicated that bandit operations, looting, and damage to the sugar companies' property appeared to be getting out of hand, the department replied to the companies' New York lawyers, saying only that, "In the event it is necessary, appropriate steps will be taken for the

---

1. Most of the letters in the State Department records were from Coudert Brothers of New York and Paris, who were counsel for six sugar companies in the Dominican Republic. A representative of Coudert asked for and was given an interview on April 26, 1912 at the department. He left the meeting apparently satisfied at what the department was doing. Memorandum of interview, W.T. Doyle, Chief of the Latin American Division; U.S., *Internal Affairs of the D.R.* In every case recorded, the State Department's response was to mail a copy of President Wilson's Declaration of Policy with no comment, or else simply to state that a U.S. ship was in the area [as had been the case more or less continually since 1910] and that the department hoped for an early return of quiet.

protection of property situated in the Romana district."[2] The lawyers made frequent reference in mid-1915 to "steps to protect the ten million dollar investment from public pillage and plunder," but the most satisfaction they ever received was a statement from Lansing that "things were normal when you wrote your letter and telegram. In the event of future disorders we will consider appropriate measures."[3] Although property damage was sustained by Americans as well as foreigners, the department made clear that it would not react to pressure. It believed the outbreaks were sporadic and not serious enough to intervene. This was also its reaction to British reports that British lives and property were threatened by civil war in and around Sánchez.

Only once did the State Department heed the sugar companies—after the marines had landed. As the closing paragraph of a message to Russell concerning congressional elections in the Dominican Republic, Lansing added almost as an afterthought: "The following sugar companies at or near Macorís request that a detachment of marines be detached to that vicinity to protect properties: Consuelo, Quisqueya, Santa Fe, San Isidro. Also Ansonia at Azua and La Romana. Transportation will be furnished by company tugs. Confer with [Rear Admiral] Caperton as to advisability of compliance."[4] Russell answered immediately after consulting with Caperton: "With present force of less than 600, it is impossible to effect disarmament of the revolutionary element throughout the country, and no force can be spared for the protection of the sugar estates. I have conferred with Admiral Caperton on this account."[5] Caperton kept himself informed about the situation in La Romana where there was the greatest amount of bandit activity, but he remained reluctant to do anything to protect the sugar estates. He even complained about the persistent requests from Mr. Van Alen Harris, manager of the Central Romana, for special consideration.[6] There appears to have been no general State Department policy to guide the American forces. Decisions were made on the scene by local commanders.

The sugar estates existed prior to 1916, but they were relatively small. Total production in 1893 from all of them, Dominican and foreign-owned, was only 35,547 tons. In 1902 total production was 45,723 tons, and by 1915 had reached only 110,005 tons annually, an increase of about 64,000 tons after 13 years.[7] By comparison, production in 1926 was 360,415 tons. The big business of the early years of this century was trade with Germany in cacao, tobacco, and sugar. American economic interests in the Dominican Republic were not of great importance in 1916, although as the first American military

---

2. Letter, Alvey A. Adee to Lorenzo Semple of Coudert Brothers, August 2, 1915, ibid. Semple even sent the department clippings from *Listín Diario*, which suggested strongly that a full-fledged revolutionary movement was forming in the eastern provinces.

3. Letter, Lansing to Semple, August 8, 1915, ibid.

4. Message, Lansing to Russell, May 17, 1916, ibid.

5. Message, Russell to Lansing, May 18, 1916, ibid. Here again, the question of protection of American property was incidental to the main point of the message, which concerned commerce and elections.

6. Letter, serial 50099–16, Commander, Cruiser Squadron, Atlantic Fleet to Secretary of the Navy, subject: "Operations of Commander Cruiser Squadron Atlantic Fleet in Haiti and Haitian waters and at Santo Domingo City from 12 May 1916–19 May 1916," ibid.

7. Junta Nacional, *Informaciones*, table 73, and Juan Sánchez Guerrero, *La caña en Santo Domingo*, passim. The latter is perhaps the best, detailed, factual study of the development of the great *ingenios* available in the Dominican Republic. Although he includes data from the colonial period, Sánchez Guerrero's unpublished, unbound work is a history of the individual sugar enterprises, commencing with the Cuban immigration of 1868. A copy was made available to me from the Vicini interests through the kindness of Dr. Freddy Prestol Castillo.

governor recorded, one could not deny that foreign sugar corporations were engaged in business in the Dominican Republic for not completely altruistic purposes.[8]

The security of the Caribbean area and the defense of the Panama Canal were key factors in the strategic planning of the United States after 1905. The minutes of the Joint Board of the Army and Navy,[9] from its inception in 1903 to its reorganization in 1919, as well as the log book of all papers acted on during this period show that military strategic planning for the Caribbean was based on the Monroe Doctrine. The development of this national military strategy in worthy of consideration.

Navy plans submitted to the joint board in 1904 contained consideration that the Caribbean would have to be protected against attack by a hostile coalition. Protection of trade—and, therefore, the Panama Canal—was to be the primary objective. The most likely enemy would be a coalition of Russia, France, and Germany. In this event, first-priority planning would provide for the defense of Puerto Rico and Cuba, occupation of Haiti and Santo Domingo,[10] capture of Martinique, achievement of dominance in Venezuela and Colombia, and defense of Panama.

Santo Domingo was not mentioned again until third-priority planning, based on the possibility of a hostile French and German coalition "attacking" the Monroe Doctrine in South America. In this contingency, navy plans contemplated the occupation, or at least defense, of Haiti and Santo Domingo. In all, there were six priority categories of plans, the lowest of which was based on operations against Germany alone in southern South America.

Army plans, also submitted to the joint board, took into account that the Roosevelt Corollary might force the United States to intervene in the domestic affairs of an independent state south of the United States for the purpose of establishing and maintaining an orderly government therein. According to the army's plan, the Monroe Doctrine, no matter what the wording with which it was originally promulgated, had been accepted by the American people, making the United States not only the pro-

---

8. I have interviewed a number of Dominican historians on this point of economic interest. A minority, of extreme liberal persuasion, insist that Wilson was guided by economic considerations but admit there is no documentary evidence. These economic historians base their argument on the record of the increase in sugar production after 1920 in the American-owned mills, which, they say, thereby demonstrates that the earlier decision to intervene had as its real objective the forming of latifundio and the economic penetration of the republic. The theory lacks credibility. A number of Dominican historians would, however, point out that the defense of the Panama Canal, the possibility of the United States entering the war, and the German influence in the Dominican Republic, where there were German citizens, newspapers, business houses, and social clubs, were elements in the State Department's and Wilson's policies, although none of these considerations had a critical influence on the decision to occupy their country.

9. The joint board was formed on July 17, 1903, by agreement between the Secretary of War and the Secretary of the Navy. In accordance with its instructions the board held such regular and extraordinary sessions as advisable for the purpose of conferring upon, discussing, and reaching common conclusions regarding all matters calling for the cooperation of the two services. The board's recommendations were forwarded to the service secretaries for appropriate action. The joint board was the forerunner of what today is the Joint Chiefs of Staff organization. Appointments to the board, four senior officers from each service, were made by the respective service secretaries. The board was greatly concerned with port and harbor defense, defense of the Panama Canal, and the military security of insular possessions and the naval base at Guantanamo, Cuba. Captain Harry S. Knapp, U.S. Navy, the first military governor of Santo Domingo, reported to the board on April 18, 1910, for duty as a member and recorder.

10. The reference here was to the country, not the capital city.

tector of independent American states against foreign conquest but the protector of the people of an American province (for example, Cuba) belonging to a foreign power (for example, Spain) against intolerable oppression by that power.

Army planners estimated that the next war would come about through one of the various applications of the Monroe Doctrine, possibly a war of intervention by the United States with a Latin American country, at the outset, with the approval of the New World, and without foreign complications. Then with intervention of a foreign power likely in order to protect the interests of its nationals, the need would arise for the U.S. to defend Puerto Rico, Santo Domingo, and Cuba. Accordingly, the following additional general planning assumptions were posted: first, that the United States would intervene in some South American country (Venezuela, for example) (a) to assist that country in ousting an assumed foreign power, or (b) against the two as allies; and second, that the theater of war would include the Caribbean Sea and the Philippine Archipelago.

The proposed army and navy strategies were considered by the joint board. Later in 1904 Admiral George Dewey, senior member of the board, issued a joint planning directive for the two services containing the basic assumption that the most probable cause of war would be some act or purpose undertaken by a European power which "conflicts with the policy enunciated by President James Monroe." The joint board recommended that the general staffs of the army and navy undertake a study based on the following additional assumptions:

> The United States finds itself obliged, for any assumed cause growing out of the Monroe Doctrine,[11] to intervene in the affairs of an independent country in the West Indies or on the mainland of Central or South America; and that the intervention is carried out under the following successive conditions:
> A. To restore order, without complications with any other foreign power;
> B. For the purpose of aiding the country in which intervention takes place against another foreign power not of this hemisphere.
> C. Against the country in which intervention takes place, assisted by a foreign power not of this hemisphere.
> D. Under the conditions of A and B, assuming an alliance of two or more foreign powers not of this hemisphere.

Under the foregoing conditions, the problems would involve a complete study of the Caribbean Sea as a theater of war and of the Philippine Archipelago as a theater of war.

The main strategy of the joint board, which was approved for further planning by the Secretaries of War and the Navy, therefore, did contemplate the possible need for intervention in the Caribbean to restore order—but as a response to a direct assault on the Monroe Doctrine.

There had to be some threat of intervention by a power from outside this hemisphere, even though the United States might have no immediate diplomatic complications with that power.[12] These considerations were the basis for U.S. Caribbean strategy until after World War I.

One more point about U.S. strategy in the Caribbean should be noted. A study by navy planners indicated by 1908 a definite need for an advanced base to protect the Panama Canal, which was still under construction. The consensus of naval authorities

---

11. Note that the date of this planning guidance generally coincides with Theodore Roosevelt's Corollary.

12. U.S., Minutes of the Joint Board of the Army and Navy, 1903–1919.

favored Guantanamo, Cuba, as the best site. After considering all the tactical and strategic factors involved, the joint board concurred with the navy.[13] This plan, which eliminated other potential base areas, was approved by Theodore Roosevelt.

One must conclude that by 1916, United States planning for the Caribbean area was sensitive to the need for political and military security of the approaches to the Panama Canal as well as the canal itself. There was no joint military contingency planning for conditions short of war, such as the unilateral intervention in 1916. Joint board plans were developed on the assumption that the United States would be forced to defend the Monroe Doctrine against foreign powers outside the Western Hemisphere. The State Department was, therefore, understandably sensitive to the financing of revolutions or corrupting of small Caribbean governments, acts which on occasion had thrown control of the governments into the hands of the European powers. In Lansing's opinion such intrusions and the "national safety"[14] of the United States required this country to intervene to aid in the establishment and maintenance of a stable, balanced government—an honest government—if no other course of action were successful. The argument of national safety—not humanitarianism—made such intervention reasonable, practical, and in full accord with the principles of the Monroe Doctrine. Lansing was convinced that too many international crimes had been committed in the name of humanity.[15]

Thus, although the defense of the Panama Canal appears to have played no direct part in the decision to intervene in the Dominican Republic in 1916, the importance to the United States of a politically stable Caribbean area was well known in the State, War, and Navy Departments. Although there were many German sympathizers in the Dominican Republic,[16] there was no direct threat in 1915 or 1916 that Germany might convert the country into a base for general military operations. President Wilson and his advisors were well aware of the capabilities of German submarines for destroying maritime commerce. It appears that if the possibility of German intervention in the Dominican Republic was discussed in high government planning councils, it must have been considered extremely remote. No exchange took place between the Department of State and the American legation in the Dominican Republic on this point during 1915 and 1916. The military government was never organized for anti-submarine warfare, nor were there any naval forces assigned to it on a regular basis for this mission.

In short, conditions in the Dominican Republic in 1916 did not constitute a direct or immediate challenge to the Monroe Doctrine, or to the security of the Panama Canal, but the U.S. strategic policy of maintaining the general stability of the Caribbean, derived from the Roosevelt Corollary, encouraged the intervention.

The United States had made perfectly clear on many occasions that it believed the Dominican government to be in repeated violation of its obligations under the con-

---

13. Joint Board Memorandum, January 29, 1908, signed Admiral George Dewey, Senior Member.

14. "National interest" might have been a more accurate expression.

15. This is the core of what Lansing called "A Caribbean Policy." A complete copy of this very interesting document is shown in Appendix 2. U.S., Department of State, *Personal and Confidential Letters from Secretary of State Lansing to President Wilson, 1915–1918.* See also U.S., Department of State, *Papers Relating to the Foreign Relations of the United States: The Lansing Papers, 1914–1920,* 2: 466–67.

16. Troncoso de la Concha says that it was public knowledge that the principal officials of the government, with the exception of Jimenes himself, were German sympathizers. *Génesis,* p. 66.

vention. From the viewpoint of the Henríquez y Carvajal government the American intervention was an exaggerated reaction to alleged Dominican violations of the 1907 Convention and a transgression of their sovereign rights. The Dominicans did not foresee in 1907 any more than did the Americans that their future governments would be so consistently crippled by internal wars. The costs of the military operations against the revolutionaries increased the financial burden on none too strong administrations; at the same time, national income, so dependent on customs revenues, was reduced by the revolutionaries' interference with customs collections. Although the servicing of the foreign debt continued, the governments from Victoria on had to resort to domestic loans and other measures such as the withholding of government salaries to avoid bankruptcy. This was the debt increase that the American government alleged was a violation of the convention. According to the Dominicans, the increase did not fall within the definition of "public debt" since it was unforeseen and unscheduled. In May 1916 the incapacitated Jimenes government was undeniably headed for another disaster despite the best of intentions on the part of Jimenes. The United States intervened because of the steadily growing internal debt brought on by revolution—the old, old story, despite financial semantics to the contrary.

The Wilson administration felt a specific, paternal obligation under the Convention of 1907 to insure the establishment of responsible, orderly government. When friendly advice augmented by strong diplomatic pressure did not achieve the ends sought, more forceful steps followed. With respect to the Convention of 1907, the United States was technically justified in landing troops in May 1916 in order to protect the function of the general receiver.

There had been no attempt in 1907 by either country to agree on a definition of terms. Later Dominican claims that the public debt had not been increased had neither more nor less validity than the American claims to the contrary. What was clear to the United States was the fact that the Jimenes government could not maintain order, and was being financially drained as had been all the preceding governments ever since Heureaux, except that of Cáceres. At hand was another revolution which would bring further financial problems. However, American diplomatic notes might well have placed more emphasis on the need to protect customs houses and the receivership, since the Dominican failure to provide security was less susceptible of debatable legal interpretation.

American refusal to recognize the duly elected Henríquez y Carvajal government is open to criticism because the refusal was actually no more than a diplomatic gambit to force the Dominicans to accede to the U.S. interpretation of the 1907 Convention. Although the United States was not obliged to recognize Henríquez y Carvajal, failure to do so was considered by the latter to be contrary to the spirit of the convention and Woodrow Wilson's own declared policy of disinterested friendship with the Latin American states. Under the convention the United States was obliged to assist the Dominican government in the collection of customs revenues. The convention did not define the legal eligibility of the Dominican government to receive the money—for example, "de jure," "de facto," "constitutional," or "legitimate." Nevertheless, the United States withheld from the Henríquez y Carvajal administration its normal share of the customs collections on the grounds that since the United States did not recognize the latter, such disbursement would be illegal. As the Dominicans saw it, this was a moral violation—a violation of the spirit—of the 1907 Convention, which left them with the extreme choices of submitting to force or starving honorably. The action of the United

States was a political expediency which, as both Russell and Stabler recognized within a matter of weeks, would not withstand for long the moral scrutiny of international public opinion.

The basis for the withholding of funds from the Dominican government was in fact a weak one. Morally it constituted a gross misuse of power. It also placed an unnecessary hardship on innocent Dominicans. The fact that this decision was taken and supported for five months highlighted the ineffectiveness of both American and Dominican diplomacy from May to November 1916.

From July to November the clash between American demands for reform and Dominican rejection of the demands led to an inevitable confrontation, as neither side indicated a willingness to depart from its basic position. All too familiar with the political history of 1911 through 1916, Russell and the State Department saw no long-range gains in any arrangement short of United States control of Dominican finances and a national constabulary. Compromise of the U.S. position would only have served to permit disorders to continue. Most Dominican political leaders felt that national dignity was at stake; therefore out of sheer pride or fear of personal criticism they would not bend. Both Jimenes and Henríquez y Carvajal feared that compromise would lead to instant revolution by the nationalists in Congress. Even many moderates believed the American government to be wrong in thinking it could suppress revolutions without "enslaving" the people. Washington, they said, was wrong if it seriously believed it could reorganize the finances and the public forces without giving some American official unlimited control over them. It should be possible, said these Dominicans, for the United States to establish the necessary political reforms and the rational control of finances and public forces needed for the maintenance of law and order, and still leave all authority in Dominican hands.

In fact, the Dominicans had been singularly unsuccessful in putting their own house in order, and they were unwilling to give the United States the authority to try. *Ni hacían ni dejaban hacer*. Washington had been attempting ever since Cáceres' death to advise the Dominican government on financial reforms with little success. Johnston's reports clearly reflected the futility of his position. Both Russell and Johnston admitted that any degree of active U.S. supervision would bring short-range benefits, but anything less than full U.S. control would fail to correct the administrative abuses which were so prevalent. Bryan's communications, especially his message of September 11, 1913, contained positive implications for Dominican leaders both in and out of government. He outlined with unmistakable clarity, if not diplomacy, the consequences of continued revolution. But were the consequences viable ones?

The condition of Dominican finances was only a reflection of political incapacities. This was a historic weakness which could not be cured by the insistent and unrealistic demands for immediate reform by Wilson and his secretaries of state. This was a weakness no amount of external pressure could correct without using force, nor could the Dominicans themselves correct it, except possibly under the leadership of another Cáceres. Ramón Cáceres understood the need for a firm, honest national government, and he possessed the will and strength of character to achieve it. Unfortunately the constitutionally elected men who followed him lacked either that strength or the necessary personal commitment to national unity based on actions, not words. Had the political leaders of 1911 through 1916 rejected the primacy of personalismo, there might well have been no American intervention and the Dominican people would have had a fair chance of enjoying a prolongation of the progressive norms of fiscal and political responsibility Cáceres had fostered. They were denied this chance by the accumulated monumental failures of their leadership.[17]

In a sense the true culprits were Pedro Santana, Buenaventura Baez, the men who senselessly overthrew Espaillat, Heureaux, the assassins of Cáceres, and those who throughout Dominican history had used official powers for their individual gain or for the personal gain of their friends and families. These men, in placing themselves above the law, time and again smothered the development of a social and political conscience in the masses of Dominicans either by the unwarranted use of force or by simply ignoring their own constitutional responsibilities as government officials or citizens. It was this "patriotic" tradition of civic irresponsibility that handicapped the growth of stable political institutions and made the peaceful, voluntary, and constitutional transfer of presidential power unique.

Not all Dominicans were blind to their own defects. Public letters written by responsible citizens, editorials in the press, and statements of some government officials during the 1912–16 period warned of direct and difficult intervention by the United States if Dominicans continued to manifest their old inability to manage their own government.[18] The true cause of bad government and, consequently, of revolution was the incapacity of most Dominicans for self-government, something for which they had neither education, training nor experience. As one American observer noted: "They do not know how to organize, to combine, to subordinate themselves one to another, to command and to obey. Unless direction and support from the outside are given, the alternate tyranny and anarchy of the past must continue."[19] Another report bearing on Dominican politics said:

> These are not a turbulent people nor sanguinary, as is so generally believed in the States, but a lovable, trusting people whose passions are easily played upon. There are a number of ambitious leaders who have managed to divide the island into factions; no one of them is strong enough to hold his own against all the others; and as the winner generally secures his political victory by either force or fraud, he generally loses it by the same method. No one American or Dominican believes there ever was a free and fair election. . . .
> The Government in power controls the machinery of election, and no Dominican can

---

17. The only salvation for the republic in 1915–16 was for the Jimenes government to have been able to resolve its internal predicament and thus meet the national crisis successfully. Instead of unifying the nation, inviting the opposition party to participate in the cabinet, putting aside party passions, and reorganizing the ineffective system of collecting revenues, Jimenes blindly not only remained at odds with the opposition but failed to reconcile the division between the two groups of Jimenistas [his and Arias']. Mejía, *De Lilís a Trujillo,* p. 118.

Pichardo touches on this same matter when he says: "The opposition was determined to overthrow the government, and certain ones involved pretended not to believe the threat which was heading our way, in order to be able to continue their maneuvers and disorderly machinations." Pichardo, *Resumen de la historia patria,* p. 376.

18. One thoughtful citizen, hearkening back to the 1907 Convention, suggested that they should take steps to end their problems by making a study of good government, bringing together the good elements in the country to try to learn something about government. They should organize an institute or center, away from the current political squabbles, to study by all available means how to regain their rights and sovereignty; they should form a nucleus of good Dominicans whose sole objective would be to prevent revolution. The only solution was a stable peace which could lead to the development of progressive forces in the country. Identified as "Marco Antonio," *Listín Diario,* September 21–22, 1914.

19. Charles M. Hathaway, American Consul, Puerto Plata, "Report on Revolution," October 6, 1913, U.S., *Internal Affairs of the D.R.*

be made to believe that it would be a safe thing for him to go up and vote against the then existing government, and to convince them there will be no danger can only be done by some outside, strong force in whose honesty and purpose they can trust.[20]

Espaillat had diagnosed this chronic disease accurately when he warned that the country would continue to suffer until the leaders learned to accept the fact that their personal goals and so-called party objectives might have to be subordinated from time to time to the greater common good of all Dominicans. How could there be decent government if the officials themselves, or their close associates, were robbing the customs houses, evading their own customs regulations, enriching themselves illegally with the connivance of higher officials, or bleeding the national treasury by outright blackmail as the price for peace? By what rationale could responsible and prominent citizens, completely honest and respectful of the rights of their neighbors, calmly and without the slightest twinge of conscience cheat the government on a wholesale scale? Was the moral standard applied to the misappropriation of government funds different from that applied to common theft from a neighbor?

The difficulties experienced by the five presidents from Victoria to Jimenes were squarely in the old tradition of irresponsible political tactics designed by one man or a few to overthrow legal government.[21] Yet not all of the irresponsibility could be attributed to government opposition leaders. There were repeated and proven charges of excessive nepotism, flagrant violation of the law, and careless and even illegal administrative practices on the part of government officials from the lowest to the very highest levels. Fraudulent elections were the rule rather than the exception.[22] In 1914 Francisco Peynado had counseled the use of agitation rather than revolution to achieve change in the political establishment,[23] but most of the people were still too illiterate and politically unsophisticated to be able to influence their leaders. Two years later the Henríquez y Carvajal government could not convince the Department of State that the reforms desired by the Americans were not still needed.

It was a conflict between a weak power vaguely supported by the frail reed of international law and its strong neighbor motivated by important national interests, in this case euphemistically defined as the fulfillment "of United States treaty obligations with Santo Domingo or its tacitly conceded obligations as the nearest friend of Santo Domingo in her relations with the rest of the world." There was only one outcome possible in 1916. In the confrontation, the poor political record of the Dominicans proved to be a far more powerful determinant than their appeals for international justice. The observations of one of the most prominent Dominican lawmakers of 1916 went directly to this point:

---

20. Letter, S.A. Agnew, Santo Domingo Light and Power Co., May 14, 1914, ibid. Voting in Dominican elections was not secret, nor, of course, was there a literacy requirement for voting. It was a relatively simple matter for voting officials to intimidate or buy the voter, especially if he was an ignorant campesino.

21. Referring to the critical events of 1915, Marrero Aristy says: "As had always occurred, in 1915 the favorite tactic of the opposition against any constituted government in Santo Domingo consisted of creating as many disorders as possible until that government burst into pieces." *La República Dominicana*, 2:257.

22. As late as the 1970 elections the Dominicans did not use official lists of registered voters in their elections.

23. *Listín Diario* published on July 7, 1914 a copy of a letter from Peynado, minister in Washington, to Ramón Lovatón, minister of foreign affairs, lamenting the frequency of Dominican revolutions and the political immaturity of the Dominican people.

The same thing that happens to men happens to nations; to the extent that the order and moral discipline of discreet conduct are strengthened and become rooted in him, his exterior presence grows and becomes more distinguished until it demands the respect of other men and the esteem of the public. It would never even occur to Uncle Sam to threaten with his Big Stick the capable and respectable little Costa Rican republic.

In view of these considerations I would dare to affirm that the intervention in our domestic affairs stems first and fundamentally from the obligation which is borne by the American government, the principle of international policing, *and that the direct and immediate cause which has brought on this intervention, we ought to be valiant enough to confess: the disorderly, incorrect life of revolutions and sacking of the public treasury, which places us outside the common law of nations. This, therefore, strips us of any authority to invoke the accepted principles governing the international relations of the peoples who live a regular and honest life.* [emphasis added]

The obligation which produced the Dominican-American Convention and the Wilson Plan are, in my opinion, no more than obvious reasons, and doubtlessly very deserving, for intervention action. It is clear that the American government, having constituted itself as the guarantor of the Dominican state because of heavy debts, could not remain indifferent to the disorder of our treasury, and within this order of ideas, would be able to arrogate to itself the exercise of this right of prescience, the eagerness with which in the present intervention they have tried to take possession of the administration of public funds.

When these funds are scrupulously administered, as they were during the administration of Sr. Velásquez [under Ramón Cáceres], all will go well and the intervening action will be reduced strictly to the limits of the convention.

The writer ends the passage with a bitter attack on those who had profited so long from revolution and illegal practices:

The mere fact of knowing that the intervention and the reforms will put an end in the republic to the sweet collection of revolutionary claims is in itself a trumpet of war which calls to combat in the terrible struggle, in the name of patriotism and to the certain injury of the public all of whom suffer, those who incite against the American intervention, the many in this land who have derived benefits and advantages from the disorder, the power, the fraud, the crimes, the injustice, the contraband, the usury, the speculation, and the innocent blood of the people spilled in torrents.[24]

There is no question but that the United States viewed Desiderio Arias as an undesirable political force who should be removed from the scene. The report from the legation on November 20, 1916, that Arias would probably gain control of the whole government, was the final touch which put the full intervention machinery in motion. Would Arias have actually gained control of the government and, if so, would his administration have been able to stabilize and reform those political institutions which had been so defective for so long?

Arias unquestionably had strong support in the Congress even before the elections. He held one cabinet portfolio and controlled another in the Jimenes government; during this period he had created a strong political base in the capital. The returns from early elections in four provinces showed that his congressional support would be even stronger after all elections were held. Brewer's message was, of course, an estimate, but it was based on enough firm data to have convinced the legation, and it convinced Stabler as well. Russell was also in Washington at the time, and available for consultation.

Arias' past record of political immorality was clear for all to read. He had lived by

---

24. Pelegrín Castillo, *La intervención americana,* pp. 9, 15.

revolution; he had shown no particular administrative ability except that which could be exerted at gunpoint. With Arias in control of the government it is likely that, instead of reform, the country would have suffered from all its old ailments on a scale not experienced since the days of Heureaux. Arias had made bitter political enemies among the Horacistas and even to some extent among the business elements in his own Monte Cristi province. The State Department reasoned apprehensively that under Arias the country would have been plunged into more chaos. Even if given full U.S. support, sooner or later Arias would have been faced with armed revolt which could have been controlled only by more active American intervention. Arias, not a cruel or bloodthirsty man personally, would have been a political disaster for the Dominican people and a continual headache for the United States government. The trend of Dominican elections in November 1916 eliminated all further hesitancy in Washington about wider American intervention. The prospect that Arias would gain control of the government made further delay highly undesirable if not dangerous, and the occupation so long threatened became a reality.

17

THE MILITARY OCCUPATION
AND ITS PROBLEMS

The Military Government of Occupation has been criticized for much that it tried to do as well as for what it failed to do. It also created recognized, long-term benefits for the Dominican people. This book will not include a review of all of the political, military, economic, and social aspects of the occupation, though such a review would be worthwhile, especially in light of events since 1924. An evaluation of the accomplishments of the occupation in two important areas will serve our purposes. These areas are public education and rural land registration; the reforms achieved were among the most significant of those placed in effect between 1916 and 1924.

Captain Harry Shepard Knapp, commander, Cruiser Force Atlantic Fleet, arrived in the port of Santo Domingo on November 22, 1916. On November 27, Knapp had an interesting and encouraging private interview ashore with Archbishop Nouel. The archbishop had not changed his opinion of Dominican politics and politicians. Nouel stated that the country was in a state of anarchy, that political parties had only one desire: to fill their pockets and obtain power. He discussed the absence of patriotic party purposes and said that parties existed for the attainment of power and for the personal needs and enrichment of the leaders. Outside aid was needed, but agreement among the politicians on how to better local conditions was impossible. Nouel himself did not want to return to politics. The archbishop said that U.S. policy ebbed and flowed like the tide, but he did not specifically say that he favored intervention. Knapp read between the lines that the archbishop, as a good Dominican, could not say that he wanted intervention and a military government. Nouel did say that Dominicans would welcome good government, and, according to Knapp, he implied that something had to be done. Knapp concluded his report of the interview with these words: "I believe that the conclusion reached in conference prior to my departure from Washington is correct."[1]

---

1. Message, Commander, Cruiser Force to the Secretary of the Navy, November 27, 1916, U.S., *Military Government* appendix to Quarterly Report of the Military Governor for the period ending December 31, 1916. Also present at the meeting with Nouel were members of Knapp's staff and Secretary Brewer of the legation. All agreed with the inferences Knapp drew.

In accordance with his instructions,[2] he issued the proclamation on November 29 from on board the *Olympia*, placing the Dominican Republic in a state of military occupation and subjecting it to military government and military law. Knapp issued the proclamation as commander of all armed forces of the United States within the territory of the Dominican Republic.[3]

It made little difference to the Dominicans that the proclamation disclaimed the objective of destroying their sovereignty. Nor did its announced intention of helping them restore internal order while enabling them to meet their international obligations prove satisfactory. To the average Dominican, the sight of the foreign flag flying in his capital for the first time since 1865 signified nothing less than a brutal invasion by superior military force. Extreme nationalists even claimed that the United States did not want a peaceful solution of the financial problems or of the frequent revolutions; the real purpose of the invasion was to occupy strategic territory until the war in Europe ended, in order to protect the Panama Canal, while dragging the Dominican Republic into the orbit of American world power.[4] But many influential leaders, such as Horacio Vásquez, Francisco Peynado, Manuel de Jesús Troncoso, Federico Velásquez, and to some extent, even Francisco Henríquez y Carvajal, although insisting that the intervention was a complete violation of international law, did not attribute any motives to the United States other than those announced by Knapp.[5]

Having set the general conditions under which the military government would administer the affairs of the republic, Knapp methodically began to attack the problems facing him. His first executive order was issued within five days of the proclamation of occupation.[6] Stating that the necessities of occupation required that the offices of secretaries of state, war and navy, and interior and police be held by officers of the U.S. forces, he dismissed the incumbents and announced that until further notice no Dominican citizen would be eligible to hold the offices. They were then vested in Colonel J. H. Pendleton, U.S. Marine Corps, who commanded forces ashore. This action was the signal for the remaining Dominicans in the provisional government cabinet to resign. Before the end of December the entire occupation, except for the judiciary and a few minor

---

2. As soon as the president had authorized the occupation, Lansing advised the secretary of the navy and requested that the Navy Department take the necessary action. At the same time that Knapp received his instructions from Daniels, the legation in Santo Domingo was advised of the decision to declare the military occupation. The American minister was told to confer immediately with Knapp and be governed in his actions by the proclamation. Message, November 27, 1916, signed Lansing, U.S., *Internal Affairs of the D.R.*

3. Proclamation of November 29, 1916, signed H.S. Knapp, ibid. The complete proclamation can also be found in U.S., *Foreign Relations, 1920*, 2:139–40.

4. Mejía, *De Lilís a Trujillo*, p. 134. Mejía was a *nacionalista* of San Francisco de Macorís.

5. The first vice-president of the Horacista party published a circular letter in April 1917 which Knapp forwarded to the secretary of the navy. The letter read in part: "We have no just reasons to consider the American intervention as a covert and artful conquest and so has it been understood by the leader of the party, whose patriotism nobody can doubt. He, not only by his remonstrance but by his example, has shown that he wishes that the period of unfruitful civil war be ended and that efforts be made to hasten the termination of the present abnormal occupation by cooperating to suppress the obstacles which prolong it. Therefore, his efforts are directed towards convincing his friends and followers of the utility of accomplishing the disarmament of private citizens. . . . " Knapp to Secretary of the Navy, Enclosure to letter, serial 647–17 K-S, April 27, 1917, U.S., *Military Government*. The Horacista letter was signed by Emilio Joubert. The reference to disarmament will be mentioned later.

6. Executive Order No. 1, December 4, 1916, ibid.

employees, consisted solely of U.S. Navy and Marine Corps personnel. The principal offices followed the Dominican pattern: foreign relations, justice and public instruction, treasury and commerce, agriculture and immigration, development and communications, war and marine, and police and interior. The officers concerned had no special training for and no particular knowledge of the Dominican Republic, its language and problems. They were for the most part members of Knapp's regular staff.[7] Special augmentation became necessary later, especially in the legal and civil engineer branches.

The American receivership of Dominican customs had been operating since April 1, 1905, first by virtue of the executive modus vivendi reached between the two heads of government and later by the Convention of 1907. During the occupation the receivership maintained its separate identity and continued to report administratively to the Bureau of Insular Affairs of the War Department in Washington. Relations between the military government and the receivership were very close. Correspondence files of the former contain copies of receivership reports to the War Department and considerable material on local matters judged by the receiver to be of interest to the military government. Of special value were trip reports submitted by officials of the receivership, copies of which were routinely sent to the governor.

The official relationship between the military government and the American legation was one of cooperation, but with clear recognition that the former was carrying on the affairs of state. Knapp and Minister Russell had worked together in Washington when the occupation plan was being formulated. Their personal and official relations in Santo Domingo were excellent. Russell, in asking the State Department to clarify his status, said: "The Dominicans are convinced that their sovereignty is not imperiled. Knapp is an excellent man for this situation. He has always conferred with me, and there is no friction whatsoever."[8] Lansing advised: "The position of the Legation should be practically the same as before the proclamation of the Military Government. And it should be understood that it is the civil representative of the American government in Santo Domingo and will advise on all points with the Military Government which is carrying on the government for the Republic."[9] Lansing added that the department would rely on Russell's ability and tact and was confident that cooperation between Russell and Captain Knapp would be "perfect."

A different picture of cooperation developed with Knapp's successors, Rear Admiral Thomas L. Snowden and Rear Admiral Samuel S. Robison. It was Knapp's wider experience in international relations which distinguished him from both Snowden and Robison. Knapp not only had a more active professional interest in Caribbean matters, but he seemed more apt in understanding Dominican problems. His successors, neither of whom was particularly pleased with his assignment, were more aloof, less flexible, and further handicapped by more vocal political opposition, at least after the immediate impact of the initial landings had worn off.[10] Unfortunately they headed a military

7. The State Department had suggested that experienced American specialists be recruited from civilian life, commissioned as officers in the Naval Reserve, and ordered to report to the military governor to help inaugurate the many reforms which were anticipated. The navy might have avoided much bitter criticism of the military government in 1921 and 1922 by supporting the idea, but Secretary Daniels rejected it rather stuffily, saying that such a procedure would be "contrary to the spirit of the law forming the Reserve of the United States Navy." Letter, serial Op 23, 27818–44, September 26, 1917, to the Secretary of State, signed Josephus Daniels, ibid.

8. Message, Russell to Department of State, Dec. 14, 1916, U.S. *Internal Affairs of the D.R.*

9. Message, December 20, 1916, 2:00 *P.M.*, Lansing to Russell, ibid.

government which by 1920, both the Dominicans and the State Department believed, was no longer serving a useful purpose. The Navy Department did not agree.

As the civil representative of the United States government, the legation initially acted as policy advisor to the military government, but by 1920 the Department of State had left the administration of the Dominican Republic to the military governor and the Department of the Navy. The navy, in turn, gave the military governor full freedom of action. The diary of Josephus Daniels contains only a few references to Santo Domingo, indicating that the secretary was more concerned—understandably so—with events in Europe. Daniels reveals little of his own personal thoughts on the intervention, except his concern with reports of the military government's inefficiency and despotism and of atrocities. He ordered several official investigations of the latter.[11]

Lack of coordination of policy matters in Washington at times placed the military governor in a conspicuous and delicate position. Occasionally neither the secretary of the navy nor the secretary of state knew what the military governor's plans were. For example, late in 1920 both secretaries criticized Rear Admiral Thomas Snowden, then the military governor, for having issued two executive orders (572 and 573) which appeared to impose a measure of unpopular censorship on the Dominicans, and for refusing to recognize a limited legislative veto authority previously conceded by the State Department to a special Dominican consultative commission. At this time the State Department was trying to devise an instrument to permit the Dominicans to participate more actively in their own government. Snowden's refusal caused the commission to resign and, in the opinion of the State Department, ruined the possibility of an entente. As a result of Snowden's actions the secretary of the navy criticized the military governor for not having advised him of the plan to issue the noxious executive orders, and the secretary of state criticized Snowden and the Navy Department for not conforming to State Department policy in the matter which caused the consultative commission to resign.[12] Theoretically the communications channels for military government

---

10. Snowden, in particular, may have appeared to many Dominicans as lacking in understanding of their traditions. Yet in 1920, unsuccessful in his efforts to administer affairs with the collaboration of a group of prominent Dominicans, he is quoted as saying that he was not serving the United States' interests and that he was trying to fulfill a social and not a political role. "I am not—[he affirmed with surprising audacity]—I am not an agent who supports himself by violence. At the moment I am nothing more than a Dominican governor anxious to emulate in their civic virtues President Espaillat and President Billini." Américo Lugo, "Emiliano Tejera," p. 313.

11. E. David Cronon, ed., *The Cabinet Diaries of Josephus Daniels, 1913–1921*, passim. Daniels' entry of April 26, 1918, indicates that the secretary of the navy may have agreed with Knapp's philosophy of paternal military government. Daniels commented that he and Knapp had "talked about our duty in San [sic] Domingo. He has large view—American view." ibid., p. 301.

12. The officer administering the department of finance and commerce of the military government was in Washington a few days later. In a series of rather incendiary conferences at both State and Navy Departments he made clear that his superior, the military governor, was ready to obey all orders given him, but that (1) the military governor had been delegated wide discretionary powers, (2) the State Department had advised the Navy Department on earlier occasions that it did not desire to be consulted on the issuing of executive orders, and (3) the secretary of the navy had never asked to be or had been consulted on the issuing of executive orders. Rear Admiral Knapp, the former military governor, was present at the meeting with the secretary of the navy and after concurring with the finance officer's comments, added a recommendation that the American minister at Santo Domingo be withdrawn. Personal handwritten letter, January 27, 1921, Lieutenant Commander Arthur H. Mayo, Supply Corps,

affairs from Washington passed through the Navy Department to Santo Domingo; that is, regardless of the source, all communications between Washington and the military government had to be handled by Navy. The State Department, of course, communicated directly with the legation on strictly departmental matters.

Knapp's policy was to conduct the affairs of government, utilizing Dominican law where possible, but overruling it unhesitatingly if it ran counter to the purposes of the occupation. His job of administration made easier by the lack of an organized Dominican Congress, Knapp turned to the immediate problem of internal security.

Internal security was a matter for the marines. Although the grim and sometimes colorful details of the pacification of the sparsely populated eastern provinces possibly merit more attention, this phase of military government operations is of minor interest here. Most of the country was brought under control with little difficulty. On the recommendation of Colonel Pendleton, Knapp issued orders to the marines to confiscate all firearms and ammunition. Except for those carrying special permits, no Dominican was authorized to wear or own firearms.[13] The excessive zeal with which these orders were carried out frequently brought marine search parties into conflict with Dominican law or hallowed customs and did little to increase respect for United States forces.

The privacy and security of a Dominican home were no less constitutionally guaranteed in Santo Domingo than in the United States. On the other hand, there were frequent cases of sniping and direct armed attack on remote marine detachments. Under these conditions one cannot censure too strongly the willingness of the marines to enforce the arms confiscation order. The major security problem was the pacification of the rough, sparsely populated provinces in the east, particularly San Pedro de Macorís and El Seibo.[14] This was a region of banditry, bushwhacking, and brutality, where confron-

---

U.S. Navy, to Rear Admiral Thomas Snowden, U.S., *Military Government*. Mayo's letter is a long one, full of details of the behind-the-scenes sniping in the Navy Department and between State and Navy Departments. It was the sort of letter that must have pleased Snowden, so far from the seat of government. Mayo's report revealed the existence of a lack of awareness by the secretary of the navy of events in Santo Domingo and the lack of working communications at times between his department and the Department of State. Mayo cites clear evidence of State Department officials deliberately bypassing the Navy Department in matters of direct concern to the military governor.

13. This was a well-conceived order. The most treasured gift a Dominican father of that period could give his son was a revolver, which, as we have seen, was the real symbol of authority in the rural areas. I have interviewed several elderly Dominicans in the Cibao who remember the occupation, not so much for the reforms or failures of the military government as for the fact that "the Americans took away my gun—a very beautiful Colt." Colonel Pendleton reported that in less than four months 9,337 rifles, 25,760 revolvers, 855 sawed-off shotguns (*patas de mulas*), 1,327 shotguns, 175, 760 rounds of ammunition, and two machine guns had been confiscated. Report of Pacification, dated April 16, 1917, signed J. H. Pendleton, U.S., *Military Government*. By far the most frequent offenses by Dominicans were unlawful possession of arms and ammunition and carrying concealed weapons. Summary of Military Court Proceedings in Santo Domingo, November 29, 1916, to December 29, 1919, p. 81, ibid.

Mejía comments on the disarming of civilians: "In the rural areas they collected thousands of revolvers, especially in the Cibao where fathers, when their sons arrived at puberty, gave them one, or they acquired one with the first money they earned. . . . The crime rate dropped extraordinarily." *De Lilís a Trujillo*, p. 145. The cooperation of Horacio Vásquez in this pacification measure was noted earlier.

14. Despite the light population, these were important provinces because the large sugar estates were located here. Bandit raids on the sugar installations were so prevalent that most of the larger companies organized their own para-military security forces for self-protection.

tations between guerrilla[15] and anti-guerrilla forces frequently brought suffering to the peaceful little villages in the region. By the middle of 1919, however, banditry had been reduced to sporadic incidents, and by 1920 the military governor reported that the country as a whole was tranquil except for some of the former political factions.[16]

The military government's preoccupation with the problems of finances, badly needed public works and sanitation projects, reforms of civil, criminal, and commercial codes, revision of export and import regulations, certain political reforms, the creation of a national police force,[17] and all of the onerous administrative details of government will be noted only by the observation that the governor and his staff, aided by the consultants they chose to seek out, constituted for all practical purposes a completely autonomous group, at least during the early years of the occupation. Although Knapp's successors, Snowden and Robison, did not display the qualities that made Knapp the

---

15. The local term for them was *gavilleros*; they had existed long before the Americans arrived on the scene. Marrero Aristy, *La República Dominicana*, 2:383. There is an undated memorandum signed by Luis Galván the Dominican chargé d'affaires in Washington, U.S., *Internal Affairs of the D.R.*, in which Galván states that American intervention did not create banditry and that Evangelista (Vicente Evangelista, one of the most notorious bandits of the eastern provinces) had been a bandit for many years and represented the revolutionary atmosphere against which the Dominican Republic had been struggling for so long. Manuel Amiama's *El terrateniente* contains several chapters devoted to local attitudes toward American marines and the gavilleros who operated in the vicinity north and east of San Pedro de Macorís.

16. United States Military Government of Santo Domingo, *Santo Domingo: Its Past and Its Present Condition*, p. 15 (hereafter referred to as *Santo Domingo*). Elsewhere in the republic living conditions had stabilized much earlier. As early as April, 1918, in the extensive and important agricultural Cibao, the military government was in reasonably good repute with the inhabitants. The small farmers were happier. Instead of cultivating their land as far as possible from roads, to protect themselves from passing bands of marauders, they were now cultivating as close to roads as possible in order to take advantage of transportation facilities. Much additional land was being cleared and placed under cultivation, and if it were not for the availability of large numbers of Haitians, labor would have been scarce. In other words, the farmers were doing well. Letter, April 2, 1918, Trip Report of Irvin I. McManus, Special Collector, Internal Revenue, to Colonel J. H. Pendleton, USMC, U.S., *Military Government*. McManus' observations were of considerable value since his duties carried him to all parts of the country where he could report on rural as well as city conditions. Observations of various officials, including the military governor himself, during the period 1917–19 led the latter to include in his summary of the occupation to date: "The native Dominican is hospitable, long suffering, and hopeful. He has been exploited and misused for centuries. The people desire peace and the opportunity to pursue their various occupations without constant molestation and robbery, as well as being forcibly enlisted in the intermittent revolutions." U. S., *Military Government, Santo Domingo*, p. 26. Written Dominican sources summarizing the generally more prosperous conditions in the rural areas during this period are not available. Knowledgeable Veganos, however, have pointed out that the campesinos' cultivating their land close to the roads was a very significant indicator of peace in the countryside.

17. Knapp's thoughts on a force for law and order should be recorded here: "Looking at international conditions, Santo Domingo is a country with a revolutionary habit. Revolutions arise not in principle or for principles but to further personal ambition. Parties here have the most rudimentary of principles and in general are not named for principles but for persons. An efficient army would serve to keep one party, one leader really, permanently in power; an inefficient army would be of no use in preventing those, as is proven by the experience of years. Either alternative is bad. What the country does need to meet the internal requirement is, in my opinion, not an army but a police force of such strength and discipline as to maintain order throughout the country, and yet not be the tool of any unscrupulous leader. . . . " Quarterly Report, Military Governor, Oct.–Dec. 1916, U.S., *Internal Affairs of the D.R.* Knapp's observations on an "efficient army" were, unhappily, confirmed in 1930.

superior governor of the three, all were well-intentioned and all addressed themselves seriously to the challenging variety of problems which confronted their administrations.

Knapp as well as Snowden, who carried on the start his predecessor had made, believed that progress and, in fact, the whole future of the country would depend on educational and land reforms and agriculture:

> I am convinced that here, as has proved to be the case in Puerto Rico, the Philippines and Cuba, the solution of the problem of good government will be found in the better education of the people. . . .
> The future material prosperity of Santo Domingo will be, I believe, principally dependent upon agriculture. Agricultural possibilities are known to be great, although they are still largely undeveloped—methods and tools are archaic. There are rich semi-arid lands, but irrigation has not yet been resorted to in any considerable degree. There are some large foreign corporations engaged in agriculture, chiefly sugar raising. That they increase the business and prosperity of Santo Domingo is to some degree undoubted; that their presence here is not altruistic is equally undoubted. The desirable thing is to show the Dominican people how to raise larger, better and more varied crops, the proceeds of which will accrue to the Dominicans themselves and not go in large measure to foreign corporations.[18]

In this same context Knapp also mentioned the need to survey the country and to clear up the land title confusion. He quickly turned his attention to these matters.

---

18. "Annual Report of the Military Governor of Santo Domingo From Proclamation, November 29, 1916, to June 30, 1917," U.S., *Military Government*, p. 12.

18

EDUCATION AND THE LAND
TAX, 1917-24

Rural education in the Dominican Republic progressed little in the thirty years preceding 1917. The central government devoted little money to school construction.[1] If there were to be any rural schools, they usually had to be built by the farmers themselves. In prosperous districts such as the provinces of Santiago, La Vega, and Espaillat, schools might be simple, one-room frame buildings; in the less prosperous districts, they might be no more than a hut similar to those used by the Indian inhabitants four or five centuries earlier. In these schools the lone teacher typically had no special training or preparation; most themselves were barely able to read and write. Rarely could a rural teacher boast of more than an eighth-grade education. Because of the lack of teacher training, local authorities often preferred older persons, not professional teachers, but those who would be more experienced in handling children. Rural teachers were usually paid about ten to fifteen pesos a month.[2] Prior to the occupation a provincial inspector of schools was paid thirty pesos a month.

Since there were never enough schools for the rural population, classes were held in two sessions, or *tandas,* one in the morning and one in the afternoon, each session accommodating about fifty children. Normally three grade levels of elementary reading and writing were offered, but since education for all children was not mandatory, many did not achieve even these capabilities. In addition, rural parents were notoriously unco-

---

1. Ministry of public education records do not reveal the inadequacies of rural education early in this century. The general description of the rural educational system of the times has been provided by a now retired, highly respected inspector of rural schools who had worked as teacher, school director, and finally as provincial inspector of schools in the provinces of Salcedo, Dajabón, and La Vega. His fifty-two years of experience with rural schools covered the period 1913 to 1965. D. Ramón Gómez, private interview, La Vega, D. R., November 7, 1969. Gómez' observations were generally confirmed by various officials in the office of the secretary of state for education and fine arts.
2. A peso was worth about one dollar.

181

operative in requiring their children to attend school even where facilities were available. Rural adult education did not exsist.

Knapp's efforts to reform the educational system stemmed directly from his philosophy of military government. He did not view either his country or himself as military conquerors. To the contrary, in the tradition of Theodore Roosevelt, he saw the relationship between the two nations as that of guardian and ward, trustee and beneficiary; and in either case, the relationship imposed on the representatives of the United States government special obligations at all political levels, especially in the provinces.[3] Knapp expected that his officers would do everything in their power officially and privately to make the people grateful to the United States for their presence. He stressed the point that such an objective could not be achieved by the mere use of force.

To help the Dominicans, no better starting point presented itself than in the field of education. Less than two months after he had established the military government, Knapp took steps to correct what in his opinion was a major weakness in Dominican institutions.[4] He found that there was no recognized national school law, that the school administration was riddled with politics, that there were no rural schools,[5] and that even the understaffed schools in the larger cities were inadequate in quantity and quality. Salaries of teachers were low; nationwide, there were no more than 18,000 pupils enrolled in school. Statistics were neither constant nor reliable, but the available data showed that of these the pupil attendance rate was about forty percent. There were only eighteen higher primary (fifth to eighth grade) schools in the country, each with about forty-five students. Twelve were public schools and six were private. There was no vocational education, unless one considered the little rural primary school garden as vocational training. The quality of teaching in the private schools was far superior to public school instruction.

The main administrative weakness of the public school system lay in the inertia of the provincial authorities. Reflecting the familiar tendency to ignore the will of central authorities, the ayuntamientos rarely made a school budget or maintained records of expenditures, as they were required to do. There were about twenty provincial school inspectors scattered unevenly throughout the country, but none had an office, kept records, or actually supervised schools.[6] Education in each of the twelve provinces was administered by a provincial superintendent of education who reported to the general superintendent in the ministry of education. His monthly salary was eighty pesos.

---

3. Confidential letter of August 18, 1918, Knapp to Phillips, State Department, U.S., *Military Government*. Knapp's exact words were: "The relationship existing between the United States and Santo Domingo is that of guardian and ward, or trustee and beneficiary, either of which relationships imposes on the United States certain obligations which officers going out to the provinces must discharge in their respective provinces. In addition to discharging obligations as trustees, their business and the business of each of them is to do everything in their power officially and privately to make the Dominican people thankful to the United States for their presence and that this objective cannot be obtained by mere use of force."

4. U.S. Military Government, *Santo Domingo*, p. 32.

5. Knapp reported that there were none, exaggerating only slightly. On the whole, Knapp's information on conditions in rural and urban schools was accurate. Ibid., p. 33.

6. Here again, Knapp was inaccurate, but not fatally so. He made a habit of visiting schools wherever he went on his official travels no matter what other business was involved. On one trip in 1918, noted in his quarterly report January 1–March 31, 1918, he visited schools in fifteen different comunes in Monte Cristi, La Vega, Puerto Plata, Samaná, San Pedro de Macorís, and La Romana. On these trips he also talked to the ayuntamientos, provincial governors, and chambers of commerce, inviting free exchange of opinion from all.

One of Knapp's major criticisms of school records was that he could find no centrally maintained data which would show the number of schools in each province, along with location, number, and quality of teachers, and number of students. In other words, there was no system; it would have been of only slight consolation to the military governor to know that ministers of education ever since the time of Bonó fifty years earlier had been complaining about the same problem. Distinguished educators such as Argentina's Sarmiento and Costa Rica's Mauro Fernández seem to have been lacking in Dominican public life, at least for a long enough period to remedy important defects. A contributing difficulty during the years immediately preceding the military occupation was the high cost of maintaining internal security, and this endemic ailment too can be traced back to the beginning of independence or even further.

In January 1917 the military government formed a commission of education composed of prominent Dominicans to examine existing conditions and make recommendations to improve the educational system.[7] After a full year of study the commission, having concluded that a complete educational reform was needed, drew up a comprehensive set of seven major school laws under the following headings: compulsory school attendance, public school administration, general studies, University of Santo Domingo, theological seminary, organic law of public education, and school revenues. The military government promulgated all but the seventh law with few modifications.

Reflecting Knapp's interest in primary education, the first law to be published made school attendance mandatory for children of both sexes between seven and fourteen years of age.[8] Parents or guardians were required to enter their children in primary school; special truant officers—*policía escolar*—under the direction of the provincial inspectors of public instruction were charged with investigating violations of the law, which carried a penalty of fine or arrest. The law also provided for a census of school age children. The first superintendent-general of education was Julio Ortega Frier, who had been secretary to the commission of education and whose knowledge of the English language enabled him to work exceptionally well with Colonel Lane. Alejandro Fuenmayor, a Venezuelan teacher, was brought in as a technical consultant.

The next five laws were promulgated on April 5, 1918.[9] Judging from their long existence thereafter, one must conclude that they were well received by the Dominican

---

7. Colonel Rufus H. Lane, U. S. Marine Corps, was the officer administering the department of justice and public instruction from December 1916 to February 1920. In addition to his military commission he had been awarded a bachelor of laws degree from Columbian Law School, now George Washington University. Lane supervised all the government's work on education, for which he was decorated later by both the United States and Dominican governments for distinguished and exceptional service. The formation of the commission was announced in Executive Order 25 of January 19, 1917; its members were indeed prominent: Archbishop Adolfo Nouel, former president of the republic, was the president of the commission; additional members were Senator Pelegrín Castillo; Jacinto R. de Castro, former provisional president of the republic; lawyer and former Senator Manuel Ubaldo Gómez, author of the 1911 Law of Partition of Communal Land; Manuel de J. Troncoso de la Concha, eminent historian, lawyer, judge, minister of the interior, and future president of the republic; and Federico Velásquez y Hernández, the brilliant minister of finance in the Cáceres cabinet and later the leader of the Progressive party. Ibid., p. 32.

8. Executive Order 114, December 25, 1917, U.S., *Military Government*. Compulsory school attendance had been established for the first time in 1907 during the administration of Ramón Cáceres.

9. Executive Order 145, ibid. Trujillo reissued the laws, but did not basically change them.

public. The education commission had written into the Organic Law of Public Instruction a provision calling for the use of the Spanish language for classroom instruction and another which prohibited the use of the classroom to disseminate doctrines contrary to public morality or to patriotic Dominican traditions. Public primary schools were free; instruction did not include religious subjects. Knapp delayed the seventh law because he had not yet been able to formulate fully a plan under consideration to revise the entire tax structure of the country, including the system for raising school revenues.[10]

The new laws streamlined the entire school administrative system. The country was divided into six school departments and each department into fifty districts. A superintendent of schools headed each department, and a school inspector headed each district. Superintendents and inspectors were provided with offices and detailed instructions on the preparation and submission of school statistics.

In formulating the laws considerable attention was paid to the selection and working conditions of teachers.[11] A nomination and appointment system based on merit and controlled completely by the department of justice and public instruction was established, thus freeing the system of the old evils of political influence. Pay scales were radically increased, which almost overnight insured the recruiting and retention of better qualified teachers.[12] By 1920, where there had been an enrollment of 18,000 students, there were now just under 100,000 youngsters in the classroom; there were 1,468 teachers, giving a teacher-pupil ratio of about 1 to 60. One indication of the greater incentive toward education was the noticeable increase in secondary school enrollment. The statistics of the military government, for example, showed that although secondary school attendance was not compulsory, the enrollment at the Eugenio de Hostos School in the capital had jumped from 42 prior to the school reform to 208 by July 1919.

Rural schools came in for special attention. At the end of the first three years of the occupation 50,000 children were enrolled in 647 rural schools. School authorities sponsored the formation of parents' associations in the rural areas; through these groups alone, some 150 small, cheap, temporary but functioning buildings were erected.

In the urban areas there were now 228 primary schools, 7 secondary schools, 6 industrial schools, 2 fine arts schools, and 2 correctional schools. In comparison with the figures previously developed in this book, the increase in numbers of urban primary schools would not appear to be proportionate to the quantum increase in students—that is, 173 schools in 1885 compared to 228 in 1919, and 6,483 students in 1885 compared to 100,000 in 1919. The school administration achieved this accommodation by consolidating facilities; small schools were combined to form fewer but larger ones in order to allow limited teaching staffs to teach larger numbers of students. Before the educational reform the largest primary school in the country had an enrollment of 92. By 1919 practically all primary schools had enrollments of over 100, and many accommodated 200 to 300 stu-

---

10. Quarterly report of Military Governor, Santo Domingo, October–December 1917, Serial 2144–17 K–F, ibid.

11. Knapp refused to bring in American teachers because he thought that the language problem and other differences in culture would not produce a net benefit to the children. He did not wish to force the English language on them. He wanted the Dominicans to develop their own educational system and to participate in it.

12. A district school inspector's salary was raised to $150 per month. Rural teachers were paid $40 to $60 per month instead of $10 to $15 as in earlier years, urban primary teachers, $60 to $100 instead of $20 to $40, secondary, normal and vocational school teachers, $100 to $115 instead of $30 to $60. U. S. Military Government, *Santo Domingo*, p. 34. (One U.S. dollar equalled one Dominican dollar.)

dents. Nearly all schools in the capital had enrollments of up to 500. The administration spent over $200,000 on school furnishings alone in 1918–19.[13] During the academic year 1920–21 over a million dollars in public funds and at least that much more from private sources was spent for schools, salaries, equipment, and supplies.[14]

In what was a major reform effort, the military government, using the plans developed by the Dominicans themselves, transformed an inadequate and inefficient educational system into a thriving cultural enterprise. A major infusion of effort, money, and man-hours was needed, but the results were startling.[15] Rural, graded, secondary, and vocational schools were opened; teaching methods patterned after the United States system were inaugurated as old methods were replaced. An elective system of studies was adopted in secondary schools, and vocational subjects were introduced.

A national system replaced an undisciplined, decentralized one. Major emphasis was placed on primary education, especially in rural areas, in accordance with Knapp's original plan. As the military governor reported in 1920:

> The Department of Education conceives its present mission to be to extend the rudimentary [rural] system until illiteracy is banished. It conceives the fulfillment of this mission to be the most important function of the government. It is assumed that the basic mission of the Military Government is to lay the foundation of a self-supporting democracy in this country. A democracy can be maintained only on an intelligent public opinion, which cannot be developed without extensive interchange of information and the exchange of views.[16]

Not all Dominicans were happy with what the Americans were attempting in the educational field. Max Henríquez Ureña, a highly respected man of letters who figured prominently among Dominican nationalists campaigning internationally against the intervention, reluctantly agreed that the military government showed good intentions in the field of education, but in the same breath observed that intentions were not everything. Henríquez Ureña recognized that the number of primary schools had been increased and was pleased to note that the military government had reestablished an agri-

---

13. During the last three months of 1919 the following schoolroom equipment was distributed: 694 single desks, 10,000 double desks, 600 reversible blackboards, 300 teachers' tables, 1,000 chairs, 800 numerical frames, 500 call bells, 400 eraser cleaners, 1,000 wastebaskets, and many other items. This delivery brought the total of desks delivered to 34,000, but there were still over 60,000 children using homemade benches. Quarterly Report of Military Governor for October–December 1919, dated January 1, 1920, U. S., *Military Government*.

14. Letter from Colonel Marix to Military Governor, file no. 6987, June 13, 1921, ibid. Colonel A. T. Marix had relieved Colonel Lane.

15. Colonel Lane conducted an early and continuous campaign for more money for the public school system. In one of his most effective arguments he pointed to the fact that the illiteracy rate was greater than ninety percent and that in many districts there was no one who could read and write. Emphasizing the importance of reducing this percentage, he reminded the military governor that there were approximately 200,000 children of school age, but that in the preceding year, 1917, the schools could accommodate only 45,000. Lane's comparative figures probably impressed the military governor even further:

Expenditures for Education	U.S.	D.R.
per capita, total population	$ 3.86	$ .80
per capita of school population	19.30	4.00

Letter, Officer Administering the Department of Justice and Public Instruction to Military Governor, signed Rufus H. Lane, serial 2–041 of November 27, 1918, ibid.

16. U.S. Military Government, *Santo Domingo*, p. 37.

cultural school and was actively promoting agricultural research and extension work. But in his opinion it had made a serious error in trying to reform the secondary school system founded in 1880 by Eugenio de Hostos. According to Max Henríquez Ureña the problem was not teaching methods but a lack of schools, and the effort to reform Latin American schools in the United States mold would lead to absurdities.[17] This was a minority voice, and a biased one at that. Regardless of their attitude toward the intervention itself, most Dominicans recall with favor the effort of the military government to educate the Dominican youth. They would agree that in three years of occupation the Americans had built more schools and were educating more Dominican children than their own government had.

During the last three months of 1917 Knapp began to explore the possibility of revising the antiquated fiscal institutions of the Dominican Republic. During the colonial period the Spanish Crown had made some exceptions in special cases, but on the whole the colonists were continually faced with taxes of every description: import taxes, export taxes, sales taxes, Church taxes, food taxes, the royal fifth, excise taxes, and the *cruzada*,[18] to list the most common ones. Many of these earlier taxes continued in existence through the national period. There was neither an income tax nor a direct land tax, however, which meant that the tax system was essentially an indirect one. Thus the poor had to bear an inequitable burden. Knapp was determined to equalize the tax load, which he did by means of a land tax plan. Since no one in military government headquarters felt competent to tackle a general revision of the tax system, Knapp prudently brought in expert assistance. On the Dominican side he asked Francisco J. Peynado to determine the feasibility of a land tax reform, and he could have made no better choice. Peynado, who was to play a key role throughout the occupation, was one of the ablest lawyers in the country. Despite the fact that he had been elected president of the ayuntamiento of Santo Domingo three times, Peynado was not a party politician. During the administrations of 1912–14 he had headed the Dominican diplomatic mission in Washington, had been the delegate to the 1915 Pan American Congress, and had been secretary of the treasury just before the occupation. As much or more than any other Dominican, he assisted the military government in a number of important administrative problems, yet always remained a patriotic citizen. His wide circle of influential friends in the United States, his broad international experience, and his excellent legal training later served him well in negotiating the final agreement under which the United States forces would

---

17. Henríquez Ureña, *Los Yanquis en Santo Domingo*, p. 232. Henríquez Ureña is in error here. The U.S. was not trying to impose a duplicate American system on the Dominicans. The military government concentrated on primary education in order to attack the problem of illiteracy, giving relatively little attention to secondary education and none to the university. U.S. Military Government, *Santo Domingo*, p. 36; and Quarterly Report of the Military Governor, October–December 1917, p. 4, U.S., *Military Government*. Mejía, in referring to the work of Frier and Lane as "brilliant" and "highly beneficial" to the country, notes that secondary and university education continued along the same path sketched by de Hostos. He says that the military government stimulated precisely that which had been neglected by earlier Dominican governments: primary education. Mejía, *De Lilís a Trujillo*, pp. 151–52. I have interviewed a number of knowledgable officials in the present ministry of education on this point. All commented favorably on the educational effort of the military government of 1916.

18. A holdover of the indulgence sold to provide funds for wars against the infidels. The cost varied in different regions, and the amount was determined by the capacity of the individual to pay, usually from a fraction of a peso up to ten pesos. Haring, *Spanish Empire in America*, p. 268.

withdraw from the Dominican Republic. Peynado represented nearly all of the large American sugar interests, but there is no evidence that these connections ever warped his political activities. Peynado accepted Knapp's invitation, as well as other important collaborative roles with the military government, along with other prominent Dominicans without "abdicating his patriotic sentiments."[19]

On the American side Knapp's choice of tax expert was Fred R. Fairchild, professor of political economy at Yale University, whom he invited to make an independent study of the complete tax structure. Fairchild visited the country early in 1918 to familiarize himself with local problems. For the proposed land tax he recommended a flat rate of one-fifth of 1 percent of the value of the land. His reasons for this rate and his comments on the actual law that was issued will be mentioned later. Armed with the Peynado and Fairchild studies, Knapp organized a land tax board within the military government to begin work on drafting a land tax law which would be the first of three new tax measures. Concurrently with the land tax, Knapp began work on a second law to provide school revenue.[20] Traditionally, funds for school support had been raised by municipal taxes. The money was collected by municipal authorities, placed in the municipal treasury, and, according to law, was supposed to be used only for education. This was the old law of *patentes*, or license fees, which actually assigned to school support not only the license fee income but a percentage of other tax monies as well.

The military governor soon discovered that many of the ayuntamientos deserved their reputation for mismanagement of funds. In the years preceding the military government's centralization of public school administration, annual total collections from the patentes averaged about $160,000. Under the centralized system, new school laws, and collections of the patentes money by the new internal revenue service of the government, proceeds from the patentes jumped to $600,000, an increase of about 370 percent. This money was left in the municipal treasuries and later disbursed for education under a budget prepared by the secretary of justice and public instruction. Shortages and irregularities continued to crop up, however, which eventually led the military government to order that all school tax money be deposited in the general treasury for direct disbursement.[21] This was the fiscal arrangement which some officials had sought since the early years of independence.

Knapp, promoted to rear admiral in April 1917, was detached from duty as military governor in November 1918, and it fell to his successor, Rear Admiral Snowden, to approve the work of the land tax board.[22] The Land Tax Law of April 10, 1919, proved

---

19. Mejía, *De Lilís a Trujillo*, p. 181. Peynado died in voluntary exile on January 1, 1933. His remains were returned in honor to the Dominican Republic and interred along with the select heroes of the nation in the Chapel of the Immortals, in the cathedral at Santo Domingo. As will be brought out later, Peynado was distinguished for his ability, rare in Santo Domingo, to harmonize the best interests of his country with those of the United States during this trying period. In his *Resumen de la historia patria*, Pichardo notes the death of Peynado, to whom he refers as the great figure of the Third Republic. Welles, who worked closely with Peynado especially from 1921 to 1924, evaluates him as a recognized prominent citizen, an outstanding jurist, and an individual possessing an insight into and comprehension of American policy. Welles, *Naboth's Vineyard*, 2:782.

20. The third, an income tax law, was never passed because of economic difficulties in 1921–22.

21. Executive Order 369, December 13, 1919, U.S., *Military Government*.

22. This was Snowden's last full tour of active duty. His previous experience had included sea duty assignments in various types of ships and a tour ashore as the hydrographer of the navy. He had no service experience which especially qualified him for the assignment as military

to be highly controversial both within the military government and in the Dominican Republic.[23] The law was a detailed and complete document consisting of sixty-nine articles, of which only the major elements need be mentioned here. The first of its kind in Dominican history, it imposed a graduated tax on land, based on area: one-half percent of the assessed value of holdings under 2,000 tareas (slightly less than 310 acres); 1 percent for holdings over 2,000 tareas but less than 10,000; 2 percent for holdings over 10,000 tareas; one-fourth of 1 percent of the assessed value of permanent improvements; and five cents for each peso or similar share of communal lands. Excluded from the definition of permanent improvements were trees, shrubs, crops, and all mechanical equipment used to cultivate the soil. Exempted from the tax were state-used or -controlled lands, common lands belonging to the comunes which were not leased, loaned, or utilized for private use, Church land, provided that it was used exclusively for religious purposes, land belonging to schools, libraries, charitable institutions, and hospitals not in excess of forty tareas, land belonging to foreign powers used for diplomatic missions, and all property of a single owner whose total tax was less than one dollar.

The owner himself was required to file a description of his property, including its value, this declaration to be used by the municipal treasurers in computing the tax due. Payment of the tax was to be the duty of every landowner; no demand or notification of taxes would be made by the government. Failure to pay tax when due would result in a ten percent delinquency surcharge, plus an additional two percent per month thereafter until payment was made.

The government's stated reasons for imposing the tax bore directly on the problem of school support and the overall philosophy of the tax reform. Reduced to their simplest expressions, the government wanted, first, to compensate the ayuntamientos for municipal tax revenues which had been or were to be abolished; second, to place the tax burdens on those best able to bear them and on those who reaped the greatest benefits from the national wealth; and, third, to abolish certain obnoxious municipal taxes in order to reduce the burden of taxation on the poor. Evidence of the first and third objectives was action by the government within the month to abolish the following municipal taxes: on foreign imported merchandise; on merchandise, cattle, carts, or other objects imported, exported, or in transit from one común or municipality to another; the alcabala, or sales tax; road taxes; entertainment taxes; taxes on entry or clearance of vessels; on production, manufacture, use or consumption of domestic articles; and taxes on houses based on value, rent, or frontage.[24] Revenue from these taxes did constitute an important fraction of municipal income, and the new law included specific compensatory provisions.[25] Thus there was a direct relation between the land tax law and school support, since the latter was dependent on municipal funds.

The first unfavorable reaction to Executive Order 282 came from the officer administering the department of development and commerce, Lieutenant Commander C. C.

---

governor of Santo Domingo in February 1919. Snowden returned to the United States in June 1921 and retired from active duty two months later.

23. Property Tax Law, Executive Order 282, the law to become effective July 1, 1919, ibid.

24. Executive Order 285, May 3, 1919, ibid.

25. For fiscal years 1919–20, 1920–21, and 1921–22, ayuntamientos were to retain from the revenue collected under the new land law an amount equal to one-fourth of the total amount of municipal revenue collected by each in calendar year 1917. For fiscal years subsequent to 1921–22 the amounts to be paid to the ayuntamientos would be determined by the national government.

Baughman. Under normal staff coordination procedures Baughman would have had the opportunity to comment on the proposed executive order before Admiral Snowden signed it into law. In the case of the land tax law, however, because of an administrative slipup, Baughman had missed the chance to talk to the land tax board or to comment on the proposed executive order while it was still in draft form. He nevertheless criticized the law after it was published, viewing it as an injustice to the owners of extensive but remote, undeveloped lands who would be heavily taxed on property which was bringing them no revenue. He felt that such taxes should not be imposed until after roads had been built and communications generally improved in the rural areas. Baughman's comments made the rounds of all principal officers of the military government, who unanimously rejected his position. A résumé of the various comments is worth mention because, taken together, they given an indication of the attitude the military government would take toward land and its development:

Taking their guidance from the policy on agricultural development that was established by Knapp in 1917, the land tax board viewed land use as a matter of public interest; that is, it was in the public interest that land be used effectively. The land must be made to produce, and it must be used to the overall advantage of the Dominican people. The imposition of a land tax would promote such requisites, because in order to meet expenses the owner of idle land would be pressed to put the land to use or transfer it to another who would be more willing or able to do so. The tax would make the owning of large expanses of idle land more expensive than smaller holdings. In short, the tax would produce an economic pressure to break up large estates and thereby permit more people to put more land into production.[26] The increase in individual participation would bring beneficial economic, social, and political advantages.

The land tax brought to a head the conflict between public and private interests. Both were of legitimate concern to the government, but in such a conflict private interests had to give way. Apart from the aspect of increased production, the graded tax would allow the poor man to pay little or no tax at all, while those landowners more affluent in terms of property would pay proportionately more. As for Baughman's comment on delaying the tax until rural areas were developed and the land therefore potentially more productive, there was very strong rebuttal. First, the tax was to be based on the assessed value of the land. If the remote lands were unproductive, their market value would be fairly assessed at a lower figure. Second, since the owners of these lands stood to gain the most from the development of roads and communications, they should be sufficiently interested in increasing the value of their lands to be willing to contribute tax money for improvements. The construction of better roads and bridges was a priority item in the national development plan, but it had to wait on collection of revenue, not vice versa.

---

26. Baughman's criticism of Executive Order 282 is contained in his letter of May 1, 1919, serial 3167, U.S., *Military Government*, which was circulated for comment. Lieutenant Commander Arthur H. Mayo, officer administering the department of finance and commerce, in commenting stated that one of the objectives of the land board was to break up large holdings. Colonel Rufus Lane, officer administering the department of justice and public instruction, also a member of the land board, rebutted Baughman's criticism, stating that idle land would have to be put to use to meet expenses, that the surtax tended to promote the public interest and that there would be "an economic pressure to break up large estates into smaller ones. Thus the product of the land is divided among a greater number of people." The comments of these two officers are contained in the military government files as endorsements of Baughman's letter; they are most significant in terms of future agrarian reform objectives.

Professor Fairchild was asked to comment on the law about a year after it had been promulgated. His criticisms followed a different line and heralded difficulties the government would soon encounter.[27] Fairchild pointed out that while the law was a good one and filled a precise need, he was not enthusiastic about the progressive tax based on area. He could, on the other hand, justify a tax based strictly on value, since a wealthy man could pay more. Basing the tax on area alone, without consideration as to the use of the land, worked an injustice. The owner of a desirable block of city real estate might possess property equal in value to large expanses of cheap rural land, yet he would be required to pay tax at a rate several times lower. The idea of discouraging the concentration of large tracts of land in the hands of a single owner was good, but did not justify discrimination against owners of less valuable land. The professor also calculated that by such subterfuges as nominal dispersion of land titles but not control, the large landholder could evade the tax. He mentioned that he had based his earlier recommendation of a low, flat tax rate in the fear that landowners would undervalue their property for tax purposes, which could invite collusion between taxpayer and assessor.[28] Fairchild's views prompted the military government to review the land tax experience over the preceding year and reconsider the concept of a progressive tax based on area. Within a short time the government amended the earlier law, levying the tax on a basis of value and reducing the rate to almost exactly that recommended two years earlier by Fairchild. A low, flat rate of 0.5 percent of the assessed value of all land was set; the tax on permanent improvements was raised from 0.25 to 0.5 percent; and the five-cent tax on peso titles remained unchanged. Fifty percent of the tax collected in each común would be paid to the ayuntamientos without prejudice to any other legal taxes which the latter might levy.[29]

The public accepted the law with relative tranquility during 1919 and 1920 when the economy was prospering. Land tax collections by the end of March 1920 reached $993,515; by December 1920 the military governor was reporting that the law had been well received.[30] As promised, fifty percent of the tax collections were assigned to the ayuntamientos to meet the costs of services, materials, and aid to education, sanitation, and public works.[31] It appeared that further planned tax reforms would achieve equal success.

Three months later the economy of the country began to suffer major setbacks as the result of the worldwide economic depression. On the international market sugar (which accounted for over sixty percent of Dominican exports) dropped by 1921 to two cents a pound from a high of twenty-two cents in the first quarter of 1920. Property tax col-

---

27. Letter, Professor Fred R. Fairchild to Military Governor, dated May 20, 1920, subject: Property tax and proposed revenues for public education, ibid.

28. Under the law, assessors would be called in if the owner failed or refused to evaluate his property or if his evaluation was obviously out of line.

29. Executive Order 545, September 20, 1920, ibid.

30. U.S. Military Government, *Santo Domingo*, p. 8.

31. The ayuntamientos finally began to submit copies of their budgets to the central government. The port city of Sánchez was one of the progressive urban centers of the country; the Sánchez budget for 1919 reflected the local popularity of the government's drive for more education. The income from patentes and other tax sources totalled $11,338, all of which was budgeted for school support. Other budget entries such as administration, police, lighting, subsistence for the local priest, and public works came to $8,987.73. Thus fifty-six percent of the city's budget was earmarked for schools. República Dominicana, *Files Military Government*, Municipal Budget, Sánchez, 1919.

lections dropped twenty-four percent by the end of March 1921; customs collections for the first six months of 1921 dropped fifty-five percent from the comparable period of 1920; other collections such as from wharfage, consular fees, and patentes dropped by as much as thirty-eight percent. By March 1921 there were still nearly a half million dollars in uncollected taxes, most of which were destined for the ayuntamientos. By the end of 1921 even a reduction of the penalty on delinquent taxes did not stimulate collections,[32] and the first protests over the land tax itself began to be heard.[33] There was little, however, that the military government could do, or desired to do, to enforce the law under the prevailing economic conditions. The government severely curtailed all operations to conform to shrinking budgets.[34] From the point of view of the progress made to date, one of the most unfortunate decisions taken was that to close all public schools. On May 20, 1921, just a month before the end of the normal school year, all school children were dismissed and all school offices were closed indefinitely. The reaction of the officer administering the department of justice and public instruction is quoted in part:

1. As a result of the falling revenues of the Dominican Government, brought about by the depressed conditions of affairs, the Military Governor directed this Department to make such economies in the school services that all schools, except the University and the two Correctional Schools, had to be closed. This action was taken by the Military Governor on the recommendation of the Department of Finances, in whose opinion it was preferable to close the schools while the crisis was on rather than to mutilate other public services which were considered more vital. . . .

32. Executive Order 692, U.S., *Military Government.*

33. One of the specific objections concerned inaccurate appraisals. The law made provision for appeal from unjust appraisals, but given the lack of trained personnel and the long experience of ineffective land law administration, the appeals machinery apparently did not function well. A whole new tax office had been established under the comptroller general to include assessors, special agents, inspectors and the necessary supporting bureaucracy. One is surprised that complaints of maladministration were as few as the military government files indicate.

Two very respected citizens of Santiago, Doctor Ramón de Lara, one of the leading surgeons in the nation, and Señor Archambault, editor of the influential Santiago newspaper *El Diario*, called on Colonel C. H. Lyman, U.S.M.C., commanding the marine detachment in the Cibao, to discuss the land tax. Both Dominicans felt that the tax was too high for many people to pay. De Lara gave two examples of high appraisals and added that while he knew of the right of appeal, most Dominicans would not resort to it because nearly all appeals had been rejected. He said that he was not sure who had done the appraisal work in the district but understood that it was a group of three men, one Dominican, one Puerto Rican, and one American, none of whom was an official appraiser. All were surveyors. They had divided the city into sections and appraised equal amounts of land at equal rates regardless of location, size, or usage. Memorandum for Record, December 9, 1921, signed C.H. Lyman, ibid.

The complaint illustrated the same point of land usage which Professor Fairchild had made. The friendly interview was conducted in Colonel Lyman's office. I have compared the Colonel's official memorandum of record with the front-page article published in *El Diario* the following day; the reporting of all parties was in agreement and unbiased.

34. The following table will show the trend of Dominican trade:

Year	Imports	Exports
1920	$ 46,525,876	$ 58,731,241
1921	24,585,327	20,614,048
1922	14,317,419	15,231,355
1923	18,245,082	26,042,821
1924	21,580,571	30,262,896

Marrero Aristy, *La República Dominicana*, 2:414.

2. If nothing is done to reopen the schools in time to finish the school year, the damage caused would be beyond calculation. About 80,000 school children have been thrown out of school. . . . But the economic damage is not the most serious that this unforeseen interruption will cause. The main accomplishment of any school system consists in the production of habits of study and the spirit of learning in the student body; such accomplishment is the result of the accumulated efforts of years, and, unfortunately, is very unstable. Thousands of children who were attending school spontaneously, not being of compulsory school age, will lose courage and give up schooling; many others may go back, but without faith or interest.[35]

The author then cited the hard work over the preceding years to build up a motivated teacher corps and the vital role of education in the political development of the Dominican people as justification for assigning a fair share of public funds to the maintenance of schools. Marix' plea was a sound and thoughtful one,[36] but the schools remained closed.[37] In the following year the government changed the title of the Land Tax Law to the School Tax Law, and added provisions which would apply the revenue from land taxes primarily to school support. This concession to education proved to be a hollow one considering the difficulty experienced by the government in collecting land taxes in 1922.

One last item concerning shrinking educational finances appears in the military governor's report to the Navy Department late in 1923. In the budget of the new provisional government, which had been installed on October 21, 1922, there was no item for schools or school officials. The military governor had concluded that the Dominican government intended to support schools out of land tax collections and that these, when properly collected, would maintain the educational system. But since the schools were closed, apparently land taxes were not being collected.[38] Such was the case. Collections dropped steadily after 1921. The American legation reported in June 1926 that practically nobody in the country was paying the land tax except the sugar estates, and they had refused to pay the tax for the year 1926–27, claiming that their financial difficulties due to low sugar prices would not permit tax payments.[39]

Even after a measure of national prosperity had been restored, collections remained low. Dominicans were not accustomed to paying a tax on land. The initiative to pay rested with the individual, and the government did not press them to comply. To com-

35. Letter, serial 6987, dated June 13, 1921, Department of Justice and Public Instruction to Rear Admiral S. S. Robison, Military Governor, signed A. T. Marix, Colonel, U.S.M.C., U.S., *Military Government.*

36. He also recommended a return of school disbursement authority to the ayuntamientos in order to protect school funds from unfavorable decisions at the national level. Knapp's experience had clearly shown this arrangement to be less efficient; furthermore, Marix was probably unaware that as in 1847, the national government could, if it desired, simply order the ayuntamientos to open their treasuries.

37. Robison could do little. Snowden had previously made the decision as a result of the large drop in government revenue, especially in the all-important foreign trade, in 1920 and early 1921. Unhappy that any cuts at all had to be made, Snowden preferred to reduce but keep alive other services such as the Land Court and the guardia nacional, even if it meant closing the schools. This is what Marix was protesting. By the time economic conditions had improved, the Americans had withdrawn, and all government was back in Dominican hands.

38. Quarterly Report of the Military Governor of Santo Domingo, Fourth Quarter, Calendar Year 1923, p. 36, ibid.

39. Report to Secretary of State on General Conditions Prevailing in the Dominican Republic, June 16–June 28, 1926, from American Legation, signed by W.M. Wilson, U.S., *Internal Affairs of the D.R.*

plete the history of land taxes, the government in 1927 modified the tax law, imposing lower rates which weakened the thrust of the original law of the military government to put uncultivated land into production.[40] The 1927 law not only permitted the owner of uncultivated land due advantage of the lower assessed value, but imposed a more favorable fifty percent lower tax rate than that on cultivated land, thus tending to lessen the pressure to make unused land productive. The effects of the law were, first, to favor the owners of uncultivated lands, who paid at a lower tax rate, and those who owned less than 5,000 tareas, who paid no tax whatsoever; second, to increase the tax shelter for owners of cultivated land by exempting taxes on land valued under $5,000; and third, as a result of the above, to reduce government revenue.

The 1927 law was a halfway measure in the direction of abolishing the land tax, but there was no deliberate intention to inhibit agricultural productivity. In fact, at the same time the tax was lowered, the government undertook to increase production by establishing a series of farm colonies on hitherto uncultivated but arable land. The first two were settled in June 1926 near Monte Cristi and Bonao.[41] In 1935 the government swept away the tax law completely, citing as a reason the unsatisfactory results produced by an "institution strange to the idiosyncrasies of the Dominican people."[42]

After the military government withdrew in 1924, the school system limped along barely alive, suffering primarily from a lack of financial support. The impetus toward education created by Dominicans for all Dominicans under the aegis of the military government vanished, along with that government's policy of defining land usage in terms of public, not private, interest.

---

40. *Ley de impuesto territorial*, No. 688, June 27, 1927, published in the *Gaceta Official*, No. 3875, July 9, 1927. One-half of 1 percent of appraised value of cultivated land, unless otherwise exempted; one quarter of 1 percent of the value of permanent improvements on cultivated land; one quarter of 1 percent of appraised value of land not cultivated; and one-half of 1 percent of appraised value of houses, buildings, or structures on urban land. Some significant changes in qualification for tax exemption were also made. The 1927 law added to the list cultivated rural properties valued at less than $5,000 belonging to one owner; uncultivated rural land of less than 5,000 tareas belonging to one owner; arid, unirrigated, uncultivated land, and urban property valued at less than $2,000 belonging to one owner. The law increased the exempted land on which stood hospitals, schools, etc., from 40 tareas to 60 tareas and added the provision that the value must also exceed $5,000.

41. Fourteen Spanish colonists and their families, residing in Cuba, were given ten acres of irrigated land in Monte Cristi; forty such families were each given twenty acres in the Bonao settlement. The Dominican government paid all the settlers' living expenses until they actually arrived at the colony sites and loaned them money for family travel if families did not accompany the colonists. The new settlers were given the usufruct of the property for life, houses, the necessary equipment to start farming, and further assistance until their farms became productive. A cooperative farm organization was planned, although never instituted.

The government planned to bring in Portuguese settlers for additional colonies to be established somewhere in the Cibao and near Samaná, a plan reminiscent of a period four hundred years earlier. Officially there was considerable satisfaction at the initially reported success of the venture, but the American legation reported that many obstacles had not yet been overcome and that not all Dominicans were as optimistic as the secretary of agriculture. U.S., *Internal Affairs of the D.R.*, Report to Secretary of State on General Conditions Prevailing in the Dominican Republic, December 22, 1926–January 4, 1927, p. 7.

42. *Gaceta Oficial*, No. 4828, September 4, 1935, Law No. 977.

19

LAND REFORM: TITLES
AND TORRENS

One of the least heralded yet most enduring of the major reforms accomplished during the occupation was in land reform, specifically the adaptation and imposition of the Torrens system of land title registration to force the partition of rural communal land. The Dominican Land Law of 1912, which required registration of all rural land titles, had not been effective,[1] even with a one-year extension of the registration deadline granted in 1915. The law of 1911 for the partition of communal land also had little or no effect. An immense amount of legal work was needed to force the registration of titles, delineation of property lines, and the fixing of legal titles in the proper person. Honest adjudication was almost certain to result in unavoidable loss to some individuals, and the dissatisfaction that would arise from the forced partition of common lands would create a crisis for the Dominican government.[2] The problem was a delicate one, yet, as the Dominicans themselves had realized, land title reform was long overdue.

This, then, was the military governor's estimate of the situation: fair and effective land laws, vigorously enforced, were needed to restore confidence in government, to protect legitimate title-holders, to prevent future land frauds, and, as a most valuable by-product, to determine the exact extent of public land so that a liberal homestead law could be enacted. In this manner the development of small, independent land-holdings could be fostered. On the settlement of these questions the duration of the occupation and the whole future progress of the republic rested.[3]

---

1. There were unconfirmed reports that many small landowners in rural areas were not even informed of the existence of this law.

2. In the aggregate there was enough land for all claimants. The density of population was only about forty-seven inhabitants per square mile, but the expected large number of fraudulent titles would logically appear in those comunes containing good land but few inhabitants. Violence could be anticipated as politically influential individuals who lost land court decisions would invoke party politics to attack the government. (The density of population noted above was confirmed by the first official census of 1921 which showed a population of 897,000.)

3. Letter, Military Governor to the Chief of Naval Operations, May 29, 1917, signed Knapp, U.S., *Military Government*.

Knapp realized that development of a general land law would be a tremendous and delicate task. For such a reform to be effective he would have to attack most if not all of the earlier relevant Dominican legislation and the whole Spanish-Dominican tradition of land ownership, inheritance, and usage. Some administrations between 1911 and 1916 had, at least on the record, tried to reform the system, but the combination of defective laws and internal political crises had prevented any meaningful progress. Now in 1917 the foreign head of an unwanted military government prepared to modernize the legal framework, something the Dominicans had not been able to do for themselves.[4] Knapp knew he would have to move slowly until he could be sure that new laws not only would cure but would be workable. His only action during the first six months was to twice extend the deadline on registration of land titles set by the Dominican Law of Inscription of Rural Land Titles. In so doing he emphasized the importance of the legal requirements already established. But he also recognized that all property-holders might not be able to comply with the order. Accordingly, as a minimum obligation in these cases, he asked for a property description, which would be useful later:

> To expedite the extremely important work of registration of titles, in conformance with the Law of Inscription of Land as passed by the Dominican Congress on December 14, 1915, the proprietors of lands who have not submitted titles for registration are called upon to do so as soon as possible. . . . Proprietors of lands who cannot file titles immediately for good and sufficient reason will send a letter for record purposes to the Land Registry Office setting forth the following data:
> Name, residence and profession of proprietor;
> Name, residence and profession of party or parties from whom property was purchased or procured;
> Date procured and by what method; whether transfer was effected before a Notary or other officer empowered to administer oaths; state name, residence and official position of same;
> Location, name, area and boundaries of property.[5]

Knapp again called on Francisco Peynado for help, which Peynado promised in the time he could spare from his extensive private law practice. This was to mean that although Colonel Lane worked closely with Peynado throughout 1918, the development of a general land law reform would be slow. Even so, Knapp was willing to accept the delay in order to avail himself of Peynado's superior services and influence.

Meanwhile Knapp was able to plan for some of the supporting actions which a broad reform would require. For reasons of economy he discarded an earlier idea that a national census was needed for effective land title registration, although he recognized that a census would be desirable from other viewpoints and should eventually be taken.[6] He also began to consider the need for a special land court, but late in 1917 decided the time was not yet ripe. The problem ran much deeper than the judiciary itself. There were, however, two measures on which he could act.

---

4. Minister Russell had as early as August 1916 been reporting to the State Department that "The enactment of some proper land title law is absolutely required for the progress of the Republic." Memorandum to State Department, August 18, 1916, signed Russell, ibid. The department notified the minister on August 26 that it was studying the problem of reforms and would advise him as early as possible.

5. Executive Order 48, April 12, 1917. In an earlier order of January 24, Knapp had extended the deadline for registration to December 1, 1917. Ibid.

6. Letter, Military Governor to Naval Operations, serial 1991–17, October 8, 1917, 2d endorsement, p. 3, ibid.

Landowners were slow in registering their titles despite the deadline extensions their government and the military government had granted. On August 8, 1918, Knapp drafted a second executive order on the subject to force compliance with the first.[7] He conceded a three-month period of grace for registration of titles at a cost of $3, without penalty. Titles could be registered during an additional, final three-month period, subject to a higher fee of $55, again without penalty. Delinquents thereafter would be severely penalized. All titles of rural communal land not inscribed would lapse and become valueless; the proprietors of any rural land that was not communal, as well as their heirs, would be incapacitated to sell, donate, divide, transfer, mortgage, partition, or defend it in court without first inscribing the title and paying fees of $110. There were additional provisions for the legal handling of delinquent cases and cases of titles found to be false or null.

The penalties of the proposed new law raised the question of constitutionality. Article 21 of the Constitution of 1844 and corresponding articles in succeeding constitutions guaranteed to all Dominicans the right to property ownership and its privileges, which could be overtaken by reason of public expediency, previous indemnification, or contrary judgment. Knapp, however, adequately protected the government's interests by obtaining a prior legal opinion from Peynado, who concluded that the proposed law was constitutional.[8]

Executive Order 195 left in effect the 1912 Law of Inscription and the 1915 amendment to it. To make sure all citizens were advised of the new law, the executive order contained a provision that the terms of the law were to be published in writing and disseminated orally in all sections of the comunes.

The second administrative action taken by the military government concerned land survey. Knapp, who was in full agreement with an earlier recommendation by Minister Russell, initiated the program, and his successors carried on with it, as did subsequent Dominican administrations. There had never been a national topographic survey or a

---

7. Executive Order 195, August 8, 1918. The three-month period of grace expired November 8. Ibid.

8. The question had been raised by Troncoso de la Concha who thoroughly approved the purposes and utility of the law but simply wondered whether it was constitutional. Peynado reasoned that although a literal interpretation of Article 21 gave the absolute right of use and disposition of property to the legal owner, a legal interpretation would validate this right only so long as the property was not being put to a use forbidden by other laws. The proposed executive order was not an act of expropriation, that is, the taking of property against the owner's will. The landowner who failed to register title had merely to obey the law in order to avoid loss of title. To allege unconstitutionality would be to ignore the fact that men are governed by laws and that the interpretation of a general clause in the Constitution was also a matter for legal interpretation. Letter to Colonel R. H. Lane, USMC, July 17, 1918, signed Peynado, ibid.

To deprive a man of his land, especially if he is a farmer, is a painful act; in actual practice the military government was rather lenient with delinquent owners. So many appeals were received asking for exceptions to the penalty provided for under the law that a special modification was published authorizing the Department of Justice to permit registration even after the deadline date of February 22, 1919, provided that the reason for nonregistration merited consideration (*causas atendibles*). Executive Order 304 of June 10, 1919, ibid. The law did not define causas atendibles, thereby leaving decisions to the discretion of the department. Snowden later commented that much more work had been thrown on the Department of Justice as a result of the June 10 law, but that the effort was probably worthwhile.

The attitude of the military government throughout the sequence of events surrounding title registration was firm but appreciative of actual conditions in the countryside.

complete cadastral survey for land registration purposes, yet accurate surveys were a prerequisite to a modern system of registration and partition of land. Neither the general descriptions of land boundaries contained in the old Spanish grants nor the vague references in later Dominican legal documents[9] were adequate for modern legal purposes. Therefore the military government arranged for complete surveys to be conducted by Dominican surveyors under the supervision of geological engineers on leave from the U.S. Coast and Geodetic Survey Service. In 1918, $300 thousand were set aside for survey operations. The topographic survey was to commence first in order to provide accurate base points to which cadastral surveys could be referred. The cadastral surveys in turn would accurately establish boundaries of political subdivisions and property lines and afford a basis for charting terrain and mineral, agricultural, and other natural resources. The officer administering the department of development (*fomento*) estimated that eight to ten years would be needed to complete the surveying.[10]

The topographic survey did not actually begin until 1919. Surveyors began in the eastern portion of the country where the large sugar estates and cattle-grazing lands were located. It was expected that title adjudication procedures would uncover many false titles in this region of relatively few inhabitants and extensive terrenos comuneros, or common lands. In the first year of surveying, over 3,000 square kilometers were completely surveyed, 7,971 kilometers of roads and trails measured, 153 permanent points of reference and 542 provisional points established, and 40 triangulation stations constructed.[11] In the following year, the area surveyed was almost tripled.

Cadastral surveys were delayed until September 1920 because of a lack of money. Using equipment available locally, however, operations in conjunction with the topographic survey already under way were started on a limited basis, quickly expanding as instruments for thirty teams began to arrive from the United States. Lack of money later in 1921 forced the engineer-in-chief to limit further expansion of his survey force, but the teams in operation continued to work steadily throughout the remaining years of the military occupation.

Under the established system, which required that all land be registered, the initiative for commencing land surveys lay with the owner of the land. Normally the landowner contracted with the surveyor, who would usually charge from fifty cents to three dollars per hectare,[12] depending on the value of the land, an open-ended arrangement that could have left room for the surveyor to overcharge for his work.

One of the earliest contracts was arranged with the large Central[13] Romana, near the town of La Romana, which at the time owned 90,000 hectares of land in parcels of various sizes. The Central advanced the funds for the survey so that about twenty-five surveyors could be added to the working force. By making additional similar contracts, the survey engineer-in-chief was able to convert his funded operations into self-supporting ones. During the first year over one hundred petitions for survey were received, about a

---

9. See Appendix 1, Article 6, for an example.

10. Letter to Military Governor, serial 2465, October 15, 1920, signed Warfield, ibid.

11. República Dominicana, *Secretario de Estado de Fomento y Comunicaciones: Memoria 1919–20*, period ending June 30, 1920, Annex 3, signed by Albert Pike, Engineer-in-Chief, ibid.

12. One hectare equals 2.47 acres.

13. A sugar plantation including a sugar mill, sometimes referred to as *ingenio de azúcar*. The cane to be ground might be grown on land belonging to the millowner or on the land of neighboring colonos who would pay the mill owner for grinding their cane. The usual price was half the individual colono's profits.

third of which were for land located in the nine priority areas,[14] seven of which were sugar zones. Sizes of parcels varied from a few hectares belonging to small landowners up to several thousand hectares for large sugar estates. The average parcel surveyed contained 142 hectares, excluding urban parcels. By the end of the second year of operations, surveys had begun in all nine districts. Some 450,000 hectares had been surveyed, or were in process, all costs borne completely by landowners.[15]

In contrast to the surveying of privately owned land, money problems of 1921 slowed the cadastral survey of public lands, finally forcing a complete suspension in April 1922. The topographic survey program had already been abolished by late 1921 for lack of funds. During the next thirty years, as sporadic progress was made by the Dominican government, the U.S. Coast and Geodetic Survey Service provided occasional supervisory assistance.

On the whole, land survey operations were executed with little difficulty and, so far as the topographic engineer-in-chief was concerned, with a high degree of accuracy.[16] There was occasional resistance from small farmers who feared that the purpose of the survey was to take their land, but the attitude of nearly all landowners was friendly and cooperative. Survey teams were careful not to become involved directly with protesting landowners, referring such cases to the national police. The teams encountered a peculiar local problem in the region around La Noria, just north of La Romana, where United States marines had been unable to clear out the gavilleros who had taken to the brush. There it was frequently necessary for the survey teams to stop work and get out of the way of gun battles between marines and gavilleros.

In accordance with the land law, surveyors were required to submit their notebooks promptly, along with the plans and descriptions of the surveyed land to the land court for use when each case came up for adjudication. Occasionally the court found it necessary to remind the surveyors of the law by ordering the guardia to escort a stubborn surveyor, notebook in hand, to the capital. The normal practice for the court was to index and note the contents of the book, then return it to the surveyor. Pages showing fraud were held for court use.[17]

Money problems continued to hamper the survey program after the departure of the military government. Cadastral surveying of privately owned land continued at a much slower pace, although it never halted completely. Since the 1920 land law remained in effect, and as private owners began to realize that their interests were protected thereby, the only real obstacle to the survey work was the cost to the landowner. By 1940 essentially all of the arable, privately owned land, especially that under cultivation, had

---

14. Pedro García, Mata Maimonal, Playa Pitre, Hatillo de Yaco, El Soco, La Romana, La Victoria, Quisqueya, and Guerra. Most were located along the south coast east of Santo Domingo City or north of Santiago.

15. At the peak of their operations during the military occupation, the land survey organization employed forty-nine surveyors for field work and twenty for office work. The total monthly payroll was $7,450.

16. República Dominicana, *Secretario de Estado de Fomento y Communicaciones: Memoria, 1921–22*, Annex 3, passim.

17. República Dominicana, *Secretario de Estado de Fomento y Communicaciones: Memoria, 1920–21*, period ending June 30, 1921, p. 194. Surveyors were also required to write the description of the land, including latitude and longitude, bearings, and distances directly on the plan drawn. This procedure prevented the registration of a plan different from the written description, a practice sometimes employed by unscrupulous surveyors or notaries to defraud the ignorant campesinos.

been surveyed. Remote or economically undesirable public lands remained unsurveyed, leaving, by 1966, about ten percent of Dominican territory unsurveyed.[18]

The military government staff worked throughout 1919 on a general land law that would not only provide for the equitable resolution of the problems created by the ancient system of terrenos comuneros, but would also establish the permanent administrative machinery for a new, modern, orderly system of land ownership. Anticipating the publication of such a law, the military government advised all Dominicans at the end of 1919 that the 1911 Law of the Partition of Common Lands was suspended, as well as any partitioning action in progress as a result of that law. The judgments on any completed partition would remain in force. Surveyors were threatened with a six-month suspension of license if they continued to survey common lands, except on those that, as of the effective date of the notice, were already occupied—that is, had buildings, railway tracks, plantations, or fenced and cultivated fields.[19] On July 1, 1920, Rear Admiral Snowden published the long-expected Executive Order for Land Registration and the Demarcation, Survey, and Partition of Terrenos Comuneros.[20] This was a major effort, the need for which had long been seen not only by earlier Dominican governments, the State Department, and the military government, but also by Dominican and American lawyers familiar with land problems.[21] The name of the new law, both in the English and the Spanish versions, indicated the area of most significant innovation—registration of titles.

The Torrens system of title registration was developed in Australia in the nineteenth century by Robert Richard Torrens. He was appointed customs commissioner and in 1852, registrar general of South Australia. Through a newspaper article published in the *South Australia Register,* he became aware of the many defects in the English system for transfer of private land titles. Compared to the procedures in use for the registry and transfer of ship titles or for the transfer of titles of public land to private purchasers, the English system was far more complicated, unsure, inaccurate, expensive, and time-consuming. Even once issued, the land title privately transferred could be challenged in court. By comparison, the sale of a ship required no expert legal advice. To discover who the legal owner was, one had merely to refer to a central register, open to the public, in which all the details of the previous sale were recorded. These entries were official ones and could not be challenged as an official act since the sale of a registered vessel originated with the state; that is, the state entered into every transaction involving transfer of title.

18. As of this writing, the national cadastral survey is about ninety-five percent complete. External boundaries of most state-owned land are fixed, although additional surveys are still needed for the subdivision of lands to be partitioned for agrarian reform purposes.

19. Executive Order 363, December 6, 1919, U.S., *Military Government.*

20. Executive Order 511, ibid. This law was republished by the Dominican government in its official version, along with minor changes, in 1928. República Dominicana, *Ley de registro de tierras con sus modificaciones* (hereafter referred to as *Ley de registro*).

21. A particularly helpful and knowledgable voluntary consultant was Frank H. Vedder, lawyer for the West Indian Sugar Finance Co., the Central Romana, and the Barahona Co. Vedder's correspondence with the military governor reflects the same legal criticisms of the Dominican land title procedures which the Dominicans themselves had been making: on terrenos comuneros legal ownership was difficult to determine because of the existence of fraudulent titles. Vedder also suggested the adoption of the Torrens system of title registration as a means of preventing title fraud. Letter, Vedder to Military Governor, subject: Registry of Land Titles, December 26, 1919, Legal Officer's files, U.S., *Military Government.*

Torrens set about to create a system for land-titling modeled on commercial navigation laws. As do many innovators, he encountered opposition to the change, but his determination to remove the confusion and uncertainty that surrounded land transfer eventually led to acceptance of his ideas as law on January 27, 1858. The Torrens system was utterly simple: as in the cases of transfer of ship registry or of title to public land from government to private individuals, all land purchases would be considered as having been made directly from the state. Legally the title would appear to have been transferred from the old owner to the state and from the state to the new owner. The legal actions, with respect to transfer of property, required that the property first be identified accurately and given exclusive and complete registration in one official registry book; that title to the property be examined carefully prior to registration to insure its clarity and legality; that all possibly interested third parties be publicly advised of the proposed transfer; and, finally, that a legally competent official transfer to the buyer in good faith a legal and official property title.

The importance of the cadastral survey and the final notarial act to all of these elements is obvious and will explain why the imposition of the Torrens system served to correct the major land title problems in Santo Domingo.[22]

---

22. Ruiz Tejada in *Estudio*, pp. 138–41, has some interesting biographical details on the campaign Torrens waged in South Australia to have his system of land title registration adopted. Additional biography can be found in Sir Leslie Stephen and Sir Sidney Lee, *The Dictionary of National Biography*, 19:995. Torrens wrote several articles, including "The South Australian System of Conveyancing," 1859; "Transfer of Land of 'Registration of Title' as now in Operation in Australia under the Torrens System," 1863; and "An Essay on the Transfer of Land by Registration," 1882.

20

THE LAW OF LAND REGISTRATION

The preamble to the 1920 Land Registration Law more than adequately established the need for the reform:

WHEREAS: it is a matter of public knowledge that land titles in Santo Domingo are in general so confused and uncertain as to handicap the development of the country, foster fraud and blackmail on a wholesale scale, and result in unjust deprivation of rightful owners of their land, thus provoking disorder and breaches of the peace, and tending to loss of confidence in the State; and

WHEREAS: this condition has been recognized in various proclamations, decrees and laws in the past, but all efforts at relief through statutes and otherwise have been inadequate and of little avail; and,

WHEREAS: to remedy this condition and restore confidence in property rights and peace to the State, a vigorous measure is necessary which will determine the true ownership of land and compel its public registration by a scientific method; and

WHEREAS: the Courts now established have their dockets crowded with criminal and civil matters, and a separate tribunal dealing exclusively with the present problem of land titles is essential to its proper solution;

NOW THEREFORE: by virtue of the powers vested in the Military Government, and the duty and power of every Government to remove obstacles to development, preserve property, restore tranquility and keep the peace, the following Order providing for the Registration of Lands and the Demarcation, Survey and Partition of *Terrenos Comuneros* is hereby dictated and promulgated.[1]

These were the administrative organs and procedures established by the law to correct the above deficiencies: The land court was composed of three justices, all of whom, to qualify, were required to have practiced law or have been a judge of a court of first instance or higher court in the Dominican Republic or a court of record in the United States. One of the justices was appointed president of the court, the others as associate justices. During its first years of existence two of the judges were American and one was Dominican. The first president of the court was Judge James A. Ostrand of the New York

---

1. Executive Order 511, July 1, 1920, signed Thomas Snowden, U.S., *Military Government*.

bar, who served until August 31, 1921, when he resigned to accept an appointment as associate justice of the Supreme Court of the Philippine Islands. Upon his departure he recommended that his Dominican associate, Judge Manuel de Jesús Troncoso de la Concha, who had served both his country and the military government in various legal and administrative capacities, be named president of the court, with Judge Robert C. Pound as associate. Accordingly, Troncoso de la Concha became the first Dominican president of the land court on January 1, 1922.

Additional judges of the same qualifications could be selected at the discretion of the executive power if needed to expedite registration of land. The court had exclusive jurisdiction over all matters relating to the registration of titles to land. It determined the validity of titles and all other matters affecting the ownership of land, and by its decree, could invest an established title in those persons it might determine to be the owners of the land. When sitting in its revisional, appellate, and administrative authority the court sat *en banc*. Two members of the court constituted a quorum, and the concurrence of two justices was necessary to pronounce a final judgment. When acting in the exercise of this authority, the court was known as the superior land court. Otherwise, court could be held by a single justice acting as a court of original jurisdiction, committed to the superior land court. The court had ample authority to summon witnesses and criminal jurisdiction to punish persons knowingly presenting false titles or giving false testimony.

The clerk of the land court, under the direction of the court, maintained custody and control of all papers filed in court proceedings. He attended all sessions and reported the proceedings. After land was registered in the manner provided for, he made all memoranda affecting the title, and entered and issued certificates of title.

The register of deeds was a new office, one to be established in the principal city of each province. Within the various provinces, all land titles then dispersed in the offices of the notarios and other officials were to be concentrated in the office of the register of deeds. The register kept a suitable record in which he entered all deeds and other instruments affecting titles and lands not yet registered. After registry he had the same authority as the clerk to make all memoranda affecting titles to such lands and to enter a new certificate of title. To promote uniformity all provincial registers of deeds were made subject to the general direction of the clerk of the land court. All records and papers filed in the office of a register of deeds were open to the public, subject to reasonable regulations prescribed by the clerk. The register of deeds was required to issue certified copies of all instruments filed and registered with him.

The president of the court was authorized to appoint a sufficient number of examiners of title to meet the needs of the court. The executive power appointed a *fiscal* (government attorney) of the land court and necessary assistants. The fiscal represented the government of the Dominican Republic and, as directed, all of the political subdivisions in any court proceedings in which the government had an interest. If the interests of a political subdivision conflicted with those of the central government, the former could retain its own counsel.

Each notary throughout the country was required to list immediately in triplicate all documents and notarial instruments in his possession pertaining to real property. Within sixty days he was required to deposit the documents, instruments, and triplicate lists with the custodian of mortgages (*conservador de hipotecas*) in the principal city of the province in which the notary was established. The secretary of each ayuntamiento possessing protocols, registers, documents, and instruments by virtue of the previous death of any notary or surveyor was required to transmit to the clerk of the land court all of the official notebooks kept by him in accordance with the Law of Survey.

After they had completed the above actions, these officials lost their qualifications to be legal custodians; the only legal depositories of original instruments affecting titles to real property would be those of the provincial registers of deeds.[2]

There were two methods prescribed whereby title cases could be brought before the land court: first, through voluntary application by persons claiming ownership of specific tracts of land;[3] second, through compulsory proceedings which the court itself could institute when it determined the settlement of all titles in a specified area to be necessary or convenient, including the partition of lands held as terrenos comuneros.

In the first method applicants filed their applications with the clerk of the land court through their local register of deeds, giving all data required on special, prepared forms. The petitioner attached to the executed form a plan of the land prepared by a public surveyor and the instruments of title. The instruments of title might take almost any form, even an ancient amparo real. As a first step, the court referred the papers to an examiner of titles who, after making a title search in the office of the register of deeds, then filed a report with the court with his recommendation. If the opinion of the examiner was adverse to the applicant, the applicant could withdraw or proceed. If in the opinion of the examiner the title was a good one, or if not and the applicant wished to proceed anyway, a general public notice of the filing of the application was made. The published notice was addressed to all persons who might claim an interest in the land to be registered, and gave them the opportunity to object prior to a fixed date or thereafter be barred. After the court hearing, if the court found that the applicant had proper title, it would order a decree of confirmation and registry to be entered.[4]

For each cadastral lot,[5] the clerk sent a certified copy of the decree of registration to the register of deeds in the province in which the land lay. The register transcribed the decree in a registration book in which a leaf or leaves in consecutive order were devoted exclusively to each title. The transcription became the original certificate of title, a certified exact copy of which, identified as "Owner's Duplicate Certificate," would be delivered to the owner. After the first certification was issued, any transaction which created or discharged encumbrances on the property was registered by filing with the register the instrument creating the encumbrance. Thereafter a note to this effect was made on the back of the original certificate and owner's duplicate.

The land court could also order compulsory registration proceedings in districts or areas where the public interest required priority action to settle and adjudicate titles. In these cases the court would refer to the secretary of development who in turn would

---

2. The custodian of mortgages was to be only a temporary custodian until the register of deeds could be appointed; thereupon, after turning over all of his records and documents to the register, the office of custodian of mortgages would cease to exist.

3. See Appendix 3 for a sample of the form eventually developed to request court permission to proceed with survey. Note that the court's permission was needed prior to conducting the survey.

4. The clerk of the land court signed every decree, setting forth full names of owner, marital status, any disability, description of the land, including cadastral numbers, and, in relative priority, all encumbrances.

5. The republic was to be divided into cadastral survey districts, each further subdivided into blocks and lots in the case of urban property and parcelas, or parcels, in the case of rural land. Using a combination of letters and numbers, all property within each cadastral district could then be identified.

initiate action to make the survey and plan of the lands involved. Should the land to be surveyed lie in a comunero district, or within the land to be surveyed should there lie a comunero district, the outside boundaries of the comunero land had to be shown, as well as the location of enclosed or cultivated land areas, pastures, buildings, and other improvements thereon, together with the names of owners or persons in possession. In addition, the surveyor made a rough topographical sketch which indicated as accurately as possible without the use of survey instruments the general character of the land, nature of the terrain, what part appeared to be arable and what part appeared to be of little or no value for cultivation, with his reasons. When the lands had been surveyed and plotted, the fiscal of the land court then filed a petition against persons owning, holding, claiming, possessing, or occupying such lands or any part, stating that titles to the land were to be settled and adjudicated in the public interest. The petition included a full description and cadastral identification of the lands. Upon receipt of the petition and accompanying plan, the clerk of the land court proceeded as in the case of voluntary registration described earlier. Parties to the registration were given ample opportunity to file objections to any part of the petition, especially to the description of the lands, and to be heard by the court, but they could not impede the actual process of registration.

The 1920 law made special provisions for the registration of lands held without title or in common title, that is, terrenos comuneros.[6] These were important provisions because they attacked the complicated landownership problem which Dominican legislators had been trying to solve for over a decade. The land court could expect to be confronted with considerable litigation over the validity of peso titles, especially if the land in question were unoccupied.

After the court had received all answers to the public notices, those individuals claiming title in the same land consulted the examiner of titles who, in addition to conducting a title search, received the written conflicting claims. When so directed by the court, he called hearings at which all parties were given the opportunity to present evidence and argument. In the absence of clear proof to the contrary, instruments of title to cover land not possessed by their claimants or their predecessors on December 13, 1919,[7] were presumed to be invalid. In the absence of like proof, titles presented in good faith to cover possessed land received a favorable presumption as to validity to the extent necessary to cover the land possessed. The law presumed good faith in absence of clear proof to the contrary. In other words, peso titles to lands not in possession were presumed invalid; peso titles supported by the fact of possession were presumed valid. Possession was essential.

During the hearing on the examiner's report, which included recommendations as to validity of each title and the proportion of common land to which each claimant with a valid title was entitled, the court could accept all or part of the report or order it recommitted for further findings. After final decision on titles the court proceeded with the partition of the land, observing the following rules:

---

6. Terrenos comuneros as used in this law were understood to mean individual tracts of land owned, or claimed to be owned, by two or more persons, the interest of each such person being represented by shares known as pesos or other rights which had reference to the value or proportionate rights, rather than to the area of land owned or claimed by such persons. Article 1. The origin of peso titles is covered in Chapter 13.

7. Article 1 defined "possession" as: (1) under actual cultivation or when put to some other beneficial use; (2) when surrounded or enclosed by fences, walls, hedges, ditches, trails, or similar means of indicating boundaries; or (3) when surveyed by a public surveyor as evidenced by a survey report (*acta de mensura*) and plan. December 13, 1919, was the date of suspension of the 1911 Law on Partition of Terrenos Comuneros.

First, if there were no persons in possession on December 13, 1919, the court, in ordering the division, would take into consideration the topographical aspects of the common land which might affect the value of the various parts. This action amounted to a simple division of land, giving to each co-owner as nearly as possible a portion of land corresponding in value to that to which he was lawfully entitled.

Second, a co-owner legally in possession on December 13, 1919, of a portion not greater than that to which he was lawfully entitled would be assigned that portion. If he were entitled to more land than he actually occupied, an additional quantity to make up the deficiency would be assigned him, if possible, adjacent to the land he already possessed. If he occupied more than he was legally entitled to, he was given the option of purchasing the excess at a price fixed by the court, which would recognize the value of any improvements he had made.[8] If he so desired, the court would note the value of the excess as an encumbrance in favor, proportionately, of other co-owners in the common land, to make full payment within one year of be foreclosed in the land court at any time thereafter. If the owner failed to purchase the excess in full either immediately or at the end of the year of encumbrance, the law directed the court to eject the owner from the excess portion possessed by him.

Third, a person not a co-owner but in possession of common land for less time than that required for the ripening of prescription[9] could either purchase the land outright from all of the co-owners or accept the price as an encumbrance and pay for it within one year. If he failed to choose either of these options, the court would order his ejection from the land thus unlawfully possessed; if he failed to pay the encumbrance on time, the court could foreclose at any time thereafter.

Fourth, if for any reason property included in a comunero district was not susceptible of equitable division and the co-owners failed to agree as to the disposition of the property, the court could order the sale of the land and improvements at public auction. The net proceeds would be distributed among the various co-owners in proportion to their interests. Only a few of these cases were contemplated, for example, small portions of valuable land not useful if divided, or where indivisible improvements were the principal value. The only equitable solution was sale of the land and division of proceeds.

In effecting the partition, the court would order the public surveyor to award each

---

8. This provision compares with a similar one in the colonial Law of *Composición*: the opportunity to buy encroached but occupied land.

9. Article 69 defined prescription as it was then currently defined by common law except that possession for ten years, including the six months immediately succeeding the promulgation of the law, would be sufficient. Under common law, a total of thirty years of uninterrupted, peaceful, public, and unequivocal occupation by an owner or his predecessors without title or document but supported by witnesses was necessary to establish prescriptive rights. If the owner possessed documentation and could prove good faith at time of acquisition such as by a bill of sale, he could satisfy the time element by twenty years of possession if he lived in another province. If he lived in the same province, he could satisfy the time element by only ten years of possession. The thirty-year period without documentation was prescribed in Article 2262 of the Civil Code, the twenty- or ten-year period by Article 2265. It should be noted that the documentation referred to in Article 2265 did not require title but only written proof of lawful acquisition. Ruiz Tejada, *Estudio*, pp. 258–59.

Under the 1920 law, then, an uninterrupted, peaceful, public, and unequivocal possession by a co-owner in a comunero district for the ten-year period was sufficient to entitle him to register the land thus possessed. Sworn opposition by another co-owner could be entered during a period of four months immediately succeeding the promulgation of the law. If the claimant could satisfy the prescriptive elements of time and legal possession, the fact of possession was transformed into the right of possession, and the Law of 1920 gave the claimant by prescription an equal right to claim title as that held by a co-owner with title.

of the parties their just proportion of land, which the court itself would determine. The surveyor's plan for equitable partition into lots and parcels would consider insofar as possible the preferences of the parties, those portions of the whole which were actually possessed, and the relative value of the various subdivisions. He was required to submit his final plan to the court for approval. If the court found the plan fair and just, it would issue a judgment accordingly. If found to be unjust, unfair, or defective, the court might accept the plan in part and issue a judgment on that part, or it might require submission of an entirely new plan.

In cases of land for which no other ownership was established, the court entered decrees in favor of the state, declaring it to be the owner of the land and ordering the issue of certificates of title to that effect.

In determining questions of title the court was required to give first consideration to claims of persons in actual possession of cultivated, fenced, improved, or staked out lands.[10] For the benefit of those in possession without instruments of title, or by virtue of such instruments if the title proved to be invalid for acquiring title by prescription, the period of possession was reduced to ten years. On the other hand, persons presenting peso titles alleged by them to be vested in lands not used, occupied, or possessed by such persons at the time the law was promulgated, had every presumption against the validity of such titles which could be overcome only by establishing beyond reasonable doubt that the titles were genuine. Where the presumption was not overcome, and this would be the case in most forged or fraudulent titles, the lands became the property of the state if there were no rightful owner.

Other conditions which rendered titles invalid were: an earlier adverse decision by a court of competent jurisdiction; decision by the land court after investigation that a title was forged, fraudulent, or invalid on account of some substantial defect or irregularity; or titles to land against which prescription had run in favor of another owner. There was also a presumption against the validity of notarial deeds or documents the originals of which were found to have been separated from the registers or notaries, against instruments of title not containing the note of inscription in the provincial book of inscriptions, and against instruments not registered in the registry of civil acts.

The Land Registration Law of 1920 provided the legal landowner with a secure title

---

10. A number of unscrupulous owners in possession sought to encroach on adjacent unoccupied land by digging ditches or erecting fences in order to fulfill the legal definition of possession. This action would later give them a basis to claim the unoccupied land of other legal but unwary owners. The distracted alcalde of Sabana de la Mar, on the south shore of the Bay of Samaná, complained of this problem to the Officer Administering the Department of Agriculture and Immigration:

> In consequence of the many quarrels which are daily brought before the Alcalde relative to trails being opened in the terrenos comuneros, persons who having only 10 or 20 pesos of title are opening trails bounding an infinite number of caballerías of land, and some of the co-owners are being shut out of their land.
> I feel obliged to submit to your consideration for you to tell me what I should do.
> [s] Angel Torres

This problem was thoroughly studied by the military government, which quickly issued an executive order warning encroaching land owners that the marks of useful occupation, such as fences and trails, were so considered only if they had been made in good faith and not for the obvious purpose of taking additional land by illegal means. Civil governors were told to "get the fences down" so that the cultivation of the soil could proceed without interruption. Letter, September 27, 1920, Files of the Legal Officer, U.S., *Military Government*.

to his land. He could be sure that his title, once registered, would stand against all bodies, including the state and any of its political subdivisions.

The law required that land titles must first be purified and then registered in an official registry book available for inspection by interested parties. The registrar who maintained the book had to certify the entry; the initial registry of title and any later modifications thereto could be made only in the official book.

To replace the many dispersed and uncoordinated notarial files, the law established one central source of title information concerning a specific property and required that any legal operation affecting title must be taken to that source and be duly noted on the original title. The act of registry required proof of the legality of the modifying documents and the identification, capacity, and authority of the individuals desiring to affect the original title.

The law endowed an original title certificate and all certified copies and the owner's duplicate copy with executive force, acceptable in any court in the republic as proven documents of whatever rights, actions and duties might appear on them.

The law made mandatory the Torrens system as adapted for use in the Dominican Republic, with the objective of bringing all land registration into conformity within ten years. Theoretically, with unlimited funds for survey operations and for operational costs of the land court and its agencies, this goal could perhaps have been achieved. In practice, progress was steady but slow. Even before the military government had been withdrawn, the lack of funds had begun to limit the activities of the land court.[11] The elements of the evolving land court system were administratively organized into: the general office of cadastral surveys which, with the necessary technical personnel, was charged with supervising, controlling, and reviewing the work of the public surveyors; the office of state lawyers, the attorneys who represented the state and acted as prosecutors in the land court; judges of original jurisdiction, charged with trying cases in the first stage of purification proceedings; a high court consisting of the president of the court and four associate justices; a general secretariat; and five registers of deeds, established in the capital, San Cristóbal, San Pedro de Macorís, Santiago, and La Vega.

There were modifications to the 1920 law, most of them not substantive: more detailed administrative procedures concerning such matters as the cadastral surveys; taking of testimony; appeals from decision of the court of original jurisdiction and from the superior court itself;[12] handling of title certificates; and eviction procedures. The current law is that of 1947[13] which superseded the original law of 1920 but retained the principal features of the latter.

The United States was generally censured for the 1916 intervention by Dominican leaders and writers, by others elsewhere in Latin America, and by a number of prominent Americans, especially Republicans during the 1920 presidential campaign. The military government of occupation was criticized for its imposition of censorship; for

---

11. Quarterly Report of the Military Governor, April 22, 1922, ibid. Rear Admiral Robison added that despite the shortage of funds, the court still functioned, proceeding with those cases in which funds for surveys had been advanced by property owners. Some eighty-four final decrees in adjudication of titles had been issued.

12. Appeals from superior court decisions may be heard by the Dominican Supreme Court, but only on grounds of possible violation of law. There is no appeal from the adjudication decisions of the superior land court.

13. República Dominicana, *Ley de registro de tierras*, No. 1542, October 11, 1947. Published in *Gaceta Oficial*, No. 6707 of November 7, 1947.

atrocities committed by U.S. marines; for manipulation of Dominican tariffs in order to benefit American industry; for increasing the Dominican national debt even though a major purpose was to pay for badly needed public works programs;[14] and for abusing rights of the individual in implanting modern sanitation systems. On the other hand, I have found no serious attack and little valid criticism of the Land Registration Law of 1920. Regarding the law, Knight, writing in 1925 and 1926, says: "The emphasis on clear, individual titles incidentally gave the sugar planters the opportunity they had sought for many years."[15] Presumably referring to encroachment on common land, he fails to mention the overriding significance and pervasiveness of false titles. However, he does admit that as a result of the registration law, "the land title situation was improved and may even be thoroughly reformed in the course of years." Knight also criticizes the law for requiring a survey that "would have taken many years and cost a vast sum, in many cases more than the land was worth." The generalization on the high costs of survey deserves closer examination. In the Cibao, where the best farm land was located, worth from fifteen to thirty dollars per tarea, the surveyor's usual charge was twelve to eighteen cents per tarea, or about one dollar an acre. In those cases where the owner could not pay in cash, the surveyor would accept an agreed percentage of the land in payment.[16]

This is not to say that with the promulgation of the law, all land frauds ceased and all surveyors, notaries, lawyers, judges, and other involved officials immediately became paragons of virtue. In the correction of a system of landownership described by Dominicans themselves as a national misfortune, there undoubtedly were cases where claimants of prescriptive rights or holders of questionable titles purchased or acquired in good faith found themselves without property as the result of an unfavorable court

---

14. Peynado was particularly upset about the tariff and debt questions. He wrote a series of lengthy articles for *Listín Diario*, analyzing the policy of the military government in these matters and calling on the United States to restore Dominican independence, but with the assurance of friendship. Specifically, he asked for three concessions. First, he hoped to correct the error committed by the military government which, without consent of the Dominicans, had modified the import tariffs in 1919. The new rates, selectively lowered, brought special benefits to American exporters but tended to handicap the Dominican economy which suffered from a lack of protection for its infant industries. Second, he urged that the United States give Dominican imports the same tariff advantage as those given Cuban products. Third, he wanted the United States to hand back the public treasury, not in the existing disastrous state (annual interest on external debts increased from $1.2 million in 1916 to $3.2 million in 1922, all under the military government) but in the same condition it was when the occupation occurred, that is, able to service the public debt without prejudice to the other administrative services. *Listín Diario*, Feb. 25; March 2, 3, 7, 1922. Peynado's last statement, of course, is the Dominican position on the definition of "public debt" and is subject to challenge, but on the whole his analysis was correct. Knight has written in detail of the United States economic penetration of the Dominican Republic in *The Americans in Santo Domingo*.

15. Ibid. pp. 104, 106.

16. I have examined several notarized contracts made in 1920 between co-owners of terrenos comuneros and surveyors in La Vega province which show the above survey cost figures. Notarial Acts of Pedro R. Pichardo, U.S., *Military Government*. Knight's failure to appreciate the need for a national land survey and his concentration on the contemporary economic situation with its heavy accent on the sugar industry indicated a lack of familiarity with the earlier defective land title registration system. He never really addresses himself to the inequities created by false titles on a national scale. His comments on landownership problems are superficial and lack historical perspective. On the whole, those owners whose titles were cloudy were the ones who complained about the required surveys. Landowners who possessed good titles were the first to take advantage of the security offered by the new 1920 law.

decision. That there would be some injustice created under the law in cases of apparently legal but opposing claims was anticipated by the military government, yet there was no alternative to drastic reform except continued chaos.[17] Any law intended to correct a longstanding inequity such as the Dominican land fraud problem could be expected to hurt someone. The situation in the Dominican Republic in 1920 was analogous to that of 1789 in the United States with respect to Alexander Hamilton's solution for funding the public debt. There was a need to establish public order based on a foundation of ethical policy if confidence in the land system was to be created. The greatest good for the greatest number of landowners over the longest period had to be the goal of the new law, even at the possible cost of some initial injustice. If there was loss of property as a result of court decisions, one should not confuse long-term justice with sympathy for the sufferers. Once incorporated into an adequate legal system, the law itself would be useful and salutary. As one Dominican surveyor wrote in 1926, in rebutting the complaints of some individuals whose peso titles, without possession, had not withstood the legal tests:

> The Law of Land Registry is good. I do not deny that it has evils as all new laws have . . . . Rule of possession was the only way to do away with false land titles expressed in peso shares or in any other units or forms. I do not pretend to make anyone believe this was the only way to avoid fraud, or that frauds have been eliminated. But now fraud is more difficult; there are fewer of them and they are of lesser importance. . . . It is lamentable if the land court is corrupted by politics. The court is alert to the matter of acquisition of lands by foreign companies and by Dominicans for the sole purpose of selling them to new foreign companies coming into the country. The problem is that lands are being lost through native Dominicans. The small landholder cannot do anything to settle his fears. He has no recourse. We need laws that will permit the formation of rural associations and urban capital to convert uncultivated and futureless land into productive and valuable land . . . . So it is that the land court in these same cases has launched all its forces to save the small rural landowners from the nets spread by Dominicans. . . .[18]

The inescapable conclusion is that the Torrens system, as adapted to the Dominican Republic in 1920, was accepted by Dominicans then as it has been ever since. The current law maintains the principles established almost fifty years ago. Prior to 1920 the land registration laws were weak and not enforced. With the 1920 reform a strong, workable, and essentially equitable law was placed in effect, was recognized by Dominicans as fair, and has since been enforced successfully and equitably. Were the law defective, it seems highly unlikely that Manuel Ramón Ruiz Tejada, professor of land law at the University of Santo Domingo, future president of the superior land court and future president of the Supreme Court would write in 1952:

> It is clear that the system implanted by our Land Registration Law offers advantages which no one can deny. It stops the uncertainty over the rights of real property and provides the holder of those rights with a certificate which is a title for the bearer, which in itself is as good as money, which no one can discount, and which is imprescriptible. . . . He who acquires a land title purified by survey has the secure ownership of what he has acquired. . . . Furthermore, the liberality of the procedures which the Land Registration Law has established are understood and proclaimed by Article 271 when

---

17. Comments by the legal officer on the forthcoming 1920 Land Law, legal files, ibid.

18. Miguel A. Fiallo, "Central Romana y Ley de Registro de Tierras," *Listín Diario*, August 31, 1926, p. 1.

it says that: "wherever possible, this law will be interpreted in accordance with the spirit in which it was given"; by the ease with which one can claim the rights possessed; the wide scope of the investigation by the land court . . . to seek the truth and grant the title to whom it belongs, even though he may not have claimed it . . . the guarantees offered all parties. . . . All this indicates a system scientifically organized to lead to the formation of a property list which recognizes only those titles which have first been cleansed and legalized.[19]

Were the law defective, the Dominicans would have changed the principles on which it was based, rejecting or reshaping it as they did with defective legislation during their colonial period. This they have not done. In one important aspect, a long history of *hecho* as distinct from *derecho*, was brought to a close by the Land Registration Law of 1920.

---

19. Ruiz Tejada, *Estudio*, pp. 423–24.

21

THE TRUJILLO PERIOD

As the American occupation wore on, the Dominicans grew more impatient. There arose the same nationalistic impulses which in their times had overthrown the French, the Haitians, and the Spaniards. By the time the military government had pacified the eastern provinces Dominican leaders of all political groups were already actively seeking a solution which would restore the control of Dominican affairs to Dominicans. "Desocupación, pura y simple" was the phrase of the day. The restoration of internal order, it was remembered, had been a major objective of the occupation.[1] Growing out of the anti-occupation campaign conducted abroad by Dominican nationalists, Latin American and European pressure on the United States to withdraw became more apparent.[2] Aware of these pressures and convinced that the military government had served its purpose, the State Department in 1919 sought to substitute a civil government as the first step toward the relaxation of control.

One of the earliest official proposals to substitute civil for military government had come from Russell shortly after the occupation had taken place. Russell recommended that there be at least one more year of military government to permit the American forces to achieve the needed reforms, to be followed by a period of control by a junta amenable to American advice.[3] Another recommendation came from General Receiver of Customs Clarence H. Baxter, in March 1918. Baxter pointed to the satisfaction of nearly all

---

1. See the reference to Proclamation of November 29, 1916, Chap. 17.
2. State Department files on the Dominican Republic for 1919–21 contain a number of communications from American diplomatic representatives in France, Mexico, Cuba, Chile, Argentina, Uruguay, and Brazil, all reporting in one form or another the desires of those countries for an end to the intervention. Political files, 1919–21, United States, *Internal Affairs of the D.R.*, passim. Henríquez y Carvajal and other active nationalists had campaigned in the Caribbean, South America, and Europe for immediate and complete evacuation of all American troops.
3. Telegram, Dec. 14, 1916, Russell to Secretary of State, ibid. Lansing concurred in a telegram dated Dec. 20, 1916, ibid.

Dominicans at the absence of fighting and political disturbance, the highest collection of revenue in the nation's history, and the generally prosperous state of business, and suggested that a civil governor be appointed. But it was not until nearly a year later that the subject was seriously discussed in Washington. By early January 1919 Russell was decidedly unhappy over conditions in Santo Domingo. Knapp had left. His regular relief had not yet appeared; and it seemed to the minister that the government of occupation should be presided over by a State Department representative, not a naval officer likely to be unfamiliar with the functions of government. Russell was now of the opinion that the Dominican Republic had passed the revolutionary stage and could gradually begin to take over its own government. In a legation report to the State Department, dated January 17, Russell supported the idea of a U.S. commission form of government which later would include Dominicans. Accordingly, a State-Navy group met at the Navy Department shortly thereafter to discuss a State Department proposal to do away with the military government. The Navy representative objected, saying that the government was not yet ready to be turned over to the Dominicans and that a civilian cabinet in a military government could not be made to work.[4]

More or less concurrently with these developments, the ousted Henríquez y Carvajal carried on a steady campaign in Washington, in writing and in person, urging in reasoned language that the government be turned back to the Dominicans. According to his calculations, Santo Domingo had been occupied for twelve years, and the time had come to remove American control. In December 1919 the chief of the Latin American Affairs Division of the State Department, noting that the military government was carrying on the greater part of its activities without reference to the Department of State, wrote that in the near future Dominican affairs should be put under civilian control, such as a provisional government.[5]

Several factors delayed progress in this direction: the Dominicans' insistence on disavowing all acts of the military government and on the evacuation of all American troops from their country as prior conditions to any negotiations; mutual distrust between the military government and the more nationalistic Dominicans; and the lack of a coordinated U.S. policy on withdrawal because of the military government's conservative estimate of the capability of the Dominicans to handle their own affairs. This last factor, the conflict in policy objectives between the two United States departments, leads to interesting conjecture. Should the United States have evacuated the Dominican Republic even though the desired reforms had not been completed? The State Department reacted to the strong currents of Dominican nationalism. The Navy, on the other hand, continued to view the problems as the United States had seen them in 1916 and believed that the Dominicans needed more time to stabilize their political institutions. Snowden estimated in 1919 that the military government would be needed for ten years longer to insure peace and prosperity. "It is the reasoned view of the undersigned that the status quo should be maintained absolutely both here and in Haiti in spite of the sympathetic agitation of other peoples in a misdirected effort to assist the Dominican people to a premature taking over of their own destinies."[6]

---

4. Memo for record of Navy Conference, January 27, 1919, signed Stabler, ibid.

5. Memorandum to the Latin American Affairs Division, subject: Policy towards Santo Domingo, signed, J. C. Dunn, ibid. Dunn thought that Minister Russell was the best-qualified candidate for the job.

6. Letter, serial 1276–19, Military Governor to Secretary of the Navy, subject: Effectiveness of *guardia nacional dominicana*, June 23, 1919, signed Snowden, ibid. Sumner Welles, who played

The Americans, for their part, insisted that all acts of the military government, including the proclamation of occupation, be recognized as valid; that national elections be called for by the military government; that there be provision for a sizeable legation guard and U.S. military mission; and that a U.S. financial advisor to the Dominican government be appointed. Neither side was willing to compromise on the major issues; the stalemate continued for almost three years.

A Dominican initiative set the stage for agreement between the two countries. Although he had announced to the Dominican press that he was traveling to New York for reasons of health, Francisco Peynado arrived in Washington early in March 1922 as a knowledgable private citizen armed with specific ideas and the strong desire to extract his people from their predicament. He participated in several meetings with Secretary of State Charles E. Hughes, Sumner Welles, who was chief of the Latin American Division, Senators Medill McCormick and Atlee Pomerene, Secretary of the Navy Edwin Denby, and Dana G. Munroe, also of the Latin American Division. Almost at once Hughes accepted Peynado's proposal to form a provisional government but categorically refused to agree to an immediate withdrawal of troops. The main issue, as seen in Washington, soon became apparent: U.S. troops would not be taken out of Santo Domingo until the validity of the acts of the military government was recognized and ratified by a responsible Dominican government. Through hard work and patience on both sides, agreement was gradually reached. An unhappy Peynado finally compromised rather than accept the alternative of prolonged occupation. On the American side, Hughes compromised on the issues of recognition of all military government acts, the calling for elections by the military government, the establishment of a legation guard and military mission, and the assignment of a financial advisor.[7]

In early summer 1922 both sides settled on the general conditions and procedures for ending the occupation. The military governor did not play a large role in this phase for several reasons. He had inherited the general hostility of the Dominicans toward the military government; there was little he could do in 1921 or 1922 to change a widespread national feeling which had been growing since about 1919. The conferences with Peynado had been held in Washington under resurgent State Department leadership. Robison was simply not in a position to influence the outcome which was more appropriately determined by the normal techniques of diplomacy. And, finally, relating to both of the above points, Robison was not especially qualified to negotiate a withdrawal

a major role in the negotiations, later commented on this point shortly after the evacuation plan had been signed. Writing to Francis White of his relations with the military governor, he said: "Relations are exceedingly friendly, but we have to face the fact that the Navy Department looks at the whole situation from a view which is radically different from ours. Our idea is, of course, to get out at the earliest possible opportunity in accordance with the conditions of the Plan. The idea of the Navy Department is to get out more or less within the provisions of the Plan (of which they all say they do not approve) at a time when the military government believes that the governmental machinery it leaves to the succeeding Dominican government is running efficiently. . . . I do not believe we need to give in to the Navy Department one step. If we do, we are immediately open to the charge of bad faith, and all the party leaders will at once withdraw from further participation with us in our program of evacuation." Letter, Welles to Francis White, Chief, U.S. Latin American Affairs Division, State Department, August 2, 1922, ibid.

7. Letter, Horace G. Knowles to Francisco Henríquez y Carvajal, July 1, 1922, H. G. Knowles files, Francisco J. Peynado papers, República Dominicana. Archivo de la Nación, Santo Domingo. Knowles, a former minister to the Dominican Republic, was a paid New York lobbyist for the ousted constitutional government of the Dominican Republic.

because he understood little of the Dominicans or their country.[8]

The proposed convention, sometimes referred to by the Americans as the Hughes-Peynado Plan and by Dominicans as the Plan for Liberation, was signed in Washington on June 30, 1922. Negotiations for final approval of the convention continued in Santo Domingo. Welles was now on the scene as U.S. commissioner with plenipotentiary powers. He, Peynado, and other like-minded Dominicans labored diligently to convince the Dominican public that the plan should be approved. At the same time Welles had the difficult task of securing the cooperation of the military government. The past tendency of the military governors to ignore the legation or the State Department, or both, in matters which had serious diplomatic implications had been a source of irritation to Welles and others of the State Department which did not facilitate working relationships in Santo Domingo, especially after Welles arrived in 1922. At one point Welles was even advised unofficially that the State Department did not trust Robison to carry out the evacuation plan.[9] Despite this added complication, by campaigning from one extreme of the land to the other, Welles and his Dominican colleagues were able to persuade the majority of political leaders and the press that the convention would serve the best interests of the Dominican Republic. The plan was officially signed by representatives of the two governments on September 13 as a treaty of evacuation.[10]

---

8. The admiral was a distinguished naval officer who, until the Dominican assignment opened, had hoped for a command at sea in the Pacific Fleet. Diverted to the troubled little Caribbean republic, he did his best to administer the military government efficiently, but he spoke no Spanish and had no particular knowledge of either Dominican or Latin American affairs. Mrs. Robison tried to adjust as best she could to life in Santo Domingo by taking Spanish lessons and planting an American vegetable garden. Both were reasonably pleased with their quarters. The admiral's personal correspondence of this period is more concerned with his interest in professional naval matters and reflects a certain irritation with Dominican intractability rather than any philosophic appreciation of the political role either he or the United States was playing. The governor was not even familiar with the physical characteristics of his "Command," writing that "the whole country is a coral rock with a thin covering of rich soil." Personal files of the Military Governor, 1921–22, República Dominicana, *Files of the Military Government.*

9. Personal letter, Francis White to Welles, September 18, 1922, U.S., *Internal Affairs of the D.R.* Welles described his relations with Robison as friendly, but his opinion of the military government as a political organization, fortunately for the agencies concerned, remained concealed in unofficial channels. He described the military government as incompetent, inexperienced, sometimes actively prejudiced, wasteful, extravagant, and inefficient. Personal letter, Welles to Francis White, September 5, 1922, ibid.

Judge Otto Schoenrich had been only slightly less critical of the military government. He described American navy and marine officers as conscientious but inexperienced and not good administrators. In the judge's opinion, the majority had shown no sympathy or interest in their work, and a few had been overbearing tyrants. Almost all had depended on Puerto Rican interpreters, who often adopted an annoying, superior, and haughty air toward Dominicans. Report of Judge Otto Schoenrich to the Department of State, July–August 1920, ibid. The judge made a special trip to Santo Domingo to report on conditions there, at the request of the State Department.

10. Peynado emerged from the 1922 negotiations quite justifiably as something of a national hero. He ran for president in the 1924 campaign, but was unable to overcome the popularity of Horacio Vásquez. Although he was sure there had been some irregularities in the voting, Peynado appealed to his followers to forget any rancors or indignation they might have. He urged them to cooperate with the new government in the interests of national unity and the need to work for the better good of the nation. *Listín Diario,* March 24, 1924, p. 1. Peynado never sought high office thereafter. The essence of his appeal, quoted from his speech after the 1924 elections, is engraved in the marble slab covering his tomb in the cathedral.

These were the principal clauses, all of which represented compromise on main issues: Dominican party leaders would set up a provisional government, which in turn would arrange for national and provincial elections; the elected government would recognize the validity of specific acts of the military government which had been published in the *Gaceta Oficial* and which had levied taxes, authorized expenditures, established rights on behalf of third parties,[11] approved contracts, and established administrative regulations; the Dominican government would recognize as legal obligations the bond issues of 1918 and 1922; the 1907 Convention would remain in effect so long as the bond issues remained unpaid; American military forces would be completely evacuated from Dominican territory coincident with the inauguration of the new constitutional government.[12]

As indicated above, one of the early ideas proposed by the Americans was that a long-term military mission be ordered from Washington to take command of the Dominican armed forces to train and develop them. The proposal was offensive to leading Dominicans, who unanimously rejected it. One cannot help but wonder how many of these same citizens in the years to come may have cursed their own sensitivity. Under such an arrangement as the above, Trujillo could never have used the army as a stepping-stone to dictatorship. But in the ebullience of the times, the editor of Santo Domingo's *Listín Diario* undoubtedly expressed the thoughts that were uppermost in the minds of most Dominican policymakers:

> But as to this military intervention which is about to end, we must see to it that it is not only the first but the last, and therefore there must be no doors left open for caprice, private interests or American imperialistic ambition to find some pretext to enter, invade our territory, and govern us paternally for our own good, our instruction, and edification. We neither desire nor do we need another lesson. The first has been more than sufficient.[13]

The Dominicans installed a provisional government on October 21, 1922, adopted a new constitution on June 13, 1924, and on that same day elected Horacio Vásquez president of the republic. He was inaugurated on July 12, 1924. By September 17, 1924, there were no United States forces on Dominican soil or in Dominican waters.[14]

Party warfare soon resumed over budget problems and a proposed loan agreement[15] with the United States, but there was no gunfire, no political imprisonment, and no forced exile. There was freedom of speech, personal liberty, and security. Within six years General Rafael Leónidas Trujillo Molina would completely reverse these conditions.

---

11. This provision was especially important to the land reform. Had there been no such stipulation, all the recently adjudicated titles could have been challenged.

12. See "Convention of Ratification between the United States and the Dominican Republic as Contained in the Agreement of Evacuation of June 30, 1922," Edward J. Trenwith, comp., *Treaties, Conventions, International Acts, Protocols, and Agreements, 1923–1937*, 4:4077–87.

13. *Listín Diario*, June 7, 1922. This was an intelligent appeal, but as events soon demonstrated the Dominicans were still incapable of governing themselves in accord with the free, democratic principles expressed in their Constitution.

14. *Listín Diario, Sept. 18*, 1924. Russell tersely reported on the same day: "Provisions of plan of evacuation have been completed and all of the forces of occupation have left the country." Telegram, Russell to Secretary of State, No. 55, Sept. 18, 1924, U.S., *Internal Affairs of the D.R.* At 1 P.M. the USS *Kittery* got underway en route to the United States with the last troop detachment on board.

15. Vásquez had criticized Ramón Cáceres' approval of the 1907 Convention which bound Dominican finances to the United States.

Vásquez launched his administration under reasonably favorable conditions. The Americans were gone, the economic depression was being transformed into prosperity, and the popular caudillo of the Cibao apparently had an open road ahead after almost twenty five years of struggle to reach the presidency. But his was the problem of many caudillos who sought power for power's sake: he had little administrative ability or capacity to rise above party politics.[16] One of Vásquez' early and perhaps greatest mistakes was to politicize the national police previously established by the military government. In the best tradition of the cacique, Vásquez made it an arm of his political party rather than of the nation.[17] He tended to place too much confidence in those who were close to him and could never effectively unite a majority of Dominican leaders to accomplish national programs. Now sixty-four, he began to display a lack of resolution and unwillingness to grapple with difficult problems. Most of his country's internal difficulties originated with the *Progresista* followers of Federico Velásquez who, although Vásquez' vice-president, did not feel constrained to cooperate with the president's policies, especially in financial matters. The Progresistas in Congress followed suit. The alliance[18] between the two men collapsed in April 1926; thereafter their two parties continued the same myopic politics that had crippled the country for generations. Even worse, the unity of the Horacistas began to disintegrate as cliques formed around individual members of the cabinet. The president's questionable[19] decision to run for reelection in 1927 created a deep political crisis which was only temporarily resolved by the convening of a special constitutent assembly by the Horacista majority in Congress. In instituting a number of reforms, the assembly bowed to Vásquez' ambition by extending the presidential term for two years as a temporary measure until elections could be held in 1930. Still not satisfied with this one-time modification, some of the more active Horacistas almost immediately began a campaign in the name of party unity to reform the constitution permanently to permit presidential reelection. The subject of reelection split the country

---

16. Sumner Welles, who spent long hours with Vásquez during the writing of *Naboth's Vineyard*, had accurately predicated what sort of president Vásquez would be. In 1923, during the presidential campaign being waged between Vásquez, Peynado, and Velásquez, Welles wrote that Vásquez was the most sincerely patriotic of the three candidates, although the other two were good men, and that he certainly was a scrupulously honest person. But his weakness of character and openness to influence made evident that any government he would head would be a disaster. Letter, April 23,1923, Welles to Department of State, ibid.

17. Before the end of 1924 Vásquez dismissed the competent officer second-in-command of the Police who had proven to be an unenthusiastic Horacista. The replacement: Major Rafael Leónidas Trujillo. Message 1069, December 10, 1924, Russell to Secretary of State, ibid.

18. They had formed a political alliance *(Alianza nacional)*, at least for the latter part of the campaign. Francisco Peynado continued to control an important minority.

19. Under the 1908 Constitution the president was elected for a term of six years and could be reelected; under the 1924 constitution the term was reduced to four years and reelection prohibited. Vásquez felt that four years was not enough, although his party had campaigned in 1923 and 1924 for the reduced term. In the March 1924 primary elections the Horacistas had won a clear electoral victory. The electors, committed to their parties, proceeded to elect senators and deputies who were seated on May 10. The Congress then drew up and approved a constitutional reform and submitted it to a constituent assembly, which approved the new constitution on June 13. The electoral college was then reconvened and, under the new constitution, elected Vásquez president. Vásquez claimed that he had actually been put into office by electors who had been picked under the 1908 Constitution and that therefore he was entitled to a six-year term. A majority of his followers supported him; the opposition claimed that reelection would be illegal. The Supreme Court was never consulted, nor was Vásquez the man to risk his high office on an interpretation of law.

even more deeply than before.[20] In October 1929, when the campaign was at its height, a sudden, dangerous attack of nephritis took Vásquez to Johns Hopkins Hospital in Baltimore for emergency surgery. At this point, Trujillo, backed by a personally loyal national army, emerged from the political semi-shadows.

Of Trujillo's undistinguished early life, we need only note here that on December 18, 1918, at the age of twenty-seven, he qualified for a direct commission as a second lieutenant in the Dominican national guard. From that point on, his rise in the guard, which became the national police and still later, the national army, was rapid. But unlike many a *general de dedo*,[21] his early promotions were merited on a record of competency.[22] In 1925 Horacio Vásquez, who was one day to regret his faith in Trujillo, promoted him to command the national police and in 1928 the national army. From 1925 on, the army became Trujillo's personal force, as officers who were prominent during the military government and who had the best records were forced out of the service. The fundamental quality Trujillo demanded of noncommissioned and commissioned officers was personal loyalty to himself; all else was secondary. He was a tough disciplinarian, resentful and suspicious of competition, and a master at dissimulation. Aided by an extensive secret police machinery which eventually pervaded the entire country, he had an almost infallible ability to sense incipient opposition.[23] Just as surely as Vásquez began to lose control of his own administration, Trujillo became more and more a potential power

---

20. Years earlier Manuel de Jesús Troncoso de la Concha had warned about the consequences of a return to the old political ways. He had urged his countrymen to understand the advisability of the United States helping the Dominicans to know how to be free, using the same power it had used to intervene. Failing in this, they could expect nothing better than that which had brought on the intervention, because the same morbid germ which had led them to their present state would remain. In this event, "the Dominicans would either return to the past times of discord *or a despotic system would be established* [author's emphasis]. And when this happens, gentlemen, we will be just as backward as before, and material benefits would bring us little, even if our hands were lavishly filled." La Vega *El Progreso*, August 28, 1918. Ironically, within a few years after he had established his dictatorship, Trujillo named Troncoso de la Concha to be president of the Dominican Republic. The appointment was not of Troncoso de la Concha's seeking or choice.

21. Literally a "finger general." The term is used to describe an individual whose military qualifications are nonexistent but who obtains a commission when his powerful patron points a finger at him and says in so many words: "You are now a general."

22. *Listín Diario* on March 21, 1924, reported that Major Rafael Trujillo had been assigned to the Cibao to command the Northern sector and congratulated him on his new duty. The paper noted that he had just been promoted from the rank of captain on the basis of his military record and wished him continued success.

Under the supervision of U.S. Marine Corps officers, Trujillo had been trained in the Dominican national guard along with the other Dominicans who were to become officers in the national constabulary. In the June 1919 register, he is shown as number 15 on a list of 16 second lieutenants. There were also seven Dominican first lieutenants in the register which contained the total guard roster of 54 officers. There is no evidence that Trujillo received any special treatment or training during the period of his service under American supervision or observation. Photostatic copies of his service record indicate that he received marks of "Excellent" in personal characteristics such as military bearing and cleanliness of person, and "Very Good" in most professional aptitudes. His lowest marks "Good" were in material maintenance and performance of duty with superior officers. Ernesto Vega y Pagán, *Military Biography of Generalissimo Rafael Leónidas Trujillo Molina*, pp. 41–54.

23. Memorandum 71–1925 signed by Colonel Rafael L. Trujillo shows how he kept himself informed. The memorandum was addressed to all national police company commanders, ordering them to submit weekly reports commencing August 31, 1915, giving information on

despite the fact that he apparently showed no interest in politics. In 1927 the American minister reported Trujillo's probable promotion and added that as a military leader with a capacity for developing and maintaining an efficient and well-disciplined organization, Colonel Trujillo was outstanding, a soldier with loyalty first to the government and with an ability thus far to avoid the pitfalls of factional politics. If he had political aspirations they had not become apparent. The minister commented that Trujillo was the individual personally and professionally best qualified to command the national police. He observed: "Continued order and stability in this country are dependent in large measure upon the maintenance of an effective police. The efficiency of that organization has unquestionably been one of the powerful deterrents of political disturbances, and the maintenance of its present efficiency is reasonable insurance against any armed disturbance. It is the opinion of the Legation that the continuance of Colonel Trujillo's command is the best assurance of its maintenance."[24]

Trujillo's firm grip on the army after 1928 made his support a prerequisite to the success of any openly ambitious leader. Nevertheless throughout 1928 and most of 1929 the American legation political summaries indicated that Trujillo was loyal to Vásquez and that his plans did not extend to a military takeover of the government. The tentative language of the reports, however, showed that no one in the legation really knew what those plans were.[25]

On December 13, 1929, again on December 24, and still again on December 26, Trujillo gave the American minister full assurances that he was completely loyal to the Vásquez government. Vásquez himself returned early in January 1930, ill, aged, but still president. He also demonstrated full confidence in his army chief, a confidence most of his cabinet refused to share. That the old warrior was completely out of touch with political reality was soon proven.[26] Trujillo did not openly strike against Horacio Vásquez in February 1930. He simply helped plan the outbreak of a small revolution in Santiago and then made sure that the few hundred ragged rebels reached the capital safely. Since the government's only defense was the troops Trujillo commanded, and since Trujillo would not move to defend the government, the bloodless, somewhat farcical revolution

political activity in the provinces under their command. The reports were to be submitted topically as follows: existing parties; work of each party; juntas organized; meetings held; registration of new members and number registered; what propaganda was being made and with what effect; list of most prominent leaders, their activities, positions, and success of their work; changes of membership from one party to another and reasons for same; political activities of public employees; and recommendations. Enclosure 3 to American Legation report on General Conditions Prevailing in Santo Domingo June 1, 1925–June 30, 1925, dated June 30, 1925, U.S., *Internal Affairs of the D.R.*

24. Minister Franklin B. Frost to Secretary of State, report no. 530, dated July 12, 1927, ibid.

25. The State Department, no doubt, was uncertain. In July 1926 the legation, in a political report, referred to Trujillo as a "clever and unscrupulous politician [who] is said to have organized the national police into a group of personal followers." Five months later the director of the Latin American Affairs Division made a memorandum record of conversation with a U.S. Marine Corps general who, after a personal visit to the Dominican Republic, thought that Trujillo was keeping a good organization, well drilled, efficient, and nonpolitical. Report on General Conditions Prevailing in the Dominican Republic, June 29–July 13, 1926, signed Warden Wilson, ibid., p. 5, and Record of Conversation with General George Richards, U.S. M.C., December 2, 1926, ibid.

26. Mejía, *De Lilís a Trujillo*, pp. 235–45. See also John Bartlow Martin, *Overtaken by Events*, pp. 43–44.

could have but one outcome.[27] Vásquez resigned on February 28, 1930, and left the country. In a "free and fair" election on May 16 Trujillo was voted president by an overwhelming majority after two months of violence and intimidation of the opposition by the army.[28] Trujillo had not been a popular candidate in any sense of the word, but his minority "party" either carried submachine guns or wore sidearms. By May 16, election day, he had no organized political opposition; the remnants of democratic constitutional organs such as the electoral board and the courts had been overwhelmed by threat of force. Trujillo even threw his unsuccessful political opponent, Federico Velásquez, in jail.

It is not my purpose to include in this study the oppressive side of the Trujillo dictatorship except as it might coincide with the established thread of land relationships and rural education and as it leads to the beginning of a formal agrarian reform program. Trujillo built bridges and roads, cleaned up the cities, erected innumerable statues to himself and his family, promoted and sponsored cultural activities on a wide scale, encouraged the economic growth of the country, and made the Dominican Republic an attractive tourist spot, but he did not ease the lot of the campesinos, as his hagiographers would have us believe.

President Trujillo came into office gifted with the personality which gives deep-rooted reality to all his words. In this lies the secret of his success. When he said: "My best friends are the workers," it was easy to believe. His inspiring example had stimulated all Dominican workers, dignified by this friendship. No other man could have done so much for Dominican agriculture, because no one else has dedicated himself with such clear vision, such faith and such enthusiasm.[29]

To render judgment on the progress of rural education during the Trujillo period is not a simple task. On one hand, Trujillo used the classrooms to distort contemporary history in order to perpetuate his own image as the greatest defender of the people in Dominican annals.[30] On the other hand, he started and continued a vigorous drive

27. On February 24 Minister Curtis advised the State Department: "The National Army and its Commander in Chief are true to the President." Revolutionary forces entered the capital on the 26th, and by that afternoon Curtis had discovered the truth: "In spite of the solemn assurances given to my predecessor and to the authorities, it is now absolutely clear that General Trujillo conspired with the revolutionary leaders and has repeatedly betrayed the Government." Telegrams, Curtis to Acting Secretary of State, February 24, February 26, 5:00 A.M., and February 26, 2:00 P.M., U.S., *Foreign Relations, 1930*, pp. 700–704.

28. Mejía, *De Lilís a Trujillo*, pp. 246–48. The American legation reported that 223, 851 votes had been cast for Trujillo and that this number greatly exceeded the total number of voters in the country. The report continued: "However, there is every reason to believe that as anticipated by the Legation, the intimidation of the followers of the Opposition had already been so great prior to the day of the elections that none was needed, and it would seem that none was practised, on the day of the elections, in order to keep them away from the polls." Message No. 91, May 19, 1930, Curtis to Secretary of State, U.S., *Foreign Relations, 1930*, p. 723.

29. Lawrence de Besault, *President Trujillo; His Work and the Dominican Republic*, p. 215.

30. Apart from strict requirements such as that his picture be prominently displayed in all Dominican homes, schools, and all public places and that he be endlessly referred to as "Doctor Rafael Leónidas Trujillo Molina, President of the Republic and Benefactor of the Fatherland," or in even more glowing terms, there is little documentary evidence to support this statement. If teachers wished to remain employed and in good health, however, they were expected to seize every opportunity in their classroom discussions to glorify the dictator, to elaborate upon his illustriousness and infallibility, and to proclaim the eternal guilt of those who had been

against illiteracy, creating an impressive number of schools. Since the bulk of the illiterates were rural inhabitants, the Trujillo "Campaign against Illiteracy" had its greatest impact in the countryside.

In 1930 the number of schools of all kinds had dropped to 526, with an enrollment of slightly over 50,000. Although the population had increased by 359,043 since 1921, the number of schools had decreased by almost 1,000 and enrollment had halved.[31]

Trujillo is quoted as saying early in his regime that "agriculture and culture at the same time is my plan of action as a governor."[32] But for ten years he did nothing to raise the cultural level in rural areas. In 1934 he established the cabinet post of secretary of state for education and fine arts, which was given responsibility for the administration of the educational system previously held by the superintendent-general of instruction. Otherwise, from an administrative standpoint, he did not significantly change the system begun in 1917. The Law of Obligatory Attendence, the General Law of Studies, the Organic Law of Public Instruction, and the Law for the Administration of Public Teaching remained in effect.[33] Minor changes in the educational system, especially in the funding area,[34] were made as the system evolved over the years, but they were the result of growth rather than important new ideas.

In 1941 the dictator announced a major shift in the educational system as a matter of national interest: the creation of a school organization of special character for the

---

condemned as enemies of the state. No one, least of all Trujillo, would complain if a certain amount of exaggeration accompanied the teacher's enthusiasm. On the other hand, failure to extol was considered a sin of omission, and sooner or later Trujillo's amazingly sensitive security net, usually the *Partido Dominicano*, would catch the delinquent. As likely as not, a chance remark by one of the pupils off the school grounds might bring the teacher down, or at least place him under suspicion as a subversive. Personal interviews with ministry of education officials, school teachers of the period, and Dominican parents, Santo Domingo, 1969–70.

31. Population in 1930: 1,256,048. República Dominicana, *República Dominicana en cifras, 1968*, p. 8 (hereafter referred to as *Cifras*).

32. November 22, 1931. Gregorio B. Palacín Iglesias, "Cien años de educación nacional," *Educación*, 74 (1944), p. 8.

33. Apart from his Emergency School Law described below, Trujillo did not decree a major law in the field of education until 1951 when Joaquín Balaguer was secretary of state for education. Basically the main law of June 5, 1951, Number 2909, combined the educational laws passed by the military government and superseded them. República Dominicana, *Colección de leyes, resoluciones, decretos, y reglamentos, 1951*, 1: 197–213. Three weeks later he decreed a law of obligatory primary education which was very similar to, but which superseded the law which the military government had passed on December 29, 1917. Ibid., pp. 350–56.

This was a law Trujillo enforced to the limit. During the "Era of Trujillo," if enrolled children failed to attend school, their parents were fined up to 50 pesos (dollars). Anyone employing children not excused from school could be fined up to 100 pesos, or 200 pesos for a second offense. Any school teacher or school inspector who falsified attendance records or granted unauthorized exceptions to the law or speculated with graduation certificates was liable to a severe fine or loss of employment. Chronic truants, openly defiant of their parents, were tried in juvenile courts and, if the case warranted, were remanded to correctional institutions. Whatever else was attributed to Trujillo, school truancy, at least in the towns and cities, was rare. The problem lay in the shortage of rural schools and teachers which prevented the enrollment of all rural children. Personal interview, former provincial school inspector, La Vega, November, 7, 1969. A number of Dominican parents, mostly rural inhabitants, wealthy and poor alike, positively confirm the above description. Personal interviews, July, October 1969.

34. The School Law of 1935 provided that the National District and the comunes must contribute to public instruction no less than seven percent of their income. Published in the *Gaceta Oficial*, No. 4764.

purpose of completing the elimination of illiteracy in the country. He would establish 5,000 rural schools to be designated as *escuelas de emergencia*. Public primary schools were accordingly placed in four categories: rudimentary and frontier, emergency, night adult, and graded.[35] The first two categories were rural, the last two urban.

Rudimentary and frontier schools were those of the three-year type already in existence in rural areas. Attendance was mixed, in three tandas: from 8 to 10 o'clock, 11 to 1, and 2 to 4. In addition to arithmetic, language, geography, history, and domestic arts, the course work included elementary agricultural studies oriented to the farming characteristics of the region. Each school had its school garden.

The new emergency school courses were similar to those of the rudimentary schools, but were greatly reduced in scope. The objective was specific, but limited: to qualify the rural youngster as literate. Trujillo considered two years of education sufficient, and the schools were organized on this basis. Students in the first year ranged from eight to eleven years old and from eleven to fourteen in the second. Instruction in the first year consisted of elementary reading and writing; the second year, some arithmetic, a bit of history and geography, and practical instruction in regional agriculture and home economics were added. Obviously, the education was a very elementary one, hardly more than the first-grade level, and the teaching staff inferior.[36] Similar courses for adults were established in 1952. Designated as "literacy schools" (escuelas de alfabetización), they utilized the emergency school houses, simple huts, for evening instruction of illiterate campesinos.

The following data, submitted with considerable hesitation, are based on the 1945 *memoria* of the ministry of education, the 1956 national budget, the 1960 census, and on 1956–60 figures provided the national planning board by the ministry of education in 1963. The planning board was aware of certain methodological deficiencies in the latter compilation. The purpose here is only to indicate the magnitude of Trujillo's rural school effort.

The school budget for 1956 was $8,263,859. This amount included $1,088,880 for rural primary schools, $92,244 for rural adult literacy schools, $562,280 for rural emergency schools, $1,757,556 for urban primary schools, and $422,019 for all secondary

---

35. The files of the department of education contain copies of the letters sent by the secretary of state for education and fine arts to selected leading (and therefore affluent) citizens, which announced the inauguration of "the Benefactor's new, socially significant program of adult education." Each citizen was given the opportunity to volunteer a contribution to this worthy program, along with warnings that late contributions would prejudice the campaign which depended on private resources, and that in the future the program must not be permitted to falter for a lack of continuing support. The letter closed with an appeal to the generosity and patriotic spirit of cooperation of the future contributor. The factor that brought such a heart-warming response to the secretary's appeal was the widely disseminated public statement made by Trujillo a day or two earlier to the effect that he who failed to support the adult education program for reduction of illiteracy was Trujillo's enemy. República Dominicana, Archivos de la Secretaría de Estado de Educación y Bellas Artes, *Educación de adultos,* circular letter of August 18, 1953, Santo Domingo.

36. In 1952 the monthly salary of an emergency school teacher was $18, compared to $40–45 for a teacher in a regular rural primary school. República Dominicana, *Presupuesto de ingresos y ley de gastos públicos 1952.*

One retired school inspector recalls having had considerable difficulty with the rural teachers who spent their time at cockfights during school hours instead of teaching. Many of these teachers were eighth graders recruited from poor schools and with no teacher training whatsoever.

Trujillo's Rural School Effort

Year	Rural Emergency Schools			Rural Primary Schools			Rural School-Age Population (8–14 yrs)
	No.	Teachers	Enrollment	No.	Teachers	Enrollment	
1945	1,136	1,136	76,206	808	. . .	79,007	. . .
1956	2,272	2,272	110,864	1,781	3,216	225,657	. . .
1960	2,288	2,288	110,574	1,872	3,488	246,945	396,277

Using the 1960 census, I calculate there were about 102,550 rural children aged 8 to 14 not in school. The enrollment figures shown here, submitted by the ministry of education, show only 38,758 not in school. Regardless of this discrepancy, the outline of the program is apparent.[37]

and normal schools.

It was patently impossible for Trujillo to provide qualified teachers for all the emergency schools and the rural rudimentary schools. Local school authorities recruited as teachers many young people who themselves had barely completed primary schooling. The following data reveal the inadequacy of the system.[38] In 1945 the combined[39] secondary and normal school output for the country was:

Bachillerato (approx. 12th grade) in philosophy and letters	31
Bachillerato in physical and natural sciences	109
Bachillerato in physical sciences and mathematics	23
Normal graduates, qualified for primary instruction (regular 9th and 10th grades plus two years of normal)	8
Normal graduates, qualified for secondary teaching (regular 9th and 10th grades plus three years of normal)	50

Thus only fifty-eight qualified teachers were turned out in 1945, eight of whom had the equivalent of a twelfth grade education and fifty with a rough equivalent of one year of college. Statistics show that over the years many of these graduates refused to teach in rural schools where the salaries were so low. Urban teaching salaries in primary schools usually ran as much as fifty percent higher. As noted above, the result was that teachers for the mushrooming numbers of rural schools had little or no teacher training.

In 1950 the first rural normal school was opened at Licey, halfway between Santiago and Moca in Santiago province, followed by two more at San Pedro de Macorís and San Cristóbal. The latter two schools were completed by about 1961. The training of the graduates of these schools consisted of six years of primary school, two years of

37. República Dominicana, *Secretaría de Estado de Educación y Bellas Artes: Memoria del año 1945*, pp. 2–3, 324–25; República Dominicana, *Presupuesto de ingresos y ley de gastos públicos, 1956*, pp. 44–50; República Dominicana, *Cuarto censo nacional de población, 1960: resumen general*, p. 59; Junta Nacional, *Informaciones*, table 11.

38. República Dominicana, *Secretaría de Estado de Educación y Bellas Artes: Memoria del año 1945*, pp. 332–33.

39. There were no schools exclusively for teacher training. The early secondary schools in Santo Domingo and Santiago offered special courses, after two years of regular study, for students interested in teaching careers.

intermediate school, and three years of normal school. The final three years of study included courses in biological sciences, including some agronomy, veterinary studies, rural arts, and domestic sciences. Enrollment at each school varied from 150 to 175. Over the next sixteen years the average annual total teacher output of the three schools was about fifty, of which eleven failed to remain in the teaching profession.

The emergency schools, Trujillo's only innovative contribution to rural education, were of dubious value. The only available statistics on their effectiveness are those Trujillo chose to release. The lack of accuracy of these statistics can be judged by his statement in 1955, that "illiteracy could be considered eliminated in children of school age."[40] By 1960 most of the children to whom he referred constituted a group of 286,040 between the ages of fifteen and nineteen. The 1960 census showed that eighteen percent of this age group alone were illiterate.[41] About eighty percent of these illiterates were rural inhabitants[42] who were supposed to have been educated in the emergency schools.

The government's attention to rural teacher qualifications was long overdue and, in consonance with the general educational effort, inadequate. There may have been an element of sincerity in Trujillo's desire to educate the campesinos, but he wanted even more to create a facade of progress and culture to impress the world. The data illustrate the main weakness of the emergency school system which he created. The "emergency education" was in effect only window dressing. Under almost any rational definition of the term, rural children did not become literate after one or two years of exposure to a poor first-grade education. And if they somehow did learn to read and write a few words, many within a short time after leaving school slipped back into illiteracy from lack of practice. Large numbers did not even complete the second year of schooling. Thus the increased enrollment was not converted into a stream. The same observation would apply to adults enrolled in the evening literacy schools. The bulk of the progress in rural education was made in the regular primary schools, but even these were poorly staffed and inadequate in size and number to accommodate the school-age population. The tiny output of rural teachers from the normal schools fell far short of meeting the needs of a country whose population in 1950 was over two million and whose growth was averaging 3.6 percent annually. By 1960 the rural school-age population had increased by about 158,000. During this period no more than about 380 new normal-school graduates entered the rural school system, a ratio of one teacher to over 400 students.[43]

To conduct an effective battle against rural illiteracy, Trujillo should have concentrated on a long-range plan to train more and better teachers and to improve the existing rural primary school system. The effort he devoted to the emergency schools was essentially misdirected. With each passing year the problem of illiteracy would become increasingly acute, despite the favorable published statistics.

In the field of rural education, Trujillo did the wrong things partially for the right reason—and did them poorly.

40. Armand Oscar Pacheco, *La obra educativa de Trujillo*, vol. 2, p. 102. Ministry of education officials in the post-Trujillo period place little confidence in earlier statistics on school attendance.

41. República Dominicana, *Cuarto censo nacional*, table 14, p. 56.

42. The Dominican government calculated that approximately eighty-two percent of the population over fourteen years old lived in rural areas. República Dominicana, secretaría de estado de educación, bellas artes, y cultos, *Plan nacional de alfabetización y educación de adultos*, p. 33.

43. This is an estimated ratio based on total population between ages seven and fourteen and the calculation that seventy percent of all inhabitants were rural.

No Latin American ruler in modern times has matched the Trujillo record for corrupt absolutism. There have been supreme dictators who have endured, such as Paraguay's Dr. José Rodríguez de Francia, but Dr. Francia's personal honesty and frugality were the antitheses of the regime that converted the Dominican Republic into a cowed feudal state and maintained it so for thirty-one years. Porfirio Díaz ruled Mexico for thirty-four years; although his internal policies permitted the continued abuse and exploitation of the neglected Indian masses, his long administration was not characterized by the frequent political assassinations and deep moral decay at all levels of government that Trujillo fostered. There were others hardly less ruthless and absolute: Juan Manuel de Rosas, Carlos Antonio López and his son Francisco Solano López, and their modern counterpart, the more paternal Alfredo Stroessner, but their regimes could not match Trujillo's for endurance. Only the rule of Juan Vicente Gómez of Venezuela came close to the Trujillo pattern in longevity and oppressiveness. Trujillo understood his people and knew how to exploit their emotions, their weaknesses, and their idiosyncrasies. He had no friends; every man of character and basic honesty was his potential enemy, an opponent to be broken by compromise, purchase, or assassination. Crassweller does not exaggerate when he observes that Trujillo's many achievements in the areas of fiscal administration, social services, and cultural enhancement were clearly outweighed by his crimes of bloody persecution and violence, extortion, and public plunder on a wholesale scale.[44]

No prosperous enterprise, no potentially lucrative investment opportunity, escaped Trujillo's eye. Operating behind the scenes as often as not, he would acquire a controlling interest or complete control in proven profit-making businesses, using the authority of the state or the threat of physical force. Where possible, as in the cases of his salt-producing company, Salinera Nacional, his chocolate factory, La Chocolatera Sánchez, and his tobacco company, Compañía Anónima Tabacalera, Trujillo would then convert his holdings into monopolies, driving all competition from the market. He and those close to him did not confine themselves to agriculturally related companies, although these constituted the backbone of their investments. A reliable and knowledgeable authority, who wishes to remain anonymous, has estimated that the Trujillos owned or controlled eighty percent of all the most profitable industries in the republic.[45] The scope of the confiscation of these properties by the Dominican government within six weeks after the last of the Trujillos had gone into exile in late 1961 indicates the breadth of the dictator's holdings and those of his family and favorites.[46]

Although he bought and sold multimillion dollar enterprises as if they were playthings, his biggest investments were reserved for the wealthiest sector of the economy—land and

---

44. Robert D. Crassweller, *Trujillo: The Life and Times of a Caribbean Dictator*, pp. 5–6.

45. Personal interview, Santo Domingo, November 7–8, 1969.

46. In order not to encumber this part of the study, I have shown in Appendix 4 the list of enterprises taken over by the state. Not included in the list are the vast expanses of land which are indicated below in this chapter. Decree 7372, December 4, 1961, published in the *Gaceta Oficial* No. 8625 of December 8, 1961; 7382 of December 7, 1961, *Gaceta Oficial* No. 8627 of December 16, 1961; 7408 of December 13, 1961, *Gaceta Oficial* No. 8626 of December 15, 1961; 7433 of December 18, 1961, *Gaceta Oficial* No. 8630 of December 29, 1961; and 5739 of December 28, 1961, *Gaceta Oficial* No. 8634 of January 8, 1962.

There is no reliable evidence of the total financial worth of Trujillo, since in addition to the list in Appendix 4, his interests were frequently hidden behind the names of apparent owners, some of whom may still act in this capacity. Trujillo himself liked to set up dummy corporations

agricultural production. Many of his family followed this example. A short summary of the Azucarera Haina venture will illustrate how Trujillo manipulated the land, the national banks, and the people for his private gain.[47] In the late 1940s Trujillo decided to corner the sugar industry. By 1952 he had built a tremendous sugar central on the Haina River, about eight miles west of the capital, and had begun to acquire the extensive cane holdings needed to feed the mill. It was to be one of the largest in the world. For some of the land he paid full market price, some he managed to obtain at bargain prices; but nearly all the sales were forced. He bought land as far north as Cotuí, Cevicos, and Boyá, and eastward almost to Samaná. He bought land and sugar mills out to the west of the capital and in and around San Pedro de Macorís. All told, he invested about $30 million. The appropriate government officials were pleased to provide Trujillo with special irrigation facilities, army labor, military trucks, exemption from his own labor code, and most important, tax exemption for the sprawling enterprise for twenty years.

In 1953, however, Trujillo began to worry about the price of sugar on the world market. He "sold" his entire investment to the Banco de Crédito Agricola e Industrial for $50 million in cash and government securities. When the price of sugar rose in 1957, Trujillo repurchased his former properties from the cooperating bank at the same $50-million price, but now on easy credit terms. With the cash from the 1953 sale, he then acquired at a fair but forced price of $35 million, four more major holdings, those of the West Indies Sugar Company. By the end of 1957, then, for an initial investment of $30 million he had become the sole owner of twelve of the country's sixteen sugar mills, controlled almost two-thirds of the annual sugar production,[48] and could show a $15 million cash profit. Not surprisingly, as soon as the country was rid of the Trujillos, the government quickly decreed[49] that Azucarera Haina, consisting of eight sugar centrales and the associated molasses production facilities, was to be turned over to the state. These holdings were the heart of the entire national economy, sixty percent of the sugar exports, and the national interest required immediate steps to preserve their security and continued operation. A second decree[50] cancelled all the tax privileges and fiscal exemptions which the Benefactor had arranged when he went into the sugar business.

In short, Trujillo used public resources to make a private profit. He would hold an investment so long as it was profitable; if a loss appeared imminent, the Dominican

---

with himself in control but not even named on the board of directors. In addition, there were foreign investments of unknown size which would have to be added to the above list, as well as the two-thirds of the entire sugar industry which he owned. It would be no exaggeration to conclude that the dividing line between Trujillo's personal properties and the national interests of the government was at best indeterminate.

47. The story of Azucarera Haina is now public knowledge. Germán E. Ornes has an impressive report on this financial venture as well as many others of the Benefactor in his *Trujillo: Little Caesar of the Caribbean.*

48. Sugar and molasses exports for 1957 exceeded $94 million. República Dominicana, *Comercio exterior de la República Dominicana,* 5 vols. (Ciudad Trujillo: Dirección General de Estadística, 1958), vol. 5, p. 81. Azucarera Haina alone had a production capacity of 220,000 tons of sugar and 14 million gallons of molasses per year. The normal 24-hour milling capacity was 12,500 tons of cane. United Nations, Food and Agricultural Organization, *Report of the Fourth Regional Conference for Latin America* (Rome, 1957), p. 17.

49. Decree No. 7347 of November 28, 1961, published in the *Gaceta Oficial,* 8626 of December 15, 1961, pp. 10–12.

50. Decree No. 7408 of December 13, 1961, ibid., p. 12.

National Bank would take over the risk and Trujillo the safe cash. Either way, the profit was his, not the nation's. As for property owned by others, the dictator used whatever leverage the situation required: offers at market price, giveaway price, or outright seizure. Stubborn and reluctant owners were softened by threat, assault, or even more extreme forms of violence. Trujillo used these same tactics to create two magnificent, adjoining cattle ranches near San Cristóbal: Hacienda María and Hacienda Fundación. His brother José Arismendi Trujillo (Petán) followed the example and forged a 40,000-tarea feudal estate around Bonao and another of at least 7,000 tareas in Monte Cristi province.

Not all Trujillo's acquisitions came about as strictly business ventures. The case of Juancito Rodríguez stands as one of the most important single land seizures of the Trujillo era, not only because of the value and the extent of the land at the time of seizure, but because of the future impact of that act on the agrarian reform program which followed the death of Trujillo.

Juan Rodríguez García was born in 1890 in Moca, the richest farming region of the entire Cibao, where his wealthy family owned land. Financed by his brother Doroteo, he began about 1907 to buy[51] and clear land in La Vega province when the region was still very sparsely settled and relatively uncultivated. There was ample land to be had for the man who wanted to acquire it.[52] According to the estate records and other testimony, Juancito purchased a total of 200,000 tareas, distributed mostly in La Vega and Sánchez Ramírez provinces, at prices varying from a little over two pesos to five pesos the tarea. He registered all the land and obtained all the titles thereto. Juancito was hard-working, intelligent, and an able administrator. None of his holdings was unoccupied, although much of the land was used for grazing livestock of the finest quality. He was the first rancher in the area to introduce and breed thoroughbred cattle[53] and horses. By the time Trujillo came to power, Rodríguez was the most influential man in the Cibao. His cattle numbered between 15,000 and 17,000; his extensive cultivated holdings included productive and well-kept cacao and plantain plantations.

Juancito was a cousin of Horacio Vásquez, whom Trujillo had overthrown. This fact probably made it easier for the dictator to distrust him, but the first serious clash between the two men did not occur until late 1943. Trujillo had approved the building of an irrigation system near Jima which would have converted over 100,000 tareas of grassy but uncultivated land into a valuable rice-producing basin. Furthermore, he wanted to buy some of the undeveloped land. The difficulty arose from the fact that Juancito, who preferred to grow cattle rather than rice, possessed 30,000 tareas of this land and hotly refused to sell it or even listen to the proposition. He might have considered that the irrigation project would markedly increase the value of the remainder of his property,[54] but his dislike for Trujillo got the better of his business judgment. The following year

---

51. There are a few Dominicans who insist that Juancito was a thief who robbed campesinos of their land or forced them to sell. Other landowners in the Cibao, some of them former neghbors of Juancito, the lawyers for the Rodríguez estate, and still other responsible citizens who have no known reason to be biased, all claim that while Juancito was a tough, stubborn hothead, he was no thief. In particular, the estate lawyers, who have studied every document and every transaction Juancito ever made, are positively convinced that he never coerced the small landholders. Personal interviews, La Vega, July and November 1969.

52. Land now worth $100,000 could be bought for $300 in La Vega province in 1915.

53. These were mostly Carnation Farms holsteins, which later were crossed with brahmas. These breeds, along with brown Swiss, seem to thrive the best in Santo Domingo.

Trujillo made an offer to buy 1,000 head of cattle from Juancito, and again the rancher refused to do business. At this point he became convinced that Trujillo should be removed, and began to plot seriously to rid the country of the dictator.

By 1945 a number of Dominican exiles in the Caribbean had developed a plan to invade their homeland. For money and leadership they looked to the wealthy Cibaeño. Under the pretext of going abroad to seek medical treatment, Juancito joined the plot. Once out of the country, he planned and commanded the well-publicized and ill-fated Cayo Confites expedition. Frustrated by the seizure of his expeditionary force by the reluctant Cuban government, Juancito tried again in 1949, this time using Guatemala as a base, and again failed. He spent his remaining years in Puerto Rico, Cuba, and Venezuela obsessed with hate for Trujillo. He finally died late in 1960, just a few months before Trujillo was assassinated.[55]

As soon as Juancito had left the country, Trujillo began to move against the Rodríguez holdings. First, Rodríguez' cattle began to disappear in dribbles. Then the family began to undergo the usual harrassment reserved for Trujillo's enemies. Several of Juancito's workers were found shot to death under mysterious circumstances. More cattle were stolen. Then one day Amable Romeo (Pipí) Trujillo, a younger brother, rode onto the Rodríguez land at the head of an armed band and drove off the entire remaining herds of cattle.[56]

Trujillo placed an embargo on all of the Rodríguez property and had the owner tried in absentia in 1948. The court imposed a fine of $13,250,000 and loss of all land.[57] Thereupon Trujillo arranged to have the state sell the land to his friends at bargain prices, two to six pesos per tarea. This was land actually worth up to forty or fifty pesos a tarea or more, and included 13,000 tareas of some of the best cacao groves in all the

---

54. The Jima idea had merit. The stream watered only 1,500 tareas, but at a cost of no more than $100,000, the proposed system would have increased the agricultural productivity of an area twenty times greater by fifty fold. These little-known details of the origin of the quarrel were told me by a knowledgable source who wishes to remain unidentified. Personal interview, January 25, 1970.

55. Interview with Dr. Osiris L. Duquela, La Vega, July 6, 1969. Duquela and his law partner are the attorneys for the Rodríguez estate and are in possession of all of the estate's papers and documents.

56. These details were provided by the eyewitness owner of the adjacent cattle ranch who watched Pipí drive the herds away. The source referrred to in note 54 above also has confirmed the event, adding that Pipí found a very profitable way to dispose of the cattle. He called in all the poor campesinos in the neighborhood and invited them to help themselves to the herd. Shortly after that had been done, the younger Trujillo then had the unsuspecting farmers arrested and jailed for possessing stolen property. Pipí and the guardia split the fines levied on the "cattle thieves."

57. The sentence was published by the Court of First Instance of the District of La Vega on June 16, 1953, in connection with a later sale of land previously registered by Rodríguez, in the following language:

> By virtue of sentence number 147 of the Civil and Commercial Court of First Instance of the judicial district of La Vega, dated 16 June, 1953, entered on the 27th day of August, 1953, at ten hours and twenty minutes in the morning under number 180, folio number 45 of Registration Book number 4, of this office, because of the property embargo imposed by the Dominican State against the contumacious Juan Rodríguez García-a-Juancito, in the sum of RD $13,250,000—thirteen million two hundred fifty thousand gold pesos—together with other properties. . . .

Dominican Republic, Province of La Vega, Común of La Vega, Book No. 28, Folio No. 97, title to parcel no 352, survey district no. 11.

Antilles. In this particular case Trujillo himself took little, if any, of Juancito's property, but he personally approved every sale. Seizure of the land hardly satisfied the always suspicious dictator. Still fearing additional plots, he ordered even remote members of the family rounded up and carted off to jail for intense interrogation. Some were tortured, but all were eventually released in the absence of any proven collusion in a political plot. The guardia swept up one unhappy neighbor of Juancito's with the others, tortured, interrogated, beat, and confined him for several months before finally releasing him. While he was in jail his livestock were run off and two of his workers killed. The fact that he was no relation to the exiled rancher made little difference to the police; his name was Rodríguez and he knew Juancito.[58]

Trujillo's confiscation of Juancito's land broke up the famous estate, but in so doing, laid the basis for what may be a legal landmark in the development of a social philosophy of land ownership in the Dominican Republic. The case of Juan Rodríguez García versus the state will be discussed later in the context of agrarian reform.

The dictator, his six brothers, and three of his four sisters,[59] their many spouses, and large *parentela*[60] overlooked no opportunity for graft, corruption, or illegal profit. Completely cowed by Trujillo's grimly repressive terror tactics, the Dominican public could only watch more or less passively as the Trujillos systematically raided the economy. Trujillo expected and received kickbacks on all public works contracts[61]; he or his brothers controlled the casino gambling, the national lottery proceeds, international numbers racket, prostitution, a fire insurance "protection" racket, and, of course, the press. He formed the National Banking Company, installed his brother-in-law, Francisco Martínez Alba, as director, and through the bank collected a compulsory ten percent contribution from all government paychecks for the Partido Dominicano. His sources of revenue were seemingly endless.

In 1944 United States Ambassador Ellis Briggs said of Trujillo and his conglomerate: "His regime is an enterprise operated primarily for the personal enrichment of himself, his relatives and his satellites. His greed results in the impoverishment of the Dominican people, economically and morally. The dictator's vanity . . . is colossal."[62]

On May 31, 1961, the day after Trujillo's assassination, President Joaquín Balaguer declared nine days of national mourning over the republic's "irreparable" loss. In the emotional funeral oration two days later, Balaguer included these words:

---

58. As a matter of fact, he confessed involvement in a plot which was just being hatched, although Trujillo had not suspected him. He was simply a round-up bonus. Personal interview, La Vega, July 5, 1969.

59. Widespread public opinion recognized that one sister, Julieta, had not participated in the national pillage.

60. Extended family, which includes all distant relatives.

61. A civil engineer has described in full detail his having been awarded a contract to build twelve kilometers of a simple, two-lane asphalt road near Puerto Plata. The budget for the job, already prepared by government officials with the assistance of some of Trujillo's immediate staff, came to $500,000. Of this amount, the engineer was required to donate ten percent to Trujillo's Partido Dominicano, five percent to Trujillo's executive secretary, five percent to the latter's brother who had helped with the budget preparation, five percent to another individual who had helped contrive the award, and still another five percent for miscellaneous but unidentified expenses within the ministry of public works. The contractor's profit, even after all the "kickbacks," was still over $200,000. And this was but one of probably hundreds of contracts which were let during the Trujillo Era. Personal interview, La Vega, July 3, 1969.

62. U.S., *Foreign Relations, 1944*, p. 1015.

Never has the death of a man produced such a feeling of consternation in a people nor fallen with a greater sensation of grief upon their collective conscience. It is that we all know that with this glorious dead man we have lost the best guardian of public peace and the best defender of the security and repose of Dominican homes. . . .

His works will remain so long as the republic remains and in it a single Dominican conscious of the meaning of the frontier treaty, the redemption of the public debt, financial independence, the achievements accomplished in the field of public works, agriculture, health and social welfare, and all the good which has emanated during three decades of long peace which has assured progress and brought well-being and tranquility to the Dominican family. . . .

As a man who had a blind faith in God and in destiny, Trujillo was fundamentally good. . . . On his shoulders fell many debts which he did not incur and whose responsibility belongs to the masters of adulation and intrigue who speculated with his good faith and with the natural passions of a man who intensely loved the sensualities of life. Trujillo wears securely on his temples, as he goes to his grave, the crown of the immortals of the fatherland. His figure enters from this solemn moment into the glorious family of our tutelar spirits. The moment is, then, propitious for us to swear on these beloved remains that we will defend his memory and that we will be faithful to his watchwords, maintaining unity and joining together with all Dominicans in an embrace of conciliation and peace.[63]

---

63. *Gaceta Oficial, Edición Extraordinaria*, No. 8577, June 2, 1961. A careful reading of the entire funeral speech reveals some exceedingly ambiguous phraseology, but the general tenor is clearly laudatory. It must be remembered, however, that son Rafael Leónidas Trujillo Martínez, "Ramfis", who commanded the armed forces which were loyal to Trujillo, and all the Trujillo family entourage were present and still in control of events in the republic.

22

LAND RESETTLEMENT AND THE AGRARIAN REFORM LAW

Credit for the first attempt in this century to legislate an agrarian reform program goes to Senator Abelardo Nanita of Moca. Nanita sponsored a project to establish farm colonies in 1926. His objectives closely paralleled those reflected in the old colonial cédulas on settlement: populate and increase production. His was not so much a social program to redistribute land as it was an integrated, economically motivated plan to improve agriculture.[1] Yet there were important social implications in the idea. The features of the plan merit mention here because of their comprehensiveness and similarity to actions the Dominican government sponsored almost fifty years later:

Any measured, surveyed, or parceled land could be used for farm colonies which would consist of poor rural inhabitants suited for farm work.

Prospective colonists must be married or widowers with children, of good reputation, in good health. The larger the family the better; bachelors would not be eligible.

Colonies would contain a minimum of twenty families selected by lot, with first preference to citizens of that común, then of the province, and finally of the country at large.

Colonists could select their own crops, but with the advice, help, and technical assistance of the department of agriculture.

---

1. These colonies have been mentioned earlier; see chap. 18 note 41. Predating, but related to, the 1926 farm colony plan, was a suggestion made in 1923 by an obscure village official near Bonao who, in trying to borrow tents and cots from the government to house a Danish immigrant family temporarily, came up with an idea for stimulating Caucasian immigration to the Cibao. He proposed to the secretary of agriculture and immigration that the government acquire land along both sides of the River Mao in western Santiago province and sell it in lots of no less than 160 tareas to Scandinavian immigrants exclusively. To attract the latter to this good rice and coffee-growing area, he recommended that the government conduct a vigorous propaganda campaign in Copenhagen, Stockholm, and Christiana. The idea was applauded and approved by both the secretary of agriculture and the provisional president, Juan B. Vicini Burgos, who agreed that there was a need to populate the fertile Cibao with competent farmers. República Dominicana, *Secretaría de Agricultura e Inmigración, Memoria*, 1923, (Santo Domingo: Impresora La Provincia, 1924), pp. 130–133. If any action was taken by the government, the results were insignificant.

230

Colonists would receive title to their land after five years, but with restrictions against alienation or subdivision.

Colonists would be exempt from all fiscal and municipal taxes for the first ten years after initial settlement.

The department of agriculture would facilitate assistance in the installation of the colony and in scientific exploitation of the land, including provision of seeds, cattle, equipment, and loans.

In each colony there would be built, as a minimum, a schoolhouse and quarters for the teacher, offices and housing for department of agriculture employees, warehouse and quarters for the chief of the warehouse guard, and a house for each settler.

A cooperative would be established in each colony to serve as intermediary in the sale of crops, making of loans, purchase of supplies and equipment, and to act as a savings bank.

Prizes and other incentives would be offered for outstanding, efficient cultivation; continued substandard farming by a colonist for three years would result in his ejection from the colony.[2]

With considerable official fanfare the first colony was formally established on June 3, 1926, at Santana, común of Guayubín, Monte Cristi province. The second colony was inaugurated a few weeks later near Bonao in La Vega province. But despite the initial flurry of optimism the two colonies suffered from a lack of consistent support by the government and the plan itself was quietly abandoned temporarily. The lesson to be deduced from this attempt at reform is that an enthusiastic secretary of agriculture alone could not successfully pursue a fairly well conceived cooperative interministerial program. In this case the head of the primary agency involved did not have adequate authority or possess the necessary resources to carry out the plan.

Trujillo revived the farm colony idea in the 1930s, but the program was handicapped even before it was well started by the political factors that motivated his decision. Of the thirty-nine colonies shown in Appendix 8, twenty-three were located on or near the Haitian border. Trujillo's objective was to populate these lightly occupied western provinces, regardless of the settlers' qualifications.[3] As a result, too many of them were selected without regard for their farming experience or aptitude. Trujillo did supply the colonists with houses, water, in some cases irrigation, and roads, but these were no more than the basic necessities of life on the rough frontier. The schools, cooperatives, extension services, marketing facilities, and other elements of an integrated settlement program were missing. In some cases the quantity of land distributed to each settler was insufficient for productive farming. The colony near the village of Carbonera in Monte Cristi, for example, consisted of 10,071 tareas divided among 225 families—an average of only 45 tareas, or seven acres, per family, which proved to be inadequate

---

2. *Listín Diario,* March 28, 1926.

3. The long history of the border quarrel over the territorial line between Haiti and the Dominican Republic can be traced back to the colonial period (see García, *Compendio,* 1:213–14), and did not legally terminate until March 1936 with the Dominican-Haitian Frontier Treaty. The 1936 treaty, however, did not put an end to difficulties between the two countries. Migrant Haitian workers had for years formed the bulk of the labor force for the cane fields at harvest time, or *zafra.* During the depression of the thirties, many stayed on as illegal immigrants; others had simply drifted across the lightly populated border in search of a bit of land on which to grow food. The climax was reached in 1937 when Trujillo after giving very short notice ordered the massacre of all Haitians found within the Dominican Republic. Thousands of Haitians were slaughtered, mostly in the western provinces.

considering the quality of the land. These colonists were gradually reduced to subsistence farming.[4]

There were eight colonies established in Dajabón, south of Monte Cristi, on a major infiltration route used by Haitians for illegal border crossing. The experiment was not successful because a majority of the colonists had been urban dwellers, many of the parcels of land were of low quality, irrigation facilities were not provided, and there was no nearby local market for any excess production. One of these colonies, of Japanese settlers, prospered at first, but the lack of a local market, plus local social pressures, demoralized the colony which by 1960 retained little economic significance. In this case each colonist had been given over 100 tareas of land.[5] Trujillo's plan failed not because of a lack of executive authority behind it, but because it was poorly conceived and incomplete.

The assassination of Trujillo started a train of events which led directly to coordinated action by the succeeding Dominican governments to redistribute land to the landless. The early architect of this effort was President Joaquín Balaguer himself. Sensing the political importance of the land issued to the rural majority, on August 4, 1961, he took the first step to redistribute some former Trujillo property.[6] He formed an official commission to distribute to individuals of scanty economic resources 356,153 tareas, much, though not all, of which had belonged to Trujillo. The membership of the commission included the secretary of state for agriculture (presiding), the secretary of state for health and social benefits, the administrator of the Bank of Agricultural and Industrial Credit, the director-general of statistics and census, the director of colonization (department of agriculture), a state surveyor, and two experts in land law. Balaguer authorized the commission to expropriate privately owned land after just indemnity had been paid to the private owners. Irrigation systems and land improvements were to be taken into consideration in determining the indemnity. There were fourteen separate tracts involved, ranging from 3,236 to 78,657 tareas. Most of the land lay near Nagua in María Trinidad Sánchez province, or in Monte Cristi province. The government stated that it sought an equitable plan of agrarian reform based on social justice whereby the state would benefit from more efficient exploitation of the land. With the national interest at stake, the government, accordingly, invoked the law of eminent domain.

The job was far too complex and the implications of its terms of reference, especially the expropriation provision, too broad for the commission to complete its work. The members soon realized that a permanent, autonomous organization specifically empowered to pursue an agrarian reform program was needed, even though they as yet had no clear idea what such a program would consist of in its entirety. Therefore, instead of redistributing the land in accordance with their instructions, they recommended the creation of an agrarian reform administration. Balaguer accepted their recommendation and on September 14, 1961, named the rector of the University of Santo Domingo, José Antonio Caro Alvarez, the first director-general of agrarian reform. Two and a half months later the president followed with another order outlining the functions, general organization, and broad guidance for the general directorate of agrarian reform

---

4. Gifford E. Rogers, *Régimen de la tenencia de las tierras en la República Dominicana,* p. 14 (hereafter referred to as *Régimen de tierras*).

5. Gifford E. Rogers, *Régimen de la tenencia de las tierras en la República Dominicana,* 1st rev., p. 11 (hereafter referred to as *Régimen de tierras,* 1st rev.).

6. Decree No. 6988, published in *Gaceta Oficial,* No. 8594 of August 16, 1961, pp. 24–29.

(DGRA). Caro, of course, had played a major role in developing this decree.[7] The responsibility for redistribution of the 356,153 tareas was passed to the DGRA, and the commission formed on August 4 was dissolved. The new group was also directed to formulate for presidential approval an agrarian reform law which, among other things, would create a Dominican institute of agrarian reform to be an autonomous and juridical organ of the government. Under an agrarian advisory council, DGRA was also instructed to plan the necessary measures to commence a rational agrarian reform program, adjusted to Dominican problems, and to execute the necessary provisions. In addition to the director-general and a subdirector, DGRA was to consist of the following divisions: administration, legal, agrarian planning, agricultural comptroller, a special technical assistant to the director, plus the necessary supporting personnel. The office of colonization and the section of roads and rights-of-way of the ministry of agriculture were ordered transferred to DGRA. These transfers encountered considerable delay, however, and were eventually modified. In September 1965 DGRA absorbed the office of colonization, but the roads and right-of-way unit went to the National Institute of Hydraulic Resources (INDRHI).

Only a few of the other major provisions of this important decree need be mentioned:

> The agrarian advisory council to the president of the republic would consist of the director-general and six members qualified by their knowledge of rural economics, customs, traditions, and problems. The council would review and approve all major agrarian reform projects.
>
> Once a plan or project was approved by the council, the director would need no further instructions to take the necessary action.
>
> Internal administration of DGRA would not be subject to intervention by the council.
>
> The director-general would submit directly to the executive branch his personnel requirements and requisitions for such expenses as publications, texts, and technical studies.
>
> The director-general was authorized to summon public officials and private citizens to official sessions of the agency; members of DGRA were authorized to enter on any property, fenced or open, or any buildings or structures located on farms, plantations, or factories; and all national, provincial, and local government agencies were ordered to cooperate with the director-general.

This was the first charter of the first formal agency organized in the Dominican Republic to carry out an agrarian reform. Three points might be noted. First, the government was anxious to organize a land redistribution program which would put unused state lands in production and provide land for the landless campesinos without delay.

Second, the director-general was given the responsibility for making plans, the authority to carry them out, and direct and periodic access to the president of the republic. Internal administration of DGRA was not to be subjected to outside interference. These were all important administrative conditions, the lack of any one of which might seriously hamper the director-general.

Third, the director-general was to act as president of the advisory council, but he possessed only moderating and coordinating authority in council sessions. This was a potential weakness in the decision-making structure, since council inactivity could block DGRA operations. Obviously the director-general would have to be energetic, diplomatic, and technically competent. Caro, the first director-general, was an architect, well known in government circles as a competent administrator. The second director-general, Freddy Prestol Castillo, who replaced Caro on December 17, 1961, was a

---

7. Decree No. 7327, November 27, 1961, *Gaceta Oficial*, No. 8626 of December 15, 1961.

prominent lawyer specializing in land law. He had been one of the members of the August commission and later subdirector of DGRA under Caro.[8]

Two developments late in 1961 contributed to the complexity, as well as the urgency, of agrarian reform:

First, the United States refused to recognize a regime which continued Balaguer as president, "Ramfis" Trujillo as chief of the armed forces, and the other Trujillos and their associates in their customary privileged positions. Under heavy diplomatic pressure from the United States, including judicious deployment of Atlantic Fleet units, the Trujillos finally abandoned the republic commencing in late November.[9]

Second, within a matter of days after the Trujillos had gone into exile, the Santo Domingo press began to publicize Balaguer's plans for the resettling of farm families. One of the first articles carried the news that the government would settle 140 families on a banana plantation in Monte Cristi on land formerly owned by "Petán" Trujillo. The Santo Domingo El Caribe carried ten articles during December 1961 concerning various resettlement projects reportedly under way in Monte Cristi, San Cristóbal, Sánchez Ramírez, La Vega, María Trinidad Sánchez, and Peravia provinces. The largest of the projects involved some 80,000 tareas near Baní, in Peravia, which Trujillo had seized from small ranchers to convert into cane fields for the Central Rio Haina. The press reported that Balaguer had instructed the director-general of agrarian reform to return this land to its previous owners as soon as possible. There is evidence, however, that the action reported by the press was some distance removed from reality. The government order to resettle the Baní land was not actually promulgated until August 1962.[10]

In addition to these first stirrings of a land redistribution program, there occurred in rapid succession a series of other events which bore on the ownership and distribution of state lands. On November 25 Balaguer ordered the army to seize Trujillo properties. In January 1962 Balaguer resigned and was succeeded by a seven-man council of state, with Rafael F. Bonnelly as president. Before Balaguer resigned, however, he approved an important but too hastily worded law passed by the Congress.[11] To rectify past seizures of property by the state for owners' political crimes or transgressions, the law called for the immediate return to their legitimate owners or successors all land adjudicated to or held by the state. In those cases where the land had been further ceded by the state (that is, by Trujillo) to third parties, the state would now take back the land, but would compensate those third parties under the new expropriation law. The indemnity would be equal to the value of the land at the time of legitimate owner's loss. Legitimate owners were given a period of two years, within which they must petition the return of their property.

8. Prestol was followed successively in DGRA by two other directors, and in May 1962 Manuel de J. Viñas Cáceres became director-general after the agrarian reform law was passed and the Dominican Agrarian Institute (IAD) created. Viñas was replaced in 1963 by Gustavo Machado when the Bosch regime moved into power, and thereafter the post was filled on a basis of political expediency.

9. John Bartlow Martin, the U.S. ambassador, describes some of the negotiations in Overtaken by Events, pp. 77–83. There is a strong possibility that the presence of U.S. naval units within sight of the capital may have had some influence on the Trujillos.

10. Decree No. 8412, August 2, 1962, issued by the council of state. Resettlement moved very slowly and was never fully completed.

11. Law No. 5719, approved by the Dominican senate on December 20, by the chamber of deputies on December 21, and by the president on December 26. Published in the Gaceta Oficial, No. 8634 of January 8, 1962.

The principal defect in the law was that it failed to recognize that some of the lands seized by Trujillo early in his regime had since been passed on or sold to new owners who acquired the land in good faith, unaware of the procedures by which the state or previous owner had come into ownership. In many cases the new owners had improved the land, incurring expenses thereby for which the law would not compensate them. Another questionable feature of the law was that many Dominicans to whom Trujillo had in his generosity ceded sequestered land still remained in the country and still owned the land. These were officials who, though not intimate collaborators of the defunct dictator, had been close enough to him to take advantage of events to enrich themselves without publicity.[12] It hardly seemed fair for the state to indemnify them, yet the law drew no apparent line of distinction between these landowners and those who had bought in good faith.

A third factor neglected by the law was the question of "squatters" who had invaded former Trujillo lands even though Trujillo might have sold them to a third party. Where Trujillo holdings had been sold piecemeal and later invaded, there were now three sets of rights to be adjudicated: those of the legitimate owners, the new owners, and the squatters who may very well have improved the land they occupied.[13]

As will be described, these defects were remedied later, but meanwhile it became apparent that the amount of land held by the state would increase sharply because of expropriation of former Trujillo property.

It was known that in many cases the legitimate owners and their heirs were no longer alive. This land would remain in the hands of the state after expropriation. The government had already decreed that the Haciendas María and Fundación in San Cristóbal, as well as all other land belonging to the Trujillo heirs, were to be turned over to the state for provisional administration by the Bank of Agricultural and Industrial Credit. Within a year the total of the confiscated Trujillo land—that is, land owned by him, his heirs, family, and satellites—came to almost 3.25 million tareas, which when added to their business enterprises amounted to an impressive empire. The landholdings were distributed as follows:

National District	227,427.17	tareas
San Cristóbal	187,939.03	//
La Vega	454,245.47	//
Dajabón	36,124.93	//
Monte Cristi	294,745.80	//
San Pedro de Macorís	5.63	//
Sánchez Ramírez	146,768.04	//
María T. Sánchez	169,332.71	//
San Juan	1,110,250.83	//
La Romana	1,717.88	//
Santiago	553,419.12	//

---

12. An excellent example of such a transaction was the purchase by a well-known provincial governor whom Trujillo allowed to buy 100 tareas of Juancito Rodríguez' land at six dollars per tarea. This individual knew full well he was buying Rodríguez land because as governor he was aware of the sentence the courts imposed on the most influential landowner in the province.

13. This was exactly what happened in Nagua in María Trinidad Sánchez province. Trujillo had forced the sale of huge extensions of land, probably over 100,000 tareas, at a cheap price and had then converted much of it into valuable rice fields. He had sold most of these holdings by 1960, but during the 1950's landless peasants had settled on undeveloped sections of the property and were permitted to remain.

Valverde	6,271.28	//
Samaná	500.00	//
El Seibo	24,672.15	//
Total	3,213,420.14	tareas

Of this sum, 1,577,912 tareas were promptly made available for agrarian reform purposes. The remainder included much of the sugar holdings or other properties to which the state wished to retain title at least temporarily.[14]

The second development in 1961 that had an impact on agrarian reform was the approval by the National Assembly on December 29 of a new constitution which emphasized the need for universal, compulsory free primary education, recognized the supremacy of social interest and public benefit over the right to own property, provided for expropriation by the state of rural land needed for the agrarian reform but only after just indemnification, and gave the right to vote to all Dominicans over eighteen, or younger if they were married or had been married.[15] Taken together, these four provisions reflected the assembly's awareness that the rural majority in the country had become a potentially powerful political force. Balaguer's haste to begin redistribution of land in the fall of 1961 was recognition of this fact.

It was these same campesinos to whom Juan Bosch and his Partido Revolucionario Dominicano (PRD) appealed. Founded as an exile party in 1939, the PRD was intended to be the vehicle for awakening the leaderless, illiterate masses of Dominicans, organizing them, and bringing them into the active political arena where they could obtain by democratic means something they had never had: liberty and social justice.[16]

Bosch quickly picked up the issue of agrarian reform. Already running hard for the presidency, he first mentioned the redistribution of land during a radio speech in December 1961, shortly after the government had decreed the formation of its agrarian reform agency. At this time neither Bosch nor the high level officials in government who were involved with the so-called agrarian reform had a clear and full idea what such a program should consist of. Nor did Bosch's main political opponent, Viriato Fiallo, of the Unión Cívica Nacional (UCN). The UCN was a party of the middle and upper classes. In U.S. Ambassador Martin's words, it lacked "a real understanding of the people's needs."[17] All, however, understood the need for increased agricultural productivity, and all saw that redistribution of land was an important element. Redistribution was an attractive campaign issue, one highly popular with the campesinos, and Bosch pushed it to the limit. He repeatedly called for redistribution of Trujillo land to

14. Rogers, *Régimen de tierras,* 1st rev., p. 43. Before he went into exile Ramfis "donated" the remainder of the sugar holdings to the state—for a price. As the owner of the sugar combination *Azucarera del Norte,* he had purchased the centrales of Catarey, Esperanza, Monte Llano, and Amistad in August, 1960, for $25 million. On November 3, 1961, just shortly before Ramfis left the country, the Bank of Agricultural and Industrial Credit repurchased these centrales, and the state took steps to dissolve Azucarera del Norte. The repurchase price was reported to be $25 million. On December 13, 1961, all of the special benefits, franchises, and exemptions which Azucarera del Norte had previously enjoyed were cancelled. The centrales concerned henceforth would pay the same taxes as other centrales. Decree No. 7408, December 13, 1961, published in *Gaceta Oficial,* No. 8626 of December 15, 1961.

15. República Dominicana, *Constitución de 29 de diciembre 1961, Gaceta Oficial,* No. 8631, December 29, 1961, Article 8, paragraphs 6 and 9, Articles 13, 14.

16. Juan Bosch, *Crisis de la democracia,* p. 24.

17. Martin, *Overtaken by Events,* p. 206.

the landless peasant at the rate of about 100 tareas each.[18] This was a major talking point in his shirtsleeve campaigning throughout 1962. In his campaign speeches, however, he essentially never went beyond redistribution as a goal. He had only the conviction that every campesino should have his own land.[19] Bosch's campaign increased the pressure on the council of state to initiate the formal agrarian program. Bonnelly (no great admirer of Bosch), as well as others, could see what was happening. The campesinos, who constituted about seventy percent of the vote but were not capable of exercising political discrimination, would rely on the individual they felt they could trust.[20] The more aggressive "Peredista" leaders were filling that role because they were talking in language the campesino understood and liked. If the PRD could consolidate the rural vote, it could elect a PRD president. The council of state pushed ahead on the preparation of an agrarian reform law.

Early in 1962, while the director-general of agrarian reform and his staff were working on the draft agrarian reform law, the Dominicans realized they lacked the experience, especially on the technical side, to set up the machinery for the reform program. Assisted by the Organization of American States, they contracted for consultants to review the needs of the nation and provide guidelines for the organizational structure. The earliest report, completed in March, was a useful survey which pointed out that agrarian reform consisted in much more than a mere redistribution of agricultural lands.[21] If the redistribution was to be beneficial, it must be accomplished in an orderly manner and be accompanied by a program to aid and develop the farm families involved. The proposed program should include the following major elements:

Redistribution of agricultural lands to new owners;
Availability of cheap credit, accompanied by technical assistance services;
Educational programs for farmers and their families;
Development of facilities and an efficient system for satisfactory production and for providing materials such as seeds, fertilizers, and farm implements;
Rapid development of facilities and efficient systems for the transportation, classification, storage, processing, and marketing of agricultural products;
Development of public and social services that contribute to a more progressive life, such as electricity, schools, clinics, recreation facilities, and churches.

The survey indicated that the efforts of the agrarian reform program should initially be directed toward the use of recently recovered state lands and only on those which could be developed effectively. Land should be given to those families who were interested in cultivating the soil or who were already employed in agricultural industries such as sugar. These were two very important points: the government should at first

---

18. In *The Unfinished Experiment*, p. 51, Bosch says he spoke on radio in December 1961 of the necessity of distributing Trujillo's land among the landless peasant families at the rate of about fifteen acres each. This was the first time he had mentioned the subject, but it became a key issue in the campaign.

19. Bosch never promised "free" land, according to his secretary for campesino affairs. The latter, himself a large landholder and one of Bosch's closest advisors, managed the campaign in the Cibao. Personal interview, La Vega, July 2, 1969. The "Establishment," however, interpreted Bosch's campaign speeches and later his presidential speeches to mean that he favored seizure of private land without indemnification, in order to satisfy the landless.

20. I have seen campesinos approach the respected owner of the ranch where they worked and simply ask: "Don A_____, for whom should I vote? I don't know what I should do."

21. Mervin G. Smith, V. Webster Johnson, and Gustavo de Pedro, *A Report on Agrarian Reform in the Dominican Republic* (Santo Domingo, March 1962).

devote to the reform program the land immediately available and thus avoid unnecessary litigation over private or contested property, and it should screen the prospective beneficiaries carefully.

The specific aims of the program were:

A pacific evolution and orderly development of rural communities composed principally of owners of family-sized farms;
The establishment of improved housing and communities for agricultural laborers;
An increase in living standards and in the social and economic independence of rural inhabitants;
An increase in efficiency of agricultural production;
An opportunity for each rural inhabitant to develop fully his production potential and to increase his contribution to the development of the nation;
A positive contribution to the political and social stability of the nation.

Here was a modern, expanded version of the agrarian principles and goals Ulises Espaillat had postulated eighty-five years earlier and which José Ramón López had repeated, pleading at the turn of the century for more rural education as the cure for the backward agricultural technology of the country that was impeding economic growth. These goals were written into the agrarian reform.

The second comprehensive agrarian reform law of the Dominican Republic appeared April 27, 1962.[22] From the point of view of agricultural economics, the law was badly needed in many respects. The economy was essentially a one-crop agricultural economy based on the exportation of sugar. A large proportion of the rapidly growing population was rural. Rural unemployment was high; rural standards of living were low. Agricultural productivity was relatively low. The land tenure picture was distorted. There were approximately 200,000 landless rural families. The following specific details will amplify these general observations.

Demographic factors. Of a total population of 3,047,070, 71 percent were rural, one of the highest proportions in Latin America.[23] The annual growth rate of rural population was 2.5 percent, which tied with Costa Rica and Nicaragua as the highest in Latin America.[24]

Fifty percent of the total population were under seventeen years of age.

The net annual population increase between 1955 and 1965 was 3.5 percent, one of the highest in Latin America (see table below).

Approximately 65 percent of all economically active males—about 495,000—were employed in agriculture; of these, 25 to 30 percent were unemployed.[25]

Density of population was 62.1 inhabitants per square kilometer, third highest in Latin America (see table below). Population densities of the provinces varied from 8.6 in Pedernales province to 139.3 in Salcedo. In the Cibao, these were the figures: Duarte,

---

22. Law No. 5879, published in the *Gaceta Oficial* Number 8671, of July 14, 1962. A complete translation is contained in Appendix 7.

23. Unless otherwise indicated, demographic data are taken from República Dominicana, *Cuarto censo nacional*.

24. United Nations, *Boletín económico de América Latina suplemento estadístico,* Secretaría de la Comisión Económica para América Latina, vol. 7, no. 1, p. 54 (hereafter referred to as *Boletín económico, suplemento*).

25. Peter Dorner et al., "Agrarian Reform in the Dominican Republic: The Views of Four Consultants," p. 1 (hereafter referred to as "Agrarian Reform").

Comparative Demographic Data

	1955–60 Population per sq. km.[a]	1955–60 Annual Population Growth, %[b]	1960 Rural Population, %[c]
Dominican Republic	62.1	3.5	71
Argentina	7.2	1.8	32
Bolivia	2.4	2.2	70
Brazil	8.3	3.5	61
Chile	9.9	2.4	37
Colombia	10.1	2.8	54
Costa Rica	26.3	2.9	62
Cuba	50.9	3.9	45
Ecuador	16.9	3.2	65
El Salvador	119.9	2.1	67
Guatemala	39.3	3.1	69
Haiti	111.2	2.9	87
Honduras	16.8	2.2	78
Mexico	17.8	3.4	46
Nicaragua	11.7	3.1	66
Panama	14.2	2.7	59
Paraguay	4.5	2.5	66
Peru	7.7	3.0	64
Uruguay	14.4	1.3	18
Venezuela	8.2	3.7	38

a. Organization of American States, Pan American Union, *América en cifras, 1963*, vol. 1, *Situación física*, table 101–04 (hereafter referred to as *América en cifras*).

b. *Boletín económico, suplemento*, table 5, p. 9.

c. Ibid., table 6, p. 10.

124.9; Espaillat, 120.3; La Vega 72.1; María T. Sánchez, 65.0; Salcedo, 139.3; Santiago, 92.5.

Land tenure structure. 54.5 percent of the arable land was in crops and pastures.[26]

Nine-tenths of one hectare (one hectare equals 2.47 acres, or 16 tareas) per inhabitant was under cultivation, the second lowest figure in Latin America.

There were 450,335 private landowners, who owned 2,154,657 hectares of land under cultivation or use. 50.2 percent of all farms were less than 1 hectare in size; farms of less than 1 hectare constituted 4.7 percent of the total farm land. Therefore, over half of the farm owners owned only 4.7 percent of the total farm land.

One percent of all farms were over 50 hectares in size; farms of over 50 hectares in size constituted 53.6 percent of the total farm land. Therefore, one percent of the farm owners owned over half of the total farm land.

Of all farms, 56.3 percent were owner-operated.

There was an increase of 173,487 individually registered farms between 1950 and 1960, but 93.9 percent of these were farms less than 2 hectares in size. The trend was toward minifundismo. [27]

---

26. Unless otherwise indicated, data are taken from Rogers, *Régimen de tierras, 1st rev., suplemento estadístico*. Data are for 1960, as adjusted by IDS statistical research.

27. Rogers, *Régimen de tierras*, p. 5.

Comparative Land Tenure Data

	1950–63 Land under Cultivation per Inhabitant[a]	1950–63 Farm Units less than 5h. in Size[b]
Dominican Republic	.9 hectare	86.2% of all units
Argentina	8.8	15.7
Bolivia	10.8	59.3
Brazil	3.7	...
Chile	4.1	36.9
Colombia	1.9	62.5
Costa Rica	2.0	...
Cuba	1.4	13.9
Ecuador	1.7	73.1
El Salvador	.6	85.1
Guatemala	1.3	...
Haiti	...	...
Honduras	1.7	57.0
Mexico	5.6	72.6
Nicaragua	2.2	...
Panama	1.7	52.0
Paraguay	...	...
Peru	2.1	82.9
Uruguay	6.4	14.7
Venezuela	4.3	...

a. *América en cifras*, vol. 3, table 311–06.
b. Ibid., table 311–04.

Comparative Economic Data

	Per Capita Income (1950 prices)[a]	1960 Index of Agricultural Gross Domestic Product per Active Person[b]
Dominican Republic	$200	87
Argentina	550	244
Bolivia	75	31
Brazil	250	80
Chile	325	111
Colombia	300	143
Costa Rica	250	200
Cuba	375	249
Ecuador	140	68
El Salvador	175	73
Guatemala	175	90
Haiti	80	31
Honduras	175	71
Mexico	200	86
Nicaragua	175	115
Panama	350	143
Paraguay	100	59
Peru	175	61
Uruguay	400	290
Venezuela	1000	147
Average	300	119

a. U.N., *Boletín económico, suplemento*, vol. 7, no. 2, table 2, p. 216.
b. U.N., *Boletín económico de América Latina*, vol. 8, no. 2, table 25, p. 165.

Economic factors. Agriculture contributed 41 percent of the Gross National Product (1961).[28]

There existed a one-crop economy. Agricultural products constituted 90 percent of all exports; sugar and sugar derivatives constituted 59 percent of all exports (1961).

Gross National Product per capita in 1961 was $244.40; net real income per capita was $230.31 (1962 prices).

Agricultural production per capita was 27 percent under the average for Latin America (see column 3 in the table, "Comparative Economic Data").

Estimated total unemployment in 1962 was 300,000.[29]

Standard of living. 12.4 percent of the rural inhabitants had tap water available in their homes; 1.9 percent had electric lights.[30]

Closely linked with poor rural sanitary conditions, the death rate from infectious and parasitic diseases was two to three times higher than in the more developed Latin American countries (see table, "Comparative Standard of Living Data").

Comparative Standard of Living Data

	1957–60, Death Rate per 100,000, Infectious and Parasitic Diseases[a]	1961–62, Death Rate per 100,000, Gastro-Ent. and Intest. Diseases[b]	1957–59, Per Capita Consumption of Meat, kg/Year[c]	1960, Food Price Index[d]
Dominican Republic	109.6	132.1	9	115
Argentina	34.3	24.5	91	78
Bolivia	. . .	21.7	. . .	99
Brazil	182.9	77.2	29	82
Chile	107.3	61.9	31	82
Colombia	139.7	127.6	41	109
Costa Rica	102.8	124.2	. . .	100
Cuba	34.0	42.7	. . .	. . .
Ecuador	302.8	130.6	15	105
El Salvador	109.2	64.2	. . .	118
Guatemala	503.8	223.5	. . .	109
Haiti	. . .	. . .	. . .	114
Honduras	184.7	42.4	. . .	99
Mexico	151.8	152.0	24	107
Nicaragua	157.1	73.7	. . .	107
Panama	110.5	44.7	. . .	105
Paraguay	98.1	60.3	48	89
Peru	149.5	83.9	18	95
Uruguay	39.7	13.6	109	91
Venezuela	55.5	48.1	25	93
Average	. . .	. . .	. . .	100

a. U.N., *Boletín económico de América Latina,* vol. 8, no. 2, 1963, table 33, p. 171.
b. *América en cifras,* vol. 7, table 202–24.
c. U.N., *Boletín económico de América Latina,* vol. 8, no. 2, 1963, table B, p. 188.
d. Ibid., table 11, p. 220. Price relatives at parity rates of exchange.

28. Unless otherwise indicated, data are taken from República Dominicana, *Cifras.* This publication contains annual statistics from 1960.
29. Gifford E. Rogers, *Agrarian Reform Defined and Analyzed,* p. 4.
30. U.N., *Boletín económico de América Latina,* vol. 8, no. 2, table 32, p. 170.

The two largest causes of death were respiratory and gastrointestinal diseases such as those commonly associated with poor standards of living.[31]

Average daily food intake was low—2,000–2,100 calories.[32]

The per capita consumption of meat was the lowest of eleven Latin American countries recorded. The main staples in the rural Dominican diet have always been plantain, beans, rice, starchy roots and tubers, and fruit (in season).

The price index of food was 15 percent higher than the average in Latin America.

Comparative Educational Data

	1953–55, Elem. Teachers per 1,000 Population Aged 5–14[a]	1957, Grads. of Higher Ed. in Agriculture per Million Inhabitants[b]	Percent Illiteracy (UN criteria) 15 years and older[c]	1959–61, Percent of National Income on Education[d]
Dominican Republic	7	1	(1950) 56.8	9.9
Argentina	30	130	(1960) 8.6	17.0
Bolivia	12	52	(1950) 68.9	9.0
Brazil	11	75	(1950) 51.4	...
Chile	—	249	(1960) 16.4	14.7
Colombia	9	54	(1951) 38.5	10.2
Costa Rica	24	567	(1963) 15.7	27.8
Cuba	16	112	(1953) 23.6	12.2
Ecuador	11	28	(1962) 69.4	14.5
El Salvador	12	6	(1961) 52.0	16.5
Guatemala	10	3	(1950) 70.3	...
Haiti	5	66	(1950) 89.3	9.9
Honduras	12	7	(1961) 55.0	11.5
Mexico	11	115	(1960) 34.6	20.4[e]
Nicaragua	13	21	(1963) 50.4	...
Panama	18	26	(1960) 26.7	18.6
Paraguay	19	3	(1950) 31.8	...
Peru	12	52	(1961) 39.9	10.0
Uruguay	17	228	(1950) 15–20	...
Venezuela	12	50	(1961) 34.2	9.0[e]

a. U.N., *Boletín económico de América Latina*, vol. 7, no. 1, table 5, p. 39.
b. Ibid.
c. Norris B. Lyle and Richard A. Calman, eds. and comps., *Statistical Abstract of Latin America, 1965*, 9th ed., table 17, p. 32.
d. Ibid., table 22, p. 40.
e. Central government only.

31. Table 202-24, *América en cifras*, shows a detailed breakdown of causes of death for each country.

32. Gifford E. Rogers, *Agrarian Reform Defined and Analyzed*, p. 4. This food intake figure is one of the lowest in Latin America. Of thirteen countries recorded, only Costa Rica was lower, with 1966 calories. U.N., *Boletín económico de América Latina*, vol. 7, no. 1, table 7, p. 221. Studies conducted in the Dominican Republic by the government have confirmed the inadequacy of the Dominican diet, especially in the rural areas. At the end of 1962 the director of statistics published a report of nutrition technicians who calculated the daily average Dominican food intake at 1,700 calories. A typical rural diet consisted of the equivalent of one meal a day. Rice was the main item; it constituted 18 percent of the campesino's income, followed by oil, beans, bread, roots, and plantain. The average daily income for a family of five was $1.34; in urban areas it was $1.60. If coffee and chocolate were included, food accounted for 53 percent of the poor man's income. There was no meat on the list of foods shown as regular diet, nor was there any cheese, fish, or other protein. *El Caribe*, January 1963.

Cultural factors. The national illiteracy rate was high, estimated at 55 percent of the population 10 years or older.[33] The proportion of these in rural areas alone was about 80 percent.[34]

Only 8.9 percent of the national income was being invested in education.[35]

The broadly written 1962 law was adequate for launching the reform program, although it did not precisely define the nation's agrarian policy, toward which the reforms would work. In language strongly resembling that of the PRD, the preamble[36] recognized the rural areas' social and economic conditions which urgently demanded reform, the weaknesses of the earlier colonization program, the nature of a truly comprehensive reform, and finally, that a primary interest of the government was the establishment of an adequate agrarian reform to accelerate the socio-economic liberation of the rural masses. The law created the Dominican Agrarian Institute (IAD) and prescribed its powers, organization, functions, capitalization, and procedures. The law also fixed the powers and functions of the directory, or board of directors, of IAD. IAD became the working element within the agrarian reform structure of the government. The director-general of DGRA became also the director-general of IAD, which was legally empowered to exercise autonomous authority.

Supported by the Constitution, the law empowered IAD to petition the state for public lands needed for reform programs; to acquire land by private gift, from legal entities, or local or international organizations; and to purchase lands, or, in accordance with law,

---

33. The estimated factor here concerns more the definition of literacy rather than the accuracy of the census. Table 14 of the 1960 census, which itself should be used with caution, shows that 34.2 percent of the population was illiterate, but these figures are based on Yes or No answers to the simple question: "Do you know how to read and write?" Presumably anyone who could write or read no more than his own name might qualify as literate. By way of comparison, Costa Rican procedures are more definitive, since they require the individual to read a simple paragraph. The focus here is on a functional literacy, and, therefore, I have arbitrarily set a requirement of third grade education or better to qualify a respondent as literate. The 55 percent figure represents that part of the population over ten years of age who had less than a third-grade education. República Dominicana, *Cuarto censo nacional*, table 15, pp. 57–58. Using his own criteria, the director of planning, secretariat of education, calculated that the 1969 illiteracy rate nationwide was close to 45 percent. Personal interview, Santo Domingo, January 19, 1970.

34. See Chap. 21.

35. Total income for 1962 was estimated at RD $126.7 million. The government budgeted RD $11.4 million for education and RD $33.4 million for the armed forces. The latter figure included RD $3.5 million for education and training within the armed forces, some of which would be transferable to civilian occupations. The largest single item in the education budget was RD $3.16 million, over 27 percent, for rural education. Primary rural education received RD $2.47 million. Secondary and normal education received RD $.84 million. República Dominicana, *Presupuesto de ingresos y ley de gastos públicos para el año 1962*, Law No. 5734, published in the *Gaceta Oficial*, No. 8632 of December 31, 1961.

36. To assist in the drafting of the reform program the council of state brought in Dr. Carlos Chardón, an eminent Puerto Rican educator-agronomist, experienced in Latin American agrarian problems. The drafters intended that the rectification of the ills and evils noted in the preamble would constitute agrarian policy, but to provide more complete guidance they might have listed policy objectives in order of priority. This omission in itself was not a fatal defect, because the law was sufficiently complete yet flexible enough to permit the director-general to develop his own priorities and to modify policies in the light of experience. The setting of specific goals in terms of increased agricultural production, numbers of new owners to be settled, numbers of new rural homes to be built, and the timetable for achieving these goals, would have provided all government agencies concerned with a clearer idea of what their tasks would be.

to solicit from the executive branch expropriation authority. A most important point is noted here. The law permitted IAD to petition the executive branch for expropriation of private lands when they were needed for IAD programs, but it did not specify which private lands could be expropriated. As written, the law did not protect private holdings, large or small, that were already producing efficiently. This omission was certain to alarm private landowners, many of whom were still suffering from the trauma of thirty one years of political and physical abuse under Trujillo. An additional point, which will be referred to later, is that IAD was given no jurisdiction over property titles or title litigation. In all questions of secure titles or title adjudication, the normal procedures through the land courts had to be followed. IAD could not grant title to redistributed or partitioned land if there were no a priori secure title on which to operate. In title litigation, then, IAD had to wait for the courts.

The first director-general of the new Institute of Agrarian Reform, Manuel de Jesús Viñas Cáceres, was appointed on May 24, 1962, and lost no time in forming a staff. The same day, Victorino F. Alvarez, of the Inter-American Development Bank (BID) in the Dominican Republic joined IAD and began the task of developing the basic organization. On September 3, with the assistance of the U.S. embassy, Viñas signed a contract with International Development Services, Inc. (IDS), an American consulting firm specializing in agrarian reform. Under the terms of the two-year contract, IDS, as technical advisors to the Dominican Agrarian Institute, assumed three important obligations, all consistent with the philosophy of the Alliance for Progress:[37] (1), IDS undertook to prepare and train Dominican agricultural technicians so that they could carry the benefits of modern agrarian techniques to all citizens dependent on agriculture for their livelihood; (2), IDS would cooperate in the initiation and operation of all projects of the agrarian reform program approved by the Dominican government, bearing in mind the overriding need to harmonize them with other developmental plans of the government; agrarian reform was not to be achieved in a planning vacuum; it would be merely a part of an overall program of national development; (3), IDS would collaborate with the IAD and other agencies of the government in the preparation of a long-term agrarian development plan for achieving major economic, social, and political advantages for the Dominican Republic.

IDS technicians immediately began a series of studies to serve as a basis for the over-all reform plan.[38] In essence, the studies were an inventory of all the human, physical, and economic resources of the Dominican Republic. IDS was well aware that available data such as census information might be inaccurate or incomplete and that detailed plans would probably require modification or perhaps even complete revision as new infor-

---

37. "To encourage, in accordance with the characteristics of each country, programs of comprehensive agrarian reform, leading to the effective transformation where required, of unjust structures and systems of land tenure and use; with a view to replacing latifundia and dwarf holdings by an equitable system of property, so that, supplemented by timely and adequate credit, technical assistance and improved marketing arrangements, the land will become for the man who works it the basis of his economic stability, the foundation of his increasing welfare, and the guarantee of his freedom and dignity." Inter-American Economic and Social Council, "Declaration to the Peoples of America," *Declaration and Charter,* Punta del Este, Uruguay, August 17, 1961. Paragraph 6, Title I, Objectives. Title II, Economic and Social Development of the Declaration outlined the national development programs which included "the strengthening of the agricultural base."

38. Water resources, land tenure and usage, human resources, natural resources, and land classification were some.

mation was accumulated. For example, a serious statistical weakness was the lack of an accurate inventory and classification of all lands. Such an inventory had to be the starting point for a reform program, yet it was a monumental task requiring years to complete. The time available and the pressures for democratic changes, however, did not permit delay. Accordingly, it was agreed that the studies would not be fully acted on until firmer data were available, and that all projects would be thoroughly checked twice.[39] As a foundation for future specific programs based on these studies, IDS defined true agrarian reform as an evolutionary process by which Dominican campesinos could find security in the land. A valid program involving the complex problem of rural security would fill two needs: a much more productive agriculture as a base for economic development, and a sense of security and participation among the rural inhabitants, which would contribute to the process of achieving internal political stability. Here was complete agreement with the Smith survey.

The plan for agrarian reform was sketched in a long-term national perspective in which the principal figures were 200,000 to 225,000 campesino families who either owned no land at all or whose small holdings were classified as minifundia—holdings of uneconomic size. Indispensable to the hoped-for political participation was the expansion of rural education. Of the many elements in the agrarian program, human and natural resources, laws and institutions, financial resources and technology, perhaps the most important was the human element. If those Dominicans involved in reform projects were to contribute intellectually to their country's growth and stabilization, they had to be educated. The average participant would be illiterate, would have little or no experience with the concept of credit for relatively large sums of money, nor would he have much experience in farm management. For the majority, success could only come through a sound educational program. Unlike laws and institutions, however, which can be modified or created quickly to meet the dynamics of an agrarian reform program, the educational process would be a long one. In committing itself to a comprehensive reform, the Dominican government made a concurrent commitment to educate the campesino. To do this, both schools and competent teachers would be needed.

By mid-1962 IAD generally accepted as reasonably attainable a set of specific objectives which were consistent with the 1962 law and the Smith survey[40] and which determined the internal organization of IAD as set up by Alvarez and, later, other former BID personnel. These were the specific goals:[41]

> Completion, as a matter of priority, of land use surveys, cadastral mapping, and title classification.
> Subdivision of state-owned property for landless farmers.
> Just and legal acquisition of idle private land for subdivision and sale to landless farmers.
> Placing land in the hands of those most qualified to handle it.
> Creation of employment opportunities for rural laborers.

---

39. The wisdom of this decision became apparent as errors in the 1960 farm census were discovered between 1962 and 1963. IDS was forced to recalculate much of the land tenure data set forth in the earlier 1962 studies. Trujillo's habit of manipulating data in order to present a favorable external facade complicated any serious work which depended on Dominican statistics.

40. See note 21 above.

41. Rogers, *Agrarian Reform Defined and Analyzed*, pp. 4–5. At this stage IDS was in effect generating the policy to be followed with, of course, the approval of the director. The latter made no significant changes in IDS recommendations.

Establishment of a sound and financially feasible long-range agricultural development plan, the basic priority element of which would be increased productivity.

Initiation of a true, supervised agricultural credit program, development of an adequate extension service, and improvement of land tenancy security for the small farmer.

Improvement of wages and working conditions for farm workers and provision of adequate, low-cost rural housing.

Development of water conservation and control measures and installation of potable water and adequate waste disposal systems throughout rural areas.

Construction of adequate access roads in all agrarian development projects and the installation of adequate educational, recreational, public health, and community facilities in all agrarian reform projects.

Installation of modern crop-handling, transportation, storage, marketing, and processing systems and facilities throughout the nation.

The original organization of IAD, which was completed by August 1962, included three main divisions:[42] project planning, project execution, and permanent assistance, each subdivided into sections as follows:

DIRECTOR

SUB-DIRECTOR

Project Planning	*Project Execution*	*Permanent Assistance*
Land inventory and classification	Land subdivision and family settlement	Cooperatives and social services
Economic and social analysis	Construction and public services	Technical assistance
Cadastral surveys and land measurement	Roads, bridges, and irrigation	Agricultural implements and machinery
Family selection	Provisional project administration	Operation and maintenance of utilities
Education	Inspection and certification	

In addition to these divisions there was a technical advisor branch which came directly under the director and such staff services as accounting and auditing, legal, public relations, general secretariat, and administrative services. The structure was modified from time to time as the reform program expanded, but the basic functions were retained. Initial personnel numbered 538, of which 237 were permanent, 101 provisional; 200 were temporary laborers. By 1965 there were 637 employees. Although IAD was autonomous by law, the secretary of state for agriculture had the responsibility for reviewing the IAD budget and submitting it with the budget of his own department.

---

42. Ibid., pp. 142–43.

23

AGRARIAN REFORM IN ACTION

With respect to government, the period from 1962 to the end of 1966 can be divided into four periods: April 1962 to March 1963, under the Council of State; March 1963 to September 1963, under the Bosch government; September 1963 to June 1966, under the Triumvirate, the Reid government, and the provisional government of Héctor García-Godoy; and June 1966 on, under the Balaguer government.[1] Frequent disruptions in national administration during these years brought corresponding changes at the top executive level in IAD. The legal autonomy of the organization was ignored with every transfer of executive power. In this short space of time there were five different directors, no one of whom held the office long enough to be able to give the new agrarian program the continuity of leadership it needed. The organization always functioned, but at times with reduced efficiency. For example, Bosch handicapped the program by appointing Dr. Carlos M. Campos as his personal advisor to IAD and giving him authority equal to that of the director-general. This split in authority, coupled with the financial problems of the Bosch government, hindered administration and in part explained the lack of progress in 1963.

The IAD began a program of reform even though it appeared that there would be a number of important problem areas such as lack of clear titles by the government to some of the state-held land, lack of detailed information on current use and occupation

---

1. The Triumvirate took over the government after Bosch was ousted: Emilio de los Santos resigned in December 1963 and was replaced by Donald Reid Cabral; Ramón Tapia Espinal resigned in April 1964 and was replaced by Ramón Cáceres Troncoso; Manuel Tavares Espaillat, the third member, resigned in June 1964. Reid ran the government until April 24, 1965, when the civil war broke out. There was considerable political opposition to Reid because of his decision to run for reelection. He had not been elected by the people, and therefore did not occupy the presidency legitimately. Héctor García-Godoy became provisional president in September 1965 when the civil war ended, and held the office until Joaquín Balaguer was elected by the people in June 1966. García-Godoy later became the Dominican ambassador to the United States. References to the Balaguer administration have been incorporated at the end of this chapter.

of state-held land, and the lack of administrative experience within the IAD itself. Nevertheless, assisted by IDS specialists in the fields of organization and administration of rural colonization, land use and land management, economics and finance, and farm cooperatives, IAD negotiated a loan agreement with the United States Agency for International Development (AID) mission in July 1962 which provided for expenditures of almost 2.5 million dollars.[2] To prepare the government, news media, and public for the program, IDS technicians worked alongside Dominican staff members of IAD in seminars, public gatherings, and press and radio interviews. It was particularly important that other government agencies understand the national scope of the reform. Programs were also set up to train Dominican technicians who would administer the farm cooperatives in each project and to orient the campesinos, who would become members in the cooperatives. The objectives of the IDS personnel were to get the program started and to train the Dominicans themselves to take over the administration of the agrarian reform projects as rapidly as possible. AID technicians were also made available for this purpose by the U.S. embassy. The Bank of Agricultural and Industrial Credit, assisted by the Inter-American Development Bank, undertook to develop, among other things, a supervised rural credit system. Other government agencies were committed to cooperate in specialty fields such as road and bridge construction, establishment of schools and clinics, and housing construction.[3]

Pending completion of long-range development plans and supporting data, IAD inaugurated the following step-by-step procedures for settling the first of the new landowners, fully realizing that such procedures might have to be modified in light of actual experience, but at the same time hopeful that the basic principles for settlement would remain valid:

Make a rapid study of the lands to be settled to classify soil and determine land usage and occupation, if any;[4]

---

2. Expenditures included $640,000 for IAD administration, $1,075,000 for the first five reform projects, $430,000 for the Nagua project, $300,000 for the next five projects; total: $2,445,000. The credit agreement was signed on May 12, revised July 19, and finally amended on July 31. Gifford E. Rogers, *The Task of the Dominican Agrarian Reform Program for the Balance of This Decade*, p. 4 (hereafter referred to as *Task of Reform*). This was to be but one of the many AID projects for the Dominican Republic. Under the Alliance for Progress, the Kennedy administration inaugurated a strong effort to keep the post-Trujillo governments afloat. Support for Dominican agriculture, including sugar quotas and agrarian reform, has ever since been a constant factor in these programs. For instance, the 1968 Dominican budget showed a total of almost $21.5 million in foreign loans, virtually all from U.S. sources ($17.68 million from AID alone). Of this amount, $4 million was for community development, $3.79 million for education, $1.36 million for public health, $6.33 million for agriculture, and $0.58 million for public works. Note that just under fifty percent was earmarked for education and agriculture.

Although the U.S. assistance programs for the Dominican Republic from 1962 on form a decisive element in U.S.-Dominican relations, a detailed analysis would not contribute materially to this study. I have, therefore, included only the data that would indicate in general the importance of the agrarian reform.

3. Foreign private industry represented by the Levantino Foreign Fruit Company of New York also cooperated with IAD by assigning a technician to assist in all phases of land preparation, cultivation, harvesting, and packing in the Matanzas area. Levantino was interested in creating a fruit and vegetable export program in the Dominican Republic, and saw the opportunity to participate in the early stages of development. Ibid., pp. 6–8.

4. IAD contemplated settlement on state-held lands only for the time being. The law of 1962 included no procedures for expropriation, although the basic options were known: cash pur-

Survey the project and plot the individual units;
Provide access road and potable water supply;
Resettle "squatters," if necessary;[5]
Select new farm families;
Loan the new families the money and equipment necessary to start their new lives;
Grant a provisional title to the land; and
Render continuing technical advice and assistance.

These were the general financial planning factors which IAD developed for the reform projects:

The average size of the parcel of land to be settled would be about sixty tareas, a family-size unit, economically sound. Five basic crops would be produced: rice, beans, peanuts, tobacco, and melons.

An annual family net income goal of close to $1,200 was set, four times greater than the per capita Gross National Product average.

The cost to IAD of the first harvests in the first five projects would be $650,000; the estimated gross value of the crops harvested would be $2,070,100.

As the number of beneficiaries of the program increased, the unit costs for administration, technical and financial assistance, and other indirect costs would decrease. The final unit cost for settling a family in a completely integrated agrarian project, hopefully, would drop to $1,000. This amount, the unit cost of development, would be recovered from the sale of the land to the new landowner, based on sixty tareas per parcel at an average value of $15 to $20 per tarea.

For the first three years, the state would have to supply the funds required for housing and operating loans. Thereafter, the operations of most projects would be self-financing as a result of cooperative savings plans, assuming that members would be willing to deposit about $100 per year in the cooperative account. Housing loans, on the other hand, would have to be amortized over a ten- to fifteen-year period.

Income to IAD from land sale and capital accumulation would be insignificant for the first five years. Low interest loans would be needed to finance the IAD loans to the new landowners until IAD could accumulate sufficient capital to finance its own projects.

Important as these factors were, the heart of the reform was the redistribution of land. On this step, more than any other, would depend the success of the program. The general concept for redistribution was developed along the following lines:

With the 1962 law providing the guidelines, IAD would be responsible for the selection and development of land sites on which to settle agrarian reform projects. A "project" was conceived to be an integrated agricultural community whose members IAD would select from among landless Dominicans. "Integrated" referred to those actions that would achieve the specific goals set by IAD for the new settlers.[6]

Since one of the basic aims of the reform was to increase productivity, idle land would

---

chase, bond offers, or a combination of these.

5. In the Nagua project, where about 800 squatters had settled on former Trujillo land, staked out their own parcels, and placed them under rice cultivation, IAD found it difficult to justify uprooting and resettling the tenants. Since the situation already existed by 1962 and since the average size of the squatter's cultivated parcels was more or less in accordance with the size IAD had established for this area and crop, the squatters were not molested. IAD prudently decided that the benefits of reform should first be brought to the squatters and that such matters as final land titles and proper subdivision could await the future. IAD hoped that continuing dialogue with the squatters would lead the majority of them to accept any necessary minor revision in land boundaries. Here was a case of "invade now and pay later" which the government accepted in the spirit of project development. Ibid., p. 12.

6. See Chap. 22 note 41.

receive top priority for development. State-owned land would be developed first. Private landowners would be advised that the best protection against expropriation was efficient production. There would be no indiscriminate subdivision of efficiently producing farm land solely for the sake of redistribution.

IAD would base family selection for new ownership primarily on need, ability, and willingness to work the land. Selection procedures would include the use of nationally distributed application forms to determine the basic eligibility of applicants; their location, in order to fix development priorities by region; second, or follow-up, contacts with applicants in order to fix priorities for selection; and finally, a review of the selections by a commission composed of IAD representatives and citizens of the area where projects were to be initiated. Successful applicants would be thoroughly briefed on their responsibilities.

IAD would first survey, subdivide, and register land to be redistributed; the land courts would then issue clear titles to the parcels. The nature of the individual project would determine the actual dimensions of parcels, but the parcels would be economically sized.[7] Land would not be given free, but after a two-year trial period would be sold under a conditional sales contract with liberal, long-term loans arranged with the Agricultural Credit Bank, as would be the settlers' homes. Article 39 of the 1962 law describes this contract which, in effect, was a provisional title only.

IAD launched the first two projects, Juma and Caracol, in the Bonao area in La Vega province on June 13, 1962. Some 500 families were to be placed. On July 3 the government announced that the first 136 farmers had each received the first weekly $25 advance on loans of $800, and the Santo Domingo *El Caribe* carried a thoughtful editorial pointing out the agrarian history of the country, the previous isolated, illiterate, and economically miserable condition of the farmers, and the need for Dominicans to find solutions to their own problems within their own resources.[8]

By the end of December 1962 IAD had started eight projects and settled 822 new landowners. The total cost of the program reached $868,000, or a little more than $1,000 per family settled, but a large part of the money was used to organize the institute itself and make the necessary capital investments for materials and equipment.

During this period the inventory and land classification section began the task of taking an inventory and classifying all exploitable lands possessed by the state and considered available for agrarian reform purposes. By the end of 1962, twelve of the twenty-six provinces had been inventoried[9] and preliminary land tenure studies completed.[10] Included in the inventories were lands confiscated from the Trujillos and their cohorts, acquired by purchase, taken for unpaid taxes, and recovered under existing irrigation and public

---

7. Definitions vary among agricultural economists. IAD used this one: of size sufficient not only to cover development costs and amortization of original land cost but also to provide sufficient surplus to enable the landowner to better his economic and cultural station in life. Ibid., p. 116.

8. *El Caribe*, July 4, 1962.

9. Landholdings were classified by size, number of parcels in each size classification, total area of each size classification, and average size in each classification. For an example, see Appendix 5 the inventory of the National District. Other provinces inventoried were Monte Cristi, La Romana, Salcedo, San Pedro de Macorís, Puerto Plata, María T. Sánchez, Samaná, Valverde, Dajabón, Santiago, and El Seibo. A total of 698,228.53 additional tareas had been confiscated in La Vega, Sánchez Ramírez, San Cristóbal, Peravia, and Azua, although the IAD inventory had not yet been completed in these provinces. These confiscated lands were assigned to IAD by the end of 1962. Rogers, *Régimen de tierras*, p. 23.

10. Included in the land tenure studies were data on land usage, ownership, productivity, and climate. See Appendix 6 for a summary of the study on La Vega province.

water laws. Under the latter, the landowner who received the benefit of state irrigation facilities was required to turn in to the state title to twenty-five percent of his land, if under cultivation, and fifty percent if not.[11] Many of these state-owned parcels were too small to be considered of economic size, and IDS recommended that wherever possible they be consolidated and distributed to qualified new settlers. If such an arrangement were not possible, IAD could sell the land to those farmers already working adjacent lands. There were approximately 12,940 tareas of these small parcels, all less than 80 tareas. At an average value of $20 per tarea, IAD stood to gain almost $259,000, enough to settle 260 landless families. The remaining inventoried state lands, nearly 1,200,000 tareas, were conservatively calculated to be worth $12 million, enough to settle at least 6,000 families. It seemed clear that a judicious combination of sale and distribution of state land could considerably augment the financial resources of IAD.

The final three months of the council of state period was so hectic politically that IAD was able to accomplish very little settlement of new landowners. Several administrative changes were indicated as a result of the first six months of activity, but before any reorganization could be made, Juan Bosch won the presidency.[12]

Bosch had been important to the agrarian reform program because he pushed for it in the long 1961–62 political campaign. As president, however, he contributed little. Whatever progress was achieved during his administration had already been planned during the council of state period.[13] Bosch's tendency to centralize decision-making processes created serious administrative problems, but none so important as the political impact of his Constitution of April 29. His philosophy on private landownership appeared to strike directly at the terratenientes. The constitution declared the possession of excessive amounts of land to be against the collective interests of the nation. Private latifundios, *no matter how they had been formed* (author's emphasis; this language could apply to large landholdings legally acquired and fully productive) were prohibited. Separate law would determine the maximum extensions of land which might be owned by an individual or a legal entity, taking into consideration agricultural, social, and economic factors. Minifundio were declared to be uneconomical and anti-social. Separate law would also define minifundio and determine the necessary measures to achieve their integration into units economically and socially exploitable.[14]

From March to July 1963 IAD settled no families. Most of its efforts were spent in

---

11. Ibid., p. 20. Law No. 5852.

12. The most important change was that IAD itself should not try to be completely self-sufficient, that is, should not attempt to build roads, bridges, and houses in the agrarian projects, but should only coordinate this construction, allowing the appropriate government ministries to do the work in their own special fields. Rogers, *Agrarian Reform Defined*, p. 139.

13. As described earlier, Bosch's main contributions were negative. He administratively blocked the director-general and then created the Presidential Coordinating Committee to bring all government institutions directly into the agrarian reform program. This move was intended to facilitate the coordinating role of IAD in areas of interministerial responsibility. Bosch's objective was a desirable one, but his solution was too sweeping and impractical. He took planning and execution responsibility out of the IAD and threw it into the hands of an unwieldy 15-man committee, each member of which had his own ideas on agrarian reform. The result was indecision and inaction.

14. República Dominicana, *Constitución de la nación dominicana 1963*, published in the *Gaceta Oficial*, No. 8758 of April 30, 1963, Articles 22, 23. Given Bosch's crusade to help the landless campesino, his constitution quickly raised the specter of wholesale expropriation of private land by the government. This threat, never actually expressed, alienated many landowners and created considerable opposition and mistrust of Bosch and his domestic programs.

collecting social and economic data from applicant families, reorganizing the training of employees, and public relations activity at grass-roots level. Between July and September, 678 families were seated, in addition to the 88 squatters already settled in the Nagua area. Discounting the Nagua squatters, from mid-1962 to the end of the Bosch period, IAD settled a total of 1,500 families on sixteen projects and conducted preliminary studies and other planning on eight additional projects. The total cost of the reform reached $2.3 million, or about $1,500 per family settled. The average unit cost on sixteen projects was about $1,250 per family, not including housing or other reimbursable items.

By the end of 1963, 1,700 families, excluding those at Nagua, were settled on seventeen projects, and the institute had developed plans for an additional eleven. The true, average, nonreimbursable unit cost including a prorated share of capital investment and central administrative costs had climbed to about $1,650 per family, considerably higher than the desired $1,000 figure set by IAD.[15]

Despite the political vicissitudes of this period the agrarian reform program continued to move ahead, although too slowly for government critics.[16] Reid Cabral obtained over $35 million in loans or credits, including $10 million from AID. The AID mission continued to provide technical assistance. After his overthrow in April 1965 Reid described his policies on agrarian reform:

> Land distribution in the Dominican Republic is not difficult. There is no need to condemn or expropriate land for agrarian reform. In the Dominican Republic the best farmlands belonged to Trujillo, and after his death they became state-owned property.
>
> Nevertheless, the Bosch government succeeded in distributing only 300 parcels of land. By contrast, in a single day—last January 24 to be exact—my administration distributed 1,500 land titles to as many landless farmers, bringing to 3,000 the number we had distributed to date.[17]

Reid went on to discuss rural infrastructure in connection with land reform. He said he had assigned an initial appropriation of $9 million for rural roads, irrigation, and electrification projects; improvement in agricultural techniques; and an expansion of the educational, financial, and technical structures to help the small farmer work his land.

By the end of 1966 only about 4,000 new landowners and their families had been settled.[18] The total amount of usable state-owned land, not all of which was under IAD

15. Rogers, *Agrarian Reform Defined*, pp. 5, 148. Total IAD expenditures from founding to December 31, 1963 were $3,130,800.

16. The leftists and the PRD felt that Reid, who was of an established "oligarchic" Santiago family, either cared little for agrarian reform or did not know how to make it effective. Franklin J. Franco Pichardo, *La República Dominicana: clases, crisis, y comandos,* p. 217. At least with respect to the PRD, this conclusion was confirmed by the PRD secretary for campesino affairs, a party founder and later sub-secretary for agriculture in the Balaguer government in a personal interview, La Vega, July 6, 1969.

Reid had told U. S. Ambassador Martin in 1962 that he was adamant against agrarian reform and would fight it both inside and out of government. Later in 1964, however, when Reid was running the government, his economic policies, including those on agrarian reform, rural road development, and agricultural production, were remarkably like the Bosch policies. Both men were faced with financial problems, Bosch because business was at a standstill, Reid because the price of sugar on the world market dropped to 2.2 cents a pound. Martin, *Overtaken by Events*, pp. 114, 638. Reid had undoubtedly come to realize in the intervening two years that agrarian reform could not be denied and that it did not necessarily involve expropriation.

17. Speech at National Press Club, July 15, 1965, Washington, D.C., quoted in James A. Clark, *The Church and the Crisis in the Dominican Republic*, pp. 220–21.

18. This is an interpolation. On July 14, 1967, IAD reported that 6,756 Dominicans had

control, varied from 5.5 to 6 million tareas during this period. The total at any given time changed as private lands were donated to the state, as IAD released land to new owners, and as IAD began to reclaim otherwise unexploitable land. Not included above as usable for reform purposes were about 4.5 million tareas of state-operated sugar lands.

The agrarian reform program was not merely land reform. The 1962 law was intended to create social, economic, and political advantages for the campesino and thereby strengthen all programs of national development; therefore the reform had to be a part of, not apart from, an overall development plan. The redistribution of land by IAD was to be the most sensitive aspect of the reform, but hardly less important were the goals of increased production, adequate housing, adequate rural education for children and adults, improved sanitation, public service facilities, and irrigation projects in rural areas, and the creation of new or increased economic opportunities for farmer and non-farmer alike. With the completion of the trial period and signing of the sales contract, it was hoped that the new owner would fully meet his obligations as a landowner and citizen. He was not expected to master, unassisted, such management problems as finance, credit, marketing, and modern farming and stock-raising techniques. In these matters IAD would provide or arrange for supervised farm credit, technical assistance, organization of farm cooperatives, and supervision of project administration until at such time as the new landowners could manage their own affairs. At this point IAD was to withdraw entirely from the project.

A particularly important joint contribution of IAD and the Credit Bank was to insure that the farmer did not assume financial obligations that exceeded his farm's production potential. In the matter of loans, which constituted the main financial vehicle for resettlement, there was to be continual supervision. The loan agent would have to work closely with the farmers, especially in the event of crop failures, to find the best solution that would keep the farmers on their land. Supervised credit administrative costs are normally higher than the usual credit arrangements. IAD considered that rather than try to recuperate the costs through higher interest rates, a more effective procedure for reducing administrative costs was to encourage group loans through cooperatives and agricultural associations. By employing the concept of project communities, IAD hoped to instill in the new landowners, as a group, a sense of civic responsibility, historically a missing element in the life of the rural poor.

IAD would undertake to do marketing studies and coordinate the construction of buildings, access roads, and bridges, but private capital would also be needed in the reform. As Trujillo's colonization plan had shown, the small farmer would benefit little from an intensive production effort if there were no outlet for his products or if he could not get his produce to the market at the right time. He had to be given an incentive to produce. From the private sector would come technical knowledge and capital investment to create small industries for processing, storing, transporting, and marketing the excess farm production. These industries would provide new markets and employment for rural inhabitants not selected for land ownership, and on a national level would reduce the need to import many processed and canned foods. Increased production and lower food prices would also improve and give variety to the average national diet. The

---

received 387, 424 tareas of land. Joseph R. Thome, "The Agrarian Reform in the Dominican Republic: Problems and Perspectives," in Dorner et al., "Agrarian Reform," p. 36. This figure was probably optimistic. In the 1968 budget for the Department of Agriculture, the statement is made of IAD that "in its 5 years of life it had settled only 5,130 families, that is, 1,026 families per year." *Presupuesto de ingresos y ley de gastos públicos, 1968*, pp. 12–20.

farmers' cooperative associations, working with private industry, would provide the channel through which the individual farmer-producer could maximize his profits and the nation could strengthen its economy.

Since most of the beneficiaries of the program could not pay the initial costs of land, house, equipment, and improvements, the agrarian reform had to be considered as a long-term social investment by the government rather than as a financial investment. As of 1963, IAD estimated that 45,000 to 50,000 landless families could be accommodated on state land assigned to farm and cattle production, but that in the next decade the number of families demanding land would easily total 70,000.[19] Such an increase would almost certainly force the government to acquire private land and to consider the possibility of reclaiming lands previously considered unsuitable for agriculture because of remoteness, quality of soil,[20] or climate.

The educational aspects of the agrarian reform were not to be oriented solely toward the training of technicians to staff the development program and to operate the supporting services such as utilities installations. The government visualized a vigorous educational program for new landowners and their children as a fundamental element in the reform. Education would give the campesino both the urge to learn modern farming methods and the ability to apply intelligently the knowledge acquired. Where schools already existed within reasonable walking distance of agrarian projects, IAD planners considered the alternative of augmenting those facilities instead of constructing new ones. The possibility of bussing children to the nearest school was also considered in the cases of more remote projects. The educational program for the projects would have to be especially well integrated into the overall national education plan because of the general shortage of rural educational facilities and teachers throughout the country.

Apart from the politically generated administrative difficulties already mentioned, IAD encountered during the first years of its existence an impressive variety of problems, only some of which had been anticipated. In 1966 the Dominican Republic, again with Joaquín Balaguer as president, seemed to be entering a long- sought and badly needed period of relative calm in which to recover from the effects of the Trujillo era and the upsets of 1963–65. A few observations on the progress of agrarian reform up to 1966 are warranted, if for no other reason than to mark the beginning of an important watershed in Dominican land history.

From a procedural point of view, the greatest single problem IAD encountered was the same one the government had been trying to correct since 1911—the survey, registration, and issuance of titles to state land. By 1962 most of the state-owned land, except for that in the extremely remote western or mountainous regions, had been surveyed and the exterior boundaries recorded. Redistribution of the lands for resettlement purposes, however, now meant that new internal surveys would be required as a basis on which to subdivide and register titles to the individual parcels. In addition, the state had taken possession of vast Trujillo lands, but the question of title had to be resolved. Much of this land had been illegally or unjustly acquired by the Trujillos, and some had subsequently been sold and resold. If the state was not to create additional injustices, title clearance proceedings through the land courts were unavoidable, and in any case, would be ab- .

---

19. Rogers, *Régimen de tierras*, 1st rev., p. 44.

20. A good example of this problem existed in Monte Cristi in the more arid sections. In one of its earliest soil classification studies IAD found that as a result of the known lack of water supply and scarce rainfall, the soil suffered from a high salt content.

solutely necessary if the lands were to be turned over to IAD for redistribution. Until the rightful owners of state-held property could be determined, final title certificates could not be issued. And even if IAD signed sales contracts pending the outcome of court decisions, new landowners were reluctant to work the land without more substantial legal protection. To be effective, agrarian reform had to offer the campesino security. In 1966 IAD did not possess registered titles to fifty percent of the land it had distributed and therefore could not sign even the provisional contracts with these settlers.[21]

A second factor, which tended to delay resettlement plans, was the time consumed in completing the classified inventory of state property as contemplated by Articles 26–31 of the Agrarian Reform Law. In addition to showing the extent of state lands, their location, accessibility, current use, and potential for development, the inventory would also reveal to what extent the lands had been invaded by private individuals, the improvements they had made, and their rights under the law. The information derived from the inventory was to be a fundamental preliminary to the selection of farm activity, the economic size and location of subdivided parcels, and the location of housing, roads, and other facilities. Land encroachment was a rural tradition extending back to the colonial times. The Spanish Crown had not been able to resolve the problem to its own satisfaction; it was not until 1920 that a formal basis for establishing prescriptive rights had been brought under land laws. Encroachment in 1962, however, did not only involve legal questions; in the case of poor, landless campesinos, there were complications of a social nature as well. Yet by 1966 IAD had inventoried less than half the state-owned lands; progress continued to be slow and intermittent.

Aggravating the expeditious settlement of both land classification and title registration undertakings was the delay experienced by IAD in clearing title cases through the land courts. The legal division of the institute had no authority to resolve title cases. When forced to wait on the overworked land courts, resettlement procedures ground to a halt.[22] There were sixteen land courts in operation in 1966, but courts and title registration offices alike were poorly financed and overloaded with work.[23] The legal problems bound up in the title registration of redistributed lands appeared to be causing a major stumbling block to rapid settlement. If resettlement projects had to wait until the courts handed down final decisions on all of the *reclamas* of all previous private owners of state lands and on the subdividing of lands to which the state already possessed clear title, the agrarian reform program would need many years to make even modest progress. Meanwhile, the landless campesinos if they followed the example of their ancestors, would simply invade the land and complicate title problems even further.

---

21. Thome, in Dorner et al., "Agrarian Reform," p. 37.

22. The Cevicos case will serve as an extreme example of how such litigation can drag. The land court in the province of Sánchez Ramírez has had pending since 1951 the resolution of the partition of communal lands of Cevicos. Some 500,000 tareas of good land, mostly sugar, was surveyed in accordance with the normal partitioning procedures. By the time the case appeared on the court docket, some of the hundreds of co-owners had sold their land or further divided it, new owners had been created, and the surveyors had to repeat their work, adjusting their laborious computations to the new situation. During the additional delays, the cycle has been repeated; the court and the surveyors have now several times been overtaken by new possessions. Personal interview with one of the legal experts of the Dominican land commission of August 1961, Santo Domingo, November 7, 1969. This particular observation has been confirmed by IAD officials.

23. C.W. Loomer, "Study Report on the Land Settlement Program of the Dominican Republic," in Dorner et al., " Agrarian Reform," p. 13.

There were already indications that invasion of unused land by landless rural inhabitants had begun. Trujillo had not authorized the sale of all of the land of Juancito Rodríguez; much of it that had been sold had not been effectively occupied by its new owners. Consequently, in 1962 the state found itself in possession of valuable property in the Cibao which would have been admirably suited to distribution under the agrarian reform except for a major obstacle: the Rodríguez heirs wanted the land that legally belonged to them. To make matters worse, one *finca*, or ranch, of 23,000 tareas was almost completely invaded by 200 campesino families. Recognizing the social injustice involved in evicting the encroachers, the Rodríguez family offered to sell the land to the state so that it could be distributed to the campesinos as part of the agrarian program. The state neither accepted nor rejected the offer, possibly because of complications with the cost. The land was worth at least $50 or $60 per tarea. The state did return 92,141 tareas of their other lands to the family, which, although not pressing unduly for settlement, nevertheless commenced legal proceedings to recover an additional 50,801 tareas worth $2.5 million and an additional sum of $1.5 million for the Rodríguez cattle which Trujillo had stolen.[24]

No less disturbing to the government was the growing criticism of the agrarian reform program by some clerics, especially those in rural areas. Traditionally (in the Latin America of a hundred years ago or even more recently in some countries) the conservative, landholding Church has sided with the landed oligarchy and the military on major political and social issues. By 1966 quite a different picture was developing in the Dominican Republic. The priests were attacking the government for moving too slowly in redistributing land to the campesinos. The centers of criticism were clearly defined: in the sparsely settled savanna ranch lands of Altagracia province in the east and in the thickly settled agricultural Cibao. The clerics most deeply committed to the social evolution of the campesino included the bishop of Higüey, Monseñor Juan F. Pepén; Father Porfirio Valdés, Father Juan Núñez, and the bishop of Santiago, Monseñor Roque Adames; the bishop of La Vega, Monseñor Juan Antonio Flores, and an energetic Spanish Jesuit, Father Cipriano Cabero, operator of Radio Santa María in the little village of Santo Cerro just outside La Vega. These ecclesiastical leaders became deeply interested in agrarian reform purely as an attempt to alleviate rural misery. Except possibly for Father Cabero, they knew little of the technical aspects of the program, seeing only that many rural workers could not feed themselves, could not send their children to schools because there were not enough rural schools, and could find no way out of their misery. In the redistribution of land the priests saw the possibility of helping the rural children.

There may also have been an element of stricken social conscience which stimulated this movement. No less than any other institution, the Church in the Dominican Republic was thoroughly cowed by Trujillo. The masses said for the continued good health of "El Jefe," and other similar attentions during the long dictatorship, offered no consolation to the oppressed.[25] It was not until 1959 and 1960 that the Church hierarchy

24. Dr. Osiris L. Duquela, estate attorney, personal interview, La Vega, July 6, 1969.

25. The bishop of La Vega commented on this point: "Under Trujillo there was no point in fighting. As the Bible says, 'before fighting the enemy, measure his strength.'" Personal interview, La Vega, July 5, 1969. Bishop Octavio Rodríguez of the cathedral at Santo Domingo explained in more detail. "Trujillo held all the cards. If a priest did attack him, Trujillo would take indirect reprisal by jailing members of the priest's family or close friends or by preventing them from obtaining work. Trujillo, of course, would disclaim all knowledge of what was happening." Personal interview, Santo Domingo, January 23, 1970.

took a stand against the dictator—just before he was assassinated.[26] By 1964 a movement had gradually crystallized within the clergy to defend the landless campesinos who had invaded some of the unoccupied state lands and who were threatened with dislodgement as rightful owners reclaimed their property.[27] The conflict in 1964 and 1965 was drawn up more between the Church and the large landowners; but as the agrarian reform appeared to be moving too slowly the Church began to include the government as a target. To be accurate, not the entire Church hierarchy was deeply involved. The archbishop of Santo Domingo, closer perhaps to the seat of government, remained on more neutral ground publicly, as did the remaining two bishops in the country and a minority of the lesser clergy. But it should be noted that they did not strenuously oppose the position taken by the more militant priests. A fair statement would be that there was no division within the Church on the need for agrarian reform; some bishops were more conservative than others, but all conceded the basic problem.[28]

The landowners' alarmed reaction to the movement on behalf of the campesino was mostly aimed at the radio priest, Father Cipriano Cabero.[29] Calculating that at least 60 percent of the rural people could be reached by radio, Cabero conducted daily counseling sessions from Santo Cerro, interspersed with classical music and standard commercial programs. He operated the radio station, which has been the property of the La Vega diocese since 1957, on a strictly business basis. Twice daily he spoke to the campesinos, urging them to support the embryo farmer's organization, *Ligas Agrarias Cristianas*, not to be exploited by the government and the large landowners, and even to invade unoccupied land and cultivate it as their social right. Cabero did not claim that outright confiscation of private land, even if unused, was just. He did not claim that campesino invasions were legal. He did claim that in the Cibao 19 families owned as much land as 80,000 families, not including the landless,[30] and that this was an unjust situation. Thus he claimed that the invasion of unoccupied, lands, state or private, by hungry campesinos was socially just.

In conducting his radio campaigns, Father Cabero, more cosmopolitan than most of the bishops, was especially concerned with the socio-political implications of the agrarian reform, because he related the growing need for land distribution to potential political

---

26. It is reported that the final break between Trujillo and the Church was caused by the archbishop of Santo Domingo's refusal to concede Trujillo the new title "Benefactor of the Church." Only Trujillo's death prevented humiliating reprisal directly against the archbishop.

27. Rafael Molina Morillo, "*El conflicto entre la iglesia y terratenientes*," *Ahora* 285 (April 28, 1969): 6–8.

28. Bishop Octavio Rodríguez, personal interview, January 23, 1970.

29. Rumors started that he was a Communist. Cabero credits the rumors to his brief stay in the Sierra Maestre in 1957 with Fidel Castro. According to Cabero, he had been officially assigned by the Church in Havana to be Fidel's military chaplain, but the real purpose was to evaluate Castro's political philosophy of which the Church was already suspicious. Cabero stayed in the mountains only one week. Castro treated him properly enough, but refused to talk informally to him. Based on what he saw and heard, however, Cabero returned to Havana convinced that Castro was a Communist. Cabero had left Spain in 1944 for Santo Domingo where he had remained until 1954. He then spent seven years in Cuba, returning to Santo Domingo in 1961. He then worked as a rural pastor in and around La Vega province. Private interviews, Santo Cerro, July 7 and November 8, 1969.

30. He did not give his source for these figures. The 1960 farm census, however, shows that in the provinces of Santiago and La Vega combined, the 21 largest landowners have as much land as about 46,000 small owners. República Dominicana, *Quinto censo nacional agropecuario, 1960*, pp. 17–18.

revolution. He felt that the government was moving far too slowly in settling the igno-rant, landless farmers; his efforts to rally the landless farmers were intended simply to preempt a future revolution led by the Communists. "If the revolution comes, and it will come," he explained, "I want the Church to be leading it, not the Communists. The Church will not fight *against* the government or the wealthy, but it will fight *for* the poor rural people."[31] Cabero and the other priests saw important social changes on the horizon and were taking the initiative to provide the leadership which, in their opinion, the government had failed to provide. To the militant Church element it appeared that the military, the politicians, and the wealthy were saying: let the rural problem lie; ignore it as it has been ignored in the past. The militants countered: we will lead the change, for it is almost upon us.

By 1966 it had been apparent to planners in IAD for some time that the Agrarian Reform Law itself should be strengthened. It was a workable law, but eventually such problems as the following would be encountered, and in regard to them the law stood mute: IAD had no control over state lands held by other government agencies; the law made no provision for land tenancy other than by sale. For example, no mention was made of the possibility of lease; there was no mention of specific methods of payment or indemnification for expropriated land, nor was there any policy for the development of criteria for expropriation.

No corrective action was taken, however, and the reason was not difficult to find. De-spite the powerful social implications of agrarian reform,the government appeared to be more concerned with the immediate political impact of the program. There was no lack of publicity concerning individual resettlement activities of IAD, especially during 1962 and after 1965. But the government never developed and publicized the long- range, overall program in specific terms of national goals. The typical media releases made vague references to a development plan, usually cited the number of new settlers and the amount of bank credit they would receive, but never provided enough analytical data for the public to judge how well land reform was going. Any Dominican who could read a newspaper or listen to a radio knew what lands were being distributed, but he had no idea of the scope, urgency, or timing of the whole program. As a result of incomplete planning and inadequate public explanation, private landowners were either cynical or mistrustful of the government's intentions. The campesinos who wanted land, but had not been able to qualify, or even worse, who saw unqualified individuals selected, quickly became disillusioned. They knew that there had been considerable publicity over land distribution, but they saw that they were no closer to owning land than before. It was "politics as usual."

There were, of course, sins of commission. IAD made mistakes during these years, al-though they were more or less expected of a new agency engaged in a new enterprise. The errors did not indicate defective reform objectives, only administrative mistakes. There were cases of selection of unqualified individuals for resettlement, of settlers who sold their land illegally, and of failures to meet settlement debts. IAD personnel recognized that the early haste to start the reform program had led to some poor decisions. The first two projects, Juma and Caracol, were probably the most trouble-ridden because the local project supervisors had had little or no administrative experience. Furthermore, there were indications that the officers of the Juma cooperative, themselves new land-

---

31. Cabero interviews, 1969. Father Cabero is now assigned to Dajabón province, along the northwest frontier with Haiti.

owners, were embezzling cooperative funds. Despite all this, the settlers at Juma were harvesting two crops of rice annually and were selling their superior produce at a price twenty percent higher than farmers elsewhere.[32] By 1966 some of the growing pains were showing signs of subsiding as IAD began to profit from earlier mistakes. One important change was the tightening of procedures for screening and selecting beneficiaries.

In a single sentence, the trouble with the reform by the end of 1966 was that it had not resettled enough campesinos to win widespread campesino support, nor had it won sufficient support and sympathy from the wealthier classes, urban or rural. With land immediately available for distribution to at least 45,000 families, in over four years IAD was able to settle only about 4,000. No community centers had been constructed in any project;[33] the land classification and survey work had practically ceased; and not a single campesino had received final, clear title to his land.[34]

The bottleneck over legal titles was most serious; if the program was to have any real social significance, either IAD would have to be given the authority to adjudicate titles or the government would have to augment the land court system in order to clear up the backlog of litigation. In either event, IAD should be able to issue clear titles to the new settlers within a few months—not years—after settlement. The necessary pride of ownership and confidence in the government will not be instilled in the campesino until he is fully guaranteed that the land is legally his. IAD bypassed the technicalities of the law in settling the Nagua project; similar techniques could be adapted to the land title problem, especially on state-held land to which the state apparently will be able to obtain a clear title when the courts finally act.

IAD encountered the same problem that besets many government agencies: lack of money. For example, in 1964 the institute received an appropriation of $1.8 million on a $5.5 million budget requirement.[35] More money would not necessarily improve the efficiency of the IAD operation, but increased appropriations would at least permit IAD to proceed with the long-range land classification and survey project which has not received adequate attention. Failure to complete this basic project could slow the resettlement process as presently inventoried land becomes settled. The possibility of

---

32. United States AID Mission experts confirmed the fact that the settlers in the rice projects were repaying full development costs with the profit from their first two harvests, as planners had expected. Personal interviews, January 26, 1970.

33. Not even one new school had been built on the reform projects. This statement does not mean that no rural schools were being built by the government. On the contrary, rural school construction was high on the government's development plan. In 1966 the government anticipated an income from internal sources of $178,232,300 and expenditures of 220,835,610 of which $29,219,254 was budgeted for education. U.S. AID support to the general educational budget added another $2,299,000. Of the total education budget, $13,873,154, by far the largest single item, was earmarked for primary education. República Dominicana, *Presupuesto de ingresos y ley de gastos públicos, 1967*, published in the *Gaceta Oficial*, No. 9019 of December 31, 1966.

34. Statement of U.S. AID-supervised credit advisor to the Agricultural Credit Bank, personal interview, January 26, 1970.

35. Rogers, *Agrarian Reform Defined*, p. 148. Commencing with the July 1962 credit agreement, the United States AID has consistently supported the Dominican agrarian reform program at the rate of about $2 million annually. For 1966 the IAD share of the national budget was $2,321,000, of which three-fourths was for overhead and salaries. For 1967 the Agrarian Institute budget totalled $2,990,000, of which $2,490,000 was provided from United States AID, credits or loans and $500,000 from the Dominican general fund. República Dominicana, *Presupuesto de ingresos y ley de gastos públicos, 1967*, p. 11.

imposing a direct land tax had been raised,[36] but the government would probably resort to this historically unpopular revenue-raising institution only if no other means of financing the reform were available. The imposition of a land tax in 1966 could have been so politically unpalatable as to be counterproductive. Such a general tax, however, should not be ruled out as a future possibility. A less potentially explosive solution might be the imposition of a tax on idle land, with an alternative of leasing the land to tenants who could place it under cultivation.

Bosch frightened large landowners with his Constitution of 1963, which seemed to threaten their traditional property rights. Although Balaguer's revisions should have quieted much of the alarm,[37] the new Constitution did not appear until late in 1966. The period between 1963 and 1966, just when IAD was beginning to function, was the precise period when some of the more influential and better organized landowners were most suspicious of the reform program. IAD needed a public relations effort to swing these landowners into sympathy with the aims of the reform. The decision to publish a specific policy on expropriation of private land was a political one, and the Balaguer government, new in 1966, understandably could have been reluctant to push the reform that far. But large landowners are most vulnerable to rural social reform involving land redistribution when they permit land to stand idle; the government might well have concentrated on this point as a preliminary to future action at a more appropriate moment. The preparation and dissemination of an expropriation policy in advance of the time it will actually be needed will permit some sort of dialogue between the private landowners and the government which might avoid a political crisis. As the government seemed to appreciate, however, premature action could trigger heavy opposition from the politically important landowners. The Balaguer government wanted agrarian reform, but not at such high cost.

Could there have been a mild historic parallel here with the Spanish Crown's decision in colonial times not to antagonize the Spanish colonists even if this meant the destruction of the Indians?

---

36. IAD had regarded a possible tax as a means of providing two economic alternatives: as additional revenue for the government (IAD) or as pressure on the owners of idle land to put their land under cultivation. Agrarian reform objectives would be benefitted under whichever option the landowner might elect. The Wisconsin consultants perceived the tax as a means to raise revenue for agrarian reform which would permit the government to give the land free and clear to the settlers immediately. IAD, however, had reservations concerning the free and clear policy, preferring to delay the granting of final title until a trial period could confirm the settler's suitability for ownership. The slowness of the land courts in granting prior title to IAD would in any event have prevented rapid title transfer to the settler in many cases. Loomer in Dorner et al., "Agrarian Reform," pp. 16–18. Neither IAD nor the Wisconsin group seemed to be aware that a direct land tax system had been tried in the Dominican Republic thirty years earlier and had failed.

37. Balaguer watered down Bosch's apparent frontal attack on private ownership. Article 13 of the 1966 Constitution stated in part: "The dedication of land to useful purposes and the gradual elimination of latifundio are declared to be of social interest. The lands which the State owns or may gradually acquire or may expropriate are designated for the uses of Agrarian Reform in the manner prescribed by this Constitution, provided that these lands are not or should not be designated by the State for other purposes of general interest." República Dominicana, *Constitución de 28 Noviembre, 1966*, published in the *Gaceta Oficial*, No. 9014, of November 29, 1966. The phrase "gradual elimination of latifundio" conveys a meaning quite different from that expressed by the Bosch Constitution of 1963. See note 14 above.

24

SUMMARY

The step marked by the passage of the Agrarian Reform Law of 1962 and subsequent creation of the Dominican Agrarian Institute was the latest in the history of almost five centuries of land settlement and, it was hoped, the birth of what could be a new era in Dominican land history. Except for a few brisk, golden decades early in the sixteenth century, the real wealth of the Dominican Republic has been its agriculture. Throughout the sixteenth, seventeenth, and eighteenth centuries there was always enough rich soil for even the poorest of farmers to feed his family. In the framework of the Spanish colonial system, no economic enterprises of any significance other than those associated with the land were permitted to develop. Dominican prosperity depended on exportation of agricultural products to pay for the importation of manufactured goods. The rural population, whether slave or free, owner, tenant, or lessee, regardless of its color, always constituted the majority. So long as exterior trade continued and so long as the farmers could work their land peacefully, the colony was reasonably well off. When commerce was stifled, as it was during much of the seventeenth century and into the eighteenth, the country as a whole suffered from a lack of capital flow and internal development. But despite the vulnerability of essentially a one-crop export economy, any Dominican who went hungry did so because he was reluctant or unwilling to scratch the soil. This point was not overlooked by the Spanish Crown. If the Dominican had no land, the fault was still his own, for even well into the twentieth century land was cheap and available for purchase, lease or outright occupation without title. There were few restrictions on ownership. On the contrary, one of the most prized constitutional guarantees gave every Dominican the right to own property, subject only to congressional authority, court decision, and the preeminence of public utility. This right, coming on top of long-standing royal policies which encouraged the immigration of settlers willing to work the soil, made the ownership of land simple, easy, and attractive. For the more affluent settler, the land meant status and wealth; for the man who could afford only modest holdings, it provided food, shelter, and frequently a profit for further investment if he desired. For the poorer, landless tenant the land meant food for his family and a financial share of the landowner's harvest.

261

Recognizing that the key to the colony's economic wealth lay in the fullest possible productive use of the land, the Spanish Crown began as early as 1503 to expand the rural labor force by subsidizing immigration to Española, by offering special financial incentives to the most enterprising farmers, by adopting liberal settlement policies based on recognition that the independent operator would probably be more productive than the communal worker, by encouraging, although ineffectively, enlightened labor practices, and by emphasizing effective occupation as a basis for distribution of free land. By the end of the colonial period the Crown had even recognized as valid the claims of settlers who had invaded royal lands, held them and placed them under cultivation.

Considering that the Crown's colonial trade policies had always been exploitative, Dominican independence should have permitted the development of favorable land tenure relationships for the campesino. The economy was traditionally agricultural; the land was rich enough to produce valuable export money crops and at the same time feed the population. In terms of the campesino's physical opportunity to work the land, the potential for economic growth was enhanced by a low density of population and the availability of all the land a man could cultivate. Independence, however, brought no real change. In terms of efficiency of agricultural production, the techniques available to the illiterate campesino were sorely limited by his ignorance. As José Ramón López observed, the Dominican farmer was not lazy; he simply failed to produce more because he was technically backward. With practically no education, his knowledge was restricted to archaic land practices and primitive equipment. But a worse evil was his lack of security.

Beginning with the Haitian invasion of 1801 and lasting until the American military occupation of 1916, Dominican farmlands and farming operations were periodically hampered by the chronic wars, revolutions, and other internal upsets which either dragged the farmer himself into military service or too often commandeered his flocks and crops. Political instability depressed the domestic economy and even inhibited the development of roads for the ready marketing of surplus products grown anywhere except near the coasts. The few visionary, progressive leaders who placed the nation's well-being above parochial interests were unable to overcome the calamities generated by the caudillos. The one historic exception to this unfortunate tradition ended with the assassination of Ramón Cáceres in 1911. The campesino's hold on the land was made insecure by a defective system of land laws and by his own humble position in the political hierarchy of the nation.

However well intended it was, the military intervention of 1916 damaged the image of the United States. Even those Dominicans who tacitly or openly approved of the military government's objectives had by 1921 become restive if not openly antagonistic to the continued occupation. After five years the American presence was no more welcome in Santo Domingo than had been that of the other invaders over the centuries. But the Americans, as the Dominicans admitted then and as they admit now, brought a measure of progress. The military government adopted a modern, effective system of land registration laws and instituted a comprehensive reform of the public school system based on laws drafted by a select commission of eminent Dominicans. Long neglected by Dominican governments, primary education, especially in rural areas, was given major emphasis in an effort to reduce the high rate of illiteracy. In restoring peace to the countryside and in providing technical assistance, the government gave the farmers the incentive to increase their production. Although there was criticism of the cost, the government constructed badly needed roads, sanitary systems, waterfront and harbor facilities and other public works the Dominicans had not been able to build for themselves.

The military government also made a conscientious effort to instill a respect for political institutions, but whatever minor success was achieved by 1924 was wiped out during the long Trujillo dictatorship. Between May 1930 and May 1961 Trujillo too was responsible for considerable material progress in the Dominican Republic. But he destroyed the nation's developing democratic institutions and left a legacy of corruption, brutality, and greed. The verdict now is that Trujillo was a national disaster, a verdict the passing years are not likely to temper.

One of the most significant political developments of the immediate post-Trujillo years was the emergence of the lowly campesino as a powerful political force. Juan Bosch proved on December 20, 1962, that the candidate who wins the rural vote in the Dominican Republic wins the election. Bosch, however, was not the first political leader to grasp this point. Joaquín Balaguer began the redistribution of land to the landless campesinos less than three months after Trujillo's death. He was followed by Rafael F. Bonnelly and the other members of the Council of State who passed the Agrarian Reform Law in 1962. This was major legislation which recognized the social evolution long overdue in the Dominican countryside. In this context the 1962 law fully supported the socioeconomic principles for development established at Punta del Este for all of Latin America. The 1962 law was also a positive step to capture the political support of the as yet unorganized rural voters. The degree to which succeeding governments or candidates will be able to influence the rural areas could depend in large measure on the success of the agrarian reform and the support given it by political leaders. Until he is better educated and able to evaluate political affairs for himself—a process that will take at least another generation—the campesino will continue to be heavily influenced by the judgment of the leader he feels he can trust. If that leader can take credit for a successful agrarian reform program, he will have much of the campesino vote. If his political opposition can fix on him the blame for a halfhearted or unsuccessful agrarian program, the leader will probably lose the campesino vote. The typical Dominican countryman is likely to be illiterate, but he is no fool. He has the vote, and he will cast it for the politician he feels will help him, just as voters do in other democracies.

The Dominican Republic is still a rural nation. Its economy is agricultural and the majority of its population depend on agriculture. In these respects the nation has not evolved substantially since 1492. In one very important respect, however, there has been a significant change: there is no longer a predictably easy surplus of exploitable land for the growing population. The social pressure for settlement of the landless and the economic need to increase agricultural productivity throughout the nation have placed a premium on farmland. The owner of unoccupied land, frequently the state itself, has been exposed to criticism for allowing the land to lie unused. In the near future the state will undoubtedly assign a higher national priority to the development of land hitherto considered unusable. Providing that the Dominican government follows democratic processes as defined by the Dominican Constitution, the manner and promptness with which the government acknowledges the above needs will be strongly affected by the rural voters. Large numbers of these are landless, poverty-stricken, still with no organized political voice. The Dominican government has created the institutions whereby the social and economic conditions of these underprivileged citizens can be bettered.

Agrarian reform is a national project. In a small, increasingly politicized country the responsibility for the success of any national reform must fall squarely on the shoulders of one individual—the president. Balaguer had initiated the agrarian reform in 1961 before it deserved the name, with motives that were more political than social, but nevertheless he moved in the right direction. The muddled history of the next four years forced succeeding administrations to concentrate almost exclusively on the bare necessities of national life. Given a second opportunity in 1966, Balaguer affirmed a philosophic dedication to the social evolution of the countryside with these words: "The stimulus and cooperation to integrate the rural population effectively into the national life is declared to be a principal objective of the social policy of the state, by means of renovating the methods of agricultural production and the cultural and technological capabilities of the rural man."[1] Formal education of the illiterate will be the first step, but alone it will not be enough. The campesino will not be integrated until he has a stake in the land itself. Education is the tool by which he can acquire that stake.

The Agrarian Law of 1962, the charter of the institute for agrarian reform, and the Constitution of 1966 are collectively identified as a legal commitment to modernize rural resettlement, to rationalize the relationship of the settler to the land he works, to the community in which he lives, to the economy which he supports and which supports him, and, finally, to the nation of which he is the mainstay. The Dominican reform program undertaken by the government was in theory a reasonably well-balanced, comprehensive plan. If vigorously supported and prosecuted, it should accomplish much of the rural evolution contemplated in the 1966 constitution. The initial successes of the Juma and Caracol projects lent some basis for optimism. On the other hand, the legal, financial, and administrative problems encountered have tended to produce an attitude of caution and at times cynicism on the part of many Dominicans who perceive only slight progress in the reform. Many are convinced that the government has embarked on nothing more than a program to redistribute a bit of land to a few not necessarily deserving but sharp operators who had friends in high places.

The Rodríguez case will be the first major confrontation between the legal rights of the private individual, on one hand, and the social values of the agrarian reform program on the other. There is no question but that the post-Trujillo Dominican state has taken considerable pains to recompense the families of those who suffered loss of life or property as a result of political persecution during the Trujillo dictatorship. This factor will make a verdict completely unfavorable to the Rodríguez heirs very difficult to achieve. A second consideration is the political awareness of the state that all private landowners will be watching the outcome of the case for an indication of what the state's policy will be toward private ownership. At the same time, however, the state will recognize that the Rodríguez heirs are wealthy and already have vast landholdings and that families of campesinos are in want because the head of the family has no land of his own and knows no other way to feed his family except by working the land. The case will force the state to clarify its land expropriation policy and decide what sort of indemnity it must offer owners of land expropriated in the future. The political implications are enormous.

If the agrarian reform is to be successful—and a judgment on this cannot be made for some time yet—the public must become more aware of the broader scope of the problem and of the supporting actions which the government knows it must take. If the comprehensive reform blueprints are not followed with precision and justice the program will suffer major setbacks. Agrarian reform is far more than a land redistribution problem, as

---

1. República Dominicana, *Constitución de 1966*, Article 13a, last sentence.

Trujillo's colonization plan showed. If the reform begun in 1962 is allowed to take the path of simple redistribution, the plan will never succeed technically nor will it ever gain the public support it must have. Without public support and understanding, IAD's problems will become increasingly complicated and difficult as resources—the supplies of land and money—become more critical. The future prosperity, peace, and stability in the rural areas of the Dominican Republic will be determined in large measure by the degree to which the modern *hecho* coincides with the *derecho*.

The landless campesino is not yet unduly restive; he is patient, but he cannot be made to wait forever.

Appendixes

APPENDIXES

1. Act of Division of Family Property

God, Fatherland, Liberty. The Dominican Republic.

Today, the 17th of September, 1853, the signatories below, the legitimate children of José Bonneau and of the deceased Inés Megías, united in a private family conference, have proceeded to verify and distribute the property which their parents held in common and of which the total was presented for distribution.

As a result of a long-established principle, one of the spouses receives half of the property and the living heirs of whom there are three adults, two unmarried males and one married female, accompanied by her husband and three minor children, two females and a male, under the guardianship of their father, receive the other half.

Article 1. 960 pesos in goods, divided in two parts: one of 480 pesos for their legitimate father and 480 for the six heirs, i.e., 80 pesos for each one of the latter: the three adults have taken the sum of their inheritance and that of the three minors their guardian has made himself responsible.

Article 2. Ninety-six cattle divided in the same form and under the same circumstances.

Article 3. Three houses, one in good condition and one in bad, located on Las Damas street, and a third on the Plaza de Armas, to be divided: the house on Las Damas street in good condition, large, 18 varas [yards] long, has been ceded by mutual agreement among the heirs to their father; and the six heirs have received for their part the house situated on the Plaza and the smaller house situated on Las Damas street.

Article 4. All of the jewels of the deceased were ceded by the father in favor of the three females, the two minors and the married one, with the exception of three pairs of gold buttons which were given to the men who divided them among themselves and were satisfied with what was theirs.

Article 5. Ten place settings and two large silver ladles in division of which the father agreed to take four settings and the two large ladles, ceding thereafter the six settings which were divided among the six as had been the goods.

Article 6. Three hundred pesos of land in a place called Hato Grande, divided in the same form.

Article 7. Eight mares, six colts, eleven stallions, two mules, six ponies, and two old horses, totaling 35 animals divided in the same form.

In the partition for which we are making this Act, being in conformance all of the interested parties and co-partitioners, in faith thereof all have signed.

NOTE: For the complete division of property there are lacking two lots located in Santiago which have not been verified, because one of them is being questioned by a Señor Gullón who claims it as his own. It is therefore added to this Act that if the decision of the Court is not in favor of the heirs, the heirs then will be required to reimburse the damages and costs derived from the legal process originating on their behalf.*

(In the handwriting of   P. Federico Bonneau
Pedro F. Bonó)

2. A Caribbean Policy

November 24, 1915

My dear Mr. President:

I have enclosed a memorandum covering the subject of the Monroe Doctrine, its application and the possible extension of the principle in a way to constitute a policy which may be termed "A Caribbean Policy," since it is limited in application to the territory in and about the Caribbean Sea.

The reason for the memorandum is this: the Monroe Doctrine is based on the theory that any extension by a European power of political control, beyond that which exists over any territory in this hemisphere, is a menace to the national safety of the United States. The means of extending political control, thus far recognized, has been by occupation of an unattached territory, by conquest and by cession.

Recently the financing of revolutions and corruption of governments of the smaller republics by European capitalists have frequently thrown the control of these governments into the hands of a European power.

To avoid this danger of European political control by this means, which may be as great a menace to the national safety of this country as occupation or cession, the only method seems to be to establish a stable and honest government and to prevent the revenues of the Republic from becoming a prize of revolution and of the foreigners who finance it.

Stability and honesty of government depend on a sufficient force to resist revolution and on sufficient control over the revenues and over the development of the resources to prevent official graft and dishonest grants of privilege.

The possession of the Panama Canal and its defense have in a measure given to the territories in and about the Caribbean Sea a new importance from the standpoint of our national safety. It is vital to the interests of this country that European political domination should in no way be extended over these regions. As it happens, within this area lie the small republics of America which have been, and to an extent, still are the prey of revolutionists, of corrupt governments, and of predatory foreigners. Because of this state of affairs, our national safety, in my opinion, requires that the United States should intervene and aid in the establishment and maintenance of a stable, balanced

---

*Notarial act taken from Rodríguez Demorizi, *Papeles de Pedro F. Bonó*, pp. 601–2.

government, an honest government, if no other way seems possible to attain that end.

I make no argument on the ground of the benefits which would result to the peoples of these Republics by the adoption of this policy. That they would be the chief beneficiaries, in that their public and private rights would be respected and their prosperity and intellectual development insured, is manifest. Nevertheless, the argument based on humanitarian purpose does not appeal to me even though it might be justly urged, because too many international crimes have been committed in the name of humanity.

It seems to me that the ground of national safety, the conservation of national interests, is the one which should be advanced in support of this policy. It is reasonable, practical and in full accord with the principles of the Monroe Doctrine.

In considering this policy, it should be borne in mind what has been done already in Cuba, Panama, Nicaragua, the Dominican Republic and Haiti, and what may have to be done in the small neighboring republics. The Danish West Indies and the colonial possessions of other European nations in the Caribbean should not be forgotten in considering this policy, as through a change of their sovereignty they might become a serious menace to the interests of the United States.

Faithfully yours,

Robert Lansing

3. Sample Form of Request for Adjudication of Title

TO THE PRESIDENT AND OTHER JUDGES COMPOSING THE HONORABLE SUPERIOR LAND COURT

Via: Office of State Lawyers

Honorable Magistrates:

The below signed (fill in name, profession, domicile, nationality, name of spouse and marital status) has the honor to address himself most respectfully to the Honorable Superior Land Court that it may concede priority to him for the purification and adjudication of titles, in conformance with the Law of Land Registry, of the following property:

(Describe property, indicating the city or section, común and province in which it is located, and its adjacent lands, its approximate area, and the existing additional rights (mortgages, privileges, etc.), indicating the names of the possessors.)

To this end are submitted as attachments to this petition the contract entered into by the undersigned and the Surveyor (fill in his name) for the execution of the cadastral survey of the property described above.

Also submitted herewith to indicate the good faith of this petition is the following documentation:

(Describe the documents which support the rights claimed) (If the petition is based on prescription, a certification of Petty Alcalde must be included if the property is rural, or of the Síndico if it is urban, which will state the number of years of possession.)

Upon making this petition, the undersigned declares himself bound by all of the dispositions of the Land Registry Law and of the current rules and regulations in this matter.*

Very Respectfully,

---

*The petition and the contract must be submitted in triplicate (Arts. 47 and 48 of the Land Registry Law).

4. Interests Confiscated by the Dominican State From the Trujillo Regime, 1961

La Azucarera Haina, consisting of the sugar centrales Rio Haina, Barahona, Ozama, Boca China, Quisqueya, Consuelo, Porvenir, Santa Fe, and the national Division of Dominican Molasses.

Fábrica Dominicana de Cemento—cement
Industria de Asbesto-Cemento—asbestos materials
Sociedad Industrial Dominicana—peanut oil
Compañía Anónima Tabacalera—tobacco, cigars, and cigarettes
Chocolatera Industrial—chocolate
Pinturas Dominicanas—paint
Molinos Dominicanos—wheat, flour mill
Domínico-Suiza—home construction
Industria Nacional del Papel—paper
Fábrica Dominicana de Calzados (FADOC)—shoes
Fábrica de Ropas y Tejidos (San Cristóbal)—clothes and fabrics
Tanería Fa-2—tannery
Caribbean Motors Co.—Representative of General Electric, Chrysler, Goodyear, Firestone, etc.
Dominican Motors Co.—Representative of Allis-Chalmers, General Motors, Ingersoll-Rand, White Motors, Ford Motor Co., Bethlehem Steel, Minneapolis-Moline International, Link-Belt Speeder Corp., Kelvinator Corp., Zenith Radio, and others
Atlas Commercial Co.—auto supplies, refrigerators, large appliances
Quisqueya Motors Co.—automobiles
Concretera Dominicana—construction
Mezcla Lista—construction
Compañía Dominicana de Hormigón Asfáltico Caliente—asphalt concrete
Fábrica de Baterías Hercules—battery manufacturing
Marmolería Nacional—marble quarries
Licorera La Altagracia—distillery
Compañía Inmobiliaria Francisco Martínez Alba—land development
Diario La Nación—newspaper
Planta de Recauchado—tire retreading
Hacienda Maralba—livestock forage
Haras Rhádames—cattle-breeding ranch
Ferretería Read—hardware
Ferretería El Marino—hardware
Negocios e Indústrias—business investments
Hornos Secadores de Madera de Santo Domingo, Constanza y Azua—wood drying kilns
Ultramar Dominicana—imports, foods, and liquors
Radio HIN—radio station
Agencia de Viajes Victor Méndez Capellán—travel agency
Nacional de Construcciones (NACO)—home construction
Fábrica de Discos—phonograph record factory
Industrialización de Frutos Dominicanos—fruit and vegetable processing
Bananera Doña Antonia—banana plantation and export

Caribbean Medical Supply—wholesale medical and surgical supply
Compañía San Rafael—commercial insurance
Dominican Sugar Company—sugar export
Compañía Distribuidora—import house
Compañía de Construcciones Ozama—house construction
Pan American Investment Corporation—holding company for Trujillo investments
Fomento Industrial, Mercantil y Agrícola (FIMACA)—finance company
Inversiones Urbanas—city land investment
Industria Nacional de Alcoholes—alcohol production
Industrias Nigua—sand and construction material
Editora Handicap—publishing house
Industria Nacional—nail factory
Marta Comercial Corporation—export-import
Marian Comercial Corporation—export-import
Mar-Mol Commercial Corporation—export of marble
Transportación Marítima—marine shipping
Altagracia Julia—large-scale farming and cattle ranch
Not included in the above list are the enterprises in which Trujillo was only part owner, such as the National Match Factory, Dominican National Brewery, Industrial Caobera (furniture manufacturing, with a monopoly on mahogany), Matadero Industrial y Planta de Refrigeración (slaughterhouse, meat-packing, soap and lard manufacture), National Glass Factory, Industrial Dominicana (animal feed), Industrial Lechera (monopoly on milk distribution), and Minera Hatillo, which controlled iron ore deposits and all mining rights in the country except bauxite. Neither does the list include those investments which Trujillo had sold to the Banco de Crédito such as the national salt monopoly and the Flota Mercante Dominicana, the national merchant marine.

5. Inventory of Land Under Exploitation, Property of Dominican Government: National District, 1962

Size (tareas)	No. of Parcels	Total Area, Each Size (tareas)	Average Size (tareas)
0–5	118	297.73	2.52
5–10	52	373.78	6.67
10–16	27	349.34	12.94
16–32	32	762.90	23.84
32–60	24	954.92	39.79
60–80	3	202.91	67.64
80–112	6	551.27	91.88
112–160	7	962.48	137.50
160–240	8	1499.33	187.42
240–320	5	1319.13	263.83
320–400	3	1004.44	334.81
400–800	6	3606.65	601.11
800–1200	2	1851.92	925.96
1,200–1,600	2	2788.32	1394.16
1,600–3,200	2	4178.51	2098.26
3,200–8,000	2	13129.14	6564.57
8,000–16,000	1	13683.00	13683.00

Total of all sizes	300	47,515.77
Confiscated land	9	164,166.99	18,240.78
Total land of government	309	211,682.76 tareas under exploitation

Note: Lands shown as confiscated are those taken from the Trujillo regime and assigned to the IAD. These are not all the lands confiscated by the government.

6. Summary, Land Tenure Study, La Vega Province, Conducted by IAD, 1962

La Vega. Eighty-one percent of its rural land is under cultivation. This is one of the most productive zones in all of the Dominican Republic. Eighty percent of all farms are of 80 tareas or less in size, and these constitute 22 percent of the area of all farms. About 59 percent of all farms are less than 16 tareas in size, and these comprise only 4 percent of the total area under cultivation. About 58 percent of all farms are owner operated.

This province is one of the main producers of citrus fruits, corn, beans, rice, cacao, garlic, onions, peanuts, coconuts, potatoes, sweet potatoes, yuca, coffee, and tobacco. Agriculture is diversified. The land tenure situation could be improved by means of better distribution of all lands now possessed by the state. Until now, the land officially confiscated from the Trujillo regime totals 115,637 tareas, about 2.6 percent of all land under cultivation in the province. Production potential may have been recognized by Trujillo when he established two farm colonies here, but it is noted that neither was placed in the most lucrative agricultural zone. One, of 8,620 tareas for 212 colonists, was founded in Constanza, and the other, 6,425 tareas for 111 families, in Jarabacoa. With an average size of 45 tareas, these parcels would not be considered of economic size. However, a total of 314 houses were constructed, a fact which will complicate any new attempt to redistribute land in these two colonies.

This province contains all of the necessary factors for high farm production: good rain, moderate temperatures, favorable topographic and soil conditions, a good transportation and communications net, proximity to large markets and seaport facilities, and abundant labor supply. With adequate technical and financial assistance by the institute, this province can continue to be one of the biggest producers of agricultural wealth.

7. Agrarian Reform Law No. 5879, Dominican Republic

THE NATIONAL CONGRESS In the name of the Republic:

NUMBER: 5879

Considering: that the present conditions of the agrarian population of the Republic, as well as the farmers of limited resources such as daily farm laborers or workers, are highly precarious;

Considering: that statistical data show that 70 percent of the total population of the country derives its subsistence from agricultural work, and that the best tillable lands suitable for intensive agricultural exploitation have been concentrated in the hands of a small number of corporations and individual latifundistas;

Considering: that it is estimated that 1 percent of the existing farms cover almost 20 percent of the total cultivable area;

Considering: that in contrast to the existing enormous concentration of holdings of cultivable land in the hands of a few, there exists an extensive minifundismo in hands of the poor rural workers;

Considering: that approximately 50 percent of all the existing farms in the country in the hands of Dominican farmers have an average area of 15 tareas or less, which is a farm of insufficient size to produce the most minimal subsistence needs for a small family;

Considering: that the concentration of the best workable lands in the hands of a small number of latifundistas has caused a constant migration to urban areas, with the result that the urban nuclei of the country have had an increase of population in the last 10 years that creates grave socioeconomic problems, as much in the urban zone as in the rural zone;

Considering: that, in general, the movement of aforesaid workers to urban centers of the country does not even offer them the economic stability necessary to sustain their lives;

Considering: that the most important factor for the life of the Nation consists in achieving the settlement of its rural population, with the objective of encouraging the creation of permanent centers of production which will increase the economic power of the Republic;

Considering: that as a result of the excessive concentration of the best lands in hands of the latifundistas a large part of the rural population in search of land has moved to mountainous regions, their activities causing considerable damage to wooded areas and even to the conditions of the soil itself;

Considering: that the aforementioned element of the rural population, settled in the mountainous regions, has contributed to the development of hillside erosion and has been the effective cause of the destruction of national forests;

Considering: that in earlier years a program of colonization was completed which was able to establish in the Republic some 37 colonies in which 11,600 families were settled;

Considering: that in spite of the fact that some of these colonies are located on excellent, cultivable land, the families settled there have not had the success expected, due to the lack of planning and inadequate settlement, as well as the lack of credit and technical assistance;

Considering: that only the conception and execution of social principles which characterize a true economic-social revolution, peacefully executed, can succeed in raising the standard of living of our large rural sector, extracting it from the misery in which it lives and leading it to a life of honest work, with the expectation of adequate remuneration which will assist the continuous progress of the rural family;

Considering: that as a consequence action is required to establish immediately an agrarian reform in the Nation;

Considering: that the Agrarian Reform, which this Law establishes, should follow by means of its programs and projects the primary objective of improving the living and working conditions of the rural sector as a merited service of social justice;

Considering: that a true Agrarian Reform involves much more than mere distribution of land to poor families;

Considering: that the failures of the so-called Agrarian Reforms, as much in our country as in others of the world, have been due fundamentally to their having been limited to mere distribution of lands;

Considering: that for it to have a good probability of success, an Agrarian Reform must include various indispensable factors such as distribution and consolidation of land in hands of good rural workers; construction of homes for farm owners as well as for daily workers; the concession of cheap credit to these farmers in conjunction with assistance and technical advice; education of farmers, rural workers, and their families; the installation of good irrigation systems that will provide the water necessary for their work; electrification; construction of highways and roads and other similar facilities; establishment and development of cooperatives which will facilitate farming operations and the education and development of the farmers for an ever greater direct participation by them in the study, discussions and solutions of their problems;

Considering: that it is the primary interest of the Government which controls the destiny of the Nation to establish by means of this law, the Dominican Agrarian Reform Law, based upon adequate provisions to accelerate in every way possible the success of its programs and the economic-social liberation of our rural masses.

HAS PASSED THE FOLLOWING LAW OF AGRARIAN REFORM

Chapter I

Creation of the Dominican Agrarian Institute

Article 1. The Dominican Agrarian Institute is created under the Secretary of State for Agriculture and with the attributes which are established below.

Article 2. The Dominican Agrarian Institute is under this law invested with legal capacity to contract, to make legal claims and to accept them in its own name and right; it will be empowered, in addition, to issue its own obligations, with the express authorization of the Executive Power, which in such cases will enjoy the unlimited guarantee of the State. It will have resources subject to its own control, consisting principally in the aggregate of properties which may be placed at its disposition by transfer made by the Executive Power of the Nation.

Article 3. The Agrarian Institute will be managed for purposes specified by this Law by a Directory consisting of the Secretary of State for Agriculture, who will be the presiding officer, the Administrator-General of the Farm Bank, the Secretary of State for Finance, the Secretary of State for Labor, and three additional members named by the Executive Power. The Secretaries of State and members of the Directory will be substituted for in case of illness, absence, or incapacity by their respective Subsecretaries who may be designated by the principals.

Article 4. The Dominican Agrarian Institute will possess the following attributes, powers, and functions:

a. As a primary function, to carry to a successful conclusion an Agrarian Reform in all of the territory of the Republic;

b. To develop specific projects believed necessary to put into effect those programs to be executed;

c. To petition the Executive Power for those properties of the State that are necessary for the development of the projected programs;

d. It will be able to acquire by gift from private citizens, from legal entities, or local or international organizations, the rights to chattel or real properties;

e. Equally it will be able to acquire property, chattel or real, by means of buy and sell contracts, by degrees, or to solicit in accordance with the law, from the Executive Power, the expropriation of any property believed necessary for the purposes of this law;

f. It will have the power to acquire leased properties;

g. It will be able to sell and further lease totally or partially the property, chattel or real, which constitute the patrimony under its direct control;

h. It will have the right to borrow money and offer in pledge or guaranty the properties under its control;

i. It will be able to make property available, and furthermore to assist economically national or international institutions for the purpose of agricultural studies and activities when it judges that these favor the evolving programs put in practice in the institute itself;

j. It will be able to cede chattel or real properties at a reduced price or give them to institutions not commercial in nature, when it judges that these grants or gifts will directly benefit the agrarian or rural population;

k. It will also be empowered to contract for purposes of the Agrarian Reform with autonomous governmental or private entities;

l. Establish local offices and space for Agrarian Reform with personnel and facilities necessary to achieve the purposes of this law;

m. It will be empowered to perform other acts and transactions of its own organization which are necessary and convenient to achieve the purposes of this law;

Article 5. The Directory of the Agrarian Institute will have the following powers and functions:

a. to determine or authorize the personnel and administrative organization for the operation of the Institute; to select and nominate a Director-General of the Institute; and to determine their functions and fix their salaries;

b. to delegate to the Director-General those powers and functions that the Directorate judges appropriate and necessary for the proper development of the programs of the Agrarian Reform;

c. select, nominate, assign functions and salary to the Secretary of the Agrarian Institute and of the Directory;

d. approve the rules that are necessary to manage the offices of the Institute of Agrarian Reform;

e. dictate the guidelines and general policy for the establishment and development of the Agrarian Reform;

f. approve the internal organization to manage the functioning of the Directory itself;

g. to meet, as its own regulations determine, to receive reports from the Director-General of the Institute on current activities and projected plans, with the responsibility of taking decisions on matters not delegated;

h. to approve programs designed for the work of the following year and to determine the budgets required by these programs;

i. to approve any other program or project which the Director-General desires to submit;

j. to approve the rules that may be submitted to it by the Director-General necessary to manage the operation of the programs and projects to be developed;

k. to be able to intervene in and if desired to take decisions on any detail or operation of the Institute of Agrarian Reform;

l. to develop other necessary functions to lead to a successful conclusion the objectives outlined in this law.

Article 6. The Director-General of the Agrarian Institute will have the following duties and attributes:

a. he will be the Executive of the Agrarian Institute;

b. he will have and will execute the powers and functions which the Directory delegates him;

c. he will place into execution the orders, instructions, and authorizations of the Directory;

d. in the name of the Institute he will make and sign the contracts, letters, and other documents that are necessary to execute the actions delegated by the Directory;

e. in the name of the Institute, he will issue, sign, and grant the contracts and documents appropriate or necessary to effect the operations and transactions specifically authorized by the Directory;

f. in the name of the Institute he will issue, grant, and sign the contracts, documents, and letters appropriate or necessary for the purchase and sale of chattel or immovable property in transactions delegated or expressly authorized by the Directory;

g. he will prepare an annual budget of the programs to be executed which will be submitted to the Directory for approval;

h. he will prepare and submit periodic reports required of him by laws and regulations;

i. he will execute all other activities and functions necessary and appropriate in order to fulfill the functions delegated and assigned him by the Directory, and all other functions needed to successfully achieve the objectives of this law.

Chapter II

The Capital of the Agrarian Reform

Article 7. Capital of the Agrarian Reform is created which will be allotted to the increase of work and programs needed to achieve the objectives of the Agrarian Reform of the Republic.

Article 8. The capital of the Agrarian Reform will consist of:

a. funds and properties until now assigned or otherwise acquired by the General Directory of the Agrarian Reform;

b. the product of the sale of chattel or immovable property assigned by the State to the General Directory of the Agrarian Reform or to the Agrarian Institute;

c. income produced by properties and activities under its control;

d. the product of the sale of the proceeds and products of the properties under its control;

e. loans from banks or other institutions;

f. grants from private citizens and from national or international institutions;

g. the sums assigned in the budget to the Agrarian Institute for capitalizing operations and investments;

h. the product of the sale of bonds which the Agrarian Institute issues with the approval of the Executive Power.

Article 9. The funds of the Agrarian Reform will be managed by the General Directory of the Agrarian Reform in conformance with the annual duly approved programs and budgets. The funds will be used solely for the objectives of the Agrarian Reform in accordance with and as authorized by this law;

Article 10. Until the Directory determines otherwise, the income produced by the operations of the Agrarian Institute are to be collected by the Tax Offices of Internal Revenue.

Article 11. The Secretary of State for Finance will carry a special account for the funds of the Agrarian Reform.

Chapter III

Goals of the Agrarian Reform

Article 12. In consonance with the agrarian policy of the state, the improvement of farm lands and regions by means of repair and construction of highways and adjacent roads, irrigation systems, sources of electricity, water, and other appropriate facilities is determined to be in the public interest.

Article 13. State-owned lands will be utilized in the form and manner that will most benefit the rural working masses, the small farm owners, and the Nation in general.

Article 14. The Agrarian Institute will establish and distribute State lands that may be assigned it, in such sizes and with such facilities so as to constitute true family units in which farm families of limited resources can be settled. To this end, when the State obtains large private farms, and if the Agrarian Institute so decides, these will be divided among farmers chosen in accordance with the provisions of this law.

Article 15. When the Institute considers it appropriate, parcels of land too small to form separate farm units will be acquired and consolidated in order to create units of adequate size.

Article 16. As a principle appropriate for a permanent and effective Agrarian Reform, the Agrarian Institute will establish homes suitable for farmers of limited resources and for rural workers.

Article 17. It will develop and help establish and operate supervised farm credit services for the new landowners, that is, low-cost credit accompanied by technical assistance and advice.

Article 18. It will establish educational and technical training programs for farmers and farm workers and their families.

Article 19. It will encourage and help establish facilities to obtain selected seeds, materials, and farm equipment.

Article 20. It will schedule and direct crop cultivation in such a manner that the new farmers invest their energy and money in crops which will most benefit them.

Article 21. It will teach and direct the classification, storage, and marketing of crops, stimulating the creation of cooperatives for these functions in the shortest time possible.

Article 22. It will promote and stimulate the establishment and development of farming industries which can utilize the farmers' crops.

Article 23. It will encourage and direct the development and operation of community facilities and services.

Article 24. It will encourage and cooperate in the development and improvement of other public sectors in such a manner as to increase its purchasing capability and thus better the market opportunities for farm products.

Article 25. To achieve the foregoing objectives, the Agrarian Institute will develop and operate as a matter of urgency the programs authorized by the law.

Chapter IV

Inventory and Classification of State-owned Properties

Article 26. The Agrarian Institute, with the cooperation of the Secretariat of State for Administration, Control and Recovery of Property, and the General Administration of National Property, will determine and create a classified inventory of State property. This inventory will establish the extent and limits of each of the State properties, including detailed information on the uses to which the land is put and the state of the land. The inventory should include detailed information on the buildings and other existing improvements on these lands.

Article 27. In the same manner, the Institute will proceed to inventory any other State-owned farm property or industry which might be of use in future programs of the Agrarian Reform.

Article 28. In proceeding with the creation of the classified inventory of State property, the Institute should study with care the titles of the State farm properties in order to ascertain if these are protected by an authentic title.

Article 29. Following the matter expressed in the previous article, the Institute is authorized to resolve any reclamation which might affect the right to the property, of the title which covers any farm, always provided that the farm has been assigned by Executive Power to programs of the Agrarian Reform, being able to agree by degrees and by accommodation to any arrangement and to accede to any document which definitely secures title to the said farm.

Article 30. If State properties that are assigned to the programs are not definitely secured by survey, the Institute will have the authority to ask for a cadastral survey of these lands, determining the area and limits, and obtaining a secure title which will avoid future unjustified reclamation.

Article 31. The Institute should make a study of all State-owned lands that have been inventoried as to adaptability of the soil for different crops, supply of water, physical characteristics of the soil, economic characteristics, and the other factors necessary to establish the bases for its operations in the form most appropriate to benefit farm laborers and farmers, as well as the community.

Chapter V

Parceling of Land into Family Units

Article 32. As a means of reaching the goals of Agrarian Reform, the Agrarian Institute will be empowered, and is hereby so authorized, to divide the land assigned to it or that it may acquire, in parcels of such size that are sufficient not only to produce the needs of the farmer and his family but that also will have the productive capacity that will permit a continuous and progressive development of the family.

Article 33. On those State lands assigned or acquired by the Institute which poor families have taken upon themselves to occupy, the Institute is authorized to give these families temporary permission either, in the case of farmers, until they gather their crops, or until the farms are divided into adequate family units, at the discretion of the Institute.

Article 34. The Institute will be empowered to erect on the parcels which may be distributed homes for the farmers, structures for the crops, and other farm facilities.

Article 35. Also, the Institute will be able, if it is believed to be more desirable, to develop farm communities, building the homes in a conglomerate within an area near the parcels which are to be distributed under the program. These communities will include facilities such as schools, health centers, buildings for religious ceremonies, and centers for social and educational meetings.

Article 36. As a consequence of the establishment of the agrarian communities, the Agrarian Institute will be empowered to establish facilities for irrigation, drainage, electrical energy, water, and means of transportation and communications.

Chapter VI

Distribution of Parcels and Selection of Candidates

Article 37. The Agrarian Institute is authorized to distribute family units or parcels among farmers of limited resources of the vicinity, in conformance with the provisions of this law and the regulations which are promulgated in accordance with it.

Article 38. The distribution of parcels to the petitioners will be accomplished as indicated below by means of a conditional sales contract at the price, period of payment and under conditions which the Institute considers most reasonable, and in the manner provided by its regulations.

Article 39. The aforementioned conditional sales contract will include restrictions to the effect that the owner of the parcel may not sell, lease, mortgage, or in any other manner dispose of or alienate the ceded parcel without previous written permission of the Institute. These restrictions will terminate as soon as the owner has obtained full ownership of his parcel.

Article 40. Any parcel which in any manner is ceded, granted or sold to a farmer in accordance with Agrarian Reform plans, will be free of all restrictions, and consequently any reclaimer to the contrary which might affect the title to the parcel will be acted upon by the State as a financial matter without affecting the title to the property.

Article 41. Any benefited *parcelero* will subsequently be able to solicit additional lands, and the Institute will have the authority to assign them if the alleged reasons justify such additional action. In addition to any others that the Institute believes appropriate to impose, the conditions for assigning additional land must include:

a. The parcelero must have a large family or number of dependents capable of working the parcel;

b. The original parcel is not sufficiently large to satisfy the needs of the parcelero's family;

c. The petitioner has demonstrated the ability to work the original parcel efficiently.

Article 42. If the parcelero dies after having obtained title or full ownership of his parcel, his heirs will have the right to remain in possession and administer the parcel as an individual unit and must continue to comply with the provisions of the Conditional Sales Contract. However, if the heirs cannot agree to the common operation of the parcel, the Institute will be empowered to recover the parcel in order to use it or redistribute it in the manner it believes most appropriate in accordance with the provisions of this law. In such cases, the Institute will compensate the heirs according to the value of the land and improvements at the time of death, after having deducted any debt to the Institute or other State agency which the owner or his heirs may have contracted.

Article 43. The Institute will be empowered to revoke the rights conceded with respect to a parcel on the following grounds:

a. Use of the parcel for purposes incompatible with the Agrarian Reform;

b. Unjustified abandonment of the parcel or his family by the parcelero. In the latter case the Institute is empowered to award the farm to the wife or children, whichever in the opinion of the Institute has the greatest capacity and ability to comply with the requisites established by this law, and with the contract.

c. Manifest negligence by the owner, demonstrated by his incapacity to work the farm, permitting the decline of its resources and the destruction of its improvements.

d. Failure to comply, without justification, with the obligations contracted in the conditional sales contract.

Article 44. To effect the revocation of the subscribed contract applicable to a specific, conceded parcel, the Institute will previously advise the parcelero of its intention although the latter may ignore the notice. In the cases of revocation of concession, the parcelero will receive payment for the current value of the parcel and the improvements which have been made, less any debt or lien to the Institute or other agencies of Public Administration awaiting payment relative to the said parcel or to any service of the Agrarian Reform.

Article 45. The debts incurred by parceleros for the purchase of seeds, draft animals, material, equipment, and other necessities of the farm, with individuals or private entities without prior official authorization of the Agrarian Institute, cannot be considered as liens against the farm.

Articel 46. To be assigned a parcel, the petitioner must meet the following conditions:

a. He must promise to work and administer the farm personally or with the help of his immediate family;

b. He must not hold or possess other land or property or income, or in cases to the contrary, these must not be sufficient to provide adequate sustenance for the petitioner and his family;

c. He must be over 18 and less than 50 years old.

Article 47. Among the petitioners who meet the conditions of the preceding article the following will have priority:

a. Lessees, labor contractors, tenants, standby workers, and workers who are cultivating land which is going to be distributed or who may be working on it;

b. Persons displaced from their land as a result of Agrarian Reform programs;

c. Farmers with experience, interest, and ability in the type of cultivation proposed to be established;

d. Heads of family not over 40 years of age, with families and dependents possessing a productive potential;

e. Persons who know how to read and write or at least who are willing to learn;

f. Persons desirous of participating in educational activities, in the formation of cooperatives and in community development.

Article 48. In all lands parceled into redistributed farms in accordance with Agrarian Reform programs being executed, the Agrarian Institute will take into consideration those displaced persons who have pending reclamas for said lands, when by so doing the pending reclamas can be resolved and full titles to the property can be established.

Article 49. The distribution of parcels among persons who meet the necessary conditions to be qualified as capable of occupying parcels will be effected by means of a lottery system in which are numbered the parcels which are going to be distributed among all the participants.

Article 50. Persons qualified to receive parcels who in the lottery of a specific area do not receive a parcel will be given a new opportunity to participate in later distributions made on nearby areas.

Chapter VII

Farm Credit and Cooperatives

Article 51. The Agrarian Institute will work diligently with the Farmers Bank to obtain credit facilities for farmers and organizations included within the development program. This credit will be supervised, that is, credit of low-interest type, accompanied by technical advice adequate for production and consumption, and if possible, to be arranged through farming cooperatives.

Article 52. If the operation of supervised credit service occasionally produces a deficit in the Farmers Bank, this amount will be included in the funds assigned the Agrarian Reform in the general Budget of the Nation, to be reimbursed to the Farmers Bank.

Article 53. The Agrarian Institute will encourage by all means possible and will help to organize credit cooperatives for consumption and marketing among farm owners and among farm workers.

Article 54. The Agrarian Institute will cooperate with the interested parties so that the credit given by the cooperatives to its members, whenever possible, be in materials and equipment rather than cash.

Chapter VIII

Communities of Farm Workers

Article 55. The Agrarian Institute, when it considers it appropriate, will build worker communities near farming industries or enterprises, such as sugar centrales, sisal industries, and others.

Article 56. The homes in the farm workers communities will be established on small lots, but with an area sufficient for a small garden, a hen house, and other facilities.

Article 57. The Agrarian Insititute will build homes of the most appropriate type whether in cooperation with the Department of Public Works or arranged through contracts with private constructors, or even with the beneficiaries themselves to whom they will supply guidance and materials, or by any other method which will be practical and economical.

Article 58. The selection of candidates or petitioners will be regulated by the Agrarian Institute. The workers selected to live in a specific community will obtain the property by means of a conditional sales contract at cost price, to be paid for in easy monthly installments, for a number of years determined to be reasonable. As in the case of distribution of parcels, selection is to be by means of lottery.

Chapter IX

Education and Training

Article 59. The Agrarian Institute will encourage and will put into practice training programs for project administrators, employees of central offices, soil technicians, persons to assist in the organization and supervision of cooperatives, farm administration technicians, extension agents and others. For the conduct of this program the Agrarian Institute will be empowered to solicit the cooperation of the various departments of the Secretariat of State for Agriculture, the Farmers Bank, and other entities of Public Administration.

Article 60. Likewise, the Institute will conduct seminars and training courses throughout the Republic for the benefit of the directive body of the organization, utilizing, if necessary, programs and courses of other countries, for the benefit of the above mentioned personnel and of Dominican students. Furthermore it will be empowered to effect programs and educational activities for directors and farmers in specific localities. To this end, training plans will be formulated and special programs will be developed, duly financed by the Agrarian Institute, whether independently or in cooperation with the various dependencies of the Ministry of Agriculture and of the Farmers Bank.

Chapter X

Article 61. In those cases which the Agrarian Institute believes most desirable and beneficial, it will be empowered to work the lands or the other properties or farm industries under its control, as a single unit, distributing among the workers, in addition to their salaries, that part of the net benefits, if there be any, that it believes reasonable, after taking out necessary reserves for depreciation, improvements, expansion, and contingencies.

Article 62. The Agrarian Institute will be empowered to encourage, establish, and operate such other agricultural programs which it believes appropriate to the objectives of the Agrarian Reform.

Chapter XI
General Provisions

Article 63. Until the Dominican Agrarian Institute is definitely organized with all of its dependencies and faculties, the Secretary of State for Agriculture is invested with all of the powers assigned by the present law, in order that he may give direction to the employees and facilities of the Secretariat, as well as to the present facilities of the Administration of the Agrarian Reform and to the programs and projects of the Agrarian Reform.

Article 64. For the present, the sum of RD $2,000,000 (two million dollars) is assigned to the Dominican Agrarian Institute to be used for the objectives and in the manner authorized by this law.

Article 65. The present law cancels and replaces any other law, decree, or regulation which might be contrary to it.

GIVEN by the Council of State, in the National Palace, Santo Domingo, National District, Capital of the Dominican Republic, on the 27th day of the month of April of one thousand nine hundred sixty-two, 119th year of Independence and 99th of the Restoration.

Rafael F. Bonnelly
President of the Republic
and of the Council of State

Nicolas Pichardo	Donald J. Reid Cabral
First Vice-President	Second Vice-President
Mons. Eliseo Pérez Sánchez	Luis Amiama Tío
Member	Member
Antonio Imbert Barrera	José Fernández Caminero
Member	Member

. . . .

NOTE: This law was officially published in the newspapers *El Caribe* and *La Nación* of Santo Domingo, editions of May 4, 1962.

Published in the *Gaceta Oficial,* Number 8671, of July 14, 1962.

Law Number 6207 which modifies article 19 of the Law of Agrarian Reform, Number 5879 of 27 April 1962.

. . . .

SOLE ARTICLE: Article 19 of the Law of Agrarian Reform No. 5879 dated 27 April 1962 is modified so as to now read as follows:

Article 19. It will encourage and help establish facilities to obtain select seeds, material, and farm equipment. For these purposes the Dominican Agrarian Institute is expressly exempted from the payment of taxes, contributions or fiscal and municipal fees, as well as from the payment of customs taxes and all classes of charges arising from the importation of office equipment, equipment for industrial and agricultural purposes, automobiles, pick-ups, trucks, jeeps, tow-cars, plows, tractors, harrows, shovels, grindstones, and all other machinery or instruments suitable for agriculture, and spare parts, accessories and tires for same, construction materials, combustibles and lubricants, fertilizers, insecticides, fungicides, seeds, food, and medicines for poultry and livestock, and any other goods which the Dominican Agrarian Institute considers useful and necessary to acquire abroad for the improvement of agriculture. The Central Bank of the Dominican Republic will provide the Dominican Agrarian Institute with all the facilities necessary to make foreign payments.

GIVEN by the Council of State, in the National Palace, Santo Domingo, National District, Capital of the Dominican Republic, on the 25th day of the month of February, nineteen hundred sixty-three, 119th year of Independence and 100th of the Restoration.

· ·

HECTOR GARCIA-GODOY IN THE NAME OF THE REPUBLIC

NUMBER: 17

IN VIEW OF ARTICLE 2 OF THE CONSTITUTIONAL ACT

HAS GIVEN THE FOLLOWING LAW:

Article 1: Article 3 of the Law No. 5879 dated 27 April 1962, modified by Law No. 44, dated 4 November 1963, is herewith modified to read as follows:

"Article 3. The Agrarian Institute will be guided toward the objectives of the provisions of this law, by a Directory consisting of the Minister of Agriculture, who will be the presiding officer, the Administrator-General of the Farm Bank, the Minister of Public Works and Communications, the Minister of Labor, the President of the Corporation for Industrial Development, the Minister of Education, Fine Arts and Culture, and three additional members who will be named by the Executive Power. The Minister members of the Directory may be substituted for in case of sickness, absence or incapacity, by the respective Vice-Ministers who may be designated by the principals.

The Executive Power will designate the Director-General, the Sub-Director-General, and the Secretary of the Dominican Agrarian Institute.

Article 2: Article 5 of the Law No. 5879 dated 27 April 1962 is hereby modified to read as follows:

"Article 5. The Directory of the Agrarian Institute will have the powers and functions which are herewith set forth in detail:

a. to determine or authorize the personnel and administrative organization under which the Institute is to operate;

b. to delegate within the Directory-General those powers and functions which the Directory judges appropriate and necessary for the favorable development of the Agrarian Reform programs, subject to the approval of the Executive Power, without which such delegation will have neither validity nor effectiveness.

All general delegation is null; delegation must be specific.

c. to approve the rules necessary to manage the offices of the Institute and of the Agrarian Reform;

d. to decree the outlines and general policy for the establishment and development of the Agrarian Reform;

e. to approve the internal regulations for managing the function of the Directory itself;

f. to meet as required by its own rules to hear reports of the Directory-General of the

Institute on developing activities and projected plans, taking decisions in those matters which are not delegated;

g. to approve programs constructed for the following year's work and to decide the budgets needed for such programs;

h. to approve such other programs or projects which the Director-General may desire to submit;

i. to approve the rules which may be submitted to it by the Director-General which are necessary to control the operation of the programs and projects to be developed;

j. to be able to intercede and, if desired, to take decision on any detail or operation of the Institute and of the Agrarian Reform;

k. to develop other functions appropriate and necessary to bring to a successful conclusion the objectives outlined in this law;"

GIVEN AND PROMULGATED . . . on the 21st day of the month of September of one thousand nine hundred and sixty-five, 122nd year of Independence, and 103rd of the Restoration. . . .

HECTOR GARCIA-GODOY

8. Farm Communities Established Prior to 1961 in Chronological Order

Name and Location	Area (tareas)	Farm Units	Houses	Nationality
Pedernales, Independencia	60,000	121	139	Foreigners
La Descubierta, Neiba	80,000	240	240	Dominican
San Juan de Ocoa, Baní	22,875	167	212	Dominican
Cabrera, M.T. Sánchez	256,000	1613	1523	Mixed
Loma de Cabrera, Dajabón	63,000	332	312	Dominican
Constanza, La Vega	8,620	212	196	Mixed
Duvergé, Jimaní	23,632	257	278	Mixed
Sosúa, Puerto Plata	10,000	400	—	Foreigners
San Fco de Macorís	210,000	473	482	Dominican
Santiago Rodríguez	30,000	122	122	Dominican
El Cercado, SJ de la Mag.	10,400	148	92	Dominican
Luperón, Puerto Plata	7,500	109	126	Dominican
Loma de Cabrera, Dajabón	27,245	400	466	Dominican
San Juan de la Maguana	20,817	399	183	Mixed
Restauración, Dajabón	6,000	45	22	Dominican
Loma de Cabrera, Dajabón	26,658	200	208	Dominican
Jarabacoa, La Vega	6,425	111	118	Foreigners
Ramón Santana, El Seibo	7,500	176	95	Dominican
Oviedo, Barahona	82,000	479	412	Dominican
Pedernales, Independencia	30,000	73	105	Mixed
Monte Cristi	10,071	225	214	Dominican
Higücy, El Seibo	187,000	251	376	Dominican
Samaná	26,000	195	195	Dominican
Dajabón	24,000	232	202	Japanese
Sabana de la Mar, Seibo	27,000	407	798	Dominican
Sánchez, Samaná	150,000	975	1188	Dominican

Restauración, Dajabón	50,000	214	230	Dominican
Las Matas de Farfán	7,800	179	286	Dominican
Pedernales, Independencia	40,000	84	123	Dominican
El Seibo	20,000	541	517	Dominican
El Seibo	19,416	219	111	Dominican
Neiba	6,303	66	42	Foreigners
Hondo Valle, Elías Piña	200,000	872	868	Dominican
Restauración, Dajabón	10,000	88	86	Dominican
Bánica, Elías Piña	8,572	182	224	Dominican
Cotuí, Sánchez Ramírez	174,613	599	618	Dominican
El Valle, S.M., El Seibo	31,491	344	342	Dominican
Restauración, Dajabón	22,000	117	119	Dominican
El Cercado, SJ de la Mag.	7,823	258	95	Mixed
Total	2,024,561	12,290	12,142	

NOTE: 3,577 houses were constructed with state funds, and 8,565 with private money. The size of the farm units varied from 25 to 750 tareas, with an average of 165 tareas.

9. Planning Factors for Agrarian Reform Project AC-1, Juma, 1962

I. The landowner. There is little doubt that rice is the proper crop for this project. The land was formerly in rice production. All basic irrigation facilities are already available. Climatic and environmental factors are favorable. The project lies approximately equidistant between the two principal cities of the republic and has first-class transportation facilities to both.

Net clear income from one crop of rice has been calculated for the individual (60 tareas of land) at about $225. To this must be added $130 which the farmer has paid for housing, land, and cooperative savings payments.[a] It is further estimated that except for land preparation, the landowner will have supplied at least 80 percent of labor costs valued at about $270. Thus the real net income to the owner is about $625 per crop. On a normal two-crop basis the annual income would reach $1,250, the goal established by IAD.

A similar analysis is made for pineapples. On a one-crop basis the net annual income would be about $1,400, assuming that no more than 50 percent of the labor would be supplied by the landowner. As for other crop possibilities, tobacco is presently a lucrative investment, but future market changes and crop loss possibilities also make it very risky. Beans are a good cash crop; corn and peanuts are good for subsistence crops only. However, the introduction of new seed varieties and modern cultivation methods could alter the production picture and lead to many changes in crop recommendations.

---

a. The net profit figure was carefully calculated: production costs (materials, seeds, planting, insecticides, and sacks) plus labor (planting, irrigation, cultivation, fertilizer application, harvesting and sacking), plus other costs (land preparation, water charges, transportation, insurance, land amortization, housing payments, short term loans, and cooperative savings) came to $1,095. Market value of the rice was $11 per hundred pounds. Estimating that 200 pounds would be produced per tarea, this gave the individual farmer a gross income of $1320. His net, therefore, was $225.

Similar figures were calculated for beans, corn, melons, peanuts, pineapple and tobacco, which were estimated to bring net incomes of $432, $97, $292, $12, $1,052 and $715, respectively. Pineapple and tobacco were to be the money crops.

II. IAD. Location: La Vega province, near Bonao, on Duarte Highway and in the Yuna River drainage area.

Economically sized Land Units:

provisional titles issued to date	191
provisional titles being processed	98
provisional titles to be initiated	11
Total	300
Average size:	60 tareas

Income Goal per Individual, Net: $1,200 per year

Principal Exploitation:

Rice	200 parcels	@60 t.	12,000 t.
Pineapple	40	@60 t.	2,400 t.
Others	60	@60 t.	3,600 t.
Total	300 parcels	@60 t.	18,000 t.

Land Value: Unit: $20 per tarea   TOTAL $360,000

Amortization: 15 years

Annual Recuperation Rate: $24,000 per year

Annual Individual Land Payment: $80 per year per unit

III. Housing. Because irrigated rice land is too valuable to be occupied by housing and does not offer the most ideal conditions for human occupancy, housing for the beneficiaries on this project will be constructed in a community in a more suitable area for human habitation. Housing will be by the "self-help" [do-it-yourself] system under a competent supervisor; costs to the individual owner will be about $600, amortized in a period of 10 years.

IV. Cooperatives. A consumers' and marketing cooperative will be organized in this project. It is estimated that at least 75 percent (225) of the landowners will wish to become members and that each one will be able to deposit $100 per year in a mutual savings fund. At the end of three years, the cooperative will have accumulated a minimum of $67,500, enough for defraying normal annual operating costs on the new farms on the project. Thus no further financing will be required from the state. IAD will be able to move out of the picture, and the project will be absorbed into the normal civic life of the nation.

Bibliography

BIBLIOGRAPHY

Notes

The Colonial Period. The remnants of the colonial records of the Audiencia of Santo Domingo were returned to Spain toward the end of the nineteenth century. Joaquín Marino Incháustegui has, in effect, brought back a valuable, selected portion of the Spanish archives adding to the older compilations of transcribed documents a highly useful five-volume unedited work, *Reales cédulas y correspondencia de gobernadores de Santo Domingo.* This is a collection of documents exclusively concerned with the administration of Española, screened and transcribed from the Archives of the Indies in Seville, the Archives of Simancas at Valladolid, and the National Historic Archives in Madrid. The Incháustegui collection, sponsored by patron President Rafael Leónidas Trujillo, was the Dominican contribution to the Third Congress of Intellectual Cooperation which met in Spain in October 1958 on the 400th anniversary of the death of Emperor Charles V. Of particular value to this book, these volumes cover the years from the regency of Cisneros to 1647 when the major problems of settlement became evident. Incháustegui's entire private collection of documents, manuscripts, transcriptions, and other source material including the results of additional work conducted in the Spanish archives is at the Catholic University of Madre y Maestra at Santiago de los Caballeros.

Although not limited to one audiencia as in the Incháustegui collection, Richard Konetzke's *Colección de documentos para la historia de la formación social de Hispanoamérica 1493–1810* admirably complements the latter. Konetzke selected and transcribed his documents for their wide socio-historical value, which means that his collection includes material relating to Española as well as other colonies. In addition to the Archives of the Indies, Konetzke also made good use of various collections of cédulas during his several years of research in Spain. A third collection of documents which provides good back-

291

ground material is the Spanish Royal Academy of History's *Colección de documentos inéditos relativos al descubrimiento, conquista, y organización de las antiguas posesiones españolas de ultramar.* Other collections of supplemental value are Antonio Muro Orejón's *Cedulario americano del siglo XVIII;* the *Compendio bulario índico 1694* of Balthasar de Tobar, edited by Gutiérrez de Arce; and the *Selección de las leyes de Indias* and *Disposiciones complementarias de las leyes de Indias*—the latter two published in Madrid by the Ministerio de Trabajo y Previsión. Where possible, I have verified the accuracy of the transcription in all collections by using microcopy of the original Spanish documents in the files of the Library of Congress.

Of the Dominican general histories covering the colonial period, *Compendio de la historia de Santo Domingo* of José Gabriel García, Antonio Del Monte y Tejada's four-volume work *Historia de Santo Domingo,* and Américo Lugo's *Historia de Santo Domingo, 1556–1608* have been useful. Cipriano de Utrera has annotated the latter. García is perhaps the most important national historian, but Lugo can claim special qualifications: unlike García, he conducted research in the Archives of the Indies and in French archives in Paris.

Another excellent history is the set of six volumes of Gustavo Adolfo Mejía Ricart, *Historia de Santo Domingo.* Clarence H. Haring's *The Spanish Empire in America* is still the outstanding work on Spanish colonial administration. Emilio Rodríguez Demorizi, currently president of the Dominican Academy of History, has edited *Relaciones históricas de Santo Domingo,* which has been useful, especially for the Church history of the colonial period. Perhaps the most extensive work in this field, however, is the rare *La historia eclesiástica* which Canon Carlos Nouel began to write in 1884. The three-volume Church history, which begins with the arrival of Fray Bernal Boyl in 1493, was finally published in 1913. Writing with consummate grace in his *Guía emocional de la ciudad romántica,* Joaquín Balaguer has included in this sketch of early Santo Domingo a perspective of Governor Ovando quite different from those usually encountered in Dominican histories. Balaguer sees Ovando as a man tough enough to forge a new culture in a new environment, an Iliadic hero whose powerful impulse to civilize transcended any of his specific actions in importance. Interestingly enough, Balaguer is critical of history which eulogizes Las Casas and ignores "the immortal work of the stern Comendador who, next to Columbus, most loved Española."

The Dominican historian, Carlos Larrazábal Blanco, now living in Venezuela, has written what appears to be a scholarly work on the history of slavery in Española. It is to be regretted, however, that *Los negros y la esclavitud en Santo Domingo* lacks scholarly apparatus. Rodríguez Demorizi has also edited a volume on the brief and unsettled period between the signing of the Treaty of Basel in 1795 and the first Haitian invasion in 1801, *La era de Francia en Santo Domingo.* This work consists mostly of topographical, demographic, and economic reports and observations of the colony, written by French officials who visited or lived in Santo Domingo. The Spanish historian José María Ots Capdequi has written a scholarly study on land tenure in Española, *El regimen de la tierra en la América Española,* based on a series of lectures and discussions held at the University of Santo Domingo. His book and Manuel Ramón Ruiz Tejada's *Estudio sobre la propiedad inmobiliaria en la República Dominicana,* provide excellent background for an appreciation of the legal aspects of land settlement and ownership during the colonial period. Ruiz Tejada is a legal authority; his analysis and interpretation of land laws, including those of the twentieth century, head the list of required reading for law students in the Dominican Republic. Alcibíades Alburquerque has also contributed to this field in his *Títulos de los terrenos comuneros de la República Dominicana.*

The Middle Period. Manuscripts and original documents bearing on land settlement during the Haitian period are all too rare. When some of the private collections, such as that of Julio Ortega Frier, are made available to the public in the new National Library, perhaps additional material will emerge. J. B. Lemonnier Delafosse, a French army officer who fought under Leclerc, has provided eyewitness reports on French military operations in early, nineteenth-century Santo Domingo. His original work, later published in 1846, was entitled *Seconde campagne de Saint-Domingue du 1er Décembre 1803, au 15 Juillet 1809; Precedée de souvenirs historiques et succints de la premiere campagne. Expédition du General en chef Leclerc, du 14 Décembre 1803, par M. Lemonnier-Delafosse, ancien officier de l'armée de Saint Domingue.* C. Armando Rodríguez translated the original French into Spanish as *Segunda campaña de Santo Domingo.* Antoine Metral has also covered some of this ground in his *Histoire de l'expédition des Français à Saint-Domingue.* Included is Metral's annotation of the memoirs of Isaac Louverture, son of Toussaint. The memoirs not only report on the French expedition but also contain the son's observations on the life of his father.

The reports of the British consul general at Port-au-Prince between 1826 and 1829 provide firsthand information on conditions under the Boyer regime and a review of the administrative policies of Boyer's predecessors. Consul General MacKenzie's *Correspondence from Haiti* includes political as well as commercial information. Other documents of the period, including battle reports, are contained in Rodríguez Demorizi's edited *Invasiones haitianas de 1801, 1805, y 1822.* Haitian historian Jean Price-Mars, in *La République d'Haiti et la République Dominicaine,* has written of the Haitian invasions as aspects of a problem of history, geography, and ethnology. The role José Núñez de Cáceres played in the history of the Dominican Republic has of course been thoroughly examined by virtually all Dominican historians of the nineteenth century. Gustavo Adolfo Mejía Ricart's *El estado independiente de Haiti Español;* Antonio Martínez Ramírez' *El Dr. José Núñez de Cáceres y la verdadera independencia dominicana;* Manuel de J. Troncoso de la Concha's reprint of his discourse *La ocupación de Santo Domingo por Haiti;* and the general works of José Gabriel García and Ramón Marrero Aristy, also cited below, are but a few examples.

For the remainder of the middle period of this study the most useful Dominican documentary sources are the *Colecciones de leyes, decretos, y resoluciones,* such as that of the early years of independence, 1844–47; the recorded proceedings of the 1851–53 Congress, *Congreso nacional 1851–1853,* which is vol. 4 of the multivolume *Colección Trujillo,* edited by Manuel Peña Batlle; and the two-part compilation of Dominican constitutions from 1844 to 1942, *Constitución política y reformas constitucionales 1844–1942,* which is vol. 2 of the *Colección Trujillo. The Report of the Commission of Inquiry to Santo Domingo* contains the recorded and translated testimony of seventy-seven witnesses who in 1871 appeared before the commission headed by the Honorable Benjamin Franklin Wade. The variety of social, economic, and political subjects touched on by the witnesses, as well as the personal observations of the commissioners and their party, give the book unusual value, provided that the student also takes time to read José Gabriel García's adverse comments on the commissioners' report. *A Brief Refutal of the Report of the Santo Domingo Commissioners* criticizes the Americans for not having been thorough enough in investigating conditions in the Dominican Republic. García's *Compendio,* the four-volume national history, is most helpful for anyone working in the early national period of Dominican history. García was not only a careful historian but had had the personal experience of fighting in some of the Haitian wars and the War of Restoration as a contemporary of Santana. The *Compendio* ends with the year 1876 and the fall of the liberal Ulises Espaillat, in whose cabinet García served as minister of justice and public instruction.

The Modern Period. The United States Department of State has microfilmed its files concerning events in the Dominican Republic from 1910 to 1929. These seventy-nine microcopy rolls, *Records Relating to Internal Affairs of the Dominican Republic,* have provided copious source material for the period leading up to the military occupation, as well as to the pre-Trujillo period thereafter. State Department *Papers Relating to the Foreign Relations of the United States* add more information on conditions in the Dominican Republic as reported by the U. S. legation. *The Records of the United States Military Government of Santo Domingo,* located in the National Archives in Washington, D. C. and in the National Archives in Santo Domingo have provided the richest source material for the occupation from 1916 to 1924. These are the complete Navy Department files of the military government; they include the correspondence and reports of the military governors, a complete collection of all executive orders issued from 1916 to 1922, correspondence from the general receiver, reports from all subordinate offices and commands to the military governors, and a number of valuable staff papers and studies. There are no separate Dominican files for these years. *The Personal and Confidential Letters from Secretary of State Lansing to President Wilson, 1915–1918* is a single microcopy roll of a special correspondence file maintained by Lansing. Apart from his interesting "Caribbean Policy" letter quoted in Appendix 2, Lansing's references to Santo Domingo in this correspondence are extremely scarce. Nearly all the file concerns the war in Europe. *The Minutes of the Joint Board of the Army and Navy, 1903–1919,* which make good reading for the military historian, also indirectly provides a valuable insight to the foreign policy adopted by the United States for the Caribbean area. The H. G. Knowles file of the Francisco Peynado Papers reveals the cool relationship between Peynado and Henríquez y Carvajal's lobbyist during the critical period of June to September 1922. There is unmistakable evidence that Peynado was avoiding Knowles. Knowles eventually became persona non grata in U. S. government cricles during this period because of his public attacks on U. S. policy in the Dominican Republic.

Four general histories covering the modern period have been of considerable background value: Ramón Marrero Aristy's *La República Domnicana;* and three by American writers, Samuel Hazard, *Santo Domingo, Past and Present,* Otto Schoenrich, *Santo Domingo,* and Sumner Welles, *Naboth's Vineyard.* Hazard's book was written in 1873, and for years was the most prominent American history of Santo Domingo. Schoenrich, who had been Professor Jacob H. Hollander's secretary, lived in the Caribbean and spent considerable time in Santo Domingo preparing his book which is excellent for general information, especially for 1850 to 1915. Sumner Welles, relatively inexperienced in Latin American affairs, was nevertheless chief of the Latin America division of the State Department in 1921 to 1922 when international pressure for the withdrawal of U. S. forces was at its peak and when negotiations became more intense. In the summer of 1922 the twenty-nine-year-old Welles was appointed U. S. Commissioner to Santo Domingo and charged with negotiating the evacuation of American forces from the country. Privately no admirer of the Dominicans, Welles gives a good firsthand account of the negotiations.

Claiming that the French sought no advantage in their involvement in Dominican financial affairs, a viewpoint not confirmed by events, the Haitian writer Alexandre Poujols, under the pseudonym Antonio de la Rosa, has produced a useful if somewhat biased history of Dominican finances during the Heureaux period and beyond to 1915. *Les finances de Saint-Domingue et le controle Américaine,* translated into Spanish as *Las finanzas de Santo Domingo y el control americano,* should be read along with Troncoso de la Concha's *La génesis de la convención dominico-americana.* Both explain the origin of the Dominican debt and the 1907 Convention, Poujols in terms of American imperialism, and Troncoso de la Concha in terms of American aggressiveness combined with Dominican political and financial frailties. Manuel de Jesús Troncoso de la Concha was an outstanding legal authority; his analysis of the events of 1905 to 1916 and his impartial criticisms of both countries are worth careful study. César A. Herrera's *De Hartmont a Trujillo* is another history of the unfortunate Dominican financial vicissitudes from 1869 on. The most authoritative study of the Dominican debt question from the American point of view is Jacob H. Hollander's own special report to President Theodore Roosevelt, *Santo Domingo Debt. Reconstrucción financiera,* vols. 15 and 15B of the *Colección Trujillo,* is an excellent reference for the financial treaties and agreements made by the Dominican Republic from 1903 to September 24, 1940, the date of the Trujillo-Hull Agreement which finally freed the Republic from foreign intervention in its fiscal affairs. Of particular relevance, these volumes contain the remarks of the concerned deputies about to vote on the ratification of the 1907 convention and the exchanges of many diplomatic notes with the U. S. during the following decade, all as recorded by the Dominicans.

Melvin M. Knight's well-known *The Americans in Santo Domingo* (1928) has been translated into Spanish as *Los Americanos en Santo Domingo* (1939). It is an attack on the American economic penetration of the Dominican Republic, which began about 1920. It lacks much scholarly apparatus, although the author claims he has a wealth of reference material and supporting data in his personal files. The book is not a history but rather a journalistic and not always accurate reporting of contemporary economic conditions. Knight visited the Dominican Republic in 1925 and 1926.

Two other Dominican authors have been most helpful. Pedro Troncoso Sánchez has written a sympathetic biography *Ramón Cáceres,* which brings out the philosophy of firm but honest government, as well as the personal qualities, of the strong Dominican president who was assassinated in 1911. Luis F. Mejía in *De Lilís a Trujillo* has filled a gap otherwise occupied only by Ramón Marrero Aristy. These two authors try objectively to give the Dominican version of the American occupation in 1916, the background, the intervention, and the aftermath. Mejía was a lawyer who entered politics just before the occupation. His work lacks some scholarly apparatus, yet it is authentic according to Dominicans who were contemporaries of the author. Mejía, himself a nationalist, makes a determined effort to give a balanced accounting of the government during the occupation; on the whole, he does a commendable job as does Marrero in this respect. Both are superior to Max Henríquez Ureña's *Los Yanquis en Santo Domingo* which is weighted far too heavily on the nationalistic side. Marrero Aristy's work is somewhat more scholarly than Mejía's but does not reflect Mejía's more intimate knowledge of political events and personalities. Mejía fled the country when Trujillo came to power but later was able to accumulate considerable material on which to complete the final chapters of his book.

With respect to the Trujillo period, I found no single fully documented source of particular importance to this study. Books about Trujillo written by Dominicans were either written in exile by his enemies or were to all intents and purposes paid for by Trujillo himself. Those who lived in the Dominican Republic either lavishly praised the Benefactor, or they did not write. Lawrence de Besault's *President Trujillo: His Work and the*

Dominican Republic is an example of this sort of hagiography. Official records and statistics from 1930 to 1960 cannot be trusted fully, although they may have limited use. Fortunately the developments leading to the agrarian reform program of 1962 do not depend too heavily on the seamy side of Trujillo's domestic politics. Personal interviews, some recorded, with knowledgeable individuals who lived during the Trujillo era have proven to be invaluable. This information, evaluated in conjunction with the published official acts of the governments that succeeded Trujillo, provide the necessary structure on which to continue the study. All important laws, decrees, and resolutions are published officially for national cognizance in the *Gaceta Òficial* including, of course, approved budgets and changes in the constitution. The *Gaceta* is indispensable for research involving government policies and actions.

A series of three articles on education published in 1944 on the occasion of the national centennial provides a usable but limited summary of the legislation dealing with Dominican education. This is Gregorio B. Palacín Iglesias *"Cien años de educación nacional,"* published in *Educación,* nos. 73, 74, 76. The reader must remember, however, that 1944 was during the Trujillo period; as a matter of self-defense Palacín Iglesias had to give Trujillo much credit where little was due, judging from the persistence of high rural illiteracy rates thereafter. A comprehensive history of Dominican education has yet to be written. The records of the nineteenth century were poorly kept, if at all, and much data carried over from the Trujillo period are suspect. Largely in response to the efforts of international organizations such as the United Nations some effort has been made during the past ten years to accumulate data in the field of education. Personal interviews of officials in the provinces and in the department of education and fine arts are still the most fruitful means of research. There is an almost complete absence of recorded data on early teacher training. The Technical Office of Educational Planning's "La enseñanza normal y primaria en la República Dominicana," (mimeographed) is one of the few documents available for anyone interested in historical research in this field.

The principal official Dominican sources for the post-Trujillo period, apart from the *Gaceta Oficial* and the statistical documents, are the records of the agrarian reform institute. The most important of these up to 1966 are the series of studies done by International Development Services, from 1962 through 1964.

Dominican newspapers have been of assistance, especially for research in the 1907 to 1916 period and from 1922 to 1930. *Listín Diario,* founded in 1889, is very reliable, except for the Trujillo period, when no Dominican periodical was free of governmental coercion. Since the death of Trujillo, *El Caribe* has had a moderately nationalistic editorial policy. From 1961 to 1963 it was in fact the only widely read reliable newspaper in operation. The weekly *Ahora,* founded in January 1962, follows a balanced editorial policy. *Ahora* is a magazine dedicated to varied reporting; articles may be historical or contemporary, dealing with any newsworthy topic. *Clío,* the irregularly published journal of the Dominican Academy of History, fulfills a role somewhat similar to that of the *American Historical Review.*

To close with a sentimentally historic note, there must be added to the list of journals the dean of the Dominican press, *El Porvenir* of Puerto Plata, whose editor, D. Alonso Rodríguez Demorizi, continues to publish weekly the small newspaper founded on January 1, 1872, *The Voice of the North.*

References

Abad, José Ramón, ed. *La República Dominicana: Reseña general.* Santo Domingo: Imprenta de García Hermanos, 1888.

Aiton, Arthur Scott. *Antonio de Mendoza, First Viceroy of New Spain.* New York: Russell and Russell, 1967.

Alburquerque, Alcibíades. *Títulos de los terrenos comuneros de la República Dominicana.* Ciudad Trujillo: Impresora Dominicana, 1961.

Alfau Durán, Vetilio. *Controversia histórica: Polémica de Santana.* Preface and notes by author. Santo Domingo: Editora Montalvo, 1968.

Altamira, Rafael. *A History of Spain.* Translated by Muna Lee. New York: Van Nostrand, 1949.

Amiama, Manuel A. *El terrateniente.* Santo Domingo: Impresora Arte y Cine, 1970.

Anderson, Charles W. "Political Factors in Latin American Development." *Journal of International Affairs* 20 (1966): 235–53.

Anonymous. *In the Tropics, by a Settler in Santo Domingo.* With an introductory notice by Richard B. Kimball. 3d ed. New York: G. W. Carleton, 1863.

Ardouin, [Alexis] Beaubrun. *Etudes sur l'histoire d'Haiti.* 2d ed. Annotated by Francois Dalencour. Port-au-Prince: Editor Dalencour, 1958.

Argentine Commission of High International Studies. *Inter-American Statistical Yearbook.* New York: Macmillan, 1940, 1942.

Aron, Raymond. *Peace and War.* New York: Doubleday, 1966.

Baker, Ray S., and Dodd, William E., eds. *The Public Papers of Woodrow Wilson,* vol. 1, *The New Democracy.* New York: Harper, 1925.

Balaguer, Joaquín. *El centinela de la frontera.* Buenos Aires: Artes Gráficas, 1962.

———. *Guia emocional de la ciudad romántica.* Santo Domingo: Ediciones Alpa, 1969.

Banco Central de la República Dominicana. *Compilación de las disposiciones legales dictadas sobre la moneda metálica en la República Dominicana.* Ciudad Trujillo, 1955.

Barceló Malagón, Javier. *El distrito de la audiencia de Santo Domingo en los siglos XVI a XIX.* Ciudad Trujillo: Editora Montalvo, 1942.

Bemis, Samuel Flagg. *The Latin American Policy of the United States.* New York: Harcourt, Brace and World, 1943.

Bemis, Samuel Flagg, and Griffin, Grace Gardner. *Guide to the Diplomatic History of the United States 1775-1921.* Washington: U. S. Government Printing Office, 1935.

Besault, Laurence de. *President Trujillo: His Work and the Dominican Republic,* 3d ed. Santiago: Editorial El Diario, 1941.

Besso, Henry V., ed. *A Guide to the Official Publications of the Other American Republics—Dominican Republic.* Washington: Library of Congress, 1947.

Billini, Hipolito. *Present Condition of the Dominican Republic.* New York: Thompson and Moreau, 1885.

Bosch, Juan. *Crisis de la democracia,* 2d ed. México, D.F.: Centro de estudios y documentación sociales, 1965.

———. *The Unfinished Experiment.* New York: Praeger, 1965.

Buehrig, Edward H. *Wilson's Foreign Policy in Perspective.* Bloomington: Indiana University Press, 1957.

Caribbean Commission. *Caribbean Land Tenure Symposium.* Washington: Caribbean Research Council, 1946.

Carlson, Fred Albert. *Geography of Latin America.* New York: Prentice-Hall, 1936.

Castillo, Pelegrín. *La intervención americana.* Santo Domingo: Imp. Listín Diario, 1916.

Center for Latin American Studies. *Statistical Abstract of Latin America.* Los Angeles: University of California, 1961, 1962.

Chamberlain, Robert S. "Simpson's The Encomienda in New Spain and Recent Encomienda Studies." *HAHR* 34(May, 1954): 238–50.

Clark, James A. *The Church and the Crisis in the Dominican Republic.* Westminster, Md.: Newman, 1967.

Contreras A., Cesareo A. *Los principios fundamentales de la ley de registros de tierras.* Ciudad Trujillo: University of Santo Domingo, 1953.

Cordero, José M. "Notes on Agrarian Reform." *Caribbean Studies* 2 (1962–63): 23–32.

Córdova Bello, Eleazar. *La independencia de Haiti y su influencia en Hispanoamérica.* Caracas: Instituto Panamericano de Geografía e Historia, 1967.

Crassweller, Robert D. *Trujillo: The Life and Times of a Caribbean Dictator.* New York: Macmillan, 1966.

Cronon, E. David, ed. *The Cabinet Diaries of Josephus Daniels, 1913–1921.* Lincoln: University of Nebraska Press, 1963.

De la Rosa, Antonio [Alexandre Poujols]. *Les finances de Saint-Domingue et le controle américain.* Paris: A. Pedone, 1915.

De Vries, Egbert, and Echavarría, José Medina, eds. *Aspects of Economic Development in Latin America.* Belgium: United Nations, Desclée et Cie, 1963.

Del Monte y Tejada, Antonio. *Historia de Santo Domingo.* 4 vols. Santo Domingo: Imprenta de García Hermanos, 1953–90.

Diffie, Bailey W. *Latin American Civilization.* New York: Octagon Books, 1967.

Dorner, Peter. "The Influence of Land Tenure Institutions on the Economic Development of Agriculture in Less Developed Countries," Madison, Wis.: Land Tenure Center, University of Wisconsin, 1968 (mimeographed).

Dorner, Peter. "Land Tenure, Income Distribution and Productivity Interactions." Madison, Wis.: LTC Reprint Series no. 5, Land Tenure Center, University of Wisconsin. Reprinted from *Land Economics,* vol. 40, no. 3, pp. 247–54, 1964.

Dorner, Peter; Loomer, C. W.; Penn, Raymond; and Thome, Joseph. "Agrarian Reform in the Dominican Republic: The Views of Four Consultants." Madison, Wis.: Land Tenure Center, University of Wisconsin, 1967 (mimeographed).

Elliott, J. H. *Imperial Spain, 1469–1716.* New York: Mentor Press, 1966.

Fabens, Joseph Warren. *Resources of Santo Domingo.* Washington, D. C.: Gibson Bros., 1869.

Fagg, John E. *Cuba, Haiti and the Dominican Republic.* Englewood Cliffs, N.J.: Prentice-Hall, 1965.

Flores, Edmundo. *Land Reform and the Alliance for Progress.* Princeton: Center of International Studies, Princeton University, 1963.

Franco Pichardo, Franklin J. *La República Dominicana: clases, crisis y comandos.* Havana: Casa de las Américas, 1965.

Gabb, William M. "On the Topography and Geology of Santo Domingo," *Transactions of the American Philosophical Society,* vol. 15, n.s. Philadelphia: American Philosophical Society, 1881.

Galíndez Suárez, Jesús de. *La era de Trujillo.* Buenos Aires: Editiorial Marymar, 1962.

Galván, Manuel de Jesús. *Enriquillo.* Santo Domingo: Imprenta Amigo del Hogar, 1970.

García, José Gabriel. *A Brief Refutal of the Report of the Santo Domingo Commissioners.* New York: M. M. Zarzamendi, 1871.

——. *Compendio de la historia de Santo Domingo.* 4 vols., 4th ed. Santo Domingo: Talleres de Publicaciones Ahora, 1968.

Gibson, Charles, ed. *The Spanish Tradition in America.* Columbia: University of South Carolina Press, 1968.

Great Britain. Foreign Office. *Communications Received at the Foreign Office Relative to Hayti.* House of Commons, February 17, 1829.

Gómez Hoyos, Rafael. *La iglesia de América en las leyes de Indias.* Madrid: Gráficas Orbe, 1961.

Hanke, Lewis. *Aristotle and the American Indians.* London: Hollis and Carter, 1959.

——. *The Spanish Struggle for Justice in the Conquest of America.* Boston: Little, Brown, 1965.

Haring, Clarence H. "Ledgers of the Royal Treasurers in Spanish America in the Sixteenth Century." *HAHR* 2 (1919): 173–87.

——. *The Spanish Empire in America.* Harbinger Books. New York: Harcourt, Brace and World, 1947; rev. ed. 1952.

——. "Trade and Navigation between Spain and the Indies: A Re-view, 1918–1958." *HAHR* 40(February 1960): 53–62.

Hazard, Samuel. *Santo Domingo, Past and Present.* New York: Harper and Brothers, 1873.

Henríquez y Carvajal, Federico. *Duarte.* Ciudad Trujillo: Imprenta San Francisco, 1944.

——. *Nacionalismo.* Santo Domingo: Imprenta de J. R. Vda García, 1925.

Henríquez García, Enriquillo. *Cartas del presidente Francisco Henríquez y Carvajal.* Santo Domingo: Imprenta Sánchez, 1970.

Henríquez Ureña, Max. *Los Yanquis en Santo Domingo.* Madrid: M. Aguilar, ed., 1929.

Henríquez Ureña, Pedro. *La cultura y las letras coloniales en Santo Domingo.* Buenos Aires: Imprenta de la Universidad de Buenos Aires, 1936.

Herrera, César A. *De Hartmont a Trujillo*. Ciudad Trujillo: Impresora Dominicana, 1953.
Herrera Bornia, O. *Creación y funcionamiento del Banco de Crédito Agrícola e Industrial de la República Dominicana*. Ciudad Trujillo: Editora del Caribe, 1958.
Herring, Hubert. *A History of Latin America*, 3d ed. New York: Alfred A. Knopf, 1968.
Hirschmann, Albert O., ed. *Latin American Issues, Essays and Comments*. New York: 20th Century Fund, 1961.
Hoepelman, Antonio, y Juan A. Senior, eds. *Documentos históricos*. Santo Domingo: Imprenta de J. R. Vda. García, 1922.
Hoetink, Harmannus. "Materiales para el estudio de la República Dominicana en la segunda mitad del siglo XIX." Parte primera. *Caribbean Studies*, vol. 5, no. 3, p. 7 (October 1965).
Holland, James M. *Tenures and Titles*. New York: privately printed, 1936.
Hollander, Jacob H. *Santo Domingo Debt*. Washington: U.S. Government Printing Office, 1905.
International Labour Organization. *Conditions of Life and Work of Indigenous Populations of Latin American Countries*. Geneva: ILO, 1949.
Inter-American Development Commission. "Report of the Dominican Commission of Inter-American Development to the Conference of Commissions." *The Economic Development of the Dominican Republic*. Washington, 1944.
Inter-American Economic and Social Council. "Declaration to the Peoples of America." *Declaration and Charter*. Punta del Este, Uruguay, August 17, 1961.
Inman, Samuel Guy. *Through Santo Domingo and Haiti*. New York: Committee on Cooperation in Latin America, 1919.
Incháustegui, J. Marino. *Historia dominicana*, vol. 1. Ciudad Trujillo: Impresora Dominicana, 1955.
————, comp. *Reales cédulas y correspondencia de gobernadores de Santo Domingo*. 5 vols. Madrid: Gráficas Reunidas, 1958.
Hussey, Roland. "Document: Text of the Laws of Burgos (1512–1513) concerning the Treatment of the Indians." *HAHR* 12 (1932): 301–26.
Jacoby, Erich H. *Inter-Relationship between Agrarian Reform and Agricultural Development*. Rome: Food and Agricultural Organization of the United Nations, 1953.
James, Preston. *Latin America*, 3d ed. New York: Odyssey Press, 1959.
Kelsey, Carl. "The American Intervention in Haiti and the Dominican Republic." *Annals of the American Academy of Political and Social Science*. 100 (March 1922):113–99.
King, James Ferguson. "Evaluation of the Free Slave Trade Principle in Spanish Colonial Administration." *HAHR* 22 (February 1942):34–56.
Kirkpatrick, Frederick Alexander. "Repartimiento-Encomienda." *HAHR* 19 (August 1939): 372–79.
Knight, Melvin M. *The Americans in Santo Domingo*. New York: Vanguard, 1928.
————. *Los Americanos en Santo Domingo*. Ciudad Trujillo: Imprenta Listín Diario, 1939.
Konetzke, Richard, ed. *Colección de documentos para la historia de la formación social de Hispanoamérica, 1493–1810*, 3 vols. Madrid: Consejo Superior de Investigaciones Científicas, 1953.
Lamb, Ursula. *Frey Nicolás de Ovando, gobernador de las Indias,1501–1509*. Comentarios preliminares por Miguel Muñoz de San Pedro. Madrid: Consejo Superior de Investigaciones Científicas, 1956.
Lara Fernández, Carmen. *Primera ciudad cristiana del Nuevo Mundo, la Isabela*. Ciudad Trujillo: Editora. Montalvo, 1947.
Larrazábal Blanco, Carlos. *Los negros y la esclavitud en Santo Domingo*. Santo Domingo: Editora del Caribe, 1967.
Las Casas, Bartolome de. *Historia de las Indias*. Estudio preliminar por Lewis Hanke. 3 vols., 2d ed. México, D.F.: Edición Fondo de Cultura Económica, 1965.
Lemonnier Delafosse, J. B. *Segunda campaña de Santo Domingo*. Trans. by C. Armando Rodríguez from the original French edition of 1846. Santiago: Editorial El Diario, 1946.
Leyburn, James G. *The Haitian People*. 1st ed., rev. New Haven: Yale University Press, 1966.
Link, Arthur S. *Wilson. The Struggle for Neutrality 1914–1915*, vol. 3. Princeton: Princeton University Press, 1960.
Livermore, Harold. *A History of Spain*, 2d ed. London: Allen & Unwin, 1966.
Logan, Rayford W. *Haiti and the Dominican Republic*. New York: Oxford University Press, 1968.
López, José Ramón. *La paz en la República Dominicana*. Santo Domingo: Emiliano Espinal, 1915.
Lugo, Américo. "Emiliano Tejera." *Boletín del archivo general de la nación* 18 (October 1941): 283–318.

————. *Historia de Santo Domingo*. Annotated by Cipriano de Utrera. Ciudad Trujillo: Editorial Librería Dominicana, 1952.

Luperón, Gregorio. *Notas autobiográficas y apuntes históricas*. Prologue and ed. Rufino Martínez. 3 vols., 2d ed. Santiago, R. D.: Editorial El Diario, 1939.

Lyle, Norris B., and Calman, Richard A., eds and comps. *Statistical Abstract of Latin America, 1965*. Los Angeles: University of California, 1966.

MacLean y Esteños, Roberto. *La reforma agraria en el Perú*. México, D.F.: Universidad Nacional, 1965.

Malloy, William M., comp. *Treaties, Conventions, International Acts, Protocols, and Agreements, 1776-1909*. 2 vols., Washington: U.S. Government Printing Office, 1910.

Manning, William R. *Diplomatic Correspondence of the United States*, vol. 6. Washington: Carnegie Endowment for International Peace, 1935.

Martin, John Bartlow. *Overtaken by Events*. New York: Doubleday, 1966.

Marrero Aristy, Ramón. *La República Dominicana*. 3 vols. Ciudad Trujillo: Editora del Caribe, 1957-59.

Martínez, Rufino. *Hombres dominicanos*, vol. 2, *Santana y Baez*. Santiago, R.D.: Editorial El Diario, 1943; vol. 3, *Rafael Leónidas Trujillo: Trujillo y Heureaux*. Santo Domingo: Editora del Caribe, 1965.

Martínez Ramirez, Antonio. *El Dr. José Núñez de Cáceres y la verdadera independencia dominicana*. Ciudad Trujillo: Imprenta Renovación, 1945.

McBride, Grorge Mc Cutchen. *Chile: Land and Society*. New York: American Geographical Society, 1936.

Mecham, J. Lloyd. *Church and State in Latin America*. Chapel Hill: University of North Carolina, 1966.

Mejía, Felix E. *Alrededor y en contra del plan Hughes-Peynado*. n.p: Imp. de la Gran Librería Selecta, 1922.

Mejía, Luis F. *De Lilís a Trujillo*. Caracas: Editorial Elite, 1944.

Mejía Ricart, Gustavo Adolfo. *El estado independiente de Haiti Español*. Santiago, R.D.: Editorial El Diario, 1938.

————. *Historia de Santo Domingo*. 6 vols. Ciudad Trujillo: Editores Pol Hermanos, 1948-52.

Metral, Antoine. *Histoire de l'expédition des Français à Saint-Domingue*. With memoirs and notes of Isaac Louverture. Paris: Fanjat Ainé, Libraire-Editeur, 1825.

Mitchell, Sir Harold. *Contemporary Politics and Economics in the Caribbean*. Athen: Ohio University Press, 1968.

Molina Morillo, Rafael. "El conflicto entre la iglesia y terratenientes." *Ahora* 285 (April 28, 1969): 6-8.

Moreno, José Antonio. "Sociological Aspects of the Dominican Revolution." Doctoral dissertation, Cornell University, 1967.

Moscoso, Rafael M. *Catalogus Florae Domingensis*. New York: L & S Printing Co., 1943.

Moya Pons, Frank. *La Española en el siglo XVI, 1493-1520*. Santiago, D.R.: Universidad Católica Madre y Maestra, 1971.

Munden, Kenneth W., comp. *Preliminary Inventory of the Records of the Dominican Customs Receivership* (National Archives publication no. 63-14.). Washington: National Archives, 1962.

Munro, Dana G. *Intervention and Dollar Diplomacy in the Caribbean, 1900-1921*. Princeton: Princeton University Press, 1964.

Muro Orejón Antonio, ed. *Cedulario americano del siglo XVIII*. Seville: G.E.H.A., 1956.

Newton, Arthur P. *The European Nations in the West Indies, 1493-1688*. London: A & C Black, 1933.

Nouel, Carlos. *La historia eclesiástica de la arquidiocesis de Santo Domingo*. 3 vols. Rome: Oficina Poligráfica Italiana, 1913.

Organization of American States. Pan American Union. *América en cifras*, 1963. Washington: Instituto Interamericano de Estadística, 1964.

————. *Fifth Inter-American Conference on Agriculture, 1960*. Washington: General Secretariat, OAS, 1960.

Ornes, Germán E. *Trujillo: Little Caesar of the Caribbean*. New York: Thomas Nelson & Sons, 1958.

Ots Capdequi, José María. *El estado español en las Indias*. México, D.F.: El Colegio de México, 1941.

————. *El régimen de la tierra en la America española durante el periodo colonial.* Ciudad Trujillo: Editora Montalvo, 1946.

Oviedo y Valdés, Gonzalo Fernández de. *Historia general y natural de las Indias.* 4 vols. Madrid: Impr. de la Real Academia de la Historia, 1851–55.

Pacheco, Armando Oscar. *La obra educativa de Trujillo.* 2 vols. Ciudad Trujillo: Impresora Dominicana, 1955.

Pacheco, Juan Rafael. *Cien años de vida universitaria.* Ciudad Trujillo: Editora Montalvo, 1944.

Palacín Iglesias, Gregorio B. "Cien años de educación nacional." *Educación* 73 (January–March 1944): 39–69; 74 (April–June 1944): 7–31; 76 (October–December 1944): 40–57.

Pan American Union. *Bibliography of Books and Magazine Articles on Relations between the United States and the Dominican Republic.* Revised to October 10, 1924. Washington, D.C., 1924.

Pan American Union. Consejo Interamericano Económico y Social. *Informe del Secretariado sobre las condiciones económicas y los problemas de desarrollo de América Latina.* Washington: PAU, 1950.

————. *Selected Economic Data on the Latin American Republics* (CB-15-E), 1948.

Pares, Richard. *War and Trade in the West Indies 1739–1763.* London: Cass, 1936.

Parparcen, R. Lepervanche. *Núñez de Cáceres y Bolívar.* Caracas: Editorial Bolívar, 1939.

Parsons, Kenneth H.; Penn, Raymond J.; and Raup, Philip M., eds. *Land Tenure.* Madison, Wis.: University of Wisconsin Press, 1956.

Parry, J. H., and Sherlock, P. M. *A Short History of the West Indies.* 2d ed. New York: St. Martin's Press, 1968.

Peña Batlle, Manuel Arturo. *La rebelión del Bahoruco.* Ciudad Trujillo: Impresora Dominicana, 1948.

Peña Batlle, Manuel Arturo, ed., *Colección Trujillo.* 16 vols. Vol. 2, *Constitución política y reformas constitucionales, 1844–1942,* issued in 2 vols.; Vol. 4, *Congreso nacional, 1851–1853;* Vols. 15 and 15B, *Reconstrucción financiera de la República Dominicana, 1903–1930;* Vol. 16, *Historia de la división territorial,* 1494–1943. Santiago, R.D.: Editorial El Diario, 1944.

Pensón, César Nicolás. "Propiedad territorial." Article published in 1899 (typewritten copy).

Phillips, John F. *The Development of Agriculture and Forestry in the Tropics.* 1st ed. rev. New York: Praeger, 1967.

Pichardo, Bernardo. *Resumen de historia patria.* 5th ed. Santo Domingo: Julio D. Postigo, 1969.

Price-Mars, Jean. *La République d'Haiti et la République Dominicaine.* 2 vols. Port-au-Prince, 1953.

Ratekin, Mervyn. "The Early Sugar Industry in Española." *HAHR* 34 (February 1954):1–19.

República Dominicana. Archivo de la Nación, Santo Domingo. *Files of the Military Government of Occupation.*

————. Archivo de la Nación, Santo Domingo. H. G. Knowles files, *Francisco J. Peynado Papers.*

————. Archivo de la Nación, Santo Domingo. *Secretaría de Estado de Agricultura, Legajos 1532, 1533, and 1534,* 1961.

————. Archivos de la Secretaría de Estado de Educación y Bellas Artes. *Educación de adultos* (circular letter). Santo Domingo: August 18, 1953.

————. *Colección de leyes, decretos, y resoluciones, 1844–1847,* vol. 1. Santo Domingo: Imprenta de Listín Diario, 1927.

————. *Colección de leyes, resoluciones, decretos, y reglamentos, 1951.* Edición oficial. 2 vols. Ciudad Trujillo: Imprenta J. R. Vda. García Sucesores, 1955.

————. *Colección de leyes, decretos, y resoluciones, 1905–1907.* Santo Domingo: Imprenta de J. R. Vda. García, 1909.

————. *Colección de órdenes ejecutivos 1918, 1919, 1920.* Santo Domingo: Imprenta de J. R. Vda. Garcia, 1919–21.

————. *Comercio exterior de la República Dominicana.* 5 vols. Ciudad Trujillo: Dirección General de Estadística, 1958.

————. Congreso nacional. *Ley de gastos públicos, 1962* (Law no. 5734). *Gaceta Oficial,* no. 8632. Santo Domingo: Imprenta J. R. Vda. García, Sucesores, December 31, 1961.

————. Congreso Nacional. *Presupuesto de ingresos y ley de gastos públicos 1952* (Law no. 3153) *y 1956* (Law no. 4347). Ciudad Trujillo: Casa Editora Arte y Cine, 1951, 1955.

————. Congreso nacional. *Presupuesto de ingresos y ley de gastos públicos, 1968.* Santo Domingo: Secretariado Técnico de la Presidencia, 1967.

————. *Cuarto censo nacional de población, 1960: Resumen general.* Santo Domingo: Oficina Nacional de Estadística, 1966.

————. *Gaceta Oficial.*

————. Junta Nacional de Planificación y Coordinación. *Informaciones estadísticas dominicanas.* Santo Domingo: Dirección General de Estadística y Censos, 1963.

————. *La frontera de la República Dominicana con Haiti.* Ciudad Trujillo: Editorial La Nación, 1946.

————. *Ley de registro de tierras con sus modificaciones.* Santo Domingo: Imp. de J. R. Vda. García Sucesores, 1928.

————. *Ley sobre división de terrenos comuneros.* Santo Domingo: Imp. de J. R. Vda. García, Sucesores, 1929.

————. *Ley sobre inscripción de títulos de terrenos rurales.* Santo Domingo: Imp. de J. R. Vda. García, Sucesores, 1912.

————. *Plan nacional de alfabetización y educación de adultos.* Santo Domingo: Secretaría de Estado de Educación, Bellas Artes y Cultos, 1965.

República Dominicana. Province of La Vega. Común of La Vega. *Registration Book no. 28, folio no. 97.*

————. *Quinto censo nacional agropecuario, 1960.* Santo Domingo: Oficina Nacional de Estadística, 1966.

————. *República Dominicana en cifras, 1968.* Santo Domingo: Oficina Nacional de Estadística, 1968.

————. Santiago de los Caballeros. *Honorable ayuntamiento de Santiago, boletín oficial Julio 10–20, 1923,* no. 1124. Santiago: Imprenta J. M. Vila Morel, July 31, 1923.

————. *Secretaría de Agricultura e Inmigración, Memoria, 1923.* Santo Domingo: Impresora La Provincia, 1924.

————. *Secretario de Estado de Educación y Bellas Artes, Memoria del año 1945.* Ciudad Trujillo: Casa Editora Luis Sánchez Andujar, 1947.

————. Secretaría de Estado de Educación, Bellas Artes y Cultos. "La enseñanza normal y primaria en la República Dominicana," Santo Domingo: Oficina Técnica de Programación Educativa, 1967 (mimeographed).

————. *Secretario de Estado de Fomento y Comunicaciones, Memoria 1919–20, 1920–21, 1921–22.* Santo Domingo: Imp. E.N. Casanova, 1920–22.

————. *Tercer censo nacional de población, 1950.* Ciudad Trujillo: Oficina Nacional de Estadística, 1956.

Rippy, J. Fred. "The Initiation of the Customs Receivership in the Dominican Republic." *HAHR* 17 (November 1937): 419–57.

Robinson, Harry. *Latin America: A Geographical Survey.* New York: Praeger, 1967.

Rodríguez Demorizi, Emilio. *En elogio de la geografía.* Santo Domingo: Editora del Caribe, 1970.

————. *Santana y los poetas de su tiempo.* Santo Domingo: Editora del Caribe, 1969.

————, ed. *Actos y doctrina del gobierno de la Restauración.* Santo Domingo: Editora del Caribe, 1963.

————, ed. *Cesión de Santo Domingo a Francia.* Ciudad Trujillo: Impresora Dominicana, 1958.

————, ed. *Documentos para la historia.* 2 vols. Ciudad Trujillo: Editora Montalvo, 1944.

————, ed. *La era de Francia en Santo Domingo.* Ciudad Trujillo: Editora del Caribe, 1955.

————, ed. *Hostos en Santo Domingo.* Ciudad Trujillo: J. R. Vda. de García y Sucesores, 1939.

————, ed. *Informe de la comisión de investigación de los E.U.A. en Santo Domingo en 1871.* Ciudad Trujillo: Editora Montalvo, 1960.

————, ed. *Invasiones haitianas de 1801, 1805, y 1822.* Ciudad Trujillo: Editora del Caribe, 1955.

————, ed. *Papeles de Buenaventura Baez.* Santo Domingo: Editora del Caribe, 1969.

————, ed. *Papeles de Espaillat.* Santo Domingo: Editora del Caribe, 1963.

————, ed. *Papeles del general Santana.* Rome: Stab. Tipografico G. Menaglia, 1952.

————, ed. *Papeles de Pedro F. Bonó.* Santo Domingo: Editora del Caribe, 1964.

————, ed. *Relaciones históricas de Santo Domingo.* 3 vols. Ciudad Trujillo: Editora Montalvo, 1957.

————. *Riqueza mineral y agrícola de Santo Domingo.* Santo Domingo: Editora del Caribe, 1965.

————. *Samaná: pasado y porvenir.* Ciudad Trujillo: Editora del Caribe, 1945.

Rogers, Gifford E. *Agrarian Reform Defined and Analyzed.* Santo Domingo, 1964.

————. *Régimen de la tenencia de las tierras en la República Dominicana.* Santo Domingo, 1962.

————. *Régimen de la tenencia de las tierras en la República Dominicana.* 1st rev. Santo Domingo: International Development Services, 1963.

————. *The Task of the Dominican Agrarian Reform Program for the Balance of this Decade.* Santo Domingo, 1963.

Rosenblat, Angel. *La población de América en 1492*. México: Colegio de México, 1967.
———. *La población indígena de América*. Buenos Aires: Institución Cultural Española, 1945.
Ruiz Tejada, Manuel Ramón. *Estudio sobre la propiedad inmobiliaria en la República Dominicana*. Ciudad Trujillo: Editora del Caribe, 1952.
Saint-Mery, Méderic Louis Elie Moreau de. *Descripción de la parte española de Santo Domingo*. Trans. from the French by C. Armando Rodríguez. Ciudad Trujillo: Editora Montalvo, 1944.
Sánchez Guerrero, Juan J. "La caña en Santo Domingo." Santo Domingo, 1893 (mimeographed).
Sánchez Valverde, Antonio. *Idea del valor de la isla Española*. Annotated by Fr. Cipriano de Utrera. Ciudad Trujillo, 1947.
Sauer, Carl Ortwin. *The Early Spanish Main*. Berkeley and Los Angeles: University of California Press, 1966.
Schoenrich, Otto. *Santo Domingo: A Country with a Future*. New York: Macmillan, 1918.
Simpson, Eyler N. *The Ejido, Mexico's Way Out*. Chapel Hill: University of North Carolina Press, 1937.
Simpson, Lesley Byrd. *The Encomienda in New Spain: Forced Native Labor in the Spanish Colonies, 1492–1550*. Berkeley: University of California Press, 1929.
Sluiter, Engel. "Dutch-Spanish Rivalry in the Caribbean Area 1594–1609." *HAHR* 28 (May 1948): 165–96.
Smith, Mervin G.; Johnson, V. Webster; and Pedro, Gustavo de. *A Report on Agrarian Reform in the Dominican Republic*. Santo Domingo, March 1962.
Smith, Thomas Lynn, ed. *Agrarian Reform in Latin America*. New York: Knopf, 1965.
———. *The Process of Rural Development in Latin America*. Gainesville: University of Florida Press, 1967.
South Australia. *An Act to Establish the Validity of Certain Registrations under the Act no. 23 of 1855–56*. Adelaide: W. C. Cox, Government Printer, 1858.
Southey, Thomas. *Chronological History of the West Indies*. 3 vols. London: Cass, 1968.
Spain, Academia Real de la Historia. *Colección de documentos inéditos relativos al descubrimiento, conquista, y organización de las antiguas posesiones españolas de ultramar*, 2d series, vol. 6, bk. 1, *Documentos legislativos*. Madrid: Impresores de la Real Casa, 1890.
———. *Colección de documentos inéditos relativos al descubrimiento, conquista, y organización de las antiguas posesiones españolas en América y Oceanía*, vols. 12, 13, 21, and 23. Madrid: Imprenta de Manuel G. Hernández, 1869–75.
———. Ministerio de Trabajo y Previsión. *Disposiciones complementarias de las leyes de Indias*. 3 vols. Madrid: Saez Hermanos, 1930.
———. Ministerio de Trabajo y Previsión. *Selección de las leyes de Indias*. Madrid: Imprenta Artística, 1929.
Sociedad de Amantes de la Luz. *Escritos de Espaillat*. Santo Domingo: Imp. la Cuna de América, 1909.
Stephen, Sir Leslie, and Lee, Sir Sidney. *The Dictionary of National Biography*. 22 vols. London: Oxford University Press, 1964.
Steward, Julian H., ed. *Handbook of South American Indians*, vol. 4; *The Circum-Caribbean Tribes*. 2d ed. New York: Cooper Square Publishers, 1963.
———. and Furon, Louis C. *Native Peoples of South America*. New York: McGraw-Hill, 1959.
Szulcz, Tad. *Dominican Diary*. New York: Delacorte, 1965.
Tansill, Charles Callan. The *United States and Santo Domingo, 1798–1873*. Baltimore: Johns Hopkins University Press, 1938.
Tavares, F. hijo. *Elementos de derecho procesal civil dominicano*. 4 vols., 2d ed. Ciudad Trujillo: Editora Montalvo, 1948..
Thornton, A. P. "Spanish Slave Ships in the English West Indies, 1660–1685." *HAHR* 35 (August 1955): 374–85.
Tobar, Balthasar de. *Compendio bulario índico*. Manuel Gutiérrez de Arce, ed., 2 vols. Seville: Escuela de estudios hispanoamericanos, 1954.
Tolentino Dipp, Hugo. *La traición de Pedro Santana*. Santo Domingo: Impresos Brenty, 1968.
Trenwith, Edward J., comp. *Treaties, Conventions, International Acts, Protocols, and Agreements, 1923–1937*, vol. 4. Washington: U. S. Government Printing Office, 1938.
Troncoso de la Concha, Manuel de Jesús. *La génesis de la convención domínico-americana*. Santiago, R.D.: El Diario, 1946.

———. *Narraciones dominicanas*, 5th ed. Ciudad Trujillo: Editorial Stella, 1960.
———. *La ocupación de Santo Domingo por Haiti*. Ciudad Trujillo: La Nación, 1942.
Troncoso Sánchez, Pedro. *Ramón Cáceres*. Santo Domingo: Editorial Stella, 1964.
Tudela, José, ed. *El legado de España a América*. Madrid: Ediciones Pegaso, 1954.
United Nations. Comisión Económica para América Latina. *Boletín económico de América Latina*, vol. 7, nos. 1 and 2. Santiago, Chile, 1962.
———. Comisión Económica para América Latina. *Boletín económico de América Latina, suplemento estadístico*, vol. 7, no. 1. Santiago, Chile, 1962.
———. Comisión Económica para América Latina. *Boletín económico de América Latina*, vol. 8, no. 2. Santiago, Chile, 1963.
———. Department of Economic Affairs. *Report of the Joint ECLA/FAO Working Party: Agricultural Requisites in Latin America.* (19500 2. G. 1), 1950.
———. Economic Commission for Latin America and Food and Agricultural Organization. *The Selective Expansion of Agricultural Production in Latin America*, 1957.
———. Economic and Social Council. Economic Commission for Latin America. *Economic Survey of Latin America*, for the years 1948, 1962, 1964, 1965 (E/CN. 12/82 series), 1949–67.
———. Food and Agricultural Organization. *Prospects for Agricultural Development in Latin America.* Rome, *ca.* 1953.
———. Food and Agricultural Organization. *Report of the Fourth Regional Conference for Latin America, Santiago, 1956.* Rome, 1957.
United States. Department of the Navy, Office of Information, Biographies Branch. Selected "Biographical Data," Washington, D.C. (mimeographed).
———. Department of the Navy. *Records of the Military Government of Santo Domingo, 1916–1924.* National Archives, Washington, D.C.
———. Department of State. *Papers Relating to the Foreign Relations of the United States, 1899 to 1945.* Washington: U. S. Government Printing Office, 1901–69.
———. Department of State. *Papers Relating to the Foreign Relations of the United States: The Lansing Papers, 1914–1920.* 2 vols. Washington: U. S. Government Printing Office, 1940.
———. Department of State. *The Personal and Confidential Letters from Secretary of State Lansing to President Wilson, 1915–1918.* Washington: National Archives (microcopy).
———. Department of State. *Records Relating to Internal Affairs of the Dominican Republic 1910–1929.* Washington: National Archives, 1965 (microcopy 626).
———. Military Government of Santo Domingo. *Santo Domingo: Its Past and Its Present Condition.* Santo Domingo City, D.R., 1920.
———. *Minutes of the Joint Board of the Army and Navy, 1903–1919.* Washington: National Archives.
———. Secretary of the Treasury. *A Report of the Commerce and Navigation of the United States*, for the years 1861, 1867, 1868, 1871, 1872, 1873, 1874, 1878, 1880, 1885. Washington: Government Printing Office, 1862–86.
United States Congress. Joint Economic Committee. Subcommittee on Inter-American Economic Relationships. *Understanding the Pressures for Land Reform*, by Raymond J. Penn. Subcommittee reprint, 87th Congress, 2d ses., May 10 and 11, 1962. Washington: U. S. Government Printing Office, 1962.
———. Senate. *Select Committee on Haiti and Santo Domingo Inquiry into Occupation and Administration.* Washington: U. S. Government Printing Office, 1921–22.
United States Senate. Committee on Foreign Relations. Subcommittee on American Republics Affairs. *Survey of the Alliance for Progress—Problems of Agriculture.* Committee Print, 90th Cong., 1st ses., December 22, 1967. Washington: U. S. Government Printing Office, 1967.
University of Santo Domingo. *Anales.* Ciudad Trujillo: University of Santo Domingo, 1955.
Urquidi, Victor L. *The Challenge of Development in Latin America.* Foreword by Frank Tannenbaum. Trans. by Marjory M. Urquidi. New York: Praeger, 1965.
Utrera, Cipriano de. *Para la historia de América.* Ciudad Trujillo: Impresora Dominicana, 1958.
Vaughan, Thomas W.; Cooke, Wythe; Condit, D. D.; Ross, C. P.; Woodring, W.P.; and Calkins, F. C. *A Geological Reconnaissance of the Dominican Republic.* Washington: Gibson Brothers, 1921.
Vega y Pagán, Ernesto. *Military Biography of Generalissimo Rafael Leónidas Trujillo Molina.* Translated by Ida Espaillat. Ciudad Trujillo: Editorial Atenas, 1956.
Velez Sarsfield, Dalmacio. *Relaciones del estado con la iglesia.* Edited by Ricardo Rojas from 2d ed., Edición Varela, 1871. Buenos Aires: Librería La Facultad, 1930.

Vergas Vidal, Pedro L. *Duarte.* Santo Domingo: Editora del Caribe, 1966.

Vicini, José D. *La isla del azucar.* Ciudad Trujillo: Editores Pol Hermanos, 1957.

Volafán, Género H. de. *Primera epístola de almirante D. Cristóbal Colón dando cuenta de su gran descubrimiento a D. Gabriel Sánchez, tesorero de Aragón.* Valencia: Imprenta de D. José Maten Garín, 1858.

Wade, Benjamin Franklin; White, Andrew D.; and Howe, Samuel G. *Report of the Commission of Inquiry to Santo Domingo.* Washington: U. S. Government Printing Office, 1871.

Walworth, Arthur C. *Woodrow Wilson,* 2d ed. rev. Boston: Houghton Mifflin, 1965.

Webster, Cyril C., and Wilson, P. N. *Agriculture in the Tropics.* London: Longmans, Green and Co., 1966.

Welles, Sumner. *Naboth's Vineyard.* 2 vols. New York: Payson and Clarke, 1928.

Wilgus, A. Curtis, ed. *The Caribbean Area.* Washington: George Washington University Press, 1934.

Yudelman, Montague. *Agricultural Development in Latin America, Current Status and Prospects.* Washington: Inter-American Development Bank, 1966.

Yuengling, David G. *Highlights in the Debates in the Spanish Chamber of Deputies Relative to the Abandonment of Santo Domingo.* Washington: Murray and Heister, 1941.

Zavala, Silvio A. *La encomienda indiana.* Madrid: Imprenta Helénica, 1935.

———. *New Viewpoints on the Spanish Colonization of America.* Philadelphia: University of Pennsylvania Press, 1943.

Maps

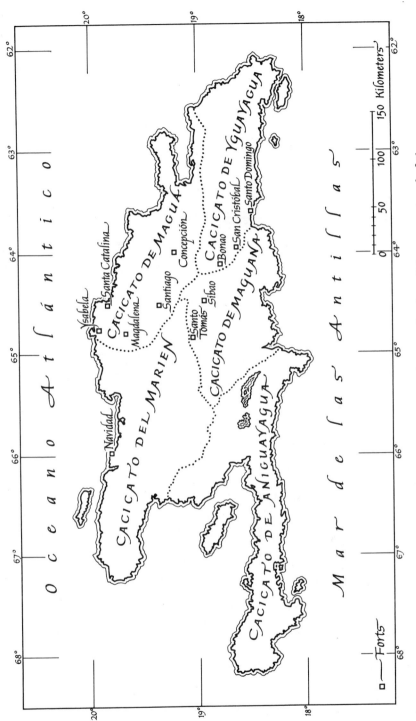

1. The island of Haiti, or Santo Domingo, at the time of the conquest and of the caciques. After an old map, courtesy of Emilio Cordero Michel.

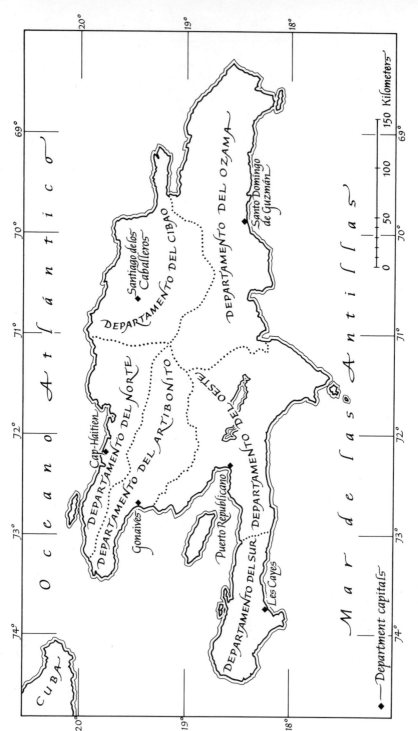

2. Santo Domingo under Haitian rule, as of July 11, 1843. After an old map, courtesy of the Director of the National Archives, Santo Domingo, D.R.

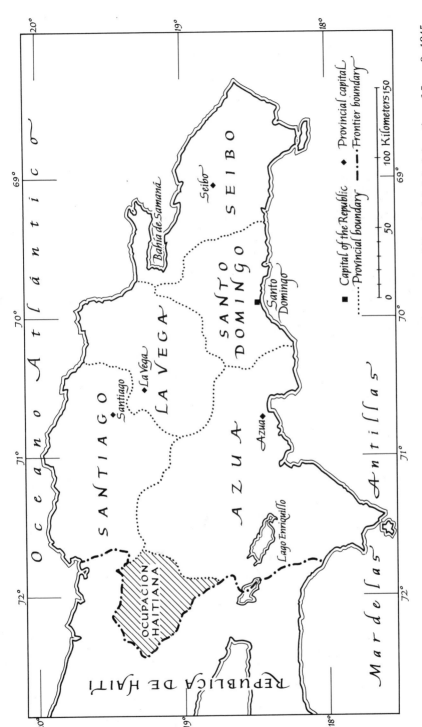

3. Dominican Republic according to the Constitution of November 6, 1844 and the Law of Provincial Administration of June 9, 1845. After on old map, courtesy of the Director of the National Archives, Santo Domingo, D.R.

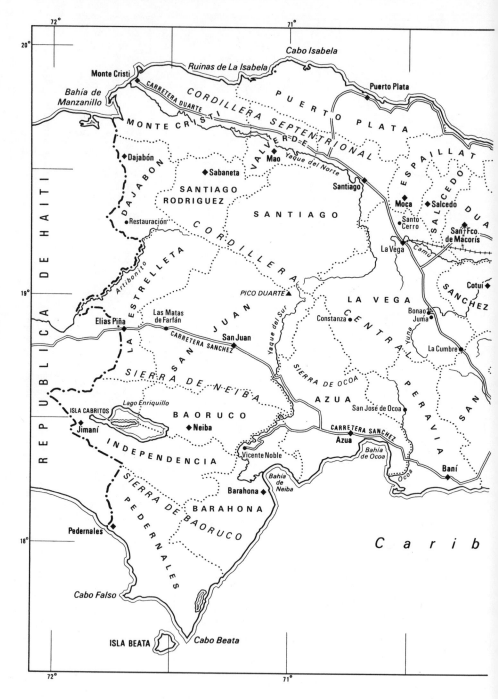

4. The Dominican Republic, 1972.

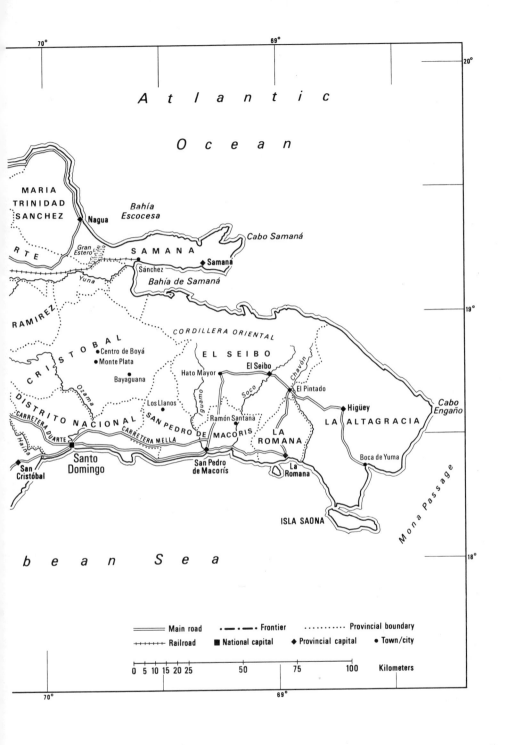

Atlantic

Ocean

MARIA
TRINIDAD
SANCHEZ

Nagua

Bahía
Escocesa

Cabo Samaná

RTE

Gran
Estero

SAMANA

Sánchez

Samaná

Yuna

Bahía de Samaná

RAMIREZ

CORDILLERA ORIENTAL

CRISTOBAL

● Centro de Boyá
● Monte Plata

EL SEIBO

El Seibo

Bayaguana

Hato Mayor

Chavón

Ozama

El Pintado

Los Llanos

Soco

Iguamo

DISTRITO

Ramón Santana

NACIONAL

SAN PEDRO DE MACORIS

Higüey

Cabo
Engaño

CARRETERA DUARTE

CARRETERA MELLA

LA ALTAGRACIA

LA
ROMANA

Haina

Santo
Domingo

San
Cristóbal

San Pedro
de Macorís

La
Romana

Boca de Yuma

Mona Passage

ISLA SAONA

bean Sea

══════ Main road	▬ · ▬ · ▬ Frontier	·········· Provincial boundary
┼┼┼┼┼┼ Railroad	■ National capital	◆ Provincial capital	● Town/city

0 5 10 15 20 25   50   75   100   Kilometers

Index

INDEX

Abad, José Ramón, 96, 98. *See also* Personalismo

Absentee ownership: early complaints and prohibitions, 58–60; under the Bourbons, 60–61. *See also* Land tenure

Adames, Monseñor Roque, 256. *See also* Agrarian reform, current

Agrarian reform. *See also* Land redistribution, state

—current: initial program, 247; procedures and planning factors, 248–49; political vicissitudes, 247, 251–53; goals of, 253–54; problems of, 254–60, 263–65

—evolution of: farm colonies of 1926, 193, 230–31; creation of reform administration in 1961, 232–34; seized Trujillo properties, 234–36; Constitution of December 1961, 236; Smith survey, 237; Agrarian Reform Law of 1962, 237–38; agricultural economics in 1962, 238–43; creation of IAD, 243–44; IAD contract with IDS, 244; IAD definition and specific objectives, 245–46. *See also* Land tenure

Agricultural production: Española and Saint Domingue, 69–70; Sánchez Valverde on, 70–72; rural guard established in interests of, 94–95; Espaillat on, 113, 170, 171, 238

Alburquerque, Alcibíades, 118

Alcabala (sales tax), 69, 188

Alcalde, 93. *See also* Personalismo

Alcocer, Canónigo Luis Jerónimo, 65. *See also* Church, Catholic

Alexander VI, Pope, 28, 54

Amparo real, 54–56. *See also* Land titles

Anacaona (ruler of Jaragua), 15

Archambault (editor of Santiago *El Diario*), 191n. *See also* Land tax

Arias, Desiderio: chronic revolutionary, 142, 143, 144, 145, 147–48; as Jimenes' minister of war and navy, 151, 152, 154; leads rebellion against government, 155, 156, 157; bandit operations, 160; and decision for occupation, 161–62; a political disaster, 172–73. *See also* United States, intervention in Dominican Republic; Personalismo

Asiento (slave contract), 42–44

Audiencia of Santo Domingo: composition of, 30; neglected Indian rights, 41; and distribution of land, 47; reconstituted at Havana in 1800, 81

Baez, Buenaventura, 88–89, 90–91, 103, 104, 109, 141, 170. *See also* Personalismo

Baez, Doctor Ramón, 129, 150

Balaguer, President Joaquín, xi, 220, 228, 232, 234, 236, 247, 260, 263–64; on Ovando, 292. *See also* Agrarian reform, current

Ballester, Miguel, 26

Baughman, Lieutenant Commander C. C., 189

Baxter, Clarence H., 211

Behechio, Cacique, 15

Benson, Admiral William B., 161

Billini, Francisco G., 110

Bobadilla, Francisco, 24

317